{ OBJECTS }

have Class!

{ OBJECTS }

have Class!

An Introduction to
Programming with Java

David A. Poplawski

Michigan Technological University

Boston   Burr Ridge, IL   Dubuque, IA   Madison, WI   New York   San Francisco   St. Louis
Bangkok   Bogotá   Caracas   Kuala Lumpur   Lisbon   London   Madrid   Mexico City
Milan   Montreal   New Delhi   Santiago   Seoul   Singapore   Sydney   Taipei   Toronto

McGraw-Hill Higher Education

A Division of The **McGraw-Hill** *Companies*

OBJECTS HAVE CLASS! AN INTRODUCTION TO PROGRAMMING WITH JAVA

Published by McGraw-Hill, a business unit of The McGraw-Hill Companies, Inc., 1221 Avenue of the Americas, New York, NY 10020. Copyright © 2002 by The McGraw-Hill Companies, Inc. All rights reserved. No part of this publication may be reproduced or distributed in any form or by any means, or stored in a database or retrieval system, without the prior written consent of The McGraw-Hill Companies, Inc., including, but not limited to, in any network or other electronic storage or transmission, or broadcast for distance learning.

Some ancillaries, including electronic and print components, may not be available to customers outside the United States.

This book is printed on acid-free paper.

1 2 3 4 5 6 7 8 9 0 QPF/QPF 0 9 8 7 6 5 4 3 2 1

ISBN 0–07–242340–4
ISBN 0–07–112258–3 (ISE)

General manager: *Thomas E. Casson*
Publisher: *Elizabeth A. Jones*
Developmental editor: *Melinda Dougharty*
Executive marketing manager: *John Wannemacher*
Senior project manager: *Gloria G. Schiesl*
Lead production supervisor: *Sandra Hahn*
Coordinator of freelance design: *Michelle D. Whitaker*
Freelance cover/interior designer: *Jamie E. O'Neal*
Cover image: *Paul Biddle/The Image Bank*
Supplement producer: *Brenda A. Ernzen*
Media technology senior producer: *Phillip Meek*
Compositor: *Interactive Composition Corporation*
Typeface: *10/12 Times Roman*
Printer: *Quebecor World Fairfield, PA*

Library of Congress Cataloging-in-Publication Data

Poplawski, David A.
    Objects have class! : an introduction to programming with Java / David A. Poplawski. — 1st ed.
      p.   cm.
    ISBN 0–07–242340–4 — ISBN 0–07–112258–3 (ISE)
    Includes index.
    1. Java (Computer program language). 2. Object-oriented programming.   I. Title.

  QA76.73.J38 P67 2002
  005.13'3—dc21
                                2001026619
                                CIP

INTERNATIONAL EDITION ISBN 0–07–112258–3
Copyright © 2002. Exclusive rights by The McGraw-Hill Companies, Inc., for manufacture and export. This book cannot be re-exported from the country to which it is sold by McGraw-Hill. The International Edition is not available in North America.

www.mhhe.com

DEDICATION

To Dick Rudzinski, who took the time to point me in the
right direction a long time ago.

Brief
CONTENTS

CONTENTS

CHAPTER 8   Program Testing 233

CHAPTER 9   Simple Class Extension 249

CHAPTER 10   Repetition 267

Here are some features to help you study programming with Java!

Chapter Objectives

Each chapter opens with a bulleted list of objectives that lets students know what they can expect to learn from the chapter. ——————

CHAPTER 3

Getting Started

OBJECTIVES

- To understand the basic concept of an object.
- To know the distinction between objects and the class that describes them.
- To understand how drawing is done in Java.
- To be able to write a class definition, with one method, for objects that draw on the screen.
- To be able to write, compile, and run a simple Java program.
- To be able to find and read documentation on Java graphics drawing commands.
- To know the basic Java language concepts of reserved words, identifiers, symbols, integer numbers, literals, declarations, commands, parameters, and arguments.
- To appreciate that the appearance of a program is important.
- To appreciate that choosing descriptive identifier names is important.
- To appreciate that program documentation is important.

3.1 OBJECTS

Objects are the essence of programming in the object-oriented programming design philosophy. Objects are things. Objects have *properties*. Objects have *behavior;* that is, they do things. Usually what they do depends on their properties. Programs that you write will have lots of objects, and the objects will interact with one another to change one another's properties and to cause things to happen. The programmer's task is to define the objects that make up the intended program—to indicate what properties each object has and what each object does in response to requests from other objects, and to organize that collection of objects into a working program.

The real world has all sorts of objects. You are an object. A ball is an object. A pencil is an object. Just about anything you can think of that you can touch is an object. These objects *are* something.

Objects have properties. For example, a ball has size, it has color, it has weight. You have all sorts of properties, such as height, weight, skin color, gender, marital status, number of toes, etc. These properties serve to identify the object, and can, over time, change. You probably don't weigh the same today as you did 10 years ago. You are still the same object, but one of your properties has changed.

In addition to properties, real-world objects have behavior. Behavior is what the object does in response to some stimulus. If you squeeze a rubber ball, it will change shape. If you squeeze a billiard ball, it might also change shape, but very little. You have lots of behaviors. If somebody tells you a good joke, you laugh. When you have to write an answer to a question on an exam, you put down what you think is correct. If you get cold, you put on more clothing. If you fall in the water, you start swimming (hopefully).

21

{Definition of Terms}
A function is a method that returns a value. This value is the result of computing the function, using the argument(s) sent to it when it was called.

{New Concepts}
Declaring a method name public makes it accessible from any method in any class. Declaring it private makes it accessible only from methods in the same class.

{New Concepts}
A method executes in the context of an object and as a result has access to all the instance variables of that object.

{Good Ideas}
Don't overspecify an abstraction. Define just those properties and behaviors that are necessary and no more. Adding extra information or constraints will only limit choices for implementations.

Points of Emphasis

Point-of-Emphasis boxes call attention to especially important definitions, concepts, and ideas, and make them stand out for later reference.

- **Definitions** give clear, concise meanings for important programming terms.
- **Concepts** explain succinctly how particular aspects of programs work.
- **Good Ideas** present guidelines that experience has shown are worth following.

Written Exercises

Written exercises, which appear at the end of almost every chapter section, allow students to test and reinforce their understanding of important material.

The receiving method can give any names whatsoever to the values it receives. It does not matter how a value was generated when it was sent, or what names the method that sends the values might have used when creating those values. For example, our draw method receives a value for the x-coordinate to draw at, and we chose to call that value x. We have no idea how the animation program generated the x-coordinate value it sent, nor what names it may have given to various values it knew about in order to generate it. It doesn't matter because only a value is sent to our draw method. This is important because it means that we can write our draw method without having to worry about using some name that is used somewhere else.

> (New Concepts)
> You can choose any names you like for parameters of a method.

You cannot, however, use a name other than draw for the method that the Animator calls to ask the object to draw the scene.

Written Exercises

1. Type in and get the BasicShape program working as described in the previous section. Now reverse the order of the parameters x and y as shown above. What do you think will happen to the animation as a result of this change? Compile and run the new version of the program. Were you right? If not, figure out why you were wrong.

2. Type in and get the BasicShape program working as described in the previous section. Then change *every* occurrence of x to across (there are three places), and compile and run the new version of the program. Is there any difference in the animation? Change *every* occurrence of y to down, and compile and run the program. Is there any difference? Change *every* occurrence of g to pen, and compile and run the program. Is there any difference? What do your answers to these three questions tell you about picking names for parameters?

3.10 BASIC JAVA LANGUAGE CONCEPTS

Now that you've seen a couple of complete class definitions and how objects described by these definitions are used by the animation program, I'll describe a few of the language concepts and rules that these examples demonstrate.

3.10.1 Reserved Words

A Java program consists of a sequence of words and symbols. Some words, such as import, class, void, and int are called **reserved words** (also sometimes called **keywords**). These are words that have a special meaning in

---

FIGURE 6.1

Animator (Objects Have Class! An Introduction to Programming with Java)

```
t = 14
x = 274
y = 192
```

```
<<<    >>>
```

```
pause    step    go    slower    faster
```

---

the label to green. The main points illustrated in this example are the use of a single class definition for both listener objects and the use of instance variables in the listener objects to record which object one listens for the red push button and which one listens for the green.

This applet is structured much like the last one. The main class defines an object whose sole responsibility is to create the required objects and add them to window. As in the previous example, each JButton object will have an associated listener object, with each JButton being told about its listener via the addActionListener method. In addition, each listener will have a reference to the JLabel object so that it can use the setBackground methods of the JLabel class to change the color of the label on the screen. The objects and their relationships are shown in Figure 6.9.

FIGURE 6.9

Animator

The Animator supports the definition and creation of interacting objects, one of the core concepts of object-oriented programming. From the very beginning, it allows students to write simple, short programs that come alive through animation.

Object Diagrams

Diagrams of objects, their instance variables, and their relationships are used to help students visualize how their collections of class definitions result in the creation of objects when the program executes.

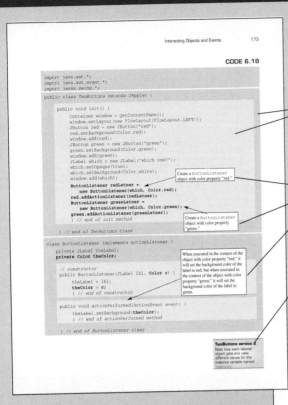

CODE 6.18

```
import java.awt.*;
import java.awt.event.*;
import javax.swing.*;
public class TwoButtons extends JApplet {

    public void init() {
        Container window = getContentPane();
        window.setLayout(new FlowLayout(FlowLayout.LEFT));
        JButton red = new JButton("red");
        red.setBackground(Color.red);
        window.add(red);
        JButton green = new JButton("green");
        green.setBackground(Color.green);
        window.add(green);
        JLabel which = new JLabel("which one?");
        which.setOpaque(true);
        which.setBackground(Color.white);
        window.add(which);
        ButtonListener redLstner =
            new ButtonListener(which, Color.red);
        red.addActionListener(redLstner);
        ButtonListener greenLstner =
            new ButtonListener(which, Color.green);
        green.addActionListener(greenLstner);
        } // end of init method

    } // end of TwoButtons class

class ButtonListener implements ActionListener {
    private JLabel theLabel;
    private Color theColor;

    // constructor
    public ButtonListener(JLabel lbl, Color c) {
        theLabel = lbl;
        theColor = c;
        } // end of constructor

    public void actionPerformed(ActionEvent event) {
        theLabel.setBackground(theColor);
        } // end of actionPerformed method

    } // end of ButtonListener class
```

Create a `ButtonListener` object with color property "red."

Create a `ButtonListener` object with color property "green."

When executed in the context of the object with color property "red," it will set the background color of the label to red; but when executed in the context of the object with color property "green," it will set the background color of the label to green.

TwoButtons version 2
Note how each listener object gets and uses different values for the instance variable named theColor.

Innovative Code Formatting

- **Intuitive Shading:** Sections of code are formatted so that classes are highlighted in one intensity and methods in another. This makes identifying and understanding the different elements of code easier for the novice programmer.
- **Author Comments:** Author tips and explanations provide detailed, even line-by-line, instruction on writing correct, workable code.
- **Program identification boxes:** Marginal boxes throughout the text name and describe each new complete program as it is introduced.

2. Why does the outer for-loop in the sort method stop when i is 2 less than the length of the array?

3. Why is a temporary variable needed to swap values between two other variables?

Programming Exercises

1. Modify the SumApplet to display the minimum value in the array.

2. Modify the SumApplet to display the second largest value in the array.

3. Write an applet with two JTextField objects and an array of 1000 String references (initially null). The first JTextField is used to enter strings. Each time a new string is entered, put a reference to it in the next empty array element. When the user enters a string into the other JTextField, search for that string in the array and set a JLabel indicating whether it was found, showing the index of the string in the array if it is found.

4. Modify the applet in the previous problem to add a third JTextField. When a user enters a string into this new JTextField, first search for it in the array, and if it is found, remove it by setting the array element to null. Modify your search method to ignore elements that have had their strings deleted (i.e., set to null) when searching.

5. Modify the sort method to display the sorted array back in the JTextField objects that were used to enter the data originally.

6. Write an applet that displays 10 JTextField objects and the minimum value, and has a button that when pushed, changes the contents of the JTextField with the minimum value to 0 and recomputes and redisplays the new minimum value (not including the 0 just inserted). Assume that all numbers entered by the user will be greater than 0 and that they will be unique (Figure 11.4).

FIGURE 11.4

before
93
10
44
74
1
23
38
20
99
7

1

delete minimum

after
93
10
44
74
0
23
38
20
99
7

7

delete minimum

Programming Exercises

These exercises give the student an opportunity to try out the programming skills that have been introduced in each chapter.

Chapter Summaries

These allow students to review key points and synthesize newly acquired information.

Summary

- Objects interact by calling one another's methods, sending argument values when they do, and returning values when those methods finish.
- Objects must have references to the other objects they interact with. These references are often passed to an object when it is created.
- An event is something that happens at an unpredictable time that should be reacted to.
- Events are handled by a listener object that implements a listener interface (e.g. `ClickListener` or `ActionListener`) by including a method of a specific name (e.g. `click` or `actionPerformed`).
- A reference to the listener object must be sent to the object that causes the event (e.g., the Animator, a `JButton`, or a `JTextField`).
- An applet is a Java program designed to be run by a Web browser.
- An applet uses a region of the screen to display various components such as text, push buttons, and boxes into which text can be typed.
- The region is associated with a browser-created `Container` object which has methods for adding objects representing text (`JLabel`), push buttons (`JButton`), and input text (`JTextField`).
- Events such as mouse clicks and text being entered cause a method called `actionPerformed` in a listener object to be called by the Web browser, giving the program the opportunity to act on them.
- Each object that can generate an event (`JButton` and `JTextField` objects) must be associated with a listener object containing an `actionPerformed` method that will act on the event.
- Displayable objects are positioned in the display region by a layout manager object.
- A flow layout manager positions displayable objects from left to right, top to bottom, much as text flows across the screen, starting a new row of objects when the next object to be added won't fit in the current row.
- A grid layout manager object positions displayable objects in a fixed number of rows and columns that are specified when the layout manager object is created. The objects are laid out from left to right as they are added to the `Container`, but the number of displayable objects in each row is fixed.
- Information is passed from one method to another when the first method calls the second.
- The information passed is always a value that may be an integer value, a double value, or a reference to an object.
- The method being called cannot change any variable appearing in the argument list of the call, but it can use and change any object whose reference is passed as an argument.

Chapter Glossaries

Key terms are listed and briefly defined at the end of each chapter.

Glossary

Applet A Java program executed by a Web browser or the appletviewer.

Container An object that represents a region of the screen in which displayable objects can be laid out and made visible.

Event Something that happens at an unpredictable time that should be reacted to, for example, an `ActionEvent`.

Flow Layout Manager A particular layout manager that lays out displayable objects from left to right, then top to bottom, similar to text flowing across and down a page, fitting as many objects as possible on each row.

Grid Layout Manager A particular layout manager that lays out displayable objects in a fixed number of rows and columns.

Layout Manager An object that positions displayable objects (`JButton`, `JLabel`, `JTextField`) within the region of the screen corresponding to a `Container`.

Listener An object containing a method that is called by the Web browser (or appletviewer) when an event occurs.

Pass by Value A manner of passing information from a calling method to a called method in which a value (not a variable or an object) is transmitted.

Primitive Type A type built into Java, and not a class. Int and double are primitive types.

this A reference to the same object that the current method is executing in the context of.

Supplements

- A CD-ROM packaged with the book contains all source code and the Animator.
- The Online Learning Center includes solutions, course notes, lab preparations and lab programming assignments, homework programming assignments, quiz material, links to professional resources, source code, and a downloadable version of the Animator.

W elcome! *Objects Have Class! An Introduction to Programming with Java* is not your typical introductory programming text. Programming is fun! And that is the first thing beginning students should learn. In this book they get to do object-oriented programming from the outset. Essential concepts are introduced through animations, allowing students to form a visual image of objects and their interactions.

Our students today come to computer science from a culture that is media-rich. *Objects Have Class!* offers them access to the powers of programming by giving them a fun-to-use, easy-to-grasp programming tool called the Animator. The Animator and the Objects Have Class! approach make both teaching and learning introductory programming a highly intuitive, more dynamic enterprise than ever before.

SPECIAL FEATURES

1. Object Orientation

Students define and use their own classes and objects from the beginning. These essential concepts of object-oriented programming begin in Chapter 3 and then are continually reinforced throughout the book. In fact, traditional programming concepts such as conditionals don't even appear until Chapter 7. Virtually every example and every programming exercise in the text involve multiple objects. Simple inheritance is introduced early (Chapter 9), but only in a very limited way by extending standard Java classes (e.g., JPanel and MouseAdapter). Inheritance is revisited more completely in Chapter 15, when students are ready to design and use their own simple class hierarchies.

2. The Animator

With the Animator students use graphics instead of textual output in the early chapters to write simple, short programs that come alive through animation. Drawing simple graphical shapes (lines, circles, rectangles, etc.) in color is intuitive to most students. Hence graphics is used instead of textual output in the early chapters. The Animator provides an environment in which objects defined by the students draw initially simple, then increasingly more complex animations in which the objects interact to vary their appearance and movement.

For example, the very first example program a student sees is this one:

```java
import java.awt*;

public class Sun extends Animator {

    public void draw(Graphics g) {
        g.setColor(Color.yellow);
        g.fillOval(10,20,40,40);
        }

    }
```

This simple class definition produces an object that draws a fixed, yellow sun in the upper left corner of the animation scene area (Figure 1).

FIGURE 1

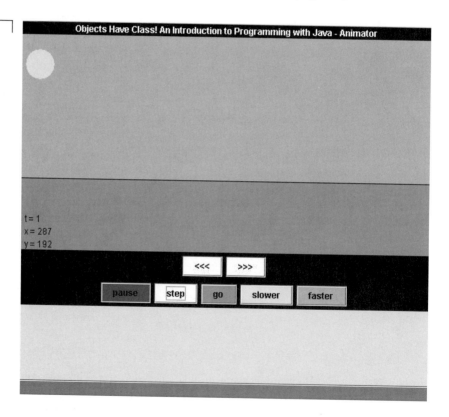

This simple program introduces the student to the concepts of classes verses objects, methods that encode the behavior of objects, and calling methods defined for another object (Graphics) to draw the yellow circle.

The key point to the animations is that each object's behavior includes drawing something in the animation scene. This one-to-one correspondence between an object and a figure in the scene makes it easy for students to *see* the effect of various code structures, and it gives them immediate, visual feedback when they make mistakes.

Successive examples involve drawing increasingly complex figures. This motivates the use of parameter values and the writing of nontrivial arithmetic expressions, conditional structures, and simple loops. Having Java objects directly represent shapes drawn in the scene also emphasizes that objects have properties (state) that must be saved, modified, and used to affect what each object draws as the animation progresses.

Programs with multiple objects, several of which are defined by the same class, again emphasize the difference between class and object and also familiarize students with creating their own objects. The example in Figure 2 (a wheel rolling behind a fence and clouds drifting through the sky) contains several student-defined objects, some moving, others not. This example also shows the simple mechanism provided by the Animator that allows programs to read and write simple textual information similar to traditional text-based, blocking input and output commands. Students need not deal with Java's awkward input and output classes until much later, making it possible for them to display debugging information and to get user input to direct various aspects of an animation.

FIGURE 2

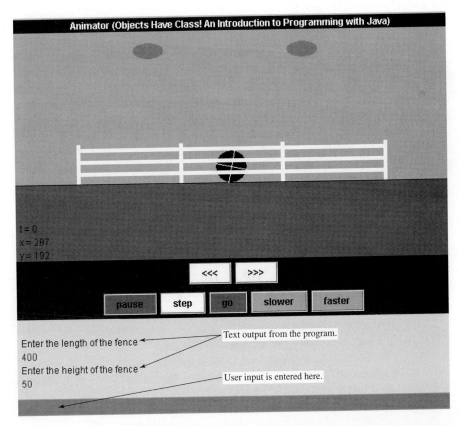

Eventually animations are defined in which several objects are created that interact with one another to exchange information via method calls, parameter passing, and return values. The example in Figure 3 consists of a fixed "person" (the tall rectangle), a balloon that can be moved from left to right (the circle), and a string (the line) between them. Each is represented by a separate object. The string object uses its references to the person and balloon objects to get their positions in the scene and then draw the line between them appropriately. Object interactions such as these are simple and provide visually based feedback to the student on whether the objects are interacting correctly. Understanding object interactions such as these is essential to understanding object-oriented programs, and the animation environment simplifies it for the student.

FIGURE 3

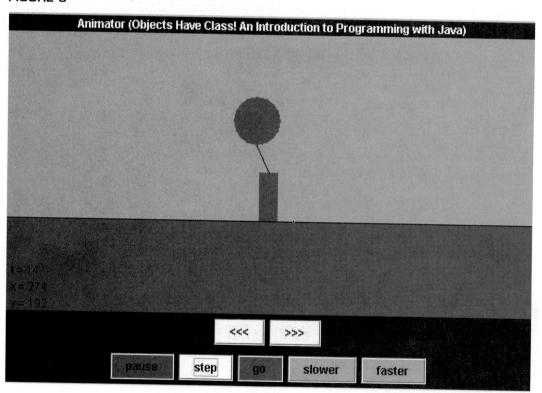

The Animator also allows the student to vary the speed of the animation, or even stop it and then single-step to see what is drawn on each refresh of the scene. When combined with the simple textual output commands, this provides a simple but fairly robust debugging environment.

Every complete animation program in the text can be retrieved from the text's associated CD and/or website and executed. Doing so will help students see exactly what an animation does and how the code makes it happen.

3. Object Diagrams

Diagrams of objects, their instance variables, and their relationships are used to help students visualize how their collection of class definitions results in the creation of objects when their program executes. Figure 4 shows the objects that define the previous balloon animation, showing in particular that the object that draws the line in the scene has references to the balloon and person objects so that it can find out their positions and thereby draw the string between them correctly.

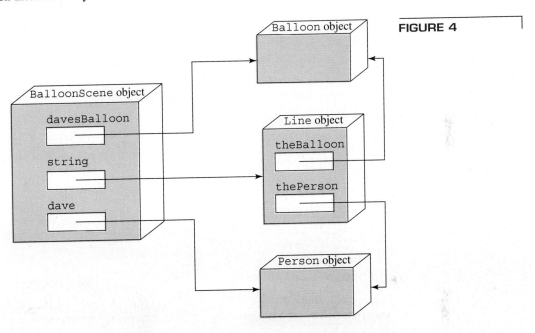

FIGURE 4

The use of such diagrams in the early design stages of a program is emphasized. In fact the student is encouraged to draw similar diagrams before writing any code.

4. Applets and Applications

All programming examples, problems, and solutions in the first several chapters use the Animator. By the middle of Chapter 6, students will have gained enough understanding and experience with multiclass programs that define multiple, interacting objects, including some that react to asynchronous events, that students can begin writing applets with event-driven buttons and text fields. Applets require the use of these same concepts, only in a different setting than animations, and hence the use of object-oriented designs in the text is continued. Applets are preferred over applications because applets can be linked to the student's own Web pages and viewed via Web browsers, increasing motivation for students who can "show off" their work to their friends and relatives. The Animator runs as an applet, too, so even the student's animations can be put on display.

Application programs are presented in Chapter 12, but designing them with graphical interfaces is emphasized. The transition to application programs with GUIs from applets is simple and natural, requiring only one new class (JFrame). Application programs then serve as the basis on which programs using Java's textual, binary, and serialized object input/output classes are built.

5. Points of Emphasis

At selected points certain aspects of the discussion in the narrative become important enough to emphasize. These points of emphasis come in three types:

• *Definitions* give clear, concise meanings to important programming terms.

{Definitions of Terms}

A *class* is a description of one or more objects. It describes the kinds of properties the objects have, but not their particular values, and it describes the behaviors of the objects.

• *Concepts* explain succinctly how certain aspects of programs work.

{New Concepts}

Objects interact by calling one another's methods. They send information via arguments and can get information returned.

• *Good ideas* are not rules, but guidelines that experience has shown are worth following.

{Good Ideas}

Incremental and unit testing helps isolate possible errors to small sections of code, thereby making debugging easier and more efficient.

Because they stand out from the text, they clearly point out what is important. They also provide a good study guide, as more extensive explanation and examples can be found nearby in the text.

6. Program Development

The basic program development process (Figure 5) is presented in Chapter 2 and reinforced throughout the book, including an emphasis on designing before coding, incremental development, and good debugging and testing techniques. Debugging hints are given in almost every chapter, and students are warned about commonly made errors. The thought processes that are involved in developing various parts of programs, and not just final products, are presented (e.g., Section 10.5, "An Approach to Writing Loops").

FIGURE 5

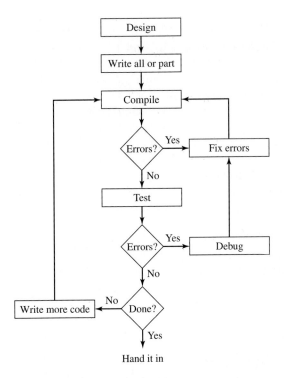

Chapter 8 is about testing, including black-and-white (or clear) box tests, unit tests, incremental testing, and drivers and stubs. Succeeding chapters apply these testing techniques in new contexts as they arise. Manual execution is presented as a method for understanding how a code segment or entire program works (or doesn't), especially when students are learning to write loops, to manipulate arrays and linked lists, and to do recursion.

7. End-of-Chapter Glossaries

Using the correct terminology to refer to programming concepts is important to understanding. Each chapter concludes with a glossary in which all new terms covered in the chapter are defined and summarized.

8. Java and Swing

This text is not about the Java language. It is about learning how to program using an object-oriented, graphical approach. Java is a great language for this purpose as it supports object-oriented design; has built-in graphical support in the form of the AWT and Swing libraries; has a clean, simple design that lends itself to use by beginning programmers; and is just plain fun to use. The Swing extensions to the window tool kit are used to keep pace with the rapid evolution of Java and its supporting libraries.

CHAPTER OVERVIEW

Chapter 1, **"Computers, Programs, and Java,"** provides background information for students with little or no computer experience. For most students this will simply be a review, although the glossary terms will make many loosely defined terms more precise.

Chapter 2, **"Writing Programs,"** defines the design, code, test, and debug cycle for developing correctly working programs, and it describes the kinds of software tools used in each step. It also makes the first strong case for spending time designing a program before jumping headlong into coding.

Chapter 3, **"Getting Started,"** guides the student through the first steps in writing simple programs consisting of a single class definition with a single method. Each object defined by one of these simple classes is used with the Animator to draw a simple shape, either static and moving, within the animation scene. The emphasis in this chapter is on distinguishing classes versus objects, and how a method describes one behavior of an object. The basic language concepts of symbols, identifiers, literals, declarations, simple parameter passing, and comments are defined, and the need for neat-looking, well-documented code is demonstrated.

Chapter 4, **"Variables, Expressions, and Assignment,"** contains fairly formal definitions of variables of the int, double, and String types as well as the evaluation of expressions using the basic arithmetic operators, type conversions, and functions from Java's Math library. All these are used to define more complex shapes and movement within the animation scene. Debugging techniques based on displaying variable and expression values are introduced to help the students identify and isolate errors in expressions.

Chapter 5, **"Defining and Creating Multiple Objects,"** is the first exposure to programs with multiple, student-defined objects, including several different objects defined by the same class. Instance variables are introduced and used to contain property values for the objects and to reference other objects. At this point object interactions are quite simple, but parameter passing is revisited in depth since this is the first time students write calls to methods that they write themselves. This is also the first time name scoping becomes an issue, and the chapter begins the discussion of the scope of instance, parameter, and local variables. Object diagrams are also introduced to help students visualize the relationships between objects.

Chapter 6, **"Interacting Objects and Events,"** begins describing how objects interact via method calls and return values. The concepts are motivated and demonstrated via animations in which objects representing shapes can exchange information about one another (e.g., position), leading to some interesting animated scenes. Passing object references is covered for the first time. The clicking of the mouse within the scene is presented as a first, simple introduction to the concept of an asynchronous event, and techniques for reacting to the event within an animation object are shown. The chapter concludes by introducing simple Java applets with labels, buttons, text fields, and the ability to react to button and text field events, thereby beginning a migration away from exclusive use of the Animator.

Chapter 7, **"Making Decisions,"** introduces the if/then/else structure, boolean expressions, equality, relational, and logical operators, and nested-if structures. Animations are still used in many examples, some of them quite complex, but applets also start appearing more frequently.

Chapter 8, **"Program Testing,"** is the first in-depth presentation of white (clear) and black box testing techniques, incremental development and testing, and unit testing. It is at this point, after the introduction of alternative paths in programs, that testing becomes more interesting, and difficult. The ideas presented in this chapter are explicitly reinforced in later chapters as they apply to new structures such as loops, arrays, abstract data types, and simple linked data structures.

Chapter 9, **"Simple Class Extension,"** is a very simple introduction to inheritance, with the students extending Java's JPanel class to draw in an applet (via the same drawing methods used in animations), and the Mouse-Adapter class to react to mouse events (via the same concept used in animations). This is a fun chapter, and it opens up the possibility of writing very interesting applets. It also, however, gives the student experience with inheritance in a simple context before approaching it in earnest in Chapter 15.

Chapter 10, **"Repetition,"** presents for- and while-loops. It has a major section on techniques for designing looping structures and testing and debugging them. Nested loops are presented, and the use of helper methods to simplify their construction is described and encouraged. String manipulations using simple string functions are introduced as another way of finding useful and challenging applications of loops.

Chapter 11, **"Arrays,"** shows students how to define and use Java's fixed-size array objects. Simple searching and sorting algorithms are used as examples to demonstrate loop structures that traverse and modify arrays. Java's Vector class is introduced, with the definition of a Vector-like class for a growable array as another array application. Arrays of two or more dimensions are also presented.

Chapter 12, **"Application Programs,"** is the first introduction to application programs as opposed to applets. The emphasis is on application programs that have a graphical user interface since students have become accustomed to them in all the applet examples and exercises in previous chapters. Java's menu classes are also used to make the GUIs more interesting.

Chapter 13, **"Input and Output,"** presents Java's mechanisms for transferring text, binary, and object data between files and the program. Since many I/O object methods throw exceptions, an introduction to Java's exception mechanism is given, but only to the extent needed to handle the required exceptions.

Chapter 14, **"Graphical User Interface Classes,"** lets the student take a breather after a series of concept-packed chapters to have some fun and learn about a few new, interesting, and useful GUI component classes. The border layout manager is presented so that the student can design complex but aesthetically pleasing arrangements of all the new components. This chapter can be skipped.

Chapter 15, **"Class Hierarchies,"** is a fairly complete introduction to inheritance. Defining superclasses and subclasses, inheriting and overriding methods, the protected access modifier, abstract and final classes and methods, and interfaces are all covered. Many examples are used to motivate and illustrate the concepts.

Chapter 16, **"Abstract Data Types and Linked Data Structures,"** defines abstraction, encapsulation and information hiding. Alternate implementations of a collection abstraction, beginning with a simple array, and continuing through several variations of a linked list, motivate the student to make use of abstraction as a program design tool. Stacks and queues are also defined as abstractions and then implemented in several ways. An important aspect of this chapter is that multiple implementations of every structure are presented, then their good and bad features are compared and contrasted in an effort to convince the student that no one implementation is always best. Documentation comments and the javadoc tool are introduced as the way to specify an abstraction for others to use.

Chapter 17, **"Introduction to Recursion,"** presents the topic in a very intuitive way. While by no means leading a student to a complete mastery of the subject, lots of examples of first simple, then increasingly more complex recursive algorithms help the student adjust to the new way of reasoning about algorithms.

SUPPLEMENTAL MATERIALS

All supplemental materials are available from McGraw-Hill's website (www.mhhe.com/catalogs/solutions/olc.mhtml). Additional material, updated more regularly, is available from the author directly at www.cs.mtu.edu/~pop/objects-have-class.

1. **Source and executable code for the Animator and all sample programs.** Source code for every complete and partial program and executables (byte codes) for every complete program are available. All applets, including animations, are directly viewable via any Swing-enabled Web browser.

2. **Solutions to all written and programming exercises.** The author's solutions to every written exercise, and solutions to every programming exercise, in both source and executable (byte code) forms, are also available. All solutions are password-protected.

3. **PowerPoint lecture slides.** Slides are available in both static and animated versions.

4. **Instructor's guide.** Teaching object-oriented programming to beginning programmers is relatively new. The author, who has taught object-oriented programming for many years, first in C^{++} and then for the last two years in Java, shares his insights into what students find helpful, what they find particularly difficult or confusing, what instructors should pay special attention to, and what pitfalls to avoid.

5. **Closed-lab exercises.** Short programming exercises, "try this and see what happens" problems, and worksheets, all class-tested, have been developed by the author over the past two years and are also available.

McGraw-Hill Online Learning Center

The book's Online Learning Center at `www.mhhe.com/catalogs/ solutions/olc.mhtml` is a "digital cartridge" that contains the book's pedagogy and supplements. Students can go online to take self-graded quizzes, access the source code, and review PowerPoint slides for the relevant topics. An instructor's section, containing password-protected solutions to problems in the text organized by chapter for easy reference, is also available.

ACKNOWLEDGMENTS

Taking on the task of writing a textbook demanded the encouragement and support of two very important people, my wife, Donna, and my daughter, Jen. They put up with my frustrations, missed me during the long hours I was glued to my computer, commiserated with my desire to finally get it done, and all the time continued in their unfailing love and continuous prayer. To them I owe my deepest gratitude.

I thank Steve Bruell, chair of the Computer Science Department at the University of Iowa and my longtime friend and colleague, for giving me the opportunity to begin work on this textbook while on sabbatical at the University of Iowa. I thank Linda Ott, chair of the Computer Science Department at Michigan Tech, for her encouragement, support, and understanding when I must have seemed like a part-time employee.

I thank the wonderful people at McGraw-Hill, especially Betsy Jones, whose encouragement gave me the confidence to take on this project and to persist when things got tough; and Melinda Dougharty, for her unbridled enthusiasm and day-to-day efforts on my behalf.

I am indebted to the few hundred Michigan Tech students who endured early drafts of the text. Many provided much needed constructive criticism. I thank my teaching assistants for their input on how to improve the presentation. Adam Diehm and Chunhua Zhao deserve special thanks for testing and debugging all the programming examples and exercises that appear in the text.

The many comments, suggestions, criticisms, and encouragement of the following reviewers are greatly appreciated:

Peter Biggs
Brigham Young University

Steve Bruell
University of Iowa

Walter Daugherity
Texas A&M University

Timothy Davis
Clemson University

Lewis E. Hitchner
California Polytechnic State University

Alan Kaplan
Clemson University

Wendy Lehnert
*University of Massachusetts,
Amherst*

Keith B. Olson
Montana Tech

Lawrence Petersen
Texas A&M University

Duane Szafron
University of Alberta

Sharon Tuttle
Humbolt State University

Richard Wiener
*University of Colorado at Colorado
Springs*

Lee Wittenberg
Kean University

And finally, but most importantly, I thank God for making all this possible and for simply being there for me day in and day out.

## CHAPTER 1

Computers, Programs, and Java

OBJECTIVES

- To understand the basic components of a computer.
- To understand what a computer program is.
- To understand how the basic components of a computer work together to execute a program.
- To know the difference between high-level and low-level languages.
- To recognize Java as a high-level language.
- To differentiate between compilation, execution, and interpretation.

1.1 INTRODUCTION

In the 1960s, computers existed mainly in air-conditioned rooms, consisted of several refrigerator-size cabinets, cost hundreds of thousands or millions of dollars each, and were used by people with extensive training. In the 1970s and 1980s the microcomputer revolution began, and computers became small, inexpensive, and easy enough to use that only minimal training was needed. By the 1990s computers have become so affordable and so easy to use that they have found application in every aspect of our society. They are in our homes, schools, businesses, and government. Many are quite visible and used directly, such as the home or business personal computer. Most are hidden and operate virtually without our knowledge, such as the ones in our cars, TVs, and VCRs. Odds are you don't even know how many there are in your own home.

So what is this thing called a computer? Well, actually not much. Most computers are made from just a few square slices of silicon, each perhaps a quarter of an inch on a side and a little thicker than a piece of paper. Of course modern technology manages to get millions of incredibly simple electric circuits and the wires connecting them onto these little pieces of silicon, and that is partially what makes them so powerful.

But the basic idea behind the operation of the computer is really quite simple. The computer has a memory in which it can store lots of information. Some of that information is actually a set of instructions (or commands) that tell the computer what to do. Each individual instruction is rather simple, such as a command to add two numbers, or to decide to do one thing or another based on a simple piece of information, such as whether one number is larger than another.

A simple analogy to a computer is that in your brain you have stored, let's say, a set of instructions on how to divide one multiple-digit number into another—long division. Let's also say that you have two numbers in mind, for example, 784 and 23, and you decide to divide the larger one by the smaller one. You now start acting as a computer acts. You follow the instructions stored in your brain to figure out, step by step, each digit of the answer. When you are done, you have the answer, also stored in your brain. Along the way you have made some decisions, such as how many times 23 goes into 78, and have done some simple calculations, such as subtraction. This is exactly what a computer does, too, except that it is probably quite a bit faster than you are. It also doesn't remember the numbers and the instructions on how to do long division in the same way as your brain does—in fact we have no clue how your brain stores this stuff. But that's not really important—the key is that the principle is the same: storing information and instructions in a memory and following those instructions to carry out some task.

What gives the computer its incredible power is that it can follow the instructions stored in its memory *very* quickly—hundreds of millions of them can be followed by a computer *every second*. If they were all additions of two numbers, that would mean that it could total all the telephone numbers in all the phone books in the United States in about a second or two (assuming all the numbers were stored in the computer's memory to start with). It's unlikely that anybody would want to know the sum of all the phone numbers in the United States, but you get the point.

However, raw speed is not the only key to the power of the computer. The other key is having a set of instructions that does something interesting. This set of instructions is called a **program.** Nobody would argue that the set of instructions (the program) that totals the numbers in phone books is very interesting, even if it can be done in a couple of seconds. But real programs are interesting. They provide the apparent intelligence that computers have. They are what make computers useful, or even fun (ask any kid at a video arcade). Without programs, computers would simply be useless.

This book is mainly about creating the sequence of instructions necessary to do something interesting, a process called **programming.** It is a fascinating task, with elements of artistic creativity and nuts-and- bolts construction. There are times of elation, such as when you find and fix an error in your creation after hours of searching, and times of frustration, such as all the hours prior to finding and fixing that error. At times it is a solitary endeavor, such as when you are sitting at a computer working on your program, and at other times a social one, say when you are part of a team working together to produce a large and sophisticated program. When your program finally works and starts being used by others, it is very rewarding. When you realize that your program is part of something that, if it works, will keep an airplane flying, and if it doesn't, could cause it to crash, it is humbling, and even scary.

To do programming effectively requires lots of talents. You need the ability to see the big picture, to break a large, complex task into smaller and more manageable pieces, and then to see how those pieces will fit together to form the whole. You need to pay minute attention to detail, as computers are not very forgiving of incredibly simple mistakes. You must have detective skills in order to track down errors that cause your program to work incorrectly, or not at all. You need perseverance, because there will be times when you will spend hours trying to figure out why your program doesn't do what it is supposed to. You must be humble, because whenever the program you created doesn't work, it is most assuredly *your* fault. You must be confident, because eventually your program will work if you put enough effort into it.

1.2 COMPUTER BASICS

To understand programming, you need to know a little bit about how a computer works—what its major components are and how they interact. You've already been shown a couple of the components in the introduction—the memory and the part that follows instructions, called the **central processing unit, or CPU.** You've probably also figured out that there must be more, and there is. Every computer needs to be able to interact with the outside world, to get information from it (input), and to send information to it (output). Figure 1.1 shows how this all fits together.

As described in the introduction, the memory is where all the information that the computer is currently working on and the instructions that the computer is carrying out are stored. Your program will be stored there when the computer is following the instructions you wrote. For those of you familiar with personal computers, this memory is often called *RAM,* which stands for *random access memory,* but it also comes in a variety of slightly different forms (DRAM, SDRAM, etc.). The differences don't matter at this level of discussion, and I'll simply refer to all of them as **memory.**

The CPU is where instructions are carried out (the carrying out of instructions is called their **execution**). For example, to add two numbers that are stored in memory somewhere and put the result somewhere else in memory, the CPU will get copies of the two numbers from the memory, then add them, then put the result back into the memory. The circuitry that does all this is part of the CPU.

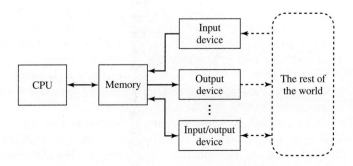

FIGURE 1.1

Remember, the instructions that the computer is executing are also stored in the memory, so when the CPU is ready to execute the next instruction, it must get the instruction from memory, figure out what it means, and then do it. This is all that the computer does, over and over. It gets an instruction from memory, figures out what it means, and then does it. And it does it hundreds of millions of times per second.

An **input device** is something that the computer uses to get information from the rest of the world. Examples are a keyboard, a mouse, a joystick, a CD-ROM drive, or a temperature or pressure sensor. The information (such as which key was typed, or what the temperature is) is put into the memory of the computer so that the CPU can use it. Although no connection is shown in the diagram, these devices interact with the CPU to tell it when new information has been put into the memory (e.g., when someone types a letter on the keyboard), or the devices get prompted by the CPU to get information (e.g., to take a temperature reading).

An **output device** is something that the computer uses to get information out to the rest of the world. Examples are a monitor (video screen), a speaker, a printer, or an actuator (something that creates movement). Again, although no connection is shown in the diagram, these devices are instructed by the CPU to take information from memory and send it to the rest of the world (e.g., to cause an actuator to move the flap of an airplane wing a certain distance).

An **input/output device** is something that does both input and output. Examples are a disk drive (floppy or hard) or a network interface to the Internet (a modem or an ethernet card). The computer uses them to both get information from the rest of the world and to send information to the rest of the world. And as before, the CPU interacts with such devices just as it does with pure input and pure output devices.

Figure 1.1 shows one input device, one output device, and one input/output device. In reality computers can have several of each. A typical home personal computer these days will have a keyboard, mouse, and CD-ROM drive for input; a monitor, printer, and speakers for output; and a floppy drive, hard drive, and modem for input/output.

Most computers that you will use while learning to write programs will have a hard drive. This is where a lot of information and programs are stored until they are needed by the CPU. Only the program being executed and the data it is using need to be in the memory of the computer. Until then, programs and information are stored on the hard drive, which, if you think about it, is just another kind of memory. Don't confuse the two. The memory shown in the diagram is used temporarily by programs that are currently being executed by the CPU. When the program finishes, it no longer needs to be in memory. If a program is to be executed again, it and all its associated information will be copied into memory from the hard drive all over again.

If you buy a program (say a game), it probably comes on a floppy disk or a CD-ROM. When you install it, you copy it from the floppy or CD-ROM onto the hard drive. You can then remove the floppy or CD-ROM from the computer—the CPU will copy the program into memory from the hard drive when you ask to execute it (i.e., to play the game).

1.3 PROGRAMS

A computer *program* is a step-by-step sequence of *instructions* that the computer follows to do some task. These instructions are very, very simple, and it takes a lot of them to do what might seem quite simple to you or me. In fact, the instructions are so simple that writing a program using these simple instructions is extremely tedious. It is actually worse than that, because the instructions, as they are stored in the memory of the computer, are just a bunch of 0s and 1s. For example, the single instruction to add two numbers on a computer with an Intel Pentium CPU is 00101110100110000110011110000001. Imagine the difficulty in writing a program that contains a few thousand instructions that all look like this! Impossible. You'd never finish, and you'd never get it right.

As a result, a long time ago (in the early 1950s, which is a long time ago by computer standards) people figured out that they could write programs in a way that was easier to understand (by humans) and then translate them into the 0s and 1s afterward. In fact, the translation itself can be done by a program. The program is called a **compiler,** and all it does is to translate a program written in a form that humans can understand to the form that the computer can execute. The computer cannot execute a program in its human-readable form. It must be translated, or compiled, into the corresponding 0s and 1s first. This human-readable form is written in a **high-level language,** and there are lots of different ones.

Programs written in high-level languages, while much easier to read than a lot of 0s and 1s, do not look like English (or French, or Chinese, etc.). It would be nice if you could just tell a computer what to do in English, but the fact is languages that are used by humans to communicate with one another are extremely complex, very imprecise, and often ambiguous.

Instead, programs written in a high-level language are relatively simple (compared to English), *very* precise, and *never* ambiguous. Most use a small collection of English words and some punctuation symbols, and there are simple but very strict rules for combining the words and symbols to instruct the computer to do something. These rules must be followed exactly, or the computer will not understand what you are trying to tell it (actually, the compiler won't know how to translate it). For example, if I say in English, "Bob is a nice person He helps people," then even though I left out a period, you can tell what I mean. If you do the equivalent in a program, you will get an error message. If I say, "I'm going to the restaurent to get something to eat," you know exactly what I mean even though I spelled *restaurant* wrong. Spell a word wrong in a program and you'll get an error message, no matter how close you were and no matter how obvious what you meant is.

The point of all this is that even though you will be writing programs in a high-level language, you must still be very precise, spelling everything exactly right, putting the appropriate symbols in just the right places, using the correct word at the correct time. This is one of the challenges of writing programs. You have to pay close attention to detail, and you must follow the rules. It can get frustrating at times, especially when you are just learning. It's complicated by the fact that compilers, which are very good at detecting a violation of a rule, are not always very good at helping you figure out what you actually did wrong. As a result, part of learning how to program is learning the rules, and part is learning to understand the compiler's often confusing, sometimes misleading responses to violations.

1.3.1 System Programs

An important set of programs, often referred to as **system programs,** are responsible for managing the hardware and making a computer easy to use by us humans. One of the most important system programs is called the operating system, which is really a collection of programs. You may already be familiar with Windows 95 (or 98), the MacOS, or Linux, all of which are operating systems.

An **operating system** handles all the minute details of direct control of the computer hardware, giving you simple, convenient ways to make the computer do what you want. For example, to run a program, all you need to do is to point the mouse and click on a small picture on the screen that represents the program, and the operating system takes care of finding the program on the hard drive, loading it into memory, and starting it running.

The operating system manages the hardware, making sure it is used correctly and efficiently. It keeps track of where programs and data are on the hard drive and where the empty space is for new programs and data. It makes sure that when two programs that are running at the same time try to print something on the printer, the output is not mixed together. It handles errors that occur in the hardware, often retrying things several times in case the error was temporary and not a permanent failure. This is but a small sample of the functions it performs.

A **windowing system,** which in some cases is part of the operating system and sometimes is separate, is another set of system programs. It provides a simple mechanism (called a **user interface**) by which the user can control the computer and the computer can communicate information to the user via the keyboard, mouse, and monitor. The most common user interface these days is a **graphical user interface** that uses pictures, shapes, and colors instead of text (or in combination with text) to convey information.

1.3.2 Application Programs

Programs that aren't system programs are usually called **application programs,** and there are thousands of them. Typical ones found on personal computers include word processors, spreadsheets, games, Internet browsers, image manipulation, and E-mail. Others are more special-purpose, with programs existing for almost any line of business or leisure imaginable. Even more are hidden, running on computers that are embedded in things you might never think would have one, such as a VCR, camera, microwave oven, automobile, or cell phone. They give the user the ability to do almost anything with a computer, and the sky is the limit. New application programs are being created daily, and new and better versions of existing ones are released all the time. In fact, the programs you write while learning how to program are considered application programs, too.

1.4 JAVA

Literally thousands of high-level languages have been invented for people to use to program computers. They range from quite simple to the rather complex. Java happens to be one of those languages, and it falls somewhere in the middle of the complexity range.

Java is a fairly new language, only having come into being in the middle of the 1990s. It was originally designed for programming what are called *embedded processors*—computers that you usually don't see that run things such as your VCR, your car, your camera, maybe even your toaster. Java was also designed to be portable, that is, for programs to be written once and work on just about every computer available. It may be hard to believe, but with most languages when you write a program, it isn't guaranteed to work exactly the same (or at all) on different computers. There are often subtle and not so subtle differences in the way each computer executes the same program. Hence that same program must sometimes be modified (usually only slightly) to work correctly on different computers. Java was intended to eliminate this problem, but unfortunately it hasn't succeeded completely. Java is still evolving, so perhaps in the near future these problems will be eliminated.

While Java was being developed, the Internet came into being and Web browsers (such as Netscape and Internet Explorer) started becoming popular. The Java developers saw an opportunity to be able to provide a mechanism, using a particular form of Java program called an *applet,* that people could use to make their Web pages dynamic and interactive instead of being simply the electronic equivalent of a piece of paper. This idea caught on quickly, and today millions of Web pages use applets to be more appealing and useful.

Java was chosen for use in this book mostly because it is fun. You can write simple programs that do fairly interesting things, that can use images, sound, and graphics; and you can interact with them in neat ways. You can do these things in other languages, too; it is just more difficult, and the programs are not quite so simple. Because Java applets can be attached to Web pages, you can fairly quickly and easily write a Java program that you can put on your Web page to impress your friends and influence people!

Java is modern, so it has the ability to express things in ways that we now think make it easier to write complex programs (the current buzzword is *object-oriented*), something that a lot of older languages either don't have or have tried to add as an afterthought. In this text you will be learning the basics of object-oriented programming, and this is another reason that Java was chosen.

It is also true that once you have learned Java, then with only a small effort you should be able to learn many other languages, should you choose to (because you are interested) or need to (because a class or your job requires it). Look at other languages, and you'll discover a lot of them look like Java. They use many of the same words and same symbols, and they have very similar rules for putting them together. They operate in much the same way. That's not to say that there aren't languages that don't look like or operate like Java. There are some of those, too. But the vast majority of programs you'll find in the world are written in languages that look and act quite a bit like Java.

1.4.1 Executing Java Programs

When a program written in just about any high-level language is compiled, it is converted to the machine language for some particular brand of computer (e.g., Intel Pentium). Unfortunately the machine language for other computers (e.g., Macintosh) is different, so the same machine language version of the program will not run on computers from other manufacturers.

Java is different. A Java program is compiled into a form of machine language, but it is not the machine language for any existing computer and hence can't be executed (directly) by any existing computer. This may seem a bit strange, as the whole point of compiling a program is to make it possible to be executed by a computer.

But Java was designed to be executed on many different computers without having to be compiled separately into the machine language of each. To do so, the designers of Java invented a new "machine language," called *Java byte codes,* that no computer can execute directly. To "execute" a program compiled into Java byte codes, a system program called a Java *interpreter* is used.

The Java interpreter is a program that simulates the execution of the Java byte codes. It causes the computer to do what the byte codes direct, without the hardware of the machine actually understanding what the byte codes mean. The interpreter is reading the byte codes and telling the computer what they mean and what to do. Here's a simple analogy to what is happening.

Suppose you (a computer) are given a recipe for baking a cake (a program that does some task), but the directions (instructions) are written in a foreign language that you don't understand (Java byte codes). You could hire an interpreter (the Java interpreter) who understands the directions (Java byte codes) and have her read the directions (Java byte codes) and tell you in your (machine) language what to do at each step: mix this, add that, bake for so long (add these numbers, multiply those, display the result). Your interpreter would not translate the entire set of directions for you all at once and give you the entire recipe in your language, but instead would just tell you what to do step by step. This is similar to what a Java interpreter does. It reads the directions (Java byte codes) and tells the computer (in its machine language) what to do at each step.

The major advantage of using an interpreter is that the Java program need only be compiled once into Java byte codes, which can then be used on any computer that has a Java interpreter (and most do). Most Web browsers (e.g., Netscape or Internet Explorer) have a Java interpreter in them, too. When you view a Web page with a Java applet on it, the browser interprets the Java applet by using its Java interpreter. Hence the creator of the Java applet need only make available one version of its compiled form (the Java byte codes), which it can send via the Internet to any computer running a Web browser with a Java interpreter. If Java byte codes did not exist, and Java applets were compiled into machine language instead, then every applet would have to be compiled into the machine language of every computer that it might be executed on, resulting in many different copies. The Web browser would also have to make sure it always got the right version to execute.

1.5 LOOKING AHEAD

The rest of this book is about programming. Even though Java is the language chosen to write programs in, this is not a book about Java. I'll not show you everything there is to know about Java. I'll explain many programming concepts that apply both to Java and to many other programming languages. You'll be able to use those concepts when you learn and use other similar programming languages, such as C++, but the main focus of this book is on writing good, working programs.

I'll guide you through the process of designing and writing programs and getting them to work correctly. You'll see examples of both well-written programs and poorly written programs, and I'll explain the difference. I'll show you how to detect, locate, and fix errors in your programs. Once you get past writing simple, short programs using just a few Java concepts, I'll talk about designing your programs before you write them. As you'll see, writing programs is more than just writing down the instructions, just as painting is more than just putting some colors on a canvas.

Here are some tips that will help you become proficient at writing programs. First, pay close attention to detail. Computers and their compilers are very picky. Second, practice, practice, practice. Practice writing lots of short programs to gain proficiency at using various programming concepts; you'll find plenty of simple exercises at the ends of the chapters to work on. Try things to see what happens. One nice thing about a computer is that it will give you almost immediate feedback, and you don't have to worry about breaking it (unless you get frustrated and pound on it).

And finally, have fun. Programming is fun, and Java is a language that makes it easy to write fun programs. This book will have you writing lots of programs that you can hang on your Web pages, and that can be fun. Graphics, animation, sound, real-time interaction—what could be better?

Summary

- Computers are made up of the following basic components: a central processing unit (CPU) that executes instructions; a memory in which the instructions and the information the computer uses are stored while the CPU is using it; and input, output and input/output devices that communicate between the computer and the outside world.

- Disks (hard drives) store programs and information when they are not being used by the CPU.

- The sequence of instructions that the computer executes is called a program.

- The power of the computer comes from how fast it can execute a program and from the complexity and sophistication of that program.

- Programming is the process humans go through to create programs for the computer to execute.

- Programs are usually written in a high-level language that is easy for humans to understand.

- Programs are translated into the simple instructions the computer can execute by a compiler.

- Java is one of many high-level languages used to program computers.

- Java is modern, useful in new environments like the Internet and Web pages, and makes writing fun programs relatively easy compared to other languages that are available.

Glossary

Application Program A program that provides some useful function, but is not a system program.

Central Processing Unit The part of a computer that follows instructions. Abbreviated CPU.

Compiler A program that translates a program written in a high-level language into the instructions that are understood by the CPU.

Execution The CPU following the sequence of instructions specified in a program.

Graphical User Interface A way of displaying information on the monitor that uses shapes, colors, images, and text, rather than just text.

High-Level Language A human-readable form of a program.

Input Device A part of the computer that is used to get information from the rest of the world.

Input/Output Device A part of the computer that is used to both get information from the rest of the world and to give information to the rest of the world.

Java The modern high-level language chosen for this book.

Memory The part of the computer where information and instructions are stored while the CPU is using it. Often referred to as random access memory, or RAM.

Operating System A collection of programs that controls the operation of the hardware and provides a convenient way to use the hardware. Abbreviated OS.

Output Device A part of the computer that is used to get information from the rest of the world.

Program A sequence of instructions that controls the operation of a computer.

Programming Creating a sequence of instructions that controls the operation of a computer. Usually done in a high-level language that is eventually translated by the compiler into the instructions that the CPU understands.

System Programs Programs that manage the hardware, thereby making the computer easier to use.

User Interface The information a user sees and the manner in which the user enters commands and information into the computer.

Windowing System Programs that make it possible for other programs to provide a graphical user interface.

Written Exercises

1. Write down what talents you think you have that will help you succeed at writing programs.

2. Computer memory comes in units called *bytes*. One byte can store one letter, digit or other character (such as a space, comma, period, semicolon). Approximately what fraction of the Christian Bible (any version) do you think will fit in the average home personal computer's memory (not disk)?

3. If you own a computer, categorize the various input, output, and input/output devices that you have.

4. What system programs do you use? What application programs do you use most often?

5. What is an advantage of writing programs in a high-level language, such as Java, over writing them in the form that the CPU can execute?

## CHAPTER 2

Writing Programs

OBJECTIVES

- To understand the process of writing a program.
- To appreciate the importance of designing before writing.
- To understand the concept of a software tool.
- To become aware of the kinds of software tools used to develop Java programs.

2.1 AN ANALOGY

Like many creative activities, becoming proficient at writing programs involves following a process. Consider writing an essay. You start with a blank piece of paper (or a blank screen on the word processor), armed only with an idea of what the essay is supposed to be about. You don't just start writing immediately, putting down the first word, then the second, etc., until you finish with the last word of the essay. Instead, first you do a little planning and organizing, perhaps creating an outline. You decide what kinds of things you want to say, and in what approximate order. You don't worry about the actual wording of anything yet. You might call this designing the essay.

When writing a program, you do the same thing. You don't start writing Java code immediately (**code** is a term used to describe the actual words and symbols in a program). You first have to get organized, perhaps by mapping out what information you will have in your program and what the information means. You outline the basic steps of how that information is going to be manipulated, what each step is going to do, and in what order. Then you might take some of that information or those steps that are a bit vague, think about them in a little greater detail, and add another level of organization.

When writing the essay, eventually you start actually putting words down on paper (or typing them onto the screen). If you are like me, you probably still don't just start with the first word and stop at the end of the essay. You write for a while, maybe a few sentences, maybe a paragraph or two; then you stop and go back and read it to see if it sounds right. You might find some mistakes in grammar or spelling, or perhaps something just doesn't sound right or fit in with the rest of what you've written. So you go back and edit, changing this, deleting that, adding something else.

Programming works the same way. You could, after doing as much design work as you think is appropriate, just start writing code, starting at the beginning and stopping only when the whole program is written. But most people don't work that way, and I don't suggest that you do either. For all but the most trivial programs of just a few lines of code, I suggest you follow the essay-writing analogy. Write part of your program, then go back and look at it to see if it has any mistakes or seems as if it might not work right. If you find something wrong, fix it and check it again until you think it's probably right. At this point you can actually do something that you can't when you are writing an essay. You can, if you have written enough, have the computer check what you have written so far to see if it is correct! At a minimum you can have it check for obvious spelling and grammar mistakes, and if you've written enough, you can execute what you've written so far to see if it works correctly. It clearly won't do everything that the program was supposed to do because you haven't written the whole thing yet, but if it works so far, you can go on to writing more code. If it doesn't, you have to do something you don't do when writing an essay—try to figure out why your code doesn't work, and then fix it so that it does. This is a process called **debugging.**

Eventually you finish writing your essay, probably after writing, reading, and fixing several different parts along the way. At this point you probably read your essay from the beginning to the end to make sure that everything is covered, that the order is right, that it flows well, and that it just plain seems to be as good as it can be. If you find something that isn't right, or that you don't like, you go back and fix it, checking the sentences and paragraphs around the fix to make sure that the change improves things, and that it fits in properly.

Eventually you finish writing your program, too. If you've been writing and testing parts of it as you go along, then by now you will be pretty close to having a complete, working program. Again, you could go back through it by hand to see if it looks as if you have everything there, in the right order, convincing yourself that it will work. But with a program the final test is to execute the whole program, trying it in various ways (i.e., giving it various inputs) to make sure that it always does the right thing in response to whatever you give it. You may find that it doesn't, even if all along the way you've been testing out parts of it and everything has worked fine so far. Don't be surprised. This happens all the time, and it just means that you'll have to go back and do more debugging.

However, and this is important, the more time and effort you spend designing your program to start with, the more likely it is that it will work correctly when you are all done. It's like the old "pay me now or pay me later" saying—a little planning up front usually saves a lot of effort at the end. In fact, the world is full of examples of programs that had to be rewritten almost from scratch because not enough design work was done up front—it became apparent that redesigning and rewriting would be easier than trying to fix the mess that was created from a poor design. This is true all the way from rather simple programs written by people just learning how to program, to large, complex software systems consisting of millions of lines of code written by teams of programmers.

The natural tendency of most people is to try to make themselves feel as if they are making progress, or convincing their boss that they are, by cutting short the design time and getting into writing code as quickly as possible. You think you are farther along because you actually have something to show for the time spent so far. You might even get parts of the program working pretty quickly. But eventually you find that although the pieces seem to work fine, when you put them together, they don't work right at all; and worse yet, figuring out why is often very difficult and very, very time-consuming. A simple analogy is that you can make the world's best square peg—perfectly square, precisely the right dimensions—and also make the world's best round hole—perfectly round, precisely the right size—only to find that when you put them together, the peg just doesn't fit in that hole very well. As the old saying goes, it's back to the drawing board.

2.2 THE PROGRAMMING PROCESS

In this section I'll describe the process that you'll be following to write your programs and get them to work correctly. This basic process is pretty much the same whether you are writing small programs as you begin to learn about programming, or you are part of a team writing large, complex software, such as a modern word processor, Web browser, or space shuttle guidance programs. With large complex systems there are more steps, both before and after those shown here, but the core process shown in Figure 2.1 is still at the heart of the programming process.

Figure 2.1 shows the steps involved in producing working programs.

Design: As I talked about in the introduction to this chapter, this is probably one of the most important steps in the process and one that you are tempted to do quickly, so that you can get to the next step. Resist. Learning how to do a good design is a major part of learning how to write programs, and we'll devote quite a bit of this book to talking about it.

Write Code: This is where you actually start writing down Java code. Some people write their code out on paper first, then type it in. Some sit right down at the computer and type it in as they create it. Do what seems right for you. Except for the simplest programs, I don't encourage you to write the whole program at this step. Write part of it, then go on to the next step. It also is a good idea to take a few minutes to read what you have just written, just as you would when writing a paper. Many simple mistakes can be found by simple inspection, and often those mistakes are more easily fixed now than later.

Compile: This step is done by the computer that you are developing your program on. It takes the file containing your Java program and translates it into a form that your computer can understand. It also finds various errors, such as missing punctuation and misspellings, and reports them to you. Do not assume,

FIGURE 2.1

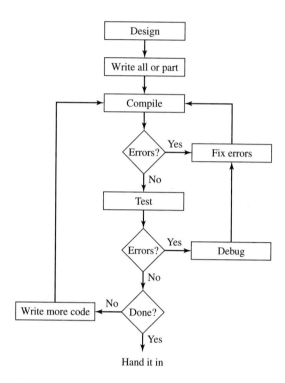

however, that if the compiler does not find any errors then your program should work correctly. In English the sentence "Buy green paint." is perfectly correct, but it is not the right thing to do if it is part of a set of directions on how to paint a house blue. The same idea applies to programs.

Fix Errors: At this point the compiler may have some errors in your program (called compilation errors); or your program may have done something illegal during execution, such as trying to divide by 0 (called run-time errors); or you may have discovered that the program doesn't do anything illegal but also doesn't work as expected. It's pretty clear what you do here—try to remove the source of problems in your program. You might fix something simple, such as a misspelled word, or do something more complex, such as rewriting a whole section of code, when there is no simple fix. Sometimes the errors aren't so easy to fix because you aren't quite sure what to do. You may have convinced yourself that something is wrong at a certain point, but you aren't sure what's right. Resist the temptation to simply try some arbitrary change in the hope that it will work. It might, but more likely it won't. Take time to think about it, and in the long run you'll almost certainly save time.

Test: In this step you have the computer execute the code you have written and compiled so far. You try various inputs to make sure it does the right thing. If it does, you gain confidence that your code is right. If it doesn't, you have to find out why. Please note that except for the most trivial pieces of code, testing will not prove that your code is correct. This is true simply because you cannot, for all but the simplest programs, test every possibility. Sometimes it would take too long (years) to try out all the millions or billions of possibilities, and sometimes there are an infinite number of possibilities. However, a well-designed set of tests can give you great confidence that your code is correct.

Debug: You wind up here when testing discovers that your code doesn't do the correct thing for one or more input possibilities. This step is where you become the detective. Sometimes it is pretty obvious where the error is in your code—consider yourself lucky. Sometimes it's not so obvious, and you'll have to dig really hard to figure out why code that looks correct to you doesn't work right. Getting good at this takes a lot of practice. Fortunately, when you are just learning how to program, you tend to make a lot of mistakes, so expect to get a lot of practice debugging.

Write More Code: Since my advice was not to write complete programs before checking them for correctness, this step simply adds more code to your program. Actually I will show you techniques whereby you can write sections of your program separately, debug and test them, and then put them all together and retest (and maybe debug and test again). As before, inspecting your new code before proceeding will often save time and effort.

2.3 PROGRAMMING TOOLS

The most basic tool used to write programs is what you use to type it in so the computer can use it. This tool is called an **editor,** and there are lots of different ones. All editors allow you to type in the characters that represent a program. All editors allow you to change (edit, hence *editor*) what you have typed in. Most editors allow you to search for various patterns of characters. And all editors allow you to save what you have typed in a file on the hard drive of your computer, and retrieve it again later. This file will be the input to the compiler.

If you are familiar with a word processor such as Word or WordPerfect, an editor is much like one. However it is usually not a good idea to use a word processor for typing in programs. The problem is that these word processors usually don't store your program in a format that the compiler can handle. Instead you should use an editor designed for writing programs, or at the very least, an editor that saves what you typed in a format that can be read by the compiler. Because there are so many different editors of this type, and because some work on one type of computer and others work on other types, I won't go into any detail about how to use one, as I probably won't pick one that you will be able to use. Instead I'll refer you to your instructor for more information on what is available and how to use it.

In addition to an editor, a wide variety of software packages exist for you to use to design, write, debug, and test your Java programs (a **software package** is a related set of programs). The simplest is the set of programs included with the Java Development Kit, or JDK, from Sun Microsystems. Four of the programs in this package (often referred to as **tools**) are of interest at this time. One is the Java compiler, which translates your Java program into a form that can be executed by your computer. Two others are programs that make the computer execute your already compiled program. As we shall see later, there are two different ways to do this, so there are two different programs to do it. The fourth tool helps you in the debugging process (inappropriately called a **debugger** since it doesn't actually debug your program, it only *helps* you debug your program—*you* are really the debugger). If you use the JDK tools to create your Java programs, then you will tell the computer to execute these tools yourself, individually.

More complex software packages for writing Java programs include the various **integrated development environments (IDEs),** such as *CodeWarrior* from Metrowerks, *JBuilder* from Inprise (formerly Borland), *Forte* from Sun, and *Visual Age for Java* from IBM. These packages integrate an editor, compiler, debugger, and tools that execute your programs, and all have a fancy graphical user interface. They can make it easier to do the various program development steps since many are automated or require just a simple mouse click on a button on the screen. Some even help you write your program, providing templates, or partially completed programs, and you just fill in the details. As with editors, because there are so many different IDEs, and because not all are available on all computers, this book will not choose one of them and show you how to use it. You'll have to depend on supplements supplied by your instructor for this.

Summary

- The process of developing a working program involves several steps: design, write, compile, test, and debug. Most of these steps are repeated many times before a finished product is created.

- Design is very important and should never be underemphasized. Avoid the temptation to plunge immediately into coding. It rarely saves time in the long run.

- Several software tools are used to develop Java programs, including an editor, compiler, and debugger.

- An integrated development environment (IDE) packages an editor, compiler, and debugger into a single tool with a fancy graphical user interface.

Glossary

Code The actual text of a program. Also a verb (to code) meaning to write a program.

Debugger A program that helps you find errors in a program.

Debugging Finding and fixing the errors in a program. Not to be confused with testing.

Editor A program that allows you to type in a program and make changes to it.

Integrated Development Environment (IDE) A collection of tools that work closely together to help you write, compile, and debug programs.

Software Package A related set of programs.

Tools Programs used to help you write programs, including at least an editor, compiler, and debugger.

Written Exercises

1. What are the reasons for spending as much time as you can designing your program before you write it?

2. Which steps of the programming process are done by a person? Which steps by a computer? In which do the person and the computer work together?

3. What programming tools do you have available to use when writing, debugging, and testing your programs? If you have an IDE, name it.

## CHAPTER 3

Getting Started

OBJECTIVES

- To understand the basic concept of an object.
- To know the distinction between objects and the class that describes them.
- To understand how drawing is done in Java.
- To be able to write a class definition, with one method, for objects that draw on the screen.
- To be able to write, compile, and run a simple Java program.
- To be able to find and read documentation on Java graphics drawing commands.
- To know the basic Java language concepts of reserved words, identifiers, symbols, integer numbers, literals, declarations, commands, parameters, and arguments.
- To appreciate that the appearance of a program is important.
- To appreciate that choosing descriptive identifier names is important.
- To appreciate that program documentation is important.

3.1 OBJECTS

Objects are the essence of programming in the object-oriented programming design philosophy. Objects are things. Objects have *properties*. Objects have *behavior;* that is, they do things. Usually what they do depends on their properties. Programs that you write will have lots of objects, and the objects will interact with one another to change one another's properties and to cause things to happen. The programmer's task is to define the objects that make up the intended program—to indicate what properties each object has and what each object does in response to requests from other objects, and to organize that collection of objects into a working program.

The real world has all sorts of objects. You are an object. A ball is an object. A pencil is an object. Just about anything you can think of that you can touch is an object. These objects *are* something.

Objects have properties. For example, a ball has size, it has color, it has weight. You have all sorts of properties, such as height, weight, skin color, gender, marital status, number of toes, etc. These properties serve to identify the object, and can, over time, change. You probably don't weigh the same today as you did 10 years ago. You are still the same object, but one of your properties has changed.

In addition to properties, real-world objects have behavior. Behavior is what the object does in response to some stimulus. If you squeeze a rubber ball, it will change shape. If you squeeze a billiard ball, it might also change shape, but very little. You have lots of behaviors. If somebody tells you a good joke, you laugh. When you have to write an answer to a question on an exam, you put down what you think is correct. If you get cold, you put on more clothing. If you fall in the water, you start swimming (hopefully).

The behavior of a real-world object often depends on the current properties of that object. A rubber ball at room temperature will change shape rather easily when squeezed. The same ball will not change shape so easily if it is frozen. The ball is still the same object, but the value of one of its properties has changed (its temperature), and hence its behavior has also changed as a result. Your behavior also can be different when some of your properties change. If you are in a good mood, you probably will laugh when told a good joke. If you are feeling sad or depressed, then you might not laugh. If you are asleep, you won't laugh at all.

Objects in the computer are very similar to real-world objects. Although you can't touch them, they do exist in the memory of the machine. They have properties, as you will see, and these properties can change. They also have behaviors that are demonstrated when the object is "stimulated," or asked to demonstrate one of its behaviors, and this behavior can vary depending on the current values of the properties of that object.

{New Concept}

Objects are the building blocks of Java programs. They have properties, which can change over time, and behaviors, which can vary depending on current property values.

Java comes with all sorts of objects all ready for you to use in constructing interesting and powerful programs. There are objects to create graphical user interfaces, to perform mathematical functions, to interact with the users, to communicate over a network, and so on. Most of these objects are constructed from other objects and/or use other objects to help them do what they need to do, just as you are an object that is constructed from other objects (bones, skin, organs, blood, etc.) and use other objects to exhibit your behaviors (such as using a pencil to write the answer to an exam question). The process of writing a program according to the object-oriented design philosophy involves the use of existing objects, the definition and creation of new objects, and making all these objects interact to carry out the task that the program is supposed to accomplish.

Written Exercise

1. Describe as many properties and behaviors of a lightbulb as you can. Be sure to include at least one property that may vary and at least one behavior that depends on the current value of that property.

3.2 CLASSES

Suppose I gave you a simple object and asked you to write down its properties (but not their actual values) and its behaviors. If it were a ball, you might write down as properties *diameter, weight, color, temperature, hardness;* and for behaviors, what it does when it is *squeezed,* or *dropped,* or *put into a bucket of water.* Clearly the behaviors depend on the properties, such as whether the ball is frozen. When writing down the bouncing behavior, you might say that it will bounce if its temperature is above freezing, but will shatter if it is below freezing. You might write down a formula from which you can compute how high it will bounce depending on its temperature. You might describe for what diameter and weight it will float versus sink in water. When you are done, you will have a list of properties (but again, *not* the values of those properties) and a set of behaviors (sometimes dependent on particular values of the properties) on a piece of paper.

Is the description you wrote on the piece of paper a ball? No, not at all. It is nothing like a ball—it is a just bunch of words on a piece of paper. But, assuming you did a very complete job of listing all the ball's properties and behaviors, what you wrote describes the behavior of balls to anyone who wants to know (Figure 3.1).

The idea of the *description* of balls is the essence of a Java concept called a *class*. A class is a description of the properties and the behaviors of one or more objects. It is not any of the objects it describes, just as the description of a ball written on a piece of paper is not any ball. This is a very important distinction, and having it clear in your mind is absolutely essential.

In Java every object has a description, that is, a class. The class tells the computer what properties and behaviors every object of that class has. If an object of a particular class is asked to do something (exhibit one of its behaviors), the computer uses the description of the *behavior in the class* and the current values of the relevant *properties of that object* to make the appropriate things happen.

Note that it is the object (not the class) that is asked to exhibit a behavior, but how the behavior works is written in the class that describes that object. You can think of the class as a set of directions for the object.

A very important aspect of a class is that it can describe a lot of objects, each of which may have different values for its properties. In the ball analogy, the actual value of the temperature of a ball is not written on the paper. The paper only says that one of the properties of a ball is its temperature. Each distinct ball has an actual temperature, but the description on the piece of paper

A ball (an object)   **A description of a ball (a class)**   **FIGURE 3.1**

red
3 in. in diameter
72 degrees
rubbery
etc.

Properties: color, diameter, temperature, hardness, etc.
Behaviors: When squeezed—if rubbery and >32 degrees,
then squish otherwise no
change
When dropped— if <32 degrees
then shatter
if >32 degrees and rubbery
then bounce high
if >32 and hard
then bounce a little
Other behaviors . . .

just says that one property of balls is temperature. Hence the description (class) written on the piece of paper can describe all sorts of balls (objects), and each one will have its own value for its temperature. This makes the piece of paper quite valuable because instead of just describing one ball (with a specific temperature), it describes the properties and behaviors of lots of different balls. The key point is that the class describes the kinds of properties (e.g., color, temperature), but the object actually has the values (e.g., red, 72 degrees).

> {Definition of Terms}
>
> A **class** is a description of one or more objects. It describes the kinds of properties the objects have, but not their particular values, and it describes the behaviors of the objects.

When you are writing programs in Java or any other object-oriented language, one of your main tasks will be to define a collection of classes that describe the objects you need in your program to make it do what you want. Depending on what the program is to do, you might first think about the steps it must take to accomplish its intended purpose (e.g., if you must write a program to *do* something), or you might first think about the objects you'll need (e.g., if you must write a program that displays a graphical interface with buttons to push, menus to choose from, and boxes to fill in). In the first case, you'll need to start thinking about the objects you'll need to do the steps you are thinking about, but in the second you already have an idea of some of the objects you need. But you'll almost immediately be thinking about the properties and behaviors of the objects you'll need to define yourself, and that will lead you to defining the classes that describe those objects.

Written Exercises

1. Write a (partial) class definition for an automobile, with three properties and three behaviors.

2. Write a (partial) class definition for a cat, with three properties and three behaviors. Make at least two of the behaviors depend on values of one or more properties.

3. Why are particular values of all the properties *not* part of a class definition?

3.3 USING OBJECTS TO DRAW AN ANIMATED SCENE

Software provided with this book includes a program that can be used to do animation. The program, called the *Animator,* draws a simple background scene consisting of grass, a surface, and sky (Figure 3.2). It then uses objects you define that have as their behavior the ability to draw one or more simple shapes (lines, rectangles, ovals, etc.) in the scene to make it more interesting.

FIGURE 3.2

Animator (Objects Have Class! An Introduction to Programming with Java)

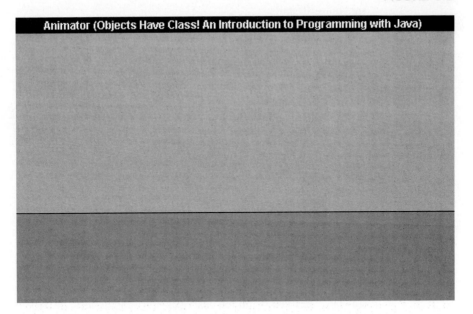

In the next two sections I'll show you how to describe a few of these "drawing" objects. The first object will simply draw a yellow circle representing the sun in the sky. The circle will remain the same while the Animator is running, so there will be no movement and hence no apparent animation. The second object, a cloud, will appear to move across the sky by being drawn repeatedly (approximately 10 times per second), each time just a little bit to the right of the previous time.

Keep in mind that the Animator uses one of these objects to draw a picture in the scene. However the Java code you will see is for a *class* that describes one these objects. The distinction is very, very important, and it is worth repeating here. The Java code is *not* the object. It is a class that describes the object, and in particular for these examples, it describes just the behavior of the object, which is to draw something when asked to do so by the Animator.

The following simple analogy may help you understand this distinction. Suppose the Java code (the class) is written on a piece of paper, and you are the object it describes. You are a very simple object and can only follow the directions written on the paper (pretend you have no other behavior). The Animator will first draw the background and then ask *you* (an object) to draw your part of the scene—it does not ask the piece of paper. When asked, you follow the directions on the piece of paper and draw whatever they say to draw where they say to draw it. When you are done, you tell the Animator you have finished. Remember, you are the *object*, not the class. The directions on the piece of paper are the class. The Animator asks *you* to draw, not the piece of paper.

The only role for the piece of paper is to tell you what and how to draw. They are your instructions.

{New Concepts}

The object does something. The class merely describes how to do it, and itself does nothing.

3.4 DEFINING A SIMPLE OBJECT IN JAVA

Our first task will be to describe a simple object by writing a *class definition* for it. The object our class defines will represent a yellow circle (the sun) and will have one basic behavior—to display (or draw) a yellow circle in the upper left part of the scene. This object will not have any properties per se, but it will have exactly one behavior. We'll add some properties and more behaviors a little later when we define more complex objects.

Let's look at the complete class definition for an object that will draw this circle when asked to do so by the animation program (Code 3.1). Keep in mind that the animation program will create an object described by this class and then use the object to do the animation. It is the object that actually does the drawing. The class definition describes how drawing is to be done (just as the behavior of a ball written on a piece of paper describes what will happen if you bounce the ball, but it is the ball itself that actually bounces).

CODE 3.1

Sun
Find and run the Animator with this shape.

```
import java.awt.*;

public class Sun extends Animator {

    public void draw(Graphics g) {
        g.setColor(Color.yellow);
        g.fillOval(10,20,40,40);
    }

}
```

At this point I will not explain in any detail the parts of the definition shown in light type. For now just assume you have to put them in every class definition you write, and I'll explain them later. Let's focus on the parts shown in **bold** type. I've also used darker shading behind some of the text to help highlight one part of the class definition in the discussion that follows.

The first (**bold**) thing that appears is text that indicates that a class is being defined. The word class lets the compiler know that what comes next is the name of the class followed by *everything* that comprises its definition, enclosed between the brace symbols {and}. Every class must have a name. In this case the class is named Sun.

This first line of code and the {and} that bracket the rest of the class definition are referred to as a *declaration*. A declaration tells the compiler something about the code, but doesn't actually do anything (i.e., cannot be executed). In a sense it provides information. The declaration above tells the compiler that a class called Sun is being defined and that everything between the {and} comprises that definition.

{Definition of Terms}
A **declaration** provides information to the compiler. A declaration is not executed.

Inside the class definition, between the first {and the last}, are listed all the properties and behaviors of objects this class defines. This particular class definition has no properties and one behavior.

{Definition of Terms}
A *class definition* gives a name to a class and contains all the properties and behaviors of objects defined by that class.

In Java we use the term *method* for the code that describes a behavior of any object defined by this class. Every method must have a name, and ours is appropriately called draw. When the animation program wants an object described by this class to draw itself on the screen, it will ask the method that describes the object's drawing behavior to do it. Using standard terminology, we say that the animation program will *call* our draw method (some use the term *invoke* instead of *call*).

When the animation program calls the draw method, it will provide some information that the method needs to use. This information is called a set of *parameters,* and they appear after the method name, enclosed in parentheses and separated by commas. For our draw method the animation program will provide just one parameter, g.

The parameter g refers to an object in the animation program that knows how to draw simple shapes such as lines, circles, and rectangles on the screen (i.e., it has methods that draw these shapes). Just as our class will define an object that draws a yellow circle of a certain size in the upper left part of the scene, the animation program has created an object that can draw all sorts of simple shapes, such as lines and ovals. That object must be told what to draw, where to draw it, what size it is, etc. The object described by our class will use g's drawing methods to draw the yellow circle of a certain size in the appropriate place.

Java requires that g be preceded by an indication of what kind of parameter it is. The term Graphics is used to indicate that it is a Graphics object, that, as I mentioned above, has all sorts of methods for drawing simple shapes on the screen. In keeping with the object/class distinction, g refers to an object that is described by a class named Graphics. The letter g can be thought of as the name of the particular Graphics object we will use to do our drawing. Be sure to be clear on the distinction between g, the name used to refer to the object, and Graphics, the name of a class that describes the object g refers to. The Graphics class is part of Java—you don't have to write it yourself.

Like a class declaration, the code defining the name of the method, the method's parameter(s), and what kind of parameters they are, and the {and} that bracket the rest of the method comprise a *declaration* of that method. They, too, merely provide information to the compiler, and as such are not executed.

In the remainder of this book I will distinguish methods from the class they are in by using a darker background. In the Sun example, the draw method has a light background while the remainder of the class definition has a dark background.

{Definition of Terms}

A **method** is a declaration that describes one of the behaviors of an object. It has a name, a list (optional) of parameters, and commands that are to be executed when the method is called.

The actual behavior of our `draw` method is enclosed between the matching braces {and}. It consists of two *commands* which are performed, or *executed,* in sequence. The commands, when executed, cause the computer to do something and are distinguished from declarations, which do not. For clarity I put each command on a separate line (which is highly recommended but not absolutely necessary).

{Definition of Terms}

A **command** causes the computer to do something. A command is executed by the computer.

The first command

```
g.setColor(Color.yellow);
```

tells the `Graphics` object referred to by `g` that it should make anything drawn by that `Graphics` object from now on yellow. When the `g.setColor` command is executed, the computer will *call* the `setColor` method of the `Graphics` object referred to by `g`. One of the properties of a `Graphics` object is the color in which it should draw things. The `setColor` method of the `Graphics` object `g` is one of the many behaviors a `Graphics` object has. The behavior is to change the color property of the `Graphics` object named `g`.

The `setColor` method needs to know what color to set, so we provide that information by sending it an *argument,* enclosed in parentheses. In this case we send it the value `Color.yellow`.[1] Note that we identify the object we want to use (`g`), the method of that object we want to call (`setColor`), and send it a value to set the color to (`Color.yellow`). The command is followed by a semicolon so the compiler knows that it is the end of this command (as a period signals the end of a sentence). Once this command has finished, one of the properties of the object referred to by `g`, the one that it uses to draw things of the right color, will be set to yellow.

---

1. Java defines the following colors: red, green, blue, yellow, orange, pink, cyan, magenta, gray, lightGray, darkGray, black, white.

The second command, which is executed after the previous one has completed, draws the circle.

```
g.fillOval(10,20,40,40);
```

Here again is a call of a method in the Graphics object referred to by g. The fillOval method draws an oval but needs to know where to draw it and how big it should be. Like the setColor method, we will send it arguments that give it this information. In this case there are four distinct arguments, each a number, separated by commas.

The first two arguments (10 and 20) tell the fillOval method where to draw the circle. Places in the scene are described by two values: the horizontal distance from the left edge of the scene and the vertical distance *down* from the *top edge* of the scene. The distance is measured in units called *pixels,* where a pixel is essentially the smallest dot of color that can be drawn on the screen.

The arguments 10 and 20 tell fillOval to draw the circle 10 pixels from the left edge and 20 pixels down from the top. Note that these values indicate the *upper left corner* of an imaginary box that contains a circle (Figure 3.3). The box is not actually drawn, but is shown in the diagram below for clarity. The next two arguments, 40 and 40, tell fillOval the width and height, respectively, of the oval.

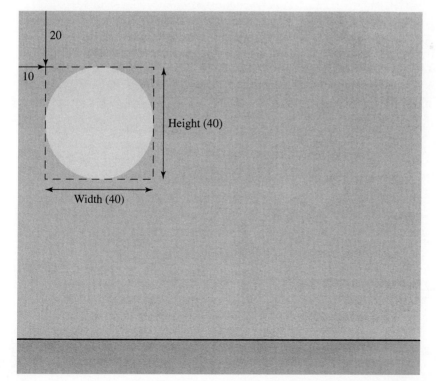

FIGURE 3.3

The fillOval method in the Graphics object referred to by g uses these four argument values, and the current value of the color property of the object referred to by g to draw a yellow circle, 40 pixels in diameter, at the indicated position.

3.5 RUNNING THE ANIMATION PROGRAM

At this time you should go to the Web page associated with this book and try out the animation program (i.e., the Sun program in Chapter 3). The scene will not be visible until you click on the green "go" button below the scene (Figure 3.4). Notice the yellow circle that now appears in the upper left corner of the scene (the scene is the area above the black band that contains the buttons "pause," "step," etc. The sun was drawn as a result of executing the draw

FIGURE 3.4

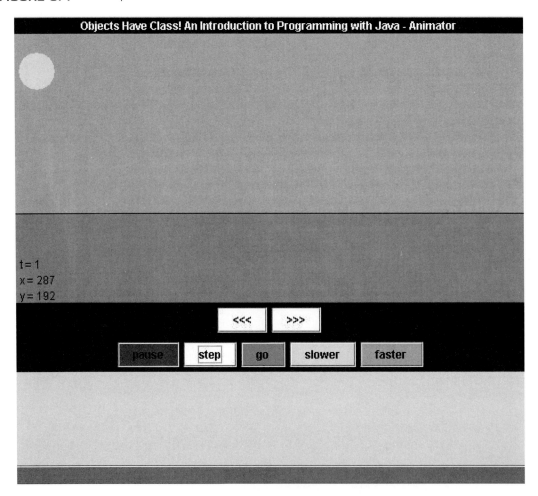

method of the Sun object (as defined in the Sun class). Everything else that you see was put there by the Animator.

Since the sun is drawn at a fixed position, nothing will change as the animation proceeds. You can tell that the animation is running by watching the number after the "t=" in the lower left part of the scene. It increases by 1 every time the Animator calls the draw method of the Sun object, which is approximately 10 times per second. To make the animation stop, click on the "pause" button. Click on "go" to make it continue. Click on "slower" to make the animation run more slowly. Each click slows it even more. Click on "faster" to make the animation run faster. If the animation is paused, clicking on "step" will cause it to make just one call to the draw method. This is a good way to see precisely what is being drawn every time the draw method is called and is useful for finding errors in your code (debugging). Again, since the sun doesn't move, these buttons aren't of much use right now; but the next object I'll define a class for will draw something that moves, and the buttons will then have a noticeable effect.

When you execute the Animator, several things happen inside the computer. Many objects are created that represent various parts of the animation and perform most of the work, and all the menus, buttons, and the background scene are drawn on the screen. An object described by our Sun class will also be created. The object that is created, the Sun object, has the behavior described by the draw method defined in the Sun class. Until the Sun object is created, the animation program cannot use the draw method because there is no object. As I mentioned earlier, the class definition describes how an object behaves, but it is the object itself that actually behaves that way. Hence the Animator must first create a Sun *object,* then ask the object to do its draw behavior by calling its draw method.

3.6 USING JAVA DOCUMENTATION

The Graphics object that I used in the Sun class above is just one of the many objects that Java provides for you to use. Many of these objects are defined by classes that exist in a package called the *Abstract Window Toolkit* (or AWT), and many more are in a package called the *Swing Components.* What the classes do and how to use them are spelled out in documentation provided by Sun Microsystems, and can be viewed via an Internet browser at the URL http://java.sun.com/j2se/1.3/docs/api/index.htm (Figure 3.5).

To find the Graphics class, use the slider for the lower left list ("All Classes") to scroll down until Graphics appears, then click on Graphics. The documentation for the Graphics class will then appear in the large area to the right. To find the fillOval method, use the slider on the far right to scroll down until you find it. You will first find an abbreviated description of the method. If you click on the method name, it will take you directly to a full description of the method (Figure 3.6).

FIGURE 3.5

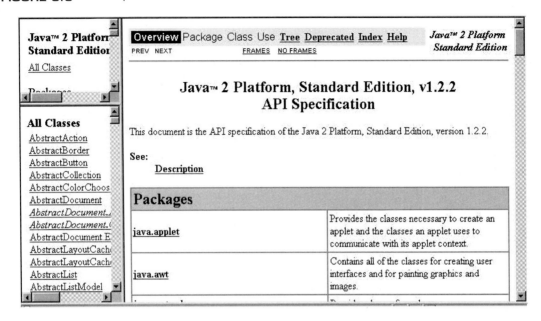

FIGURE 3.6

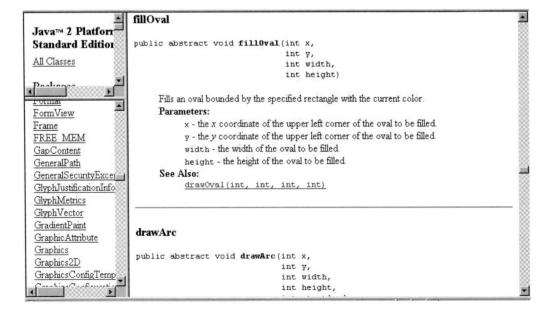

At this point a lot of the information provided may not make much sense. But you should see the exact spelling (including capitalization) of the name of the method; a list of its four parameters, which it calls x, y, width, and height, in that order; a description of what the method does; and then a repeat of the list of parameters and what each means.

Written Exercises

1. Find the fillOval and drawOval methods in the Graphics class in the Java AWT documentation. What is the difference between them?

2. Find the fillRect method in the Graphics class. Describe what it does in terms of its four parameters.

3. Find the setColor methods in the Graphics class. Then click on the parameter type "Color." What happens?

4. What is one of the properties of a Graphics object?

3.7 ENTERING, COMPILING, AND RUNNING YOUR OWN PROGRAM

It is now time to type in an animation program yourself, compile it, and run it. Let's simply enter the Sun animation that we are already familiar with, rather than write a completely new program.

Several things need to be done to enter, compile, and run your program. If you are using an IDE, follow the directions that come with it. Since there are so many different IDEs, with new ones coming out and changes to existing ones being made all the time, it isn't possible to describe them all in this textbook. However, the general flow of things is the same (as in Figure 2.2), so I'll focus here on the common steps and leave the details to the instructions that come with the IDE you use, or to your instructor.

A program is created with an editor and put into a file. In general, the name of the file you put a Java program in must have the same name as the class being defined, with ".java" appended. Hence for the Sun class the file must be called Sun.java. There can be no spaces in the file name.

Type in the Sun program, exactly as shown. Be sure that you capitalize everything exactly as shown. Exact spacing is not crucial, so don't worry if you have an extra space or are missing a space anywhere.

A second file is also needed to run your program. It specifies the name of the program to run and the size of the window the program will run in. Many IDEs create this file for you, providing default sizes and program name. If you are not using an IDE, then use your editor to create a file called Sun.html and put into it the single line of text:

```
<applet code=Sun.class width=600 height=600> Sun </applet>
```

Notice that the name of the executable version of the program is `Sun.class`, and that the width and height of the window should be 600. If you use an IDE and find that the window it gives you by default is not big enough, you'll have to use your IDE's own mechanism to change the size.

Now compile the program. Hopefully you typed it in correctly, and the compiler did not find any errors. If you did get one or more error messages from the compiler, see if you can understand them and then use them to find and fix the errors in the program. Unfortunately the Java compiler doesn't always give you very good error messages, so it might be difficult to interpret what they mean. If you can't figure out what the error messages mean, compare carefully what you typed in with the code shown in this book. If you still can't find the error, ask someone for help. Eventually you will have to comprehend the compiler's error messages, however, so don't give up until you at least try to make sense of them.

If you had errors, find and fix them; then compile your program again. Repeat this until you get no more error messages. At this point you will have a program that is ready to execute.

Now execute the program. After a few seconds the animation window should appear, and you can control the animation as described earlier. Hopefully everything looks and works the same as when you ran my version. It is possible, however, that your program is not correct even though it compiled without errors. For example, if you typed one of the numbers wrong in the fillOval command, as in,

```
g.fillOval(10,20,40,4);
```

then the sun will be longer than high (it will be a long but very flat ellipse). There is no way the compiler could have detected such an error. By running the program you have essentially tested it, and you have discovered that something isn't right. Now you need to go back to the code, find what is wrong, fix it (in this case, change the 4 to 40), recompile the program, and then run it (test it) again.

3.7.1 Java Compiler Error Messages

As I indicated above, and perhaps by now you have experienced, the error messages you get from the compiler don't always help you find the error in your program. Sometimes they tell you one thing is wrong when in reality it is something else. Sometimes they just don't make any sense, especially when you are just getting started. Sooner or later you'll have to learn to comprehend them, or at least to be able to use them, no matter how misleading, to find your error. Here's an approach to becoming familiar with and being able to use the compiler's error messages to find and fix errors in your program.

Take an existing program (like the `Sun` program) and purposely make an error. Then compile the program and see what error message you get. Perhaps the message will pinpoint the error exactly. If not, learn to associate the error message you get with the error you made. Fix that error, make a different one, and repeat the process. Do this for all sorts of errors. Leave out various things like a semicolon, one of the braces, or parentheses, or an entire word. Spell a word wrong. Capitalize a word incorrectly. Insert an extra character or word.

The more you do this now, the easier it will be later when you are trying to get your programs to work. You probably won't be able to get the compiler to give you every possible error message it can, and you probably won't make every possible mistake that causes a specific error message. But this sort of practice, while seemingly a waste of time, will pay off. In the future you will almost certainly make the same kinds of errors unknowingly when you are writing Java programs, and being able to effectively interpret the compiler's error messages will make it much easier to get your program to compile without errors.

Programming Exercises

1. Using your own development environment, type in the Sun program above and get it to work. Be very careful to type it exactly as shown, and be especially careful to capitalize and not capitalize where indicated. Exact spacing is not important however, so a few extra or a few missing spaces is OK.

2. Type in the Sun class, and make each of the following errors (independently) to see what error messages you get.
   - Spell "class" incorrectly (e.g., "clas").
   - Spell "Sun" incorrectly (e.g., "sun").
   - Spell "draw" incorrectly (e.g., "draaaw").
   - Spell "Graphics" incorrectly (e.g., "Graphs").
   - Spell the parameter name "g" incorrectly (e.g., "gg") after "Graphics".
   - Write just "yellow" instead of "Color.yellow".
   - Leave out the first } symbol.
   - Leave out the second } symbol.
   - Leave out "void".
   - Spell "fillOval" incorrectly (e.g., "filloval").
   - Leave out one of the semicolons.
   - Leave out the) in the setColor command.
   - Put in two consecutive commas where there now is one.
   - Leave out the "g." in front of setColor.
   - Leave out the word "public" in front of "class".
   - Leave out the word "public" in front of "void draw".
   - Leave out the first line (i.e., the one starting with the word "import").

3. Modify the setColor command in the Sun class so that the sun is drawn in a different color.

4. Modify the fillOval command in the Sun class to draw the sun roughly in the upper right corner of the scene. You'll have to experiment a little to find out what the distance from the left edge is.

5. Look up the fillRect command in the AWT documentation. Then write a new class definition called Box for an object that draws a 100-by-100 black square somewhere near the middle of the scene.

6. Write a new class called Tree that defines an object that draws a simple tree consisting of a green oval for leaves and a brown rectangle for the trunk. Position it so that the bottom of the trunk is in the grass, the top of the trunk and the leaves are against the sky.

7. Write a new class called Scene that defines an object that draws a sun, a tree, and a gray cloud (a long, thin oval) that partially covers the sun.

3.8 DEFINING A SIMPLE MOVING SHAPE

Our second program will be a class definition for a simple object that represents a black circle with a line through it. Like the sun, it will have one basic behavior—to display (or draw) a black circle 40 pixels in diameter with a white horizontal line through it on the screen (Figure 3.7).

The major difference between this shape and the sun is that the user will be able to tell the Animator to make this shape move to the left or right by clicking on the arrow buttons below the scene. The Animator makes this happen by varying the position in the scene where the shape is drawn. From this object's point of view, the position at which to draw the shape is provided by the Animator rather than being built into the fillOval command as it was with the Sun object. That is, the sun will always be drawn in the same place, but this shape will be drawn in a different place each time as the Animator causes it to appear to move across the scene (Code 3.2).

Note that this class definition is very similar to the one for the sun. The first real difference other than the name is that three parameters (x, y, and g) are sent to the draw method instead of just one (g). Since the draw method needs to know where to draw the shape each time, the Animator will send it that information *every* time it calls the draw method.

FIGURE 3.7

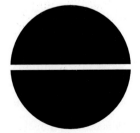

The shape drawn by this object

```
import java.awt.*;

public class BasicShape extends Animator {

    public void draw(int x, int y, Graphics g) {
        g.setColor(Color.black);
        g.fillOval(x-20,y-40,40,40);
        g.setColor(Color.white);
        g.drawLine(x-20,y-20,x+20,y-20);
    }

}
```

CODE 3.2

BasicShape
Use the arrow keys to move
the shape left and right.

The information the `draw` method needs is how far across and down from the upper left corner of the scene to draw the shape. The Animator is designed to send that information to the `draw` method as two numbers. The `draw` method gives names to those numbers, with x being the name for the distance from the left edge and y being the name for the distance from the top. The Animator sends these two numbers with the assumption that they specify the bottom, middle of where the shape should be drawn this time.

As with g, both x and y must be preceded by an indication of what kind of parameter each is. The term `int` is used to indicate that each represents an integer, or whole number, such as 1, 23, −10, or 0.

When our `draw` method is called by the animation program, the values sent to it will be associated with each of the parameters. Parameters x and y will have integer values associated with them representing where in the scene our shape should be drawn (i.e., the coordinates of the bottom middle position), and as before, g will refer to a Graphics object that we can use to do our drawing.

The first two commands in the list draw a black 40-by-40 circle.

```
g.setColor(Color.black);
g.fillOval(x-20,y-40,40,40);
```

As before, the first command tells the Graphics object referred to by g that it should make anything drawn from now on black. The second command tells the object referred to by g to draw a 40-by-40 circle, but instead of writing two numbers indicating where to draw the circle, we write something else.

Remember that the `fillOval` method expects the horizontal and vertical coordinates of the circle to refer to the upper left corner of an imaginary square that contains the circle. However the x and y parameters provided to the `draw` method by the Animator are the coordinates of the bottom middle of the circle (Figure 3.8).

As a result, we must subtract 20 from the x coordinate of the bottom middle to get the x coordinate of the left corner of the box (written x-20) and we

FIGURE 3.8

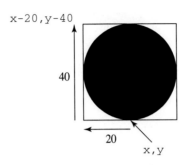

must subtract 40 from the y coordinate of the bottom middle to get the y coordinate of the upper corner of the box (written y-40). The resulting call of the fillOval command of the Graphics object referred to by g is

```
g.fillOval(x-20,y-40,40,40);
```

The use of x-20 and y-40 tells the fillOval method to draw a circle whose enclosing box's upper left corner coordinates are 20 less than x, which is the x coordinate of the middle of the circle, and 40 less than y, which is the y coordinate of the bottom of the circle.

When the computer is executing your program and it gets to the fillOval command, it will send four values to the fillOval method. The first value is computed by taking the current value associated with x and subtracting 20 from it; the second is computed by taking the current value associated with y and subtracting 40 from it; and the third and fourth values are simply 40 and 40. For example, if at some particular time the Animator called our draw method and associated the value 100 with x and 150 with y, then the value that would be computed for x-20 would be 100 − 20, or 80, and the value that would be computed for y-40 would be 150 − 40, or 110. Take special notice that when x-20 or y-40 is computed, neither the value associated with x nor the value associated with y is changed.

Having drawn the circle part of the shape, the next two commands draw the white line through the middle. We again call the setColor method of g to make it draw everything from now on white. Then we call the drawLine method of g to draw the line across the middle of the circle. Similar to the previous command, we say g.drawLine and provide the appropriate arguments. In this case the arguments are the horizontal and vertical coordinates of one end of the line followed by the horizontal and vertical coordinates of the other end of the line. From the following diagram you can see that the left end of the line will be 20 pixels to the left of (less than) the middle of the circle (x-20), and the right end will be 20 pixels to the right of (greater than) the middle of the circle (x+20). Likewise the left and right ends of the line will be 20 pixels above (less than) the bottom of the circle (y-20) (Figure 3.9).

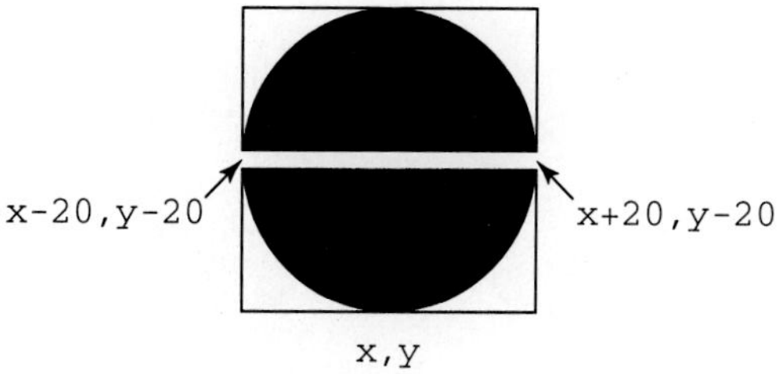

FIGURE 3.9

Here is the code:

```
g.drawline(x-20,y-20,x+20,y-20);
```

3.8.1 Running the Animator with a Moving Shape

When you now run the Animator with the `BasicShape` class, you can cause the shape to move to the left or right by clicking on the left (<<<) and right (>>>) buttons below the scene. Every time you click on one of the direction buttons, it causes the shape to move faster in that direction. If the shape is moving in one direction, then clicking on the opposite-direction button will cause it to slow down (or stop if it is moving slowly enough). Note that the shape will never disappear since the Animator will stop it (by not changing x any more) when the middle of the shape reaches either edge of the scene. Note also that even though the shape may not be moving at any particular time, the animation is still running as long as the value after the `t` is changing.

Now look at the text at the lower left corner of the scene. It shows the values sent to the `draw` method when it is called. When the shape is not moving, the values shown next to `x` and `y` remain constant. When the shape is moving to the left, the `x` value is decreasing; and when the shape is moving to the right, the `x` value is increasing. The `y` value does not change because there is are no up/down buttons. The `y` value will always be equal to the distance from the top of the scene to the top surface of the grass.

Get the shape moving as slowly as possible to the right (using the arrow keys), then click on "pause." Notice that everything stops, including increases to the `t` value. Now click on the "step" button once. You'll see the `x` and `t` values increase by 1 and the shape is redrawn 1 pixel to the right. You have just caused the Animator to call the draw method once and then pause again. As you begin to write your own animations, you'll find that stepping the animation one draw call at a time will be useful in finding errors.

Programming Exercises

1. Modify the BasicShape class to define an object that draws a moving 40-by-40 red square with black lines going between opposite corners (i.e., making an X inside the square).

FIGURE 3.10

2. Write a class definition called TwoBoxes that defines an object that draws two moving 100-by-100 boxes, one red, one green, side by side. Assume the parameters x and y specify the lower right corner of the red box and the lower left corner of the green box, respectively.

3. Write a class definition called Car that defines an object that draws a moving solid blue rectangle (the car's body) with a blue rectangle (the car's windows) and two black circles (the car's wheels). Use the drawRect command for the windows. It should look something like Figure 3.10.

4. Write a class definition called Scene that defines an object that draws a yellow sun, a gray cloud that partially obscures the sun, the moving car from the previous problem, and a tree. The car should go behind the tree as it moves.

3.9 PARAMETERS VERSUS ARGUMENTS

I used the terms *parameter* and *argument* in several places so far. It is important to keep these terms straight in your mind. The two terms are related, but making sure you use the proper terminology and understanding the difference will help keep clear what is meant when each term is used.

A *parameter* (of a method) is a *name* that is associated with a value when the method is called. That name can be used throughout the method whenever the value it was given is needed. All the parameters of a method appear in a list following the name of the method. A method *receives* information in its parameters.

{Definition of Terms}

A **parameter** is a name associated with a value sent to the related method. A method receives information in its parameters.

An *argument* is the *value* that becomes associated with a parameter when a method is called. The value comes from the code that is *calling* the method. It can be written simply as a number (e.g., 40), or it can be the result of computing something (e.g., x-20). A call *sends* information as arguments.

{Definition of Terms}

An **argument** is a value sent to a method when it is called.

Let's relate this to the draw method in our BasicShape class. The method receives three parameter values and chooses to name them x, y, and g. x is the name we use in the draw method to refer to the x-coordinate value of where the Animator wants to draw the shape. Likewise y is the name we use in the draw method to refer to the y-coordinate value of where the Animator wants to draw the shape. And g is the name of a reference to a Graphics object that we can command to draw simple shapes on the screen.

A simple analogy to how this works is as follows. Suppose you are the draw method, and the Animator sends you three values written on three pieces of paper. You receive the three pieces of paper *in order*—the first piece of paper has a value for the x coordinate, the second for the y coordinate, and the third for a reference to a Graphics object. There are no names on the pieces of paper, only values (e.g., 100). When you receive these three pieces of paper, you choose to write the name x on the first, y on the second, and g on the third. Then when you execute commands in your method and you see x written, you go to piece of paper with the name x on it and use the corresponding value. You do likewise for y and g.

The method sends arguments, such as Color.black to setColor, x-20, y-40, 40, and 40 to fillOval, etc. Arguments are values that are sent to other methods. The exact value to send either is explicitly stated (e.g., 40) or is computed from other values and names of other values (e.g., x-20). An important point is that *values* are sent from one method to another. To use the paper analogy again, when the fillOval command is executed, four pieces of paper with four numbers written on them are sent to the fillOval method in the Graphics object. The fillOval method does not care how we determined those numbers.

It is also important to remember that values are sent in a specific order. This means, for example, that you cannot define the draw method in the BasicShape class beginning with the line

```
public void draw(int y, int x, Graphics g) {
```

and expect the animation to work correctly. The Animator sends the x-coordinate value, the y-coordinate value, and the reference to the Graphics object in that order. If you define the draw method as above, you will get the two values backwards.

{New Concepts}

The order of parameters is important. Values are always sent in an order determined by the method sending them, not by the receiver.

The receiving method can give any names whatsoever to the values it receives. It does not matter how a value was generated when it was sent, or what names the method that sends the values might have used when creating those values. For example, our `draw` method receives a value for the x-coordinate to draw at, and we chose to call that value `x`. We have no idea how the animation program generated the x-coordinate value it sent, nor what names it may have given to various values it knew about in order to generate it. It doesn't matter because only a value is sent to our `draw` method. This is important because it means that we can write our `draw` method without having to worry about using some name that is used somewhere else.

{New Concepts}

You can choose any names you like for parameters of a method.

You cannot, however, use a name other than `draw` for the method that the Animator calls to ask the object to draw the scene.

Written Exercises

1. Type in and get the BasicShape program working as described in the previous section. Now reverse the order of the parameters `x` and `y` as shown above. What do you think will happen to the animation as a result of this change? Compile and run the new version of the program. Were you right? If not, figure out why you were wrong.

2. Type in and get the BasicShape program working as described in the previous section. Then change *every* occurrence of `x` to `across` (there are three places), and compile and run the new version of the program. Is there any difference in the animation? Change *every* occurrence of `y` to `down`, and compile and run the program. Is there any difference? Change *every* occurrence of `g` to `pen`, and compile and run the program. Is there any difference? What do your answers to these three questions tell you about picking names for parameters?

3.10 BASIC JAVA LANGUAGE CONCEPTS

Now that you've seen a couple of complete class definitions and how objects described by these definitions are used by the animation program, I'll describe a few of the language concepts and rules that these examples demonstrate.

3.10.1 Reserved Words

A Java program consists of a sequence of words and symbols. Some words, such as `import`, `class`, `void`, and `int` and are called **reserved words** (also sometimes called **keywords**). These are words that have a special meaning in

Java, and you cannot use them for any purpose other than for what they are intended. Appendix A has a list of all the reserved words in Java. You don't need to memorize this list. If you use a reserved word where you aren't supposed to, the Java compiler will tell you that you made a mistake. Note that all the letters in every reserved word are *lowercase*.

3.10.2 Identifiers

Nonreserved words are used to identify (or name) things and hence are called **identifiers.** In the example `BasicShape` is the name of the class; `draw` is the name of the method; `x`, `y`, and `g` are the names of the parameters of the method; `Graphics` is the name of a class that defines an object that draws simple shapes; and `setColor`, `fillOval`, and `drawLine` are names of methods in the `Graphics` class.

When writing a Java program, you can choose your own identifiers as long as you follow some simple rules. First, an identifier must begin with a letter or the character _ (underscore). After that you can use zero or more letters, digits, or underscore in any order you like.[2] Identifiers can be as short as a single letter or as long as you like. You can use uppercase or lowercase letters, but be aware that Java is case-sensitive, so the identifiers `draw` and `Draw` are not the same. Likewise, `class` is a reserved word, but `Class` is a legal identifier (but I don't suggest you use it because it is too easy to confuse it with `class`). You cannot put a space or tab between characters of a single identifier, so while `BasicShape` is a single identifier, `Basic Shape` (with a space between the c and S) is two consecutive identifiers, `Basic` and `Shape`.

The rules of Java say you can chose identifiers in any way you like. Instead of naming one of the classes I defined `BasicShape`, I could have named it Rocket, Irene, or even ZbqXrPL. The computer could care less. The reason I chose the name `BasicShape` is because I wanted to choose a name that conveyed some sort of meaning to people. Even fairly small programs will have many distinct identifiers, and keeping them straight would become very difficult if I didn't try to use identifiers that were somewhat descriptive of what they name. Making programs easy for people to understand is an important part of being a good programmer, and it is something that I'll talk about several times in this book.

> **{Good Ideas}**
>
> Use descriptive identifier names. If you don't, your programs will be very difficult to understand.

---

2. Java is an international language, and the definition of what constitutes a letter, digit, or special character includes things from many different alphabets. In this book we'll only use letters from the English alphabet, the digits 0 through 9, and the special character _ (underscore) in identifiers.

Many Java programers have also adopted self-imposed rules (sometimes called *conventions*) about the capitalization of identifiers. All letters in an identifier are lowercase, except that if the identifier consists of two or more run-together words, then the first letters of all words after the first are capitalized (e.g., `fillOval`). If the identifier is a class name, then the first letter of the identifier is also capitalized (e.g., `BasicShape` or `Graphics`). Other uses for identifiers that will appear later will follow different capitalization conventions. I'll point them out when they come up.

3.10.3 Symbols

In addition to reserved words, many nonletter characters (symbols) also have special meanings in Java. You've already seen {, }, (,), +, −, ,, and ;. Some are used for grouping, such as { } and ( ), and always appear in matched pairs. Some, for example, +, indicate that a calculation should be performed. Others are used as separators (e.g., the comma) or as terminators (e.g., the semicolon). Although I didn't use them in the `Sun` or `BasicShape` classes, Java defines certain two-symbol sequences to have a single meaning (e.g., <=). When you use them, the two symbols must be adjacent, with no spaces or anything else between them.

3.10.4 Integer Numbers

Numbers are another thing you can write in a Java program. I used the numbers 20 and 40 in the `Sun` and `BasicShape` class. Java recognizes different kinds of numbers, but at this point I'll only describe integer numbers. First, an integer number (or simply, an integer) is a contiguous sequence of one or more digits 0 through 9. The first digit shouldn't be a 0, unless you mean the number 0. You can put a minus sign in front of the first digit to form a negative number. You can also put a plus sign in front of the first digit to mean positive, but there is no need since a number without a plus sign is assumed not to be negative.

The computer sets aside a fixed amount of space in memory to store numbers that are used in your program, so there is a limit on the size of integers you can write. Integers cannot be greater than 2147483647 or less than −2147483648. You *cannot* put commas in integers (e.g., 2,147,483,647), even though it would make them easier to read.

You can also write bigger numbers, numbers with decimal points, numbers in a form of scientific notation, and numbers in different bases (8 and 16). The rules for writing these will come later.

3.10.5 Literals

Java uses the term **literal** for all the different numbers you can write in a program. The term *literal* is used because it literally means what you write. When you write 7, you mean the number 7 and nothing else. Java has other kinds of literals, such as single characters and strings (sequences of characters), but the rules for these will come later, too.

3.10.6 Program Appearance

Java is very specific about the *order* of the words and symbols in a program. However it doesn't care at all how those words and symbols appear otherwise, except that you must separate two consecutive words (reserved words and/or identifiers) with at least one space or tab, or put them on separate lines, or have one or more symbols between them. For example, Code 3.3 is a perfectly legal version of the BasicShape class that will work exactly the same as the previous one.

```
import java.awt.*;public class BasicShape extends
Animator{public void draw (int x,int y,Graphics g){g.
setColor(Color.black);g.fillOval(x-20,
y-40,40,40);g.setColor(Color.white);g.drawLine
(x-20,y-20,x+20,y-10);}}
```

CODE 3.3

I think you'll agree that this is a lot harder to read than the previous version. So while the appearance of a Java program makes no difference to the Java compiler, it does make a big difference to people.

{Good Ideas}

It is absolutely essential that a program be easy to read. A consistent, neat appearance makes a world of difference.

Here are a few simple guidelines for making your programs easy to read:

- Put the information that defines the name of the class on a single line by itself.
- Put the information that defines the name and parameters of a method on a single line by itself.
- Put one command per line.
- Indent everything inside the definition of a class by a certain amount. Make that amount the same everywhere.
- Indent everything inside the definition of a method by a certain amount. Make that amount the same everywhere.

Occasionally the name and parameters of a method, or a single command, will not fit on a single line in your editor. If this happens, continue it on the next line (or several lines if necessary). However, indent the continuation lines considerably to the right so as not to confuse them with the next thing that appears (Code 3.4).

The amount to indent is not that important, as long as it is consistent. Indenting just one space probably isn't enough to be visible, even two may not be. Four spaces is a common choice. More than four is OK, but as you'll see with more complex programs that have more things indented within things that are already indented, pretty soon there won't be much room at the right.

CODE 3.4

```
import java.awt.*;

public class BasicShape extends Animator {

    public void draw(int x, int y,
                     Graphics g) {
        g.setColor(Color.black);
        g.fillOval(x-20,y-40
                40,40);
        g.setColor(Color.white);
        g.drawLine(x-20,y-20
                x+20,y-20);
    }

}
```

The placement of the { and } that begin and end class and method definitions is something that there is no general agreement on by programmers and educators alike. In fact, great debates have taken place over which way was best. I like to put the { at the end of the line that begins a class or method definition. Others think it is better to put it at the beginning of the next line, some of them think it should be indented just as everything else in the definition is indented, and still others think it should line up with the first word in the definition. A few people will put code following on the same line as a { at the beginning of a line, but most don't. These placements are illustrated in the code skeletons below:

```
public class BasicShape extends Animator {
public class BasicShape extends Animator
    { some put code on this line, most don't
public class BasicShape extends Animator
{ some put code on this line, most don't
```

The closing } can also be in different places depending on your taste. Almost everyone puts it on a separate line as I have shown. Those who choose the second or third placements of the {always indent the} by the same amount, so they line up.

The bottom line on the placement of { and } is this. There is no "right" way. Your instructor may insist that you place them a certain way; if so, do it that way. Some editors will automatically place them for you. If you can choose, then pick one that feels right to you and that you think makes it easy to understand your programs. Just make sure you are consistent and use the same rule of placement everywhere in your program.

3.10.7 Comments

When you are writing short pieces of code as has been done so far, it is usually pretty obvious from the code itself what is going on. However, when you define lots of classes, with lots of methods, and the code inside the methods gets longer and more complicated, your code will become harder and harder to understand. Hence Java provides a way to insert **comments,** or text that is ignored by the compiler, into your code. You can use comments to make it easier for people (you or others) to understand what you have written.

Java gives you three ways to put comments in your code. First, if you put two consecutive slashes (//) anywhere in your code, then everything that appears after them up to the end of that line is ignored by the compiler (don't confuse these with backward slashes \\). If your comment will not fit on one line, then you can continue it on the next line as long as you precede the second line of comments with //, too.

Second, if you put the consecutive symbols /* anywhere in your code, then everything that appears after them up to and including the consecutive symbols */ is ignored by the compiler, even if the */ that signals the end of your comment is on a different line. Code 3.5 is an example of the use of both comment structures.

CODE 3.5

```java
import java.awt.*;
/*-----------------------------------------------

BasicShape - a class for drawing a black circle
             with a white line across the middle
Written by: David A. Poplawski
Written on: April 8, 1999

-----------------------------------------------*/
public class BasicShape extends Animator {

    //-----------------------------------------------
    //
    // draw - draw a 40x40 black circle with
    //        a horizontal white line across
    //        the middle
    //
    // parameters
    //     x - the horizontal coordinate (an int)
    //     y - the vertical coordinate (an int)
    //     g - the Graphics object to use
    //
    //-----------------------------------------------
    public void draw(int x, int y, Graphics g) {
        // draw a black 40x40 circle
        g.setColor(Color.black);
        g.fillOval(x-20,y-40,40,40);

        // draw a white line across the
        // middle of the circle
        g.setColor(Color.white);
        g.drawLine(x-20,y-20,x+20,y-20);
    } // end of draw method

} // end of BasicShape class
```

In this text I'll show comments in *italic* to make them easy to distinguish from actual Java code. In actual Java programs they look the same as everything else. It is likely that the editor you use to type your programs into the computer will show comments in a different color than the Java code in order to make them easy to distinguish.

The third Java comment structure is like the second, but starts with the three consecutive characters /** (but ends with */ just as the second structure does). I'll defer talking about this structure until later.

There are no rules which say which comment structure to use, and people will disagree about which is best. My advice is always to use the structure that begins with //, even though typing // at the beginning of every line of your comment might seem like extra work. Here's why I give that advice.

When you use the /* comment structure, it is very easy to either forget or accidentally delete the */ that marks the end of the comment. If you do, then the Java code that you have written after the nonterminated comment will be considered part of your comment by the compiler. The compiler will continue to ignore your code until it finds an */ somewhere in your program (probably terminating the next comment in your code) or it gets to the end of the file your code is in. In the first case you may or may not get an error message from the compiler, depending on exactly what code got ignored. In the second case you will get an "unterminated comment" error message from the compiler. Code 3.6 is an example in which the code `class BasicShape {` is ignored by the compiler (the whole single comment is shown enclosed in a dashed-line box).

If you get an error message from the compiler, consider yourself lucky. If you don't, it will be much harder to find the error during the testing of your program (in fact if you don't test your program very well, you might not discover the error at all—but someone who uses your program probably will). Even if you do get an error message, the place where the compiler tells you it found the error might be quite far removed from the actual place where the error occurred. The compiler is not smart enough to guess where you should have ended your comment. The problem is compounded by the fact that the message that the compiler gives you will probably give no clue that the problem was an unterminated comment. So in either case, finding and fixing the error may be quite difficult.

As much as I would like to, providing complete comments for every example in this book would take up considerable space (complete comments appear in the code on the Web pages associated with this book). As a result, I'll only include comments that help explain the code under consideration. Do not take this as an excuse to leave out comments in code you write.

3.10.8 Documentation

Program **documentation** is the sum total of all your comments. It helps explain your code both to you, when you come back to the code months after you wrote it and cannot remember what it does or how it works, and to others who use your code or have to modify it. The entire documentation of your program

CODE 3.6

```
import java.awt.*;
```

```
/*-------------------------------------------------

BasicShape - a class for drawing a black circle
             with a white line across the middle

Written by: David A. Poplawski
Written on: April 8, 1999
```

> The comment should have ended here.

```
-------------------------------------------------

public class BasicShape extends Animator {
```

> This line of Java code becomes a comment.

```
    /*--------------------------------------------

    draw - draw a 40x40 black circle with
           a horizontal white line across
           the middle

    parameters
        x - the horizontal coordinate (an int)
        y - the vertical coordinate (an int)
        g - the Graphics object to use
    --------------------------------------------*/
```

> Instead it ends here.

```
    public void draw(int x, int y, Graphics g) {
        // draw a black 40x40 circle
        g.setColor(Color.black);
        g.fillOval(x-20,y-40,40,40);

        // draw a white line across the
        // middle of the circle
        g.setColor(Color.white);
        g.drawLine(x-20,y-20,x+20,y-20);
    } // end of draw method

} // end of BasicShape class
```

might also include other information that is not part of the file your program is in but is related to it (a description of the purpose of your program, a set of requirements that your program satisfies, etc.).

The first comment in the program provides information about the entire class, what it does, who wrote it, and when. It, or something similar to it, should precede *every* class definition. It should be simple yet convey the essential information about the objects that this class defines.

The block of comments in front of the draw method describes what the method does, what its parameters are and mean, and what kind of parameter each one is. People who use this class should be able to read this collection of comments and know exactly what the method does and how to call it. They do not have to read the code inside the method, nor should they have to. Another person should be able to call your method correctly if all you gave that person was a copy of just the documentation.

Documentation is always required by anyone who pays you to write code, and it is always required by your instructor when you are learning to program, so you might as well get used to putting it in your programs. Different people and organizations have different "rules" for documenting your program, and you'll have to learn the specifics in each situation.

Beginning students (and some experienced programmers) have a tendency to avoid writing documentation until they are all done writing their code. They think that writing comments is a waste of time in the early stages because it doesn't look like they are making progress, or that the comments they put in before they write the code will probably have to be changed once they figure out what the code is supposed to do and how it actually does it.

This is usually a mistake, for much the same reason that you should never skip the design stage of writing a program. In fact, writing much of your documentation before you code is one part of doing a good design. Writing documentation (especially your class and method descriptions) before you write code helps to solidify in your mind what you are supposed to do. When you are defining a class, writing the description of the class and the description of the behavior and parameters of each method will help you write code that does the right thing. When you are writing the code inside a method, writing comments describing each step will help you write code that does the right thing. In the long run, doing documentation early will pay off because you will probably write code that has fewer errors and requires less time to debug.

{Good Ideas}

Write comments in your code as you write it. It will help you write better, more correct code in shorter time.

Written Exercises

1. Which of the following are legal identifier names?
   - notsobasicshape
   - _enD_
   - I_Love_Lucy
   - my salary
   - aBcDeFgHiJk
   - public
   - Class

2. Which of the following identifiers follow the convention for naming classes?
   - BasicShape
   - NotSoBasicShape
   - squareShape
   - Notashape

3. Which of the following identifiers follow the convention for naming things other than classes (e.g., methods or parameters)?
   - BasicShape
   - maritalStatus
   - abrahamLincoln
   - JohnDoe
   - g
   - G

4. Why is it important to pick identifier names that have some relation to what they identify?

5. Why is it important to document your code?

Summary

- Objects, which have properties and behavior, are the building blocks of Java programs.
- Classes describe objects, but are not the objects themselves.
- Classes are descriptions of collections of similar objects that may have different values for their properties, but all have the same general behavior.
- The Java Graphics class describes an object that can draw simple shapes on the screen.
- A Graphics object has a color property and several methods that draw a shape of that color.
- A parameter is a value received by a method when that method is called.
- An argument is a value sent to a method when that method is called.
- Java programs consist of reserved words, identifiers, symbols, numbers (and other literals), comments, and the space in between.
- Java programs should be written to be clearly understood by people.
- Java programs should have good program documentation, use descriptive identifiers, and appear in a form that makes each class definition, each method within a class, and every command within each method easy to see and understand.

Glossary

Argument A value sent to a method when it is called. Sometimes called an *actual parameter.*

Class A definition of the properties and behaviors of a collection of similar objects.

Command Java code that can be executed and causes something to happen.

Comment Text in a Java program that is ignored by the compiler. Comments help humans understand the program better.

Declaration Java code that provides information to the compiler. Declarations are not executed.

Documentation The sum total of all the comments that appear in a program, plus any associated information that is not part of the program but relates to it.

Identifier A word used to name something in your program.

Keyword Another term for *reserved word.*

Literal A sequence of characters that literally means exactly what it says.

Method Java code that describes a behavior of an object.

Object An entity with property values and behaviors.

Parameter The name given to values received by a method when it is called. Sometimes called a *formal parameter.*

Reserved Word A word that has a special meaning in a Java program and can only be used for the purpose intended (also called a *keyword*).

CHAPTER 4

Variables, Expressions, and Assignment

OBJECTIVES

- To be able to create and use integer, real, and string literals and variables.
- To be able to define and use local and parameter variables.
- To be able to write and evaluate Java expressions.
- To understand the order of evaluation of expressions.
- To understand the assignment of values to variables.
- To understand type conversions in expressions and assignment.
- To be able to use predefined functions in expressions.
- To be able to write methods using variables and expressions.

4.1 VARIABLES AND ASSIGNMENT

A very important use of identifiers in Java programs is to give a name to a value. In the `draw` method of the `BasicShape` class, the identifiers x, y, and g give names to values. The values associated with these names are provided to the `draw` method by the animation program, and each time the animation program calls the `draw` method, the identifiers x and y are associated with different values (and, as a result, the `draw` method draws the shape in a different place each time, thereby simulating movement). For this reason, x and y are called **variables** because they name something that can vary—the value that is associated with them. The identifier g is also a variable, but the animation program always associates the same Graphics object with it, so in a sense it doesn't appear to vary from the point of view of the `draw` method.

Since the value associated with a variable can change, the computer needs a way to keep track of the value associated with the variable at any particular time. It does this by using space in the memory of the computer. In that space is stored the current value associated with the variable (from now on I will just say "the value *of* the variable" instead of "the value *associated with* the variable"). If a program decides to change the value of the variable, it simply changes what is stored in that place in memory. The identifier is really just a name for a place in memory, and anytime you want to use the value of a particular variable (by writing its name), the computer gets the value from the place in memory that the identifier names.

> {New Concepts}
>
> A variable gives a name to a value. The value associated with a variable name may change during the execution of the program. The current values of variables are stored in the computer's memory.

FIGURE 4.1

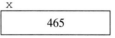

x

465

In this text I will be drawing diagrams of what the memory of the computer has in it at a particular time during a program's execution and will show how those values change as the program executes. To represent a variable, I will draw a box and put a label above it. Inside the box I will put the current value of that variable. If the value changes, I'll put the new value inside the box. Figure 4.1 is an example of the integer variable x with the current value 465.

As indicated above, the draw method in the BasicShape class has only three variables, all of which are parameters to the method. You can also define and use your own variables any time you like. As an example, Code 4.1 is a slightly modified version of the BasicShape class that defines four new variables with identifiers xLeft, yLeft, xRight, and yRight. These variables are used to represent the x and y coordinates of the left end of the white line and the right end of the white line, respectively. The changes from the original class definition are shown in bold.

CODE 4.1

BasicShape Version 2
The inclusion of more variables makes the code easier to read but has no effect on the appearance of the circle when it is displayed.

```
import java.awt.*;

public class BasicShape extends Animator {

    public void draw(int x, int y, Graphics g) {
        // draw a black 40x40 circle
        g.setColor(Color.black);
        int xLeft = x-20;
        int yLeft = y-40;
        g.fillOval(xLeft,yLeft,40,40);
        // draw a white line across the middle
        // of the circle
        g.setColor(Color.white);
        yLeft = y-20;
        int xRight = x+20;
        int yRight = y-20;
        g.drawLine(xLeft,yLeft,xRight,yRight);
        } // end of draw method

    } // end of BasicShape class
```

> Create new variables xLeft and yLeft and give them initial values.

> Use variables xLeft and yLeft in call.

> Give existing variable yLeft a new value.

Let's look at the first two new lines (commands). Each one begins with the reserved word int. This indicates that a new variable will come into existence at the time the program executes this command, and that the values that the variable can have at any particular time will always be integers. Following int is the name of the variable being created.

As soon as a variable is created, it can be given an initial value by following the name of the variable with an equals sign followed by something that represents the value. The initial value for xLeft will be the value of the (parameter) variable x at that time, minus 20. The initial value for yLeft will be the value of the (parameter) variable y at that time, minus 40. If at a particular time the value of x were 128, then the initial value of xLeft would be 108. If the value of y were 300, then the initial value of yLeft would be 260.

> **{New Concepts}**
>
> An integer variable with an initial value is created by a command that starts with int followed by the name of the variable followed by an equals sign and an initial value for the variable.

Once these two variables have been created and given initial values, they can be used later in the draw method whenever we like. In this example, the next line of the method has been changed to use xLeft instead of x-20 and yLeft instead of y-40. Although the program now looks a little different, it will still draw the same shape since xLeft will have the same value as x-20 did in the original version, and yLeft will have the same value as y-40 did in the original version.

Now consider the line

```
yLeft = y-20;
```

Notice that this time the reserved word int *does not* appear before yLeft. This is because a new integer variable is *not* being created this time. Instead the existing integer variable called yLeft that was created earlier is being given a new value, computed by subtracting 20 from the value of y. This new value *replaces* the old value associated with yLeft. The old value is lost, and from this point on in this method the new value of yLeft will be used whenever yLeft appears. This type of command is called an **assignment** because it assigns a new value to the variable.

Do not confuse the assignment command with the mathematical sense of equality. Consider the command

```
x = y;
```

In mathematics this means that x and y are equal, forever. In Java they may not be equal prior to executing the command, they will be equal after executing the command, but will become unequal again if a new value is assigned to x. Consider the following sequence of commands:

```
int y = 5;
int x = 7;
x = y;
y = 44;
```

The first command creates a variable y and gives it the initial value 5. The second command creates a variable x and gives it initial value 7. At this point x and y are not equal. The third command changes the value of x to 5. At this point x and y are equal. The fourth command changes the value of y to 44, but does not cause the value of x to change. At this point x and y are not equal. The key point is that an assignment command changes only the value of a single variable.

{Definition of Terms}

An *assignment* command gives a new value to a single existing variable. The old value of that variable is lost forever. No other variables are changed.

Since the command

```
int xLeft = x;
```

creates a new variable called xLeft when it is executed, you might wonder what happens when the animation program calls the draw method a second time. Clearly the same commands will be executed again. Is another xLeft created, or does it use the one that it created the last time? The answer is that all variables that are created in a method are gotten rid of when the method is complete and execution returns to the animation program; so every time the method is called, a new xLeft variable is created and given a new initial value. This may seem confusing—how can a variable repeatedly be given a different initial value? The answer is simple. A new variable (with the same name) is created each time, so each new version gets a new initial value. The key point is that the memory space used to hold the current value of any variable created in a method is allocated when the command is executed. When the method finishes, that space is made available for other purposes (e.g., holding the value of some other new variable). This happens automatically.

An analogy to this would be if you had a pile of pieces of paper to keep track of the current values of variables. When the draw method is called and a command that creates a new variable is executed, you take one of those pieces of paper, write the name of the variable and its initial value on it, and put it aside where you can refer to it easily. When the draw method finishes, you take all the pieces of paper you used for keeping track of the variables in the draw method, erase the names and the values written on them, and put the (now clean) pieces of paper back onto the pile. When the draw method is called again, you repeat this process.

Variables that are created inside a method are called *local variables* because they don't exist other than when the computer is executing the code in that method; that is, they are *local* to the method. The code has commands to create them, and they automatically disappear when the method finishes, only to be recreated if the method is called again.

{Definition of Terms}

Variables created in a method are called **local variables.** They are created anew every time the method they are in is called, and they disappear when the method finishes.

A similar thing happens to the parameter variables of the `draw` method. They are created when the Animator calls the `draw` method, and the Animator gives them their initial values. When the `draw` method finishes, the parameter variables disappear, just as local variables do.

{New Concepts}

Parameter variables are created and given initial values when the method they are in is called. They are variables and can be changed in the method. They disappear when the method finishes.

When our `draw` method calls the `setColor`, `fillOval`, or `draw-Line` method, it provides the initial values for the parameter variables of those methods. For example, suppose that when `draw` was called by the Animator, it created the parameter variables `x` and `y` and gave them initial values of 100 and 200, respectively. Then when our `draw` method calls the `fillOval` method, it will create four parameter variables for the `fillOval` method and make their initial values 100, 200, 20, and 20, respectively.

4.1.1 Picturing the Variables

It is often useful to draw a picture of the variables of a method and their values at any particular point during the execution of that method. This helps visualize what is happening inside the computer. The picture can be changed as execution progresses, and often this is a good way to discover that a particular piece of code isn't working correctly.

Figure 4.2 is a picture of the variables and their values when the `draw` method of the `BasicShape` class begins execution and before any commands within the method are executed.

Draw method

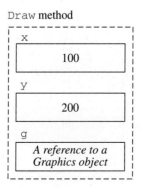

FIGURE 4.2

The dotted-line box encloses all the variables of the `draw` method and is labeled with the name of the method. Eventually you may want to show the variables and their values for more than one method at the same time, so putting a box around those from each will help keep things clear. Each box inside is labeled with the name of the variable and contains a value. Notice that the three parameter variables of the method are shown. The two integer parameters `x` and `y` are shown with initial values of 100 and 200, respectively. The parameter variable `g` is a little different because it represents a reference to a Graphics object. I showed it here only to demonstrate that it is a variable of the method. In a later chapter I'll draw a more accurate picture. Note also that variables `xLeft`, `xRight`, `yLeft`, and `yRight` are not shown at this point because they have not yet been created.

Now suppose the first three commands of the `draw` method are executed. The color to draw the circle has been set, and the two integer variables `xLeft` and `yLeft` have been created and given initial values. Figure 4.3 shows the picture so far.

Now boxes for `xLeft` and `yLeft` are shown with their initial values inside. For example, `xLeft` has value 80, which was computed by subtracting 20 from `x`. When the next command is executed, the values of `xLeft` and `yLeft` (80 and 160, respectively) will be sent as arguments to the `fillOval` method. Again, notice that `xRight` and `yRight` are not yet shown because the commands that create them have not been executed.

Finally, the Figure 4.4 shows the variables and their values just before the last command (the call of `drawLine`) is executed.

Now all the variables created in the method are shown. Note particularly that the value of `yLeft` is different than in the previous picture. This is

FIGURE 4.3

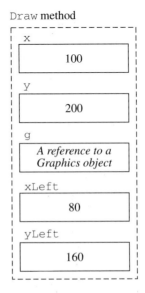

Draw method

Draw method

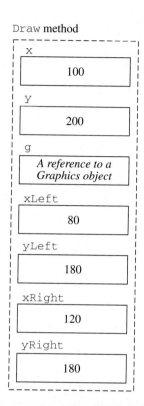

FIGURE 4.4

because the command

```
yLeft = y-20;
```

was executed, causing the old value of yLeft to be discarded and a new value to take its place.

Remember also that when the draw method finishes, all the variables (local and parameter) cease to exist. If the draw method is called again, a new set of variables is created. When drawing pictures, you should throw away what you have for the draw method when it finishes and start a new picture when it is called again.

Written Exercises

1. How does the computer keep track of the value of a variable?

2. What happens to a local or parameter variable of a method when the method finishes?

3. Draw a picture of the local and parameter variables and their values of the draw method in the BasicShape class at the following times.

Assume x was given an initial value of 150 and y was given an initial value of 100.

a. Just after `draw` is called.

b. Just after the circle was drawn.

c. Just after the line was drawn.

Programming Exercise

1. Write a class definition called `Ex` that draws a yellow 50-by-50 square with black lines going between opposite corners (i.e., making an X inside the square). The arguments in the calls of the fillRect and drawLine methods must contain only variables or literals (i.e., they must not contain anything of the form `x-20`, `y+40`, etc.). Instead, use local variables to give names to things such as `x-20`.

4.2 EXPRESSIONS

In the `BasicShape` example above, when the local variable `xLeft` is created and given an initial value, the initial value is determined by taking the current value of the parameter variable `x` and subtracting 20 from it. This is written as `x-20` and is one example of what Java terms an **expression.** Expressions are used all the time in Java to compute new values by adding, subtracting, multiplying, and dividing variables and literals.

Expressions are written almost exactly as in normal algebra, except that everything must appear as a simple sequence of identifiers, literals, and symbols (called **operators**) that represent addition ($+$), subtraction ($-$), multiplication ($*$) and division ($/$), and parentheses. Since an entire expression must be a sequence, an algebraic expression like $\frac{a}{b}$ cannot be written in Java in this form. Instead, Java requires that you convert it to the form a/b, which is now a sequence (an identifier followed by a division symbol followed by an identifier).

In normal algebraic notation, if x and y are two variables, then the product is written simply xy. Since the rules for identifiers in Java say that any sequence of letters is an identifier, Java will think that `xy` is a single variable and not the product of two variables. You must use the * symbol whenever multiplication is desired, so x times y must be written `x*y`.

4.2.1 Expression Evaluation

When a command that has an expression in it is executed, the expression will be *evaluated* by the computer. This is called **expression evaluation.** Evaluating an expression involves performing the operations indicated by the operators, using the values of variables at the time the expression is being evaluated. After an expression is evaluated, a single value will result. This value will be used as appropriate depending on where the expression is (e.g., it might be the initial value for a local variable or an argument value sent to some other method). It is very important to realize that the values of any variables used in the expression are *not* changed when the expression is evaluated. For example, given the expression x+y, with x having value 7 and y having value 9, the result of evaluating the expression will be 16, but x will still have value 7 and y will still have value 9.

{New Concepts}

Expressions are evaluated to produce a single value. The values of any variables used in the expression will not be changed.

The evaluation of an expression is always done in a very specific order, and understanding that order is important if you want expressions that you write to be evaluated correctly. The rules for expressions involving the four arithmetic operators and parentheses are as follows:

- Operations are performed from left to right, except:
- Multiplication or division is done before addition or subtraction.
- Any subexpression enclosed in (matching) parentheses is evaluated before its value is used in an operation.

Although this may seem confusing, it is exactly the same as ordinary algebra. Here are some examples:

```
a+b*c
```

The value of b and the value of c are multiplied, and then the value of a is added to the result.

```
(a+b)*c
```

The value of a and the value of b are added, and then the result is multiplied by the value of c.

```
17+b*(c+2*(e+f))-5
```

The value of e and the value of f are added, the result is multiplied by 2, the value of c is added to that result, which is then multiplied by the value of b; then 17 is added to that result; and finally 5 is subtracted from that result.

Note how the rules apply in this example. You try to add 17 and b, but multiplication must be done before addition, so you can't. You try to multiply b and (c+2*(e+f)), but the subexpression c+2*(e+f) must be evaluated first because it is enclosed in parentheses. So then you try to add c and 2, but again multiplication must be done before addition. You try to multiply (e+f) by 2, but again you can't because of the parentheses. So finally you add e and f, then multiply that by 2, then add c, multiply by b, add 17, and finally subtract 5.

Figure 4.5 depicts the evaluation of the third expression. Assume that the values of variables b, c, e, and f are 1, 2, 3, and 4, respectively.

FIGURE 4.5

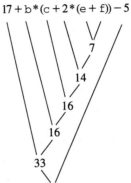

$17 + b * (c + 2 * (e + f)) - 5$

28 = result of evaluating the expression

Figures 4.6 and 4.7 are two more examples of expressions and the order in which they will be evaluated. Assume that the values of a, b, c, and d are 1, 3, 5, and 7, respectively.

```
(a+b)*(c-d)+1
```

FIGURE 4.6

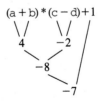

$(a + b) * (c - d) + 1$

```
a+b*(a*c)-(d+(1+a))
```

FIGURE 4.7

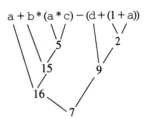

$a + b * (a * c) - (d + (1 + a))$

Notice that a*c is forced to be done before b*a because of the parentheses.

4.2.2 A Note on the Division of Integers

So far the only kinds of numbers we have seen are integers. When the computer is evaluating an expression and does an arithmetic operation, if the values on both sides of the operation are integers, then the value that results from the operation will be an integer. For addition, subtraction, and multiplication this is pretty obvious—if you add, subtract or multiply two integers, you will get a result that is obviously an integer.

When doing division, however, you might think that you won't get an integer result. For example, if the value of integer variable a is 7, then the result the computer will produce when it evaluates the expression

```
a / 2
```

will *not* be 3.5, because 3.5 is not an integer. Remember, integers are whole numbers with no fractional parts. What the computer will do is to produce a value that *is* an integer, which in this example will be the value 3.

The effect of the division of one integer value by another is that any fractional part that may exist is simply thrown away. This is called **truncation** and is not the same as rounding. It doesn't matter how big the fractional part is, it will be discarded. Hence if the computer divides 199 by 100, the result will be the integer 1 (the fractional part of the exact answer 1.99 is discarded).

{New Concepts}

When one integer is divided by another, the result will be an integer. Any fractional part is automatically truncated (not rounded).

Expecting integer division to produce a result that has a fractional part is an error that is commonly made by beginning programmers. No error message is given by the compiler, and the only way to discover the error is when the program is tested. Even then it might not turn up unless the test cases are quite thorough. For example, the expression n/2, where n is an integer variable, will seem to work as if it is giving you a result with a fractional part if all the tests have even values for n. Only a case that has an odd value for n will not work as you probably, but erroneously, expected. Be careful!

4.2.3 The Remainder Operator

Java provides an operator that gives you the remainder after dividing one integer by another. The symbol for this operator is the percent sign (%). For example, 9 % 2 = 1 (i.e., since dividing 9 by 2 results in 4 with a remainder of 1). The remainder operator acts just as multiplication and division do in terms of order of evaluation. For example, in the expression

```
a + b % c * d
```

b % c is evaluated first, then the result is multiplied by d, and finally that result is added to a.

The remainder operator is very handy in many circumstances, and we'll see it used several times in the rest of this book. Here is one particularly useful application. Suppose you have an integer variable n and you want to know if it's value is even or odd. If you write the expression

```
n % 2
```

then the result will be 0 when n is even and 1 when n is odd. In general, if you want to know if an integer n is evenly divisible by another integer m, just write

```
n % m
```

The result will be 0 if n is evenly divisible by m.

4.3 EXAMPLES

Here are a few examples that use various expressions to make objects move across the animation scene in different ways.

4.3.1 A Varying-Size Cloud

Let's make a cloud (a gray oval) appear bigger when it is on the right side of the scene and smaller when it is on the left. This is simply done by making the width and height of the oval depend on the parameter variable x sent to the draw method by the Animator. For this example, suppose the cloud is twice as wide as it is high (Code 4.2).

CODE 4.2

Cloud Version 1
The cloud is twice as wide as it is high, and it gets bigger as it moves to the right.

```java
import java.awt.*;

public class Cloud1 extends Animator {

    public void draw(int x, int y, Graphics g) {
        // draw a gray oval
        g.setColor(Color.gray);
        g.fillOval(x,50,2*x,x);
    } // end of draw method

} // end of Cloud1 class
```

The upper left corner is 50 pixels down from the top.

It gets bigger as it moves to the right

Notice that 2*x was used to specify the width while just x was used to specify the height. Hence the cloud will be twice as wide as it is high.

This cloud is not very appealing because it gets a little too large when it is far to the right. Let's modify the draw method so that the cloud increases in size one-fourth as fast. This is simply done by modifying the expressions for the width and height to be divided by 4 (Code 4.3).

```
import java.awt.*;

public class Cloud2 extends Animator {

    public void draw(int x, int y, Graphics g) {
        // draw a gray oval
        g.setColor(Color.gray);
        g.fillOval(x,50,2*x/4,x/4);
    } // end of draw method

} // end of Cloud2 class
```

The width and height are one-fourth as big as before.

CODE 4.3

Cloud Version 2
The cloud grows one-fourth as fast as it moves from left to right.

Finally, notice that the cloud completely disappears when it is at the left edge. Let's modify the `draw` method again to make the cloud have a minimum size of 50 across by 25 high, and this time we make it grow a little more slowly (one-sixth as fast as the original) as it moves to the right (Code 4.4).

```
import java.awt.*;

public class Cloud3 extends Animator {

    public void draw(int x, int y, Graphics g) {
        // draw a gray oval
        g.setColor(Color.gray);
        g.fillOval(x,50,50+2*x/6,25+x/6);
    } // end of draw method

} // end of Cloud3 class
```

The width will be at least 50 and the height at least 25.

CODE 4.4

Cloud Version 3
The cloud grows one-sixth as fast as before as it moves from left to right.

Notice when evaluating the expression $50+2*x/6$ that $2*x$ is done first, then the resulting value is divided by 6 (integer division), and then 50 is added to that to produce the final value for the width.

4.3.2 A Cloud that Moves on Its Own

We've seen two variations on the kind of `draw` method so far. One has a single Graphics parameter for drawing things that don't move, the other has two additional integer parameters that provide the x and y coordinates for an object that can be drawn in different places on the screen, under control of the user via the left and right buttons. There is yet another variation of the `draw` method. It has a single integer parameter that starts at 0 when the Animator starts running and increases by 1 every time the `draw` method is called (which is roughly 10 times per second). This parameter increases whether anything is moving or not. Since it acts somewhat like a clock, I'll call the parameter `clock`.

In this example I'll use this version to create an animation in which a fixed-sized cloud continuously moves from left to right across the screen, and when it goes off the screen on the right, it reappears at the left and moves across again.

The key is to use the remainder (%) operation to get a value that increases from 0 to some maximum (600 for this example), then goes back to 0 and starts all over again. Consider the expression `clock % 600`. As `clock` increases from 0 to 599, the remainder after dividing it by 600 will increase from 0 to 599. However when `clock` becomes 600, the remainder after dividing it by 600 will be 0 again (600 divided by 600 is 1 with a remainder of 0). Then as `clock` continues to increase from 600 to 1199, `clock % 600` will increase from 0 to 599 again. When clock becomes 1200, the remainder is 0 again, increasing to 599 as `clock` continues to increase to 1799. We can use the value of this expression to specify the x coordinate of the cloud (Code 4.5).

CODE 4.5

Cloud Version 4
The cloud moves repeatedly across the screen on its own.

```java
import java.awt.*;

public class Cloud4 extends Animator {

    public void draw(int clock, Graphics g) {
        // draw a gray oval
        g.setColor(Color.gray);
        g.fillOval(clock%600,50,50,25);
    } // end of draw method

} // end of Cloud4 class
```

4.3.3 A UFO

Figure 4.8 shows a class that defines an object that draws a UFO that swoops down to the surface, then up again as it moves across the screen. It consists of a black oval with three colored lights (red, green, and blue). It moves in a path described by a parabola, where the altitude is essentially the square of the x coordinate, adjusted to make the altitude be zero near the center of the scene.

The class uses another variation of the `draw` method. It has three integer parameters, the clock, the x and y coordinates, and a reference to a `Graphics` object. This version essentially provides the `draw` method with all the information it needs to draw the UFO correctly. The UFO moves independently of the arrow buttons, so the x coordinate is not used. However, to get the UFO to just barely touch the surface, the code I will use is the y coordinate.

To make the code easier to understand, I'll create three local variables. One's value will be the coordinate of the left edge of the UFO, another will be the altitude of the bottom of the UFO (the distance above the surface), and the third will be the coordinate of the top of the UFO.

I arbitrarily chose to make the UFO 70 pixels wide and 20 pixels high. Assuming the scene is 600 pixels wide, to make it enter the scene from the left and disappear off the right, it will traverse 670 pixels from left to right. The

FIGURE 4.8

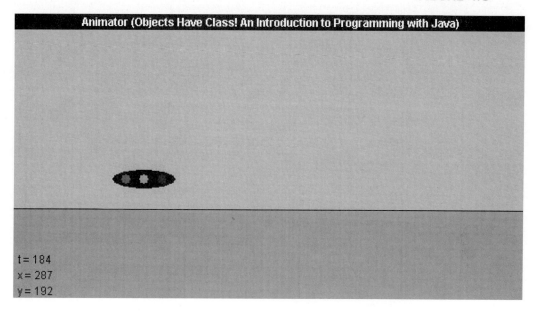

coordinate of the left edge will start at -70 and increase to 599 before returning to -70 and starting all over again. The command is

```
int leftOfUFO = clock%670 - 70;
```

As `clock` increases from 0, `clock%670` will increase from 0 to 669, then repeat. Therefore `leftOfUFO` will increase from -70 to 599 as desired.

I want the UFO to touch the surface at the middle of the scene (i.e., when the x coordinate is 300). Since the UFO is 70 pixels wide, the UFO will be in the middle of the scene when `leftOfUFO` is $300 - 70/2 = 265$. Hence `leftOfUFO-265` will be zero when the UFO is in the middle of the scene. Squaring this expression will give us a parabolic shape, but the parabola will be too steep. Dividing it by 1000, a value that I determined by experimentation, gives a nicely shaped path for the UFO.

```
int altitude = (leftOfUFO-265)*(leftOfUFO-265)/1000;
```

Finally the top of the UFO is the y coordinate of the surface, minus the altitude (to the bottom of the UFO), minus the height of the UFO (20):

```
int topOfUFO = y-20-altitude;
```

The rest of the code simply uses these variables to draw the various parts of the UFO (Code 4.6).

CODE 4.6

```java
import java.awt.*;

public class UFO extends Animator {

    public void draw(int clock, int x, int y, Graphics g) {
        // compute the upper left corner of UFO
        int leftOfUFO = clock%670 - 70;
        int altitude = (leftOfUFO-265)*(leftOfUFO-265)/1000;
        int topOfUFO = y-20-altitude;

        // draw the UFO
        g.setColor(Color.black);
        g.fillOval(leftOfUFO,topOfUFO,70,20);

        // draw the lights
        g.setColor(Color.red);
        g.fillOval(leftOfUFO+10,topOfUFO+5,10,10);
        g.setColor(Color.green);
        g.fillOval(leftOfUFO+30,topOfUFO+5,10,10);
        g.setColor(Color.blue);
        g.fillOval(leftOfUFO+50,topOfUFO+5,10,10);
    } // end of draw method

} // end of UFO class
```

> `leftOfUFO` will vary from −70 tp 599.

> `Altitude` will be 0 when the UFO is near the middle of the scene, greater than 0 in either direction from there.

UFO
The UFO repeatedly moves across the scene along a path that resembles a parabola.

Using local variables with descriptive names as was done above makes the code easier to understand. It is a good habit to get into when you write your own code.

Written Exercises

1. Evaluate the following expressions. Assume that the value of a is 5, the value of b is 14, and the value of c is 25.

   a. a * 2 + b

   b. a * (2 + b) + c

   c. (a + 1) * (a − 1)

   d. b/5

   e. (b + c)/5

   f. a − (b + c)/10 + 1

   g. (a + b − c)/(10 + 1)

   h. 100/(a + b + c)/2

2. Convert the following to Java expressions.

   a. $\dfrac{a+1}{b+1}$

   b. $\dfrac{1}{1/x + 1/y + 1/z}$

3. The remainder operator is convenient but not required. Write an expression that will evaluate to the same thing as `a % b` without using the `%` operator. *Hint:* the solution involves integer division.

Programming Exercises

1. Modify the `Cloud1` class to define an object that displays a gray cloud that is 100 wide, but its height starts at 0 when x is 0, increases to 150 when x is 300, the decreases back to 0 when x is 600. An expression for the height is $x - x^2/600$. Don't forget that x^2 is x times x.

2. Modify the `Cloud4` class so that the whole cloud does not suddenly pop into the sky at the left of the scene but instead slides in little by little. The cloud should still slide off the scene on the right as before.

3. Write a class called `RainDrop` that draws a small blue circle (diameter 10) that drops from the top of the scene to the ground, then disappears and reappears at the top again, repeatedly. Use the clock version of the `draw` method.

4. Write a class called `Smoke` that draws a fixed smokestack (a gray rectangle, 20 by 100) and a puff of smoke (a black circle, diameter 20) that rises 100 units above the smokestack, then disappears and reappears at the top of the smokestack again. As a variation, make the puff get smaller as it rises, becoming diameter 0 just before it disappears 100 units above the smokestack.

4.4 REAL NUMBERS

You've probably figured out by now that computers must be able to represent and do calculations with numbers that have fractional parts. If so, you are right. Numbers with fractional parts can be stored in the memory of the computer, and the CPU has the circuitry to add, subtract, multiply, and divide such numbers.

Numbers with fractional parts are often thought of as "real" numbers. In reality, computers only store approximations to real numbers. For example, the real number one-third, written $0.33333 \cdots$, is not stored exactly. The computer allocates a fixed amount of space in memory to store such numbers, and there simply isn't enough room to store an infinite number of 3s. As a result, it stores a number that is a close approximation to one-third. In Java the closest approximation you can get to one-third is 0.33333333333333331.

You might think that the computer should be able to store the number one-tenth exactly. After all, it is written 0.1 and has no infinite sequence of repeated digits. But it can't. Computers do not use the base-10 number system internally; they use the base-2, or binary number, system. It is beyond the scope of this book to get into the details of the binary number system or how a computer stores approximations to real numbers. It simply suffices that you assume that any real number will not be stored exactly, even though some can be. In case you were wondering, the closest Java can come to representing one-tenth is 0.10000000000000006.

Java uses the term **floating-point number** to describe numbers that are approximations to real numbers. To create a floating-point variable (i.e., a variable that can have a value associated with it that is a floating-point number), use the reserved word `double` wherever you would have used `int` to create an integer variable. This will cause the computer to allocate enough space to store a reasonable approximation to real numbers (accurate to about 16 digits).

{New Concepts}

The computer stores approximations to real numbers, accurate to approximately 16 decimal digits.

A floating-point literal can be written in several different ways. One is as a sequence of the digits 0 through 9 with a decimal point. The decimal point can precede the digits, follow the digits, or be somewhere in the middle. For example, 47.395, −2956.4582, 36., and .726 are all legal floating-point literals. Note that 36. (with a decimal point) is a floating-point literal, while 36 (no decimal point) is an integer literal.

Floating-point literals can also be written in a form that is similar to scientific notation. For example, 6.023×10^{23} as a Java literal is 6.023e23 (or 6.023E23). The "e" (or "E") is used to denote "times 10 to the power of." There cannot be any space between the first number, the "e" or "E," and the second number. The first number need not have a decimal point. The second number can be preceded by a minus sign to denote a negative power of 10. The second number can even be missing (the compiler will assume you meant 0 in this case). Some examples of floating-point literals and the numbers they represent are

- 1e5 = 1×10^5 = 100000.0
- −0.000257E9 = $−0.000257 \times 10^9$ = −257000.0
- 4.167e−3 = 4.167×10^{-3} = 0.004167
- 367e = 367×10^0 = 367.0

A floating-point literal written in the forms shown above (with or without a power of 10) is assumed by the compiler to be a double. It allocates the same amount of space in memory that it does to store a double variable. In the discussion that follows, these literals will be called *double* literals.[1]

Written Exercises

1. Write the following numbers as Java literals.
   a. 1.23×10^7
   b. $−67.0 \times 10^{-5}$

---

1. If there is *double,* you might think that there should be *single.* There isn't. Double is short for *double-precision,* which is about a twice as accurate approximation to an arbitrary real number as *single-precision* (and takes twice as much space in memory to store it). Java supports numbers that are single-precision, but instead of using the reserved word `single` to specify one, the reserved word `float` is used. Floats aren't used all that often, but if you can deal with less precise numbers, are tight on memory, or must do calculations faster, then you probably should consider using them.

2. Write the following Java literals in scientific notation.

   a. 1.01e5

   b. 10001E−6

   c. 2e1

4.5 EXPRESSIONS REVISITED

When you are writing an expression in a Java program, it is not uncommon to have a mixture of double and integer variables and/or literals. This is allowed in Java, but you must understand how such an expression will be evaluated by the computer. Of course, if an expression consists only of integer variables or literals, then the results of all arithmetic operations will be integers; and if the expression consists only of double variables or literals, then the results of all arithmetic operations will be doubles. This is simple and straightforward. Note in particular that dividing one double value by another double value will give you a double result; so, for example, if x is a variable with value 7.0, then the expression $x/2.0$ will evaluate to 3.5.

An expression that has a mixture of integer and double variables or literals is called a **mixed-mode expression.** A mixed-mode expression is evaluated in exactly the same *order* as it would be if all the variables or literals were of the same type, but various conversions of values from one type to another will be done along the way. To explain the rules, let's refer to the value on either side of an arithmetic operator as an **operand** value (whether it is a literal, the value of a variable, or the result of evaluating a subexpression). The rules are as follows:

- If both operand values of an operation are integers, then integer arithmetic will be done and the result of the operation will be an integer value.

- If both operand values of an operation are doubles, then floating-point arithmetic will be done and the result will be a double value.

- If one operand value is a double and the other is an integer, then the integer value is (automatically) converted to a double value, floating-point arithmetic will be done, and the result will be a double value.

{New Concepts}

The operands of each operation, and nothing else, determine whether integer or floating-point arithmetic will be done.

Here are a few examples. Assume that x is a double variable with value 8.6 and n is an integer variable with value 7.

```
x + n
```

evaluates to 15.6 because the value of n is converted to the double value 7.0 and then added to 8.6. Note that the variable n is still an integer and still has integer value 7.

```
x + n / 2 + 3.2
```

evaluates to 14.8 because n/2 is done first, and since both the value of n and 2 are integers, integer division is done to get 3. Then 3 is converted to 3.0 and added to 8.6 to produce 11.6, and finally 3.2 is added to 11.6.

```
(x + n) / 2
```

evaluates to 7.8 because n is converted to the double value 7.0 and added to 8.6 to produce 15.6. Then 2 is converted to a double (2.0) and divided into 15.6.

```
(n + 2) / 2 + 3.0
```

evaluates to 7.0 because n and 2 are added to produce the integer 9, which is then divided by 2 to produce the integer 4. Then 4 is converted to 4.0, and 3.0 is added to it.

Note that in all four examples the resulting value was a double. Also note that just because one or more variables or literals in an expression are doubles, integer arithmetic might still be done during the evaluation of the expression (as in the second and fourth examples). The key concept is that the operands of each operation are inspected at the time the operation is to be performed, and only those operand values determine the type of arithmetic performed. Integer arithmetic is done only if both operands are integers; otherwise floating-point arithmetic is done. If one operand is an integer and the other a double, then the integer is converted to a double before the floating-point operation is performed.

4.5.1 Assignment of Different Types

When the result of evaluating an expression is an integer and that value is then assigned to a double variable, the integer is automatically converted to a double and stored. Hence

```
double temperature = 32;
```

will result in 32.0 stored in temperature.

However, it is an error to try to assign a double value to an int variable. The reason is that the double would have to be converted to an integer, but there is no intuitively obvious way to do this. Should the double be rounded to the nearest integer, or should the fractional part be ignored? What if the double is too big to fit into an integer (e.g., 1.5×10^{57})?

However, it is still possible to convert a double to an integer by writing the following:

```
int x = (int) (expression);
```

The *expression* will be evaluated, and assuming it results in a double, it will then be converted to an integer by ignoring the fractional part (e.g., 6.9 will become 6). If the resulting value is larger than the maximum integer value, the maximum integer value will be assigned instead. Hence

```
int x = (int) (1.5e57);
```

will assign 2147483647 to x. The parentheses around *expression* are not needed if expression is a single literal or variable. The example above could also be written

```
int x = (int) 1.5e57;
```

It easy to forget the parentheses when you need them, however, so make it a point to remember the parentheses when you want to convert the value of a more complex expression to an integer.

Forcing a conversion from a double to an int is called a **cast.** It informs the compiler that you are willing to accept the loss of the fractional digits and possibly even get a much smaller value if the double is too large.

A cast can be used anywhere you like in an expression. For example, suppose angle is a double variable, then

```
int n = 1 + (int) ((angle+1.2)/2.0) * 2;
```

will first compute angle + 1.2 (a double), then divide the result by 2.0, then convert the new result to an integer, then multiply that integer by 2, then add 1, and finally assign the result to n.

{New Concepts}

A *cast* is a forced conversion of one type to another. When a double is cast to an integer, the fractional part is ignored; and if the resulting value is too large, the maximum integer value is used instead.

If you have a double variable, say x, and you want to round it before converting it to an integer, write the following:

```
(int) (x+0.5)
```

Suppose the value of x is greater than or equal to 3.0 and less than 3.5. Then x + 0.5 will be less than 4, which the cast will convert to 3. If the value of x is greater than or equal to 3.5 and less than 4, then x + 0.5 will be greater than or equal to 4, which the cast will convert to 4. Hence normal rounding takes place.

A cast can be used in an expression to force an integer to be converted to a double. For example, suppose r and s are both integers, you want to compute r/s, but you do not want integer division. Then you can use a cast to force either r or s to be a double, which will then result in double division being done:

```
(double) r/s
```

Note that you do not put parentheses around r/s.

Written Exercises

1. Evaluate the following expressions. Assume that a, b, and c are double variables and n is an integer variable. Assume that the value of a is 10.4, b is 9.6, c is 2.1, and n is 8.

   a. a + 3.5 * n

   b. b + n/2 + c

   c. 1.0 * n/5

   d. (a + n)/10

   e. (n + 1)/2.0

2. Assume x is a double variable with value 1.5. What value is assigned to n in the following commands?

   a. int n = (int) (3.1416);

   b. int n = (int) 0.99999999;

   c. int n = (int) (x + 0.5);

   d. int n = (int) x + 5;

   e. int n = 10 * (1 + (int) (x + 3.6)/2);

4.6 FUNCTIONS

The four basic arithmetic operations of addition, subtraction, multiplication, and division are all you need to compute anything you like. Remainder is useful but not absolutely necessary. However, there are many other useful operations that aren't quite as simple. For example, finding the square root of a number is a common operation, but most people do not know how to compute it for arbitrary numbers.

In the early days of programming, every programmer who needed to compute the square root in a program had to learn how to do it, then write the code to do it using addition, subtraction, multiplication, and division. It wasn't long before these programmers discovered that they could use the code that somebody else wrote for doing the square root and not have to write it themselves. This quickly led to the construction of a notebook containing the code for the square root and all sorts of other fairly complex operations. Eventually the collection of codes for these operations was stored on the computer itself.

This is the situation today. The code for doing all sorts of mathematical operations (called *functions*) exists on just about every computer that has a compiler on it, and all the programmer has to do is use the appropriate function when necessary (using essentially the same mechanism that is used to call a method). Java has such functions, too, which are really just methods that expect arguments to be sent to them but that, unlike the methods we've seen so far, return a value representing the result of computing some function using the arguments sent.

{Definition of Terms}

A **function** is a method that returns a value. This value is the result of computing the function, using the argument(s) sent to it when it was called.

Consider the square root function as an example. This function expects you to supply it with a number (a double), and it will return to you a number that is the square root of that number (or a very close approximation if it can't express it exactly). For example, if x is a double variable, then executing the following Java command will create a new double variable y whose initial value is the square root of the value of x:

```
double y = Math.sqrt(x);
```

Math.sqrt is the name given to the square root function. When this command is executed, the value of x is sent to the square root function as an argument, the function computes the square root of that value, and the value is *returned* as the value of the function; it is called the **return value.** This value is then made the initial value of the variable y.

A call to a function can be put anywhere you would put a variable or literal in an expression. When the expression is evaluated, whenever the value of the function is needed for some operation, the function is called, it computes some value and returns it, and the returned value is used in the next operation. For example, the command

```
double y = 1.0 + Math.sqrt(x)/2.0;
```

computes the square root of x, divides the result by 2.0, adds 1.0, and makes the resulting value the initial value of y.

The argument value that is sent to the function (x in the example above) can also be the result of evaluating an arbitrary expression (even including other function calls). That expression is evaluated before the function is called, and the value of that expression is sent to the function as the argument. For example, the following command creates a new double variable y that is one-half of the square root of the value of x plus 1.0.

```
double y = Math.sqrt(x+1.0)/2.0;
```

If the value of x were 8.0, then $x+1.0$ would be evaluated first to produce the value 9.0, then 9.0 would be sent to the square root function which would compute 3.0 and return it as its value, and then 3.0 would be divided by 2.0 to produce 1.5, which would be the initial value of variable y.

{New Concepts}

A function is called when the value it computes is needed. But before it is called, expressions that comprise the argument(s) are evaluated to produce the value(s) sent to the function.

Java has many other mathematical functions that you can use besides square root. Table 4.1 lists some of them. For each, the type of argument(s) that the function expects is shown, and the type of value that is returned is indicated. For more functions and their explanations, see the Java documentation.

The functions that require a double argument type will also accept an integer. The integer will be automatically converted to a double, and the double

Table 4.1

Name	Argument(s) Type	Return Type	Description
Math.sin	double	double	trigonometric sine function, angle in radians
Math.cos	double	double	trigonometric cosine function, angle in radians
Math.tan	double	double	trigonometric tangent function, angle in radians
Math.toRadians	double	double	converts the argument from degrees to radians
Math.sqrt	double	double	square root, argument cannot be negative
Math.log	double	double	natural logarithm, argument cannot be negative
Math.exp	double	double	exponential (e^x)
Math.pow	double, double	double	the first number raised to the second number's power
Math.rint	double	double	the argument rounded to the nearest integral value
Math.abs	double	double	absolute value
Math.abs	int	int	absolute value
Math.random	none	double	a different value between 0.0 and 1.0 on each call

value will be sent to the function. For example, if you write

```
double y = Math.sqrt(16);
```

then 16 will be converted to 16.0 and sent to the square root function, which will return 4.0 and then assign it to `y`.

Notice that there are two `Math.abs` functions, one with double argument and return type and one with int. Java figures out which one you want to use by the type of argument being sent to it. If the argument expression evaluates to an int, then the int version of `Math.abs` is called and an int result is returned. If the argument expression evaluates to a double, then the double version of `Math.abs` is called and a double result is returned.

The `Math.rint` function returns a double that is the rounded version of its argument, but still as a double. For example, `Math.rint(3.4)` is 3.0 and `Math.rint(6.5)` is 7.0. Use a cast to convert the result of this function to an int [e.g., `(int) Math.rint(x)`] where an int is needed.

4.6.1 Animator Functions

The Animator provides three useful functions to determine the size of the scene and the position of the surface within the scene (Table 4.2).

Here's an example of a command that creates a new variable `halfWayUp` with initial value equal to the `y` coordinate of a point halfway between the top of the scene and the surface.

```
int halfWayUp = Animator.getSurface() / 2;
```

Note that the function name is still followed by parentheses even though there are no arguments. Failure to use parentheses even when there are no arguments is an error.

We can also modify the `Cloud4` class to use the `Animator.getSceneWidth` function instead of the literal 600 so that the cloud will traverse the entire scene no matter how wide the scene is (Code 4.7).

Table 4.2

Name	Argument Type	Return Type	Description
Animator.getSceneWidth	none	int	the current width of the scene, in pixels
Animator.getSceneHeight	none	int	the current height of the scene, in pixels
Animator.getSurface	none	int	the current distance of the surface from the top of the scene, in pixels

CODE 4.7

```
import java.awt.*;

public class Cloud5 extends Animator {

    public void draw(int clock, Graphics g) {
        // draw a gray oval
        g.setColor(Color.gray);
        g.fillOval(clock%Animator.getSceneWidth(),50,50,25);
        } // end of draw method

    } // end of Cloud5 class
```

Cloud5

The cloud will traverse the scene exactly, no matter how wide the scene is, without having to change the code.

The advantage of writing it this way instead of using 600 is that the code will never need to be modified and then recompiled if you want to draw a moving cloud in a narrower or wider scene.

Written Exercises

1. Convert the following to Java expressions.
   a. $2\cos(x) - 1$
   b. $(\sin x)^2 + \cos(x^2)$
   c. $\dfrac{-b + \sqrt{b^2 - 4ac}}{2a}$ (Assume *ac* means *a* times *c*.)

2. Evaluate the following expressions. Assume x, y, and z are double variables with values 2.5, 17.0, and 6.38, respectively.
   a. `x * (1.3 + Math.sqrt(y - 1.0)) + z`
   b. `Math.sqrt(Math.sqrt(x + 13.5))`
   c. `Math.abs(x - y)`
   d. `Math.rint(z + 0.5)`

4.7 MORE EXAMPLES

Here are a few examples that use floating-point numbers and functions to make shapes move across the animation scene in different ways.

4.7.1 Random Circles

This animation draws a circle every time draw is called, but the position is determined randomly each time (Code 4.8).

Since `Math.random` returns a double between 0.0 and 1.0, multiplying it by the width of the scene will result in a (double) value that is between 0.0 and the width of the scene. Converting it to an integer gives us an integer variable x whose value is between 0 and the width of the scene.

CODE 4.8

```
import java.awt.*;

public class RandomCircles extends Animator {

    public void draw(Graphics g) {
        // generate random x and y coordinates
        // somewhere in the scene
        int x = (int) (Math.random()*Animator.getSceneWidth());
        int y = (int) (Math.random()*Animator.getSceneHeight());

        // draw the circle
        g.setColor(Color.red);
        g.fillOval(x, y, 20, 20);
        } // end of draw method

    } // end of RandomCircles class
```

Use `getSceneWidth` and `getSceneHeight` to make the animation work, no matter what size the scene is.

The product must be enclosed in parentheses because it must be done before the cast to an integer.

RandomCircles
Circles are drawn in random places in the scene every time the draw method is called by the Animator.

Note that the arguments to the `fillOval` command must be integers, not doubles. Hence commands such as

```
double x = Math.random()*Animator.getSceneWidth();
g.fillOval(x, y, diameter, diameter);
```

are not legal. That's why I cast the random `x` coordinate double value to an integer before using it.

4.7.2 A Bouncing Ball

The next example is an animation of a ball bouncing across the scene. It uses the `Math.sin` function to compute the height above the surface. The `Math.sin` function returns a value between -1.0 and 1.0, so to get the ball to bounce higher, I multiply it by the distance between the top of the scene and the surface minus the diameter of the ball. I then take the absolute value of the result to keep the ball from going below the surface (Code 4.9).

Notice that the `Math.sin` function expects an argument expressed in radians. I used the clock value as the number of degrees, adjusted to vary between 0 and 359, and then converted it to radians as needed.

The use of many local variables is intentional here to make the code easier to read. Code 4.10 is another version of the program that draws exactly the same thing, but uses no local variables. Hopefully you will agree that the first version is much easier to understand.

4.7.3 Making the BasicShape Roll

The animated version of the `BasicShape` looks a bit odd as it moves across the screen. If you think of the circle as a wheel and the line as spokes, then you would expect it to roll across the screen instead of slide. To get the shape to

CODE 4.9

```java
import java.awt.*;

public class BouncingBall extends Animator {

    public void draw(int clock, Graphics g) {
        // set the diameter
        int diameter = 30;
        // compute the coordinate of the left side of the ball
        int left = clock % (Animator.getSceneWidth()+diameter)
                    - diameter;
        // compute the height of the ball at any time
        int maxHeight = Animator.getSurface()-diameter;
        double angle = Math.toRadians(clock%360);
        int height =
            (int) Math.abs((maxHeight * Math.sin(angle)));
        // compute the coordinate of the top of the ball
        int top = Animator.getSurface() - height - diameter;

        // draw the ball
        g.setColor(Color.magenta);
        g.fillOval(left, top, diameter, diameter);
    } // end of draw method

} // end of BouncingBall class
```

BouncingBall
The ball follows a path similar to a sine curve except that it doesn't go below the surface.

appear to roll, the line through the middle of the circle needs to be drawn at a different angle as the circle moves back and forth.

I don't want to go into all the mathematics of figuring out how to do this (try it if you know some trigonometry). However, consider the following. Suppose the center of the circle has x coordinate xc and y coordinate yc. Then xc

CODE 4.10

```java
import java.awt.*;

public class BouncingBall2 extends Animator {

    public void draw(int clock, Graphics g) {
        // draw the ball
        g.setColor(Color.magenta);
        g.fillOval(clock % (Animator.getSceneWidth()+30) - 30,
            Animator.getSurface() -
            (int) Math.abs(((Animator.getSurface()-30)*
            Math.sin(Math.toRadians(clock%360)))) - 30,
            30, 30);
    } // end of draw method

} // end of BouncingBall2 class
```

FIGURE 4.9

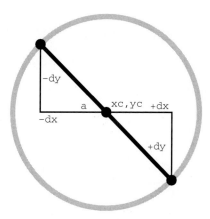

is the same as parameter x of the draw method, but yc is 20 less than the y parameter since y specifies the bottom of the circle.

The angle that the line is drawn at relative to horizontal is simply x/20. Now let dx be equal to 20*cos(angle) and dy be equal to 20*sin(angle). Then the coordinates of one end of the line are (xc-dx, yc-dy), and the coordinates of the other end of the line are (xc+dx, yc+dy). Figure 4.9 shows these relationships.

Now all we need to do is to modify the BasicShape program to incorporate this new information. Code 4.11 is a modification of the BasicShape class that uses new variables, expressions, and the use of the math functions sin and cos to draw the rotating line.

The parts shown in bold are the changes from the original version. First the angle is computed and becomes the initial value of the variable angle. Then since the x and y coordinates of both ends of the line are very similar, the sin and cos functions are called just once and their return values multiplied by 20. Then those results are rounded to the nearest integer and made the initial values of variables dx and dy. These variables are used later in the expressions that comprise the arguments to the call of the drawLine method.

Let's trace what happens when the draw method is called by the Animator. First, the circle is drawn just as it was in the original version. Next, the variable angle is created and given the value x/20.0. It is important that integer division is *not* used here, as you want an angle that is as precise as possible. Hence x is converted to a double and divided by the double literal 20.0. If x/20 were written instead, integer division would be done and the result would not be very accurate (even though the integer value that resulted would be converted to a double before being made the initial value of angle).

Next, the two integer variables dx and dy are created and given initial values. The expression for the initial value of dx is computed as follows. First,

CODE 4.11

```
import java.awt.*;

public class RollerShape extends Animator {

    public void draw(int x, int y, Graphics g) {
        // draw a black circle
        g.setColor(Color.black);
        g.fillOval(x-20,y-40,40,40);

        // draw a white line that rotates
        g.setColor(Color.white);
        int xc = x;
        int yc = y-20;
        double angle = x/20.0;
        int dx = (int) Math.rint(20*Math.cos(angle));
        int dy = (int) Math.rint(20*Math.sin(angle));
        g.drawLine(xc-dx,yc-dy,xc+dx,yc+dy);
    } // end of draw method

} // end of RollerShape class
```

xc and yc are the coordinates of the center of the circle.

Here angle is the angle and dx and dy are the offsets from the center.

Draw the line using the center and offset variables.

RollerShape
The circle appears to roll instead of slide this time because the angle the line is drawn at changes as the position of the circle changes.

the value of angle is sent as the argument to the Math.cos function, the cosine is computed, and the resulting value (a double) is returned. That value is multiplied by 20.0 and then rounded to the nearest integral value by the Math.rint function and then converted to an integer by the cast.

Let's use even more variables to make the code for the RollerShape as readable as possible. First, notice that in the original version the value 20 was really the radius of the circle being drawn. By creating a new integer variable called radius, setting its value to 20, and then using the variable radius instead of the literal 20 throughout the rest of the method, the code becomes much more readable. Likewise 40 is the diameter, which is always twice the radius, and can be replaced with the use of a new variable called diameter whose initial value is set not to 40, but to radius times 2. Not only does the introduction and use of these two new variables make the code easier to understand, it also makes it much easier to change should the draw method need to be modified to draw a circle of a different size (Code 4.12).

One important change that is easily overlooked occurs in the expression for the initial value of angle. The original expression simply divided the integer parameter variable x by the double literal 20.0, thereby forcing the division to be done as a double and producing an accurate angle. If 20.0 were simply replaced by the *integer* variable radius, integer division would result, producing a very inaccurate result. To avoid integer division, x is first cast (converted) to a double. Now the division will be done using double arithmetic and will produce the accurate value needed for the angle.

CODE 4.12

```
import java.awt.*;

public class RollerShape extends Animator {

    public void draw(int x, int y, Graphics g) {
        int radius = 20;
        int diameter = 2*radius;

        // draw a black circle
        g.setColor(Color.black);
        g.fillOval(x-radius,y-diameter, diameter,diameter);

        // draw a white line that rotates
        g.setColor(Color.white);
        int xc = x;
        int yc = y-radius;
        double angle = (double) x / radius;
        int dx = (int) Math.rint(radius*Math.cos(angle));
        int dy = (int) Math.rint(radius*Math.sin(angle));
        g.drawLine(xc-dx,yc-dy,xc+dx,yc+dy);
    } // end of draw method

} // end of RollerShape class
```

> Create new variables `radius` and `diameter` to make the code more readable and easier to modify.

> Use `radius` and `diameter` instead of 20 and 40.

> Cast `x` to a double to avoid integer division.

4.7.4 Adding Spokes

The `RollerShape` class forms the beginning of a wheel that I will use in later chapters. Now let's draw another line across the circle, except let's make it at right angles to the existing line, as shown in Figure 4.10.

Mathematically all that needs to be done is to add 90° to the angle computed in the original `RollerShape` class, recompute new values for `dx` and `dy` based on this new angle, and then draw another line using the new values for `dx` and `dy`. Since `angle` is in radians and not degrees, I'll use the `Math.toRadians` function to convert 90° to the appropriate number of radians to be added to `angle` (Code 4.13).

The first new line of code computes a new value for the angle. It does so by first evaluating the expression `angle+Math.toRadians(90.0)` to get a new value by using the existing value of `angle`. This new value is then made the current value of `angle` because of the equals sign, which commands

FIGURE 4.10

CODE 4.13

```
import java.awt.*;

public class Wheel extends Animator {

    public void draw(int x, int y, Graphics g) {
        int radius = 20;
        int diameter = 2*radius;

        // draw a black circle
        g.setColor(Color.black);
        g.fillOval(x-radius,y-diameter,diameter,diameter);

        // draw a white line that rotates
        g.setColor(Color.white);
        int xc = x;
        int yc = y-radius;
        double angle = 1.0*x/radius;
        int dx = (int) Math.rint(radius*Math.cos(angle));
        int dy = (int) Math.rint(radius*Math.sin(angle));
        g.drawLine(xc-dx,yc-dy,xc+dx,yc+dy);

        // draw a second white line 90 degrees from the first
        angle = angle + Math.toRadians(90.0);  ◄
        dx = (int) Math.rint(radius*Math.cos(angle));
        dy = (int) Math.rint(radius*Math.sin(angle));
        g.drawLine(xc-dx,yc-dy,xc+dx,yc+dy);
        } // end of draw method

    } // end of Wheel class
```

Add 90° to the angle before recomputing dx and dy.

Wheel
The second line is perpendicular to the first, but also changes angle as the circle "rolls."

the computer to replace the old value of angle with the new one. For example, if the value of angle before this command is executed is 0.0, then the value of angle after this command is executed is 0.0 + 1.5708, or 1.5708 (1.5708 is the number of radians equivalent to 90°).

4.8 TESTING AND DEBUGGING ANIMATIONS

It is not always an easy task to get the expressions written correctly so that the animations look right. Sometimes it is handy to be able to look at the values that are being computed and assigned to various variables during execution. This is especially true if the shape being drawn wanders out of the scene or if it exhibits very unusual behavior.

Most IDEs have a debugger that will allow you to step through the code of a method, stopping when you like and displaying the current values of variable. Use it if you have it.

If you don't, the Animator has a method called Animator.write that expects a single argument, either an integer or a double. When it is called, the value sent is displayed at the bottom of the Animator's window (in the light gray area below the buttons). They scroll up as more and more values are displayed, so only the last few values can be seen at any time.

If you put a call to `Animator.write` in your `draw` method, and the animation is running at normal speed, values will be printed 10 times per second, and they will be almost impossible to read. Pause the animation, then single-step it. Each single step will result in one call to the `draw` method, resulting in one call to `Animator.write`. Of course if you have several calls to `Animator.write` to display the several values, then each step will print several values.

Code 4.14 is a version of the `RandomCircles` animation, modified to use `Animator.write` to display the values of x and y on each call.

CODE 4.14

```
import java.awt.*;

public class RandomCircles2 extends Animator {

    public void draw(Graphics g) {
        // set diameter of the circle
        int diameter = 20;

        // generate random x and y coordinates
        // somewhere in the scene
        int x = (int) (Math.random()*Animator.getSceneWidth());
        int y = (int) (Math.random()*Animator.getSceneHeight());

        // display x and y
        Animator.write(x);
        Animator.write(y);

        // draw the circle
        g.setColor(Color.red);
        g.fillOval(x, y, diameter, diameter);
    } // end of draw method

} // end of RandomCircles2 class
```

Show the current values of x and y below the animation scene every time the draw method is called.

RandomCircles2
The x and y values are displayed below the scene for debugging purposes.

Note that I also added the variable `diameter` to make the code easier to read and modify. Figure 4.11 shows the animation window after a few steps of execution.

Written Exercise

1. Draw a picture of the local and parameter variables and their values of the draw method in the Wheel class at the following times. Assume x was given an initial value of 150 and y was given an initial value of 100.
   a. Just after `draw` is called.
   b. Just after the first line was drawn.
   c. Just after the second line was drawn.

FIGURE 4.11

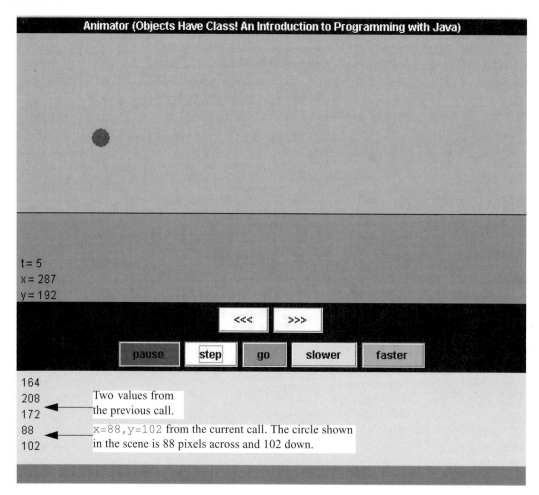

Programming Exercises

1. Modify the RandomCircles class to define an object that draws two red circles in random places in the scene and connects their centers with a blue line.

2. Modify the RandomCircles class to define an object that draws a 200-by-200 solid black square in the middle of the scene (resting on the surface), and make the red circles be drawn randomly but completely within the box.

3. Modify the BouncingBall class to define an object that draws a bouncing ball that does not move left or right but stays in the middle of the scene (i.e., bounces in place).

4. Modify the BouncingBall class to define an object that draws a 40-by-40 solid black box that slides along the surface always just below the ball. The ball should appear to go into the box and disappear as it hits the surface.

5. Modify the Wheel class to define an object that draws a wheel with four equally spaced lines drawn through it (i.e., eight spokes instead of four).

6. Write a class definition for an object that draws a gray circle whose diameter varies back and forth between 10 and 20. Base the diameter on the clock, and use the sin function to make it vary smoothly. The circle's diameter should make a complete cycle every 20 ticks of the clock. If it is done right, the circle should look like it is throbbing.

4.9 STRINGS

In addition to int's and doubles, Java provides the ability to express, store, and manipulate a sequence of characters, usually referred to as a **string.** A string literal is any sequence of characters, preceded by a double-quote character (not to be confused with two consecutive single quote characters) and followed by another double-quote character. For example, `"Dave"` is a string literal consisting of the four characters `D`, `a`, `v`, and `e`, in that order. You can put whatever characters you like between the double quotes, including spaces, symbols, punctuation, etc. You cannot, however, begin a string literal on one line and finish it on another—both double quotes must be on the same line.

> {Definition of Terms}
>
> A *string literal* is any sequence of characters, on one line, enclosed between two double-quote characters.

Java does not interpret anything in a string literal as anything other than a sequence of characters. For example, if you put the string literal `"class"` in your program, Java does *not* confuse it with the reserved word `class`. If you write the string literal "a+b/2", Java does *not* think it is an expression.

Now, suppose you want to construct a string literal that has a double-quote character in it. If you try `"a string with a "` in it", then Java will think that the second double quote (between `a` and `in`) is the end of the literal, then think that `in` and `it` are two identifiers, and that the third double quote is the beginning of a second string literal.

To solve this problem, Java requires that you precede any double-quote character you want in a string literal by the backward slash (\) symbol. The backward slash symbol (or *backslash*) is used to indicate that the next character that appears in the string literal is special and not to be interpreted in the same way that it usually is (i.e., the double quote is not to be interpreted as the end of the string literal). Hence the proper way to write the string literal shown above with a double quote in it is to write `"a string with a \"` in it". The backslash character itself is not part of the string, but the double quote that follows it is. To get a backslash character to be part of a string literal, write two consecutive backslashes. For example, `"a string with a \\ in it"` is a string literal containing a single backslash character between the a and in. The backslash character can also be used to put other special characters into string literals. See Appendix B for a complete list.

A string variable is defined much in the same way an int or double is. For example,

```
String name = "Dave";
```

is a command that creates a string variable called `name` with the initial value the string `"Dave"`. Note that `String` is capitalized. Like int and double variables, string variables can have new values assigned to them.

Let's now modify the `RollerShape` class to display the string `"Roller"` at the far left of the screen just below the surface. The `drawString` method of the Graphics class can be used to display a string on the screen. It has three parameters—the string to display, followed by the x and y coordinates of where to display it. The coordinates describe the place on the screen to put the lower left corner of the first character of the string, as shown in Figure 4.12.

Code 4.15 is a modification of the **RollerShape** class that displays the string.

4.9.1 Expressions Involving Strings

While it makes no sense mathematically, Java allows an expression to contain string variables and literals. When an expression involving a string variable or literal is evaluated, the resulting value will always be a string. However, some unexpected things happen during the evaluation of such an expression.

First, only the + operator can be used when one operand and/or the other operator is a string. You'll get an error if you try to use −, *, /, or %. The + operator doesn't mean addition, however, when one or both of its operands are a string. Instead, + means **concatenation;** that is, a new string value is constructed that begins with the string on the left of the + and ends with the string on the right. For example, the expression `"john"+"son"` evaluates to the string value `"johnson"`. Likewise, if `first` is a string variable whose value is `"pitts"` and `second` is a string variable whose value is `"burgh"`, then `first+second` evaluates to the string value `"pittsburgh"`.

Java will automatically convert an int or double that is the other operand of the + operator to a string variable or literal to a string value. As a result, if you write the expression `"x ="+x`, and if x is an integer variable with value

CODE 4.15

```java
import java.awt.*;

public class LabeledRoller extends Animator {

    public void draw(int x, int y, Graphics g) {
        int radius = 20;
        int diameter = 2*radius;

        // draw a black circle
        g.setColor(Color.black);
        g.fillOval(x-radius,y-diameter,diameter,diameter);

        // draw a white line that rotates
        g.setColor(Color.white);
        int xc = x;
        int yc = y-radius;
        double angle = 1.0*x/radius;
        int dx = (int) Math.rint(radius*Math.cos(angle));
        int dy = (int) Math.rint(radius*Math.sin(angle));
        g.drawLine(xc-dx,yc-dy,xc+dx,yc+dy);

        // draw the string "Roller" in black
        g.setColor(Color.black);
        g.drawString("Roller",0,y-10);
    } // end of draw method

} // end of LabeledRoller class
```

LabeledRoller
The characters "Roller" are drawn below the surface at the left side of the animator region.

17, then the result of evaluating the expression will be the string value "x=17". You must be careful to remember the rules for the order in which expressions are evaluated. For example, the expression "x+y="+x+y and the expression "x+y"+(x+y) evaluate to completely different values. In the first case the variable x will be converted to a string value and concatenated with the string value "x+y="; then y is converted to a string value and concatenated to the end of the first concatenation. If x has value 17 and y has value −6, then the result will be the string value "x+y=17-6". In the second case, x and y will be added (integer addition) to produce the integer value 11, which will then be converted to a string value and concatenated with the string value "x+y=" to produce the string value "x+y=11".

{New Concepts}

If one of the operands of + is a string, then the other operand will be converted to a string (unless it already is) and the two strings will be concatenated to form a single, new string.

A common error is to think that the expression "7"+8 evaluates to the integer value 15, or perhaps to the string value "15". According to the rule, one of the operands of the + operator is a string ("7"), so the other (the integer literal 8) is first converted to the string "8" and then the two strings are concatenated to produce the string value "78".

Armed with strings and string-valued expressions, now we modify the `RollerShape` class definition further to add the display of the current x coordinate of the shape immediately underneath the circle such that the value being displayed follows the circle as it moves (Code 4.16).

CODE 4.16

```java
import java.awt.*;

public class PositionRoller extends Animator {

    public void draw(int x, int y, Graphics g) {
        // set the radius and diameter
        int radius = 20;
        int diameter = 2*radius;
        // draw a black circle
        g.setColor(Color.black);
        g.fillOval(x-radius,y-diameter,diameter,diameter);
        // draw a white line that rotates
        g.setColor(Color.white);
        double angle = 1.0*x/radius;
        int xc = x;
        int yc = y-radius;
        int dx = (int) Math.rint(radius*Math.cos(angle));
        int dy = (int) Math.rint(radius*Math.sin(angle));
        g.drawLine(xc-dx,yc-dy,xc+dx,yc+dy);
        // draw the string "Roller" in black
        g.setColor(Color.black);
        g.drawString("Roller",0,y-10);
        // show the x coordinate sent by the Animator
        g.drawString("x="+x,x,y-10);
    } // end of draw method

} // end of PositionRoller class
```

PositionRoller
The x coordinate of center of the circle is displayed below the circle as it moves.

4.9.2 Converting a String to Int or Double

Strings can be converted (sometimes called parsed) to int or double values by using special functions. You *cannot* cast a string to an int or double. To convert a string to an int, use the `Integer.parseInt` function and send it the string you want converted as an argument.

```java
int n = Integer.parseInt(str);
```

Converting to a double is similar:

```java
double d = Double.parseDouble(str);
```

will create a new double variable d with an initial value converted from the string variable str. Of course any expression that evaluates to a string can be put where str is.

Written Exercises

1. Write Java string literals for the following sequences of characters.
   a. Ward said: "Hi June!."
   b. A backslash (\) is a backward slash.
2. Evaluate the following expressions. Assume that a is a double variable and n is an integer variable. Assume that the value of a is 10.4 and n is 8.
   a. n + "is eight"
   b. "a/2 is equal to " + a/2

Programming Exercises

1. Modify the RollerShape class to put your full name in the lower right corner of the display. Use the Animator functions to position it properly.
2. Modify the RollerShape class to show the coordinates of the center of the circle as it moves. Show them in the upper right corner of the display, with parentheses around them and separated by a comma [e.g., (145,200)].
3. Modify the RollerShape class to show the angle the line is currently drawn at (in *integer* degrees, not radians). Show it above the circle so that it moves along with the circle. Convert an angle in radians to degrees by multiplying it by 360 and dividing it by 2 times pi.
4. Write a class description for an object that displays all the items listed below.
   a. A sun in the upper left corner of the sky.
   b. A cloud that moves continuously across the sky, sometimes obscuring the sun partially.
   c. A smokestack with smoke coming out of it continuously.
   d. A tree (a brown rectangle for the trunk and a green circle for the leaves).
   e. A raindrop that falls from the cloud.
   f. A white wheel with four black spokes (two lines) that moves according to directions from the left/right buttons.
   g. Your name in the lower left corner.

   Make the rain fall in front of everything; make the wheel appear in front of the smokestack but behind the tree.
5. Write a class description for an object that draws a scene of your own design. Try to incorporate all sorts of interesting things that use all the concepts of this chapter.

Summary

- A double is a value that represents an approximation to a real number.
- A string is a value that represents a sequence of characters.
- A variable is an identifier that has a value associated with it. The value can change during the execution of the program.
- The current value associated with the variable is used whenever the variable name appears in an expression.
- Expressions are combinations of variables, literals, and operators that can be evaluated to produce a single value.
- An assignment command changes the value of a variable.
- Mixed-mode expressions involve combinations of integer, double or string variables, and/or literals. If both operands of an operator in an expression are of the same type (int or double), then arithmetic will be done in that type (e.g., the division of two integers results in an integer). If the types are different, first the int is converted to a double, and then double arithmetic is done.
- A cast can be used to force a conversion of an int to a double or a double to an int.
- Functions are segments of code that produce values that depend on their parameters. Many common mathematical functions such as square root, sine, and cosine are supplied with Java.
- If one of the operands of the + operator is a string, then first the other operand is converted to a string and then the two are concatenated to produce another string.
- Use lots of meaningfully named local variables to make your code easier to understand.

Glossary

Assignment A command that changes the value of a variable.

Cast Force a conversion between one type and another.

Concatenation Creation of a new string value from two other string values, consisting of the characters in the first string followed by the characters in the second string.

Expression A combination of literals, variables, operators, and functions that can be evaluated to produce a single value.

Expression Evaluation Computation of the value of an expression by performing the operations indicated in the prescribed order, using the values of the literals and variables and the return values of functions.

Floating-Point Number A number that approximates a real value.

Function Code that is already written, usually used to compute something rather complex.

Local Variable A variable that is created inside a method and disappears when the method finishes.

Mixed-Mode Expression An expression that contains a mixture of int, double, and/or string literals, variables, or functions.

Operand One of the values used in an arithmetic operation.

Operator A symbol that denotes an arithmetic operation ($+$, $-$, $*$, $/$, $\%$).

Return Value A value that is computed by a function.

String A sequence of characters.

Truncation Creation of an integer value by dropping any fractional part.

Variable An identifier that has a value associated with it that can be changed as the program executes.

CHAPTER 5

Defining and Creating Multiple Objects

OBJECTIVES

- To define and use instance variables.
- To write programs with multiple class definitions.
- To create and use objects.
- To understand the scope of instance, parameter, and local variable names.
- To understand what constructors are and how they are used.

5.1 INSTANCE VARIABLES

The Sun animation program in Chapter 3 drew a yellow circle with diameter 40 in the upper left corner of the animation scene. If you decided that you wanted the diameter of the circle to be something other than 40 (say, 55), then you would have to change the code and recompile it. From then on, the larger sun would be drawn every time you ran the animation.

Suppose you wanted to be able to specify a different size for the sun every time you run the animation. Then you'd have to modify the code and recompile it before every run. That's a lot of work. It would be easier if the program itself could ask you how big to make the sun. Then every time you run the program, you could respond with the desired diameter, the program would proceed to draw the sun that big, and recompiling wouldn't be necessary.

The Animator has facilities to allow you to do just that. It has a method called Animator.readInt[1] that will wait for the user to type in an integer and then return that value to the program.

```
int sunDiameter = Animator.readInt();
```

This command does not tell the user that the program is expecting an integer to be entered, so you could combine this with Animator.write to prompt the user to enter the diameter (so the user knows that the program is

---

1. The Animator also has Animator.readDouble and Animator.readString methods for reading doubles and strings, respectively.

expecting it):

```
Animator.write("Please enter the diameter of the sun");
int sunDiameter = Animator.readInt();
```

Now the question is, Where should we put this code? If we put it in the draw method, it will be executed *every* time the Animator calls the draw method. This would mean that we would have to enter the size of the sun over and over. What we want is for the user to enter the size of the sun just once, before the animation begins.

To do this, we must include a second method in the Sun class. This method, called startup, is called by the Animator just once before it starts repeatedly calling the draw method to do the animation. Code 5.1 is a new version of the Sun program. It includes the startup method with the code to prompt the user and then read the diameter of the sun.

CODE 5.1

```
import java.awt.*;

public class UserDefinedSun extends Animator {

    public void startup() {
        // prompt for and input the diameter of the sun
        Animator.write("please enter the diameter of the sun");
        int sunDiameter = Animator.readInt();
    } // end of startup method

    public void draw (Graphics g) {
        // draw the sun
        g.setColor(Color.yellow);
        g.fillOval(0,0, sunDiameter, sunDiameter);
    } // end of draw method

} // end of UserDefinedSun class
```

> This method is called once by the Animator before it starts calling the draw method.

> The compiler will give you an error message indicating that sunDiameter is not defined.

Unfortunately, when you compile this program, you will get an error message stating that the variable sunDiameter in the call to fillOval is undefined. The reason is that a variable created in a method can only be referred to (i.e., used) in that same method.[2] That is why it is called a local variable. It can only be used locally in the method it is created in. A local variable also disappears when the method it is created in finishes, and as a result the value that variable has also disappears.

---

2. The rules on where a local variable can be used are slightly more restrictive, but for now just assume that this is the case.

When the Animator calls the `startup` method, it will create the local variable `sunDiameter` and give it the initial value read from the user. But immediately thereafter, `sunDiameter` and its value disappear because the `startup` method finishes. Hence, by the time the Animator calls the `draw` method, there will be no `sunDiameter` variable to use.

What we need is a variable that is created outside both methods yet can be used inside both methods. In Code 5.2 I do just that.

CODE 5.2

```
import java.awt.*;

public class UserDefinedSun extends Animator {
    // instance variables
    private int sunDiameter = 0;

    public void startup() {
        // prompt for and input the diameter of the sun
        Animator.write("Please enter the diameter of the sun:");
        sunDiameter = Animator.readInt();
    } // end of startup method

    public void draw (Graphics g) {
        // draw the sun
        g.setColor(Color.yellow);
        g.fillOval(0,0,sunDiameter,sunDiameter);
    } // end of draw method

} // end of UserDefinedSun class
```

sunDiameter is created and given the initial value 0 when the UserDefinedSun object is created.

sunDiameter is assigned the value entered by the user.

The sun will be drawn with the diameter specified by sunDiameter.

UserDefinedSun
Prompts the user for the diameter of the sun before starting drawing.

Any variable declared inside a class but outside a method will be created when an object of that class is created, will continue to exist as long as the object exists, and can be referred to by any method in the class. This is just what we want.

When the `UserDefinedSun` program is started, the Animator will create a `UserDefinedSun` object. In doing so, the variable `sunDiameter` will be created as part of the object. Then when the Animator calls the `startup` method, the user will enter a value that will be assigned to `sunDiameter`. When the `startup` method finishes, the `sunDiameter` variable will continue to exist and have the value entered by the user. From then on, every time the Animator calls the `draw` method, it will use the value of `sunDiameter` that was given to it by the user via the `startup` method.

A variable declared inside a class but outside any method in that class is called an *instance* variable. This term comes from the notion that when an object is created, it is an *instance* of the class that defines it.[3] Returning to the ball

---

3. Some use the term *instantiating* an object to mean *creating* an object. The term *instantiate* means to create an *instance*.

analogy of Chapter 3, we see that each different real ball is an instance of the ball class. Another example is that you, your family, your friends, and everybody else in the world are instances of a HumanBeing class.

{Definition of Terms}

Every object is an **instance** of some class. The class defines the properties and behaviors of every one of its instances.

Any variable that is declared in the class, but not any method in the class, becomes an actual variable in every object instance. In the ball analogy, the ball class indicates that every ball object will have a property called temperature. Clearly each ball object will have its own temperature, and hence each ball object will have its own temperature "variable" to keep track of its current temperature.

Instance variables are used in Java to record values of properties of objects. In the `UserDefinedSun` class, instance variable `sunDiameter` is used to keep track of a property of the sun—its diameter.

{Definition of Terms}

An **instance variable** keeps track of a property of an object. It is declared inside the class but outside of any method in the class.

In the example above, I used the new reserved word `private` in front of the declaration of `sunDiameter`. Simply put, `private` means that the associated instance variable cannot be referred to from any other class. Generally you should get in the habit of making all your instance variables `private`. I'll explain why in later chapters.

You can declare as many instance variables you like in a class. They can be ints, doubles, strings, and other kinds of variables that I haven't presented yet. You should use them whenever you need to keep track of something (e.g., a property of an object) between calls of the methods of the class.

You should *not* use instance variables as replacements for local variables. Local variables should be used to record temporarily used values that are not needed between the completion of one call of a method and the beginning of a call of another. Using an instance variable when a local variable will suffice will work, but is not a good programming practice. It can make your code more confusing. Someone else reading it for the first time will get the wrong idea about the purpose of the variable.

{Good Ideas}

Do not use an instance variable when a local variable suffices.

5.1.1 Initial Values of Instance Variables

Java does not require that you give an initial value to an instance variable when you create it. Hence I could have simply written

```
private int sunDiameter;
```

and not given it the initial value of 0. In fact, giving it an initial value of 0 is a waste of time because as soon as the program starts running, the `startup` method is called and the user supplies its desired value.

In this case it is good programming practice *not* to give `sunDiameter` an initial value. By not doing so you indicate that `sunDiameter` will be getting its initial value from a command in one of the methods in the class. Explicitly giving it a useless value that will be almost immediately replaced by a useful one is misleading.

{Good Ideas}

Do not give a useless initial value to an instance variable if code in one of the methods of the class will give it an initial value.

Despite all that I just said, Java will, by default, give every instance variable an initial value if you don't. Ints default to the initial value 0, doubles to the initial value 0.0. Strings are a little different, and I'll explain why shortly.

As a result, even though you don't give `sunDiameter` the initial value 0 explicitly, it will get the initial value 0 anyway. Of course it doesn't really matter that Java gives `sunDiameter` the initial value 0 since the startup method changes it to the user-entered value before it is used for anything.

Now suppose you *want* the initial value of some instance variable to be 0. Should you explicitly give that variable the initial value 0, or should you simply count on Java to give it the default initial value 0? If you let Java do it, then there is no way by simply looking at the declaration of the variable to know whether it is a variable that will be given an initial value in one of the methods or is a variable whose initial value is supposed to be 0. Hence, even though Java will initialize the instance variable to 0 for you, it is clearer if you do so explicitly.

{Good Ideas}

Explicitly give an instance variable an initial value (even if it is the same as the default) unless that variable will be given an initial value by one of the methods in the class.

5.1.2 Named Constants

Instance variables can also be used to give names to fixed properties of objects. For example, let's reconsider the `BouncingBall` class from Chapter 4. In the `draw` method, I created the variable `diameter` and gave it the value 30. Technically, `diameter` is a fixed property of the ball being displayed. *It never changes.*

Every time the `draw` method is called, a new `diameter` variable is created and given the value 30, and when the `draw` method finishes, `diameter` goes away. Code 5.3 shows a better way to write the `BouncingBall` class.

Not only does this version avoid the repeated creation of the variable `diameter` (i.e., it is slightly more efficient), but also it puts a property of the

CODE 5.3

```
import java.awt.*;

public class BouncingBall extends Animator {
    // properties
    private int diameter = 30;

    public void draw(int clock, Graphics g) {
        // compute the coordinate of the left side of the ball
        int left = clock % (Animator.getSceneWidth()+diameter)
                    - diameter;
        // compute the height of the ball at any time
        int maxHeight = Animator.getSurface()-diameter;
        double angle = Math.toRadians(clock%360);
        int height =
            (int) Math.abs((maxHeight * Math.sin(angle)));
        // compute the coordinate of the top of the ball
        int top = Animator.getSurface() - height - diameter;
        // draw the ball
        g.setColor(Color.magenta);
        g.fillOval(left, top, diameter, diameter);
    } // end of draw method

} // end of BouncingBall class
```

Putting diameter here makes the program more efficient and easier to understand. The comment also helps make it clear that diameter is a property of BouncingBall objects.

BouncingBall
A new version using an instance variable to record the diameter.

BouncingBall object where it can be more easily seen. This has the benefit of making your code easier to understand.

To make it even clearer that diameter is a fixed property of BouncingBall objects, we can tell the compiler that any code that tries to change the value of diameter should be flagged as an error. To do so, replace the declaration of diameter with

```
private final int diameter = 30;
```

The reserved word final tells the compiler that you don't want the variable diameter to be changed via the execution of any command in this program, either accidentally or intentionally. This makes it possible for the compiler to detect and report an error, should you or anyone else modify your program and insert code that tries to change diameter. It also makes it clear to anybody looking at your program that diameter is an unchanging property of the BouncingBall class.

Variables declared with the reserved word final are unchangeable, and hence not "variable." Java uses the term *named constant* to refer to such things. The identifier diameter in this example gives a name to the constant value 30 and hence is a named constant.

{Definition of Terms}

A **named constant** is a descriptive name given to a constant value. Technically, it is an instance variable that can be assigned a value only once (its initial value).

Let's redo the `UserDefinedSun` class to make not only the diameter, but also the position of the sun be properties of a `UserDefinedSun` object. To do so, I'll declare named constants for the x and y coordinates of the upper left corner of the sun, as shown in Code 5.4.

CODE 5.4

```
import java.awt.*;

public class UserDefinedSun2 extends Animator {
    // properties
    private int sunDiameter;
    private final int sunLeft = 0;
    private final int sunTop = 0;

    public void startup() {
        // prompt for and input the diameter of the sun
        Animator.write ("Please enter the diameter of the sun:");
        sunDiameter = Animator.readInt();
    } // end of startup method

    public void draw (Graphics g) {
        // draw the sun
        g.setColor(Color.yellow);
        g.fillOval(sunLeft, sunTop, sunDiameter, sunDiameter);
    } // end of draw method

} // end of UserDefinedSun2 class
```

> Upper left corner position of the sun is a fixed property of a `UserDefinedSun2` object.

UserDefinedSun2
Uses named constants to define fixed properties (the position) of the sun.

5.1.3 Picturing an Object with Instance Variables

In Chapter 4, I drew pictures of parameter and local variables of a method. Each variable was a rectangle, with the name of the variable above it and its current value inside. The collection of parameter and local variables was put inside a dashed-line box to indicate that they were all part of the same method.

The same sort of picture can be drawn for objects and their instance variables. The only difference is that I'll put the instance variables inside a three-dimensional cube, doing so to indicate that the instance variables are part of that object. Figure 5.1 shows a `UserDefinedSun2` object with its three instance variables and their values just after the object is created (but before the `startup` method is called).

I put a question mark in the `sunDiameter` instance variable box, even though by default it will be 0, just to show that no useful value has been assigned to it yet. A picture of the `UserDefinedSun2` object *after* the

FIGURE 5.1

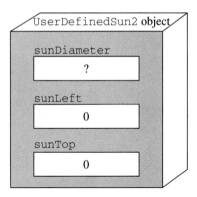

startup method is called would have the value given by the user shown in that box instead.

Written Exercises

1. What is the difference between a local variable and an instance variable?
2. When should an instance variable be used instead of a local variable?
3. Why are named constants useful?
4. Why are named constants "final"?

Programming Exercises

1. Modify the BouncingBall class from Chapter 4 to ask the user to define the diameter of the bouncing ball.
2. Modify the UFO class from Chapter 4 to ask the user to define the width and height of the UFO. Make the diameter of the colored lights be one-half the height of the UFO, and spread them evenly across the UFO. Draw a three-dimensional picture of your UFO object showing the values of all instance variables just after the user has given them values (assume the user enters 100 for the width and 30 for the height).
3. Write a class definition for an object that draws a 10-pixel-wide black post, with the bottom even with the surface. The height should be a fraction of the distance from the surface to the top of the scene, determined by a number between 0 and 1 (a double) supplied by the user. For example, if the user enters 0.25, then the post should go one-fourth of the way from the surface to the top. Use named constants as appropriate. Use Animator.readDouble to read a double from the user. Draw a picture of your object showing the values of all instance variables (including named constants) after the user has entered 0.69.
4. Write a class definition for an object that draws a string (entered by the user via the Animator.readString command) in the upper left corner of the scene. Prompt the user to enter his or her name for that string.

5.2 MULTIPLE OBJECTS

The essence of object-oriented programming is the creation and use of many objects. To motivate the use of multiple objects, let us first consider the class definition SunAndCloud in Code 5.5. It draws both a sun and a cloud, essentially combining the commands from the draw methods of the Sun and Cloud classes from Chapter 4 into a single draw method.

```
import java.awt.*;

public class SunAndCloud extends Animator {

    public void draw(Graphics g) {
        // draw the sun
        g.setColor(Color.yellow);
        g.fillOval(0,0,40,40);

        // draw the cloud
        g.setColor(Color.gray);
        g.fillOval(30,20,50,25);
        } // end of draw method

    } // end of SunAndCloud class
```

CODE 5.5

SunAndCloud
A single class definition for an object that draws a sun and a nonmoving cloud.

While this approach *will* work, consider this. We've already defined a Sun class and a Cloud class, so why should we define a new class and copy much of the code from the other two into it? Wouldn't it be nice if we could write a simple program that uses the already existing Sun and Cloud classes? Wouldn't it be nice if there were a library of classes like Sun and Cloud that we could use every time we wrote an animation that needed them, and not have to rewrite them every time?

Java allows you to do exactly that. In fact, it encourages it. Writing a class once and using it over and over saves a lot of work. The math functions are part of a Math class that somebody wrote once and now you and everybody else who write Java programs use over and over. This saves a lot of work, not just in writing the code, but in designing, testing, and debugging, too. The term used for this concept is *code reuse,* meaning simply that you reuse code that was written and tested before instead of writing everything from scratch.

{Definition of Terms}

Using previously written classes in a new program, rather than writing them from scratch, is called **code reuse.** It makes it much easier to write a correctly working program.

The new, multiple-object version of the SunAndCloud program above will have three objects. A Sun object, defined by the existing Sun class (slightly modified as described below); a Cloud object, defined by the existing Cloud class (also slightly modified); and a new SunAndCloud class that defines an object whose task is to create the Sun and Cloud objects and ask each of them to exhibit their drawing behavior. Notice that the new SunAnd-Cloud class has taken over some of the responsibility of the Animator. That is, while the Animator will create the SunAndCloud object and call its draw method, the Animator will *not* create the Sun and Cloud objects and call *their* draw methods.

Code 5.6 defines the modified Sun class to be used in this program. It embodies the good programming practices mentioned earlier in this chapter by using named constants for the diameter and position of the sun. I've also given the name drawSun to the method that draws the sun, and the name sg to the parameter variable for reasons that I'll explain later in this section.

CODE 5.6

```
public class Sun {
    // properties
    private final int sunDiameter = 40;
    private final int sunLeft = 0;
    private final int sunTop = 0;

    public void drawSun(Graphics sg) {
        // draw the sun
        sg.setColor(Color.yellow);
        sg.fillOval(sunLeft,sunTop,sunDiameter,sunDiameter);
    } // end of drawSun method

} // end of Sun class
```

Code 5.7 defines the modified Cloud class, also using named constants as appropriate. Note also the new names for the method that does the drawing and its parameter.

CODE 5.7

```
public class Cloud {

    // properties
    private final int cloudWidth = 50;
    private final int cloudHeight = 25;
    private final int cloudLeft = 30;
    private final int cloudTop = 20;

    public void drawCloud(Graphics cg) {
        // draw the cloud
        cg.setColor (Color.gray);
        cg.fillOval(cloudLeft,cloudTop,cloudWidth,cloudHeight);
    } // end of drawCloud method

} // end of Cloud class
```

Notice that these declarations of the `Sun` and `Cloud` classes *do not extend Animator*. Only one class can do so, it being the one that the Animator will use to create an object and call that object's `draw` method.

5.2.1 Creating New Objects

Next I'll write a class definition for the object that the creates `Sun` and `Cloud` objects and then calls the `drawSun` and `drawCloud` methods to get the sun and cloud drawn in the scene. Let's first look at how new objects are created.

Creating new objects is quite simple in Java. You simply need to write the reserved word `new` followed by the name of the class that defines the object you want to create, followed by opening and closing parentheses. For example, to create a `Sun` object, you write

```
new Sun ()
```

When a new `Sun` object is created, the computer allocates some space in memory to store information about the object, including the values of all the instance variables the object has (if any). Once it is created, you need a way to refer to this object. This is done by a command very similar to that used to create a new integer or double variable.

```
Sun theSun = new Sun();
```

When the command above is executed, a variable called `theSun` is created (any name will do). Then a new `Sun` object is created. Finally the initial value of `theSun` is set to be a *reference* to the `Sun` object that was just created. Putting the class name `Sun` before the variable name `theSun` tells the compiler that `theSun` will be a variable that is a reference to a `Sun` object. The variable `theSun` is the name by which we can refer to the new `Sun` object that was just created. In a sense it gives a name to that object, just as your name is a reference to the object "you."

It is important to note that the creation of a variable that is a *reference* to an object is similar to the creation of an int or double variable. Space is allocated in both cases, and something is stored in that space. However, the similarity ends there. With an int or double, the value associated with the variable is stored in the space that was allocated (for example, 7, or 3.84). For a variable that is a reference to an object, the object itself is *not* stored in the space allocated for the variable. Instead, space is allocated somewhere else in memory for the object, and the space that is allocated for the variable itself is filled with a reference to the object. This can be pictured as shown as in Figure 5.2, where the arrow stands for the reference to the `Sun` object.

{Definition of Terms}

A **reference variable** stores a reference to an object, not the object itself.

FIGURE 5.2

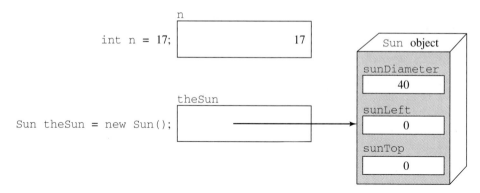

Code 5.8 is a first cut at the `SunAndCloud2` class. It only creates the new `Sun` and `Cloud` objects, and does not yet have code to ask the two new objects to draw themselves (i.e., to call their methods that do the drawing). Hence, when the `draw` method in the `SunAndCloud2` object is called by the Animator, nothing will be drawn.

CODE 5.8

```
public class SunAndCloud2 extends Animator {

    // properties
    private Sun theSun = new Sun();           ◄———
    private Cloud theCloud = new Cloud();     ◄———

    public void draw(Graphics g) {
        // tell the Sun and Cloud objects to draw themselves
        // (code to be added)
        } // end of draw method     ◄———

    } // end of SunAndCloud2 class
```

> The `SunAndCloud` object will have instance variables that refer to `Sun` and `Cloud` objects.

> Nothing will be drawn since there is no code to draw or to call the drawing methods in the `Sun` or `Cloud` object.

When the Animator creates the `SunAndCloud2` object, it executes the commands that create the instance variables. This will cause the creation of a `Sun` object and an instance variable `theSun` whose initial value will be a reference to the newly created `Sun` object. It will then cause the creation of a `Cloud` object and an instance variable `theCloud` whose initial value will be a reference to the newly created `Cloud` object. The instance variable declarations are commands that are executed when the `SunAndCloud2` object is created.

Now we need to add the code to get the `Sun` and `Cloud` objects to draw themselves. We use the same approach that was used to get the `Graphics` object to draw an oval, rectangle, or line. That is, we call the methods in the `Sun` and `Cloud` classes that do the drawing (`drawSun` and `drawCloud`, respectively). To do so, we write the name of the reference to an object, followed by a period, followed by the name of the method to call, followed in parentheses by any arguments that need to be sent to the method when it is called. Code 5.9 completes the `SunAndCloud2` class definition.

CODE 5.9

```
public class SunAndCloud2 extends Animator {
    // properties
    private Sun theSun = new Sun();
    private Cloud theCloud = new Cloud();

    public void draw(Graphics g) {
        // tell the Sun and Cloud objects to draw themselves
        theSun.drawSun(g);         ◄————————  Call the drawSun method in the
        theCloud.drawCloud(g);     ◄————————  Sun object and the drawCloud
        } // end of draw method                method in the Cloud object.

    } // end of SunAndCloud2 class
```

Let's dissect the first command in the `draw` method. It is a call of a method called `drawSun`. The definition of that method can be found in the class definition for the object referred to by `theSun`. Since the value of `theSun` is a reference to a `Sun` object, the `drawSun` method will be found in the `Sun` class definition. The `drawSun` definition in the `Sun` class has a single parameter, a reference to a `Graphics` object it uses to set the color and draw the oval. Hence we must send the `drawSun` method a reference to a `Graphics` object. Fortunately the `draw` method (of the `SunAndCloud2` class) receives a parameter that is a reference to a `Graphics` object (`g`). The reference will be sent to the `drawSun` method, and the method will use the same `Graphics` object to do its drawing (Figure 5.3).

FIGURE 5.3

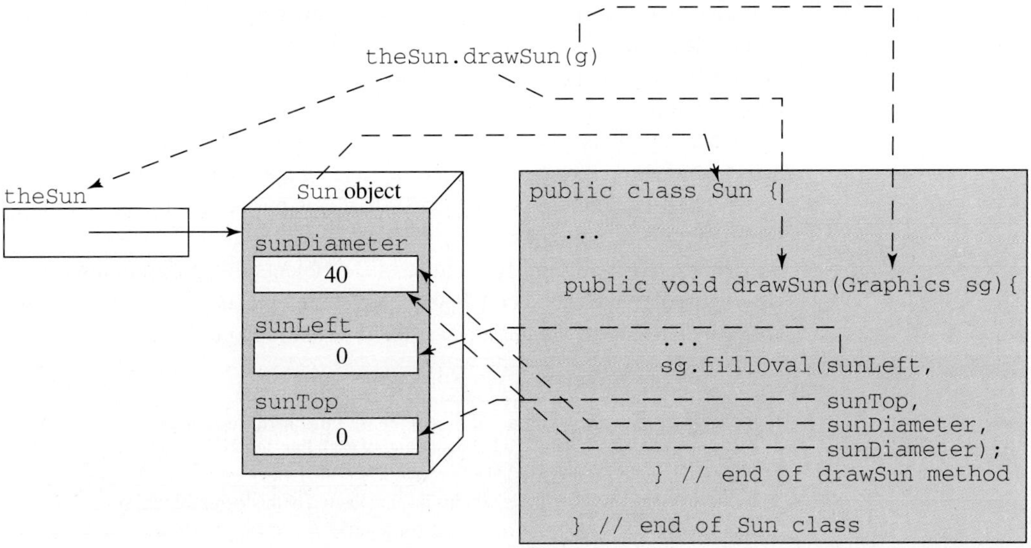

This general pattern for calling a method is always followed. The reference variable (theSun) is used to find an object (Sun), which is defined by a class (Sun). The method being called (drawSun) is defined in that class (Sun). If it isn't, then there is an error. The method (drawSun) is called, and when it is executed, it uses the values of the instance variables that occur in the object referred to by the reference variable (theSun). It also uses any parameter values sent to it by the calling method (a reference to a Graphics object).

5.2.2 Programs with Several Class Definitions

We now have three class definitions: Sun, Cloud, and SunAndCloud2. These must be combined into a single program, and there are two ways to do it.

One way is to put all three class definitions in a single file, one following the other, and then compile that file (and hence all the class definitions within) in one step. The other is to put each class definition into a separate file and compile each file (and hence each class definition) separately. Putting them in one file is simpler, but for large programs, it is not the most efficient way to go. Since it is simpler, and because you are just learning Java, it is the way I'll discuss at this time.[4]

When you put several classes into the same file, you must observe the Java rule that only one class in the file can be declared public. The remaining classes cannot be "public," which is accomplished by simply omitting the reserved word public in the class declaration. Java also requires that the file containing the class definitions be named for the public class (i.e., SunAndCloud2.java). The Animator also requires that the public class be the one that extends Animator.

The class definitions can appear in any order in the file, although it is recommended that the public class come first. Each class definition should be defined from beginning to end before the next class is defined. Do not put one class definition inside another or mix up their code in any way.[5]

Code 5.10 is a complete Java program file for the three-class SunAndCloud2 program. Notice that the import line is needed only once.

Since the main class, SunAndCloud2, is public, the file containing this program must be called SunAndCloud2.java.

Figure 5.4 is a complete picture of the objects this program uses (not including the Animator objects). It shows all three objects and their instance variables. It also shows, via the arrows, the references from the SunAndCloud2

---

4. Putting each class definition in a different file isn't that hard. Just make each class public, put "imports java.awt.*;" at the beginning of each file, and give each file the same name as the class with ".java" appended. Only the main class should "extend Animator".

5. It is legal to put one class definition inside another, but at this point we will not do so.

CODE 5.10

```java
import java.awt.*;
```
This line is needed only once.

```java
public class SunAndCloud2 extends Animator {
```
Only the main class is public and extends Animator.

```java
    // properties
    private Sun theSun = new Sun();
    private Cloud theCloud = new Cloud();

    public void draw(Graphics g) {
        // tell the Sun and Cloud objects to draw themselves
        theSun.drawSun(g);
        theCloud.drawCloud(g);
        } // end of draw method

    } // end of SunAndCloud2 class
```

```java
class Sun {
```
All other classes are *not* public and *do not* extend Animator.

```java
    // properties
    private final int sunDiameter = 40;
    private final int sunLeft = 0;
    private final int sunTop = 0;

    public void drawSun(Graphics sg) {
        // draw the sun
        sg.setColor(Color.yellow);
        sg.fillOval(sunLeft,sunTop,sunDiameter,sunDiameter);
        } // end of drawSun method

    } // end of Sun class

class Cloud {
    // properties
    private final int cloudWidth = 50;
    private final int cloudHeight = 25;
    private final int cloudLeft = 30;
    private final int cloudTop = 20;

    public void drawCloud(Graphics cg) {
        // draw the cloud
        cg.setColor(Color.gray);
        cg.fillOval(cloudLeft,cloudTop,cloudWidth,cloudHeight);
        } // end of drawCloud method

    } // end of Cloud class
```

SunAndCloud2
A complete program in a single file that uses three objects to draw the scene.

FIGURE 5.4

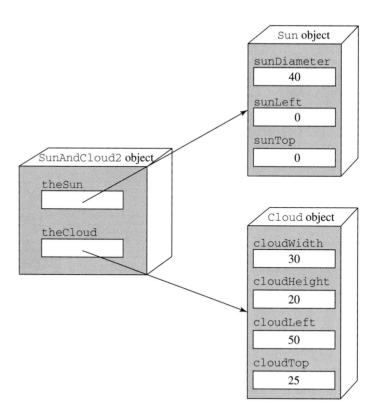

object to the Sun and Cloud objects. Diagrams like these are useful when you are trying to understand the relationships between objects in programs that create and use many objects. In fact, we'll be using diagrams like these as design aids *before* we write the code for many programs shown later in this text.

5.2.3 Another Example

Code 5.11 is an example of a program that draws two moving clouds, one 200 pixels ahead of the other. Both clouds will reappear at the left after going off the scene on the right. As in the previous example I'll define a class for each cloud and a main class that creates each cloud object and then calls their drawing methods to get them drawn.

Recall from Chapter 3 that argument values are sent from one method and received as initial values of parameter variables in the method being called. In this example, when the first command in the draw method in the TwoCloud class calls the drawCloud1 method in the Cloud1 object (as defined in the Cloud1 class), it will send it two argument values—an integer value equal to the current value of clock and a reference to a Graphics object g. The drawCloud1 method will then execute with a parameter variable clock1, which will be equal to the value of clock sent from the draw method,

CODE 5.11

```java
import java.awt.*;

public class TwoClouds extends Animator {
    // properties
    private Cloud1 firstCloud = new Cloud1();
    private Cloud2 secondCloud = new Cloud2();

    public void draw(int clock, Graphics g) {
        // tell the Cloud objects to draw themselves
        firstCloud.drawCloud1(clock, g);
        secondCloud.drawCloud2(clock, g);
        } // end of draw method

    } // end of TwoClouds class

class Cloud1 {
    // properties
    private final int cloud1Width = 40;
    private final int cloud1Height = 20;
    private final int cloud1Top = 15;
    private final int offset1 = 0;

    public void drawCloud1(int clock1, Graphics g1) {
        // draw the cloud
        g1.setColor(Color.gray);
        int cloud1Left = (clock1+offset1)%
            (Animator.getSceneWidth()+cloud1Width)-cloud1Width;
        g1.fillOval(cloud1Left,cloud1Top,cloud1Width,cloud1Height);
        } // end of drawCloud1 method

    } // end of Cloud1 class

class Cloud2 {
    // properties
    private final int cloud2Width = 40;
    private final int cloud2Height = 20;
    private final int cloud2Top = 15;
    private final int offset2 = 200;

    public void drawCloud2(int clock2, Graphics g2) {
        // draw the cloud
        g2.setColor(Color.gray);
        int cloud2Left = (clock2+offset2)%
            (Animator.getSceneWidth()+cloud2Width)-cloud2Width;
        g2.fillOval(cloud2Left,cloud2Top,cloud2Width,cloud2Height);
        } // end of drawCloud2 method

    } // end of Cloud2 class
```

and another parameter variable g1, which will be a reference to the same Graphics object used by the draw method. It is always important to remember that when a method is called, *values* are sent from the calling method to the called method. The names the two methods give to those values are completely unrelated.

I made the two cloud classes as identical as possible. Except for different class and variable names, the only significant difference is the values for the named constants offset1 and offset2. As I will show you later, it is possible to use a single class definition for both cloud objects, but I haven't shown you yet how to make the two objects differ in just that constant.

5.2.4 A Note about Strings

Strings are not primitive types like int and double. They are objects. The only difference between them and all other objects is that you do not have to use "new" to create a string object. Instead, every time you write a string literal, Java automatically creates a string object with the specified characters as its "value" and gives you a reference to that object. Hence when you write something like

```
String message = "hello there";
```

a string object is created with the value "hello there" and the variable message is made to refer to it.

Written Exercises

1. What is code reuse?
2. What is the difference between an integer variable and a variable like theSun?
3. How is a string variable different from an integer variable?
4. In what class is the code for a method named doit found when the following command is executed?

```
theThing.doit(99);
```

Assume that theThing is a variable that contains a reference to a Thing object.

Programming Exercises

1. Redo problem 2 of the programming exercises Section 3.8, using separate objects for the two boxes.
2. Redo problem 3 of the programming exercises Section 3.8, using separate objects for different parts of the car.

3. Redo problem 4 of the programming exercises Section 3.8, using separate objects for the sun, cloud, car, and tree.

5.3 THE SCOPE OF NAMES

The use of the instance variable `sunDiameter` in the `UserDefinedSun` class was forced, in part, by the fact that a local variable can be referred to only in the method it is created in. This is one example of a *scope* rule for names. The scope of a name is the region of code in which the thing (local variable, parameter variable, instance variable, named constant, method, class) the name is associated with can be referred to.

{Definition of Terms}

The **scope** of a name is the region of code in which the thing (local variable, parameter variable, instance variable, named constant, method, class) the name is associated with can be referred to.

Java has scope rules for everything that can be named. These rules are designed to make it easier to write correct programs and to make code reuse easier. For example, since a local variable can only be referred to in the same method it is created in, you can choose any name you like without worrying about whether that name was used for a local variable in a different method. If you happen to use the same name, say, `width`, in two different methods, then any reference to `width` in one method is guaranteed to be a reference to `width` created in that method and not the one in the other method. This is because `width` defined in the other method cannot be referred to in this method.

As a result, you can name local variables without any concern that the same local variable name was used in any other method that is part of your program. This includes methods in the same class or in other classes, and it includes methods in classes that you didn't write yourself. If fact, you probably can't find out what names were given to local variables in methods in, say, the `Graphics` class. Imagine the problems you'd have if this were not the case. You'd have to know every name of every local variable in every method your program uses, so that you could choose a unique name for each local variable in your new method.

The scope of parameter variable names works in the same way as local variables. They are known only in the method they are parameters for. The rationale is the same—to allow you to pick names for your parameters without having to avoid using names that were used in other methods.

In the three-class `SunAndCloud2` program, I used different names for the parameter variables in all three classes. Because of the scope rules, however, I could have just as easily written the program as shown in Code 5.12.

Even though there are three parameter variables called `g`, each one is a different variable, and references to `g` in each method are to the parameter named `g` in that same method. So don't get confused about the three different

CODE 5.12

```java
import java.awt.*;

public class SunAndCloud2 extends Animator {
    // properties
    private Sun theSun = new Sun();
    private Cloud theCloud = new Cloud();

    public void draw(Graphics g) {
        // tell the Sun and Cloud objects to draw themselves
        theSun.drawSun(g);
        theCloud.drawCloud(g);
    } // end of draw method

} // end of SunAndCloud2 class
```

The references to g in this method are to the parameter g of this draw method.

```java
class Sun {
    // properties
    private final int sunDiameter = 40;
    private final int sunLeft = 0;
    private final int sunTop = 0;

    public void drawSun(Graphics g) {
        // draw the sun
        g.setColor(Color.yellow);
        g.fillOval(sunLeft,sunTop,sunDiameter,sunDiameter);
    } // end of drawSun method

} // end of Sun class
```

The references to g in this method are to the parameter g of this drawSun method.

```java
class Cloud {
    // properties
    private final int cloudWidth = 50;
    private final int cloudHeight = 25;
    private final int cloudLeft = 30;
    private final int cloudTop = 20;

    public void drawCloud(Graphics g) {
        // draw the cloud
        g.setColor(Color.gray);
        g.fillOval(cloudLeft,cloudTop,cloudWidth,cloudHeight);
    } // end of drawCloud method

} // end of Cloud class
```

The references to g in this method are to the parameter g of this drawCloud method.

parameter names g. They just happen to have the same name, but they are different parameter variables and can potentially have different values. It's somewhat like two different families living in two different states, unknown to each other, both with a child named Donna. Even though the two children have the same name, they are different people. When relatives in one family uses Donna's name, they are referring to their Donna, not the other one. Each name Donna only makes sense in the corresponding family.

> **{New Concepts}**
>
> The scope of a parameter is just the method it is a parameter of. That parameter cannot be referenced from anywhere other than in that method.

> **{New Concepts}**
>
> Parameters of two different methods can have the same name. Each only makes sense in the method it is a parameter of.

5.3.1 Local Variable Names

The scope rule for local variables is almost the same as for parameters. The only difference is that the scope of a local variable begins when it is created, which might not be the first command in the method. If you try to use a local variable before it is created, you will get an error, as shown in the following example:

```
public void draw(int x, int y, Graphics g) {     Error—radius has
    int diameter = radius*2;                      not been created yet.
    int radius = 40;
    ...                                           radius is created here
                                                  and its scope extends to the
                                                  end of the draw method.
    } // end of draw method
```

The use of radius in the first command is an error because the local variable radius is not created until the second command. The scope of radius begins with the second command and continues until the end of the draw method (shown inside the box in the code above).

The following example shows another error caused by forgetting the reserved word int before radius:

```
public void draw(int x, int y, Graphics g) {
    radius = 40;                          Error—this does not create
    int diameter = radius*2;              the variable radius. It
    ...                                   assumes that radius has
                                          already been created.
    } // end of draw method
```

The first command tries to set an *existing* variable called `radius` to 40 rather than to create a new variable and then set it to 40. Since no variable called `radius` exists at that point, the first command is an error. Also, since `radius` is not created by the first command, the second command, which tries to use it, will be an error, too.

{New Concepts}

The scope of a local variable begins at the point it is created and ends at the end of the method.

Anytime the scope of a local variable of a given name overlaps the scope of another local variable of the same name, you'll get an error. For example, the following code has overlapping scopes for the variable `temp`:

```
public void draw(int x, int y, Graphics g) {

    int temp = 7;
    ...
    int temp = 9;
    ...

} // end of draw method
```

Error—the scope of the first `temp` overlaps with the scope of the second one.

Parameter variables and local variables in a given method also cannot have the same name, as illustrated in the following example:

```
public void draw(int x, int y, Graphics g) {

    ...
    double y = 8.6;
    ...

} // end of draw method
```

Error— the scope of the local variable `y` overlaps the scope of parameter variable `y`.

{New Concepts}

A local variable cannot have the same name as a parameter variable of the same method.

In summary, scope rules for parameter and local variables let you choose names in each method completely independently of any other method. You never have to worry about the Java compiler confusing the use of the same name in different methods. The names chosen for one method are only accessible in that method, and parameter and local variables defined in one method cannot be accessed from any other.

5.3.2 Method Names

When a method is defined as

```
public void draw( ...
```

it means that the name of the method (`draw`) is known not only within the class it appears in, but also in other classes. That is why the reserved word `public` is used. The scope of a method name defined as `public` is *everywhere.* You could replace `public` with the reserved word `private` if you didn't want any other class to be able to know about this `draw` method. Using `private` instead of `public` makes it inaccessible from anywhere but inside this class.

{New Concepts}

Declaring a method name *public* makes it accessible from any method in any class. Declaring it *private* makes it accessible only from methods in the same class.

However, just because a method name is public and accessible from other classes, you cannot simply use the name of the method when you want to call it. For example, in the `draw` method in the `SunAndCloud2` class, the `drawSun` method was called via the command

```
theSun.drawSun(g);
```

and *not* the command

```
drawSun(g);
```

This is because Java requires you to specify the name of an object that the `drawSun` method will execute "in the context of." By this, I mean that when the `drawSun` command executes, it will use named constants defined in some object, and in particular the object referred to by `theSun`.

In general, a method always executes in the context of some object. In doing so it has access to all the instance variables that are part of that object. Remember, the class is only a definition of an object and is not an object itself. Hence a method does not execute in the context of a class, but in the context of an object.[6]

{New Concepts}

A method executes in the context of an object and as a result has access to all the instance variables of that object.

Because you must always preface the name of a method with the name of a variable that references an object, it is possible to use the same public name for two different methods in two different classes (but not in the same class). For example, consider the version of the `SunAndCloud2` program shown in Code 5.13.

---

6. There are exceptions to this, but they are beyond the scope of this text.

CODE 5.13

```
import java.awt.*;

public class SunAndCloud3 extends Animator {
    // properties
    private Sun theSun = new Sun();
    private Cloud theCloud = new Cloud();

    public void draw(Graphics g) {
        // tell the Sun and Cloud objects to draw themselves
        theSun.draw(g);
        theCloud.draw(g);
        } // end of draw method

    } // end of SunAndCloud3 class

class Sun {
    // properties
    private final int sunDiameter = 40;
    private final int sunLeft = 0;
    private final int sunTop = 0;

    public void draw(Graphics g) {
        // draw the sun
        g.setColor(Color.yellow);
        g.fillOval(sunLeft,sunTop,sunDiameter,sunDiameter);
        } // end of draw method

    } // end of Sun class

class Cloud {
    // properties
    private final int cloudWidth = 50;
    private final int cloudHeight = 25;
    private final int cloudLeft = 30;
    private final int cloudTop = 20;

    public void draw(Graphics g) {
        // draw the cloud
        g.setColor(Color.gray);
        g.fillOval(cloudLeft,cloudTop,cloudWidth,cloudHeight);
        } // end of draw method

    } // end of Cloud class
```

This is a call of the draw method defined in the Sun class.

This is a call of the draw method defined in the Cloud class.

There are now three public `draw` methods. When the code in the `draw` method in the `SunAndCloud3` class executes the command

```
theSun.draw(g);
```

it knows that the `draw` method in the `Sun` class is the one to call, and not the one in the `Cloud` class or the one in the `SunAndCloud3` class. This is because `theSun` is a reference to a `Sun` object, and hence the `draw` method in the `Sun` class is the correct one. Similarly, when the command

```
theCloud.draw(g);
```

is executed, the `draw` method in the `Cloud` class is the one to call because `theCloud` is a reference to a `Cloud` object.

Hence it is legal for method names to have overlapping scopes outside of the class. Inside a single class definition, method names must be unique (although I'll show you an exception to this rule later on). When a method is called and there are two or more definitions of that method with the same name, the reference to an object that precedes the method name in the call will always resolve which definition applies.

{New Concepts}
Use of two or more public methods with the same name but defined in different classes is legal. The one being called at any point is the one in the class that defines the object that the method executes in the context of.

5.3.3 Instance Variable and Named Constant Scope

Instance variables and named constants may be declared public or private. If they are declared public, then they are accessible from code in other classes, just as methods can be called from other classes. However, for general purposes making them public is not a good programming practice, especially for instance variables. Because of this I will, for now at least, declare all instance variables and named constants to be private.

Private instance variables and named constants are accessible only within the class they are declared in. Their scope is the entire class, including the code inside methods defined in that class. They must have unique names within the class.

Since private instance variables and named constants are accessible only within the class they are declared in, the same names can be used in other classes without confusion (just like local and parameter variable names). Code 5.14 is yet another version of the `SunAndCloud3` program, this time using the same names for many of the named constants.

Even though the same names were used for `left` and `top` in both classes, it is clear that `left` and `top` defined in the `Sun` class are properties of `Sun`

CODE 5.14

```java
import java.awt.*;

public class SunAndCloud4 extends Animator {

    // properties
    private Sun theSun = new Sun();
    private Cloud theCloud = new Cloud();

    public void draw(Graphics g) {

        // tell the Sun and Cloud objects to draw themselves
        theSun.draw(g);
        theCloud.draw(g);
    } // end of draw method

} // end of SunAndCloud3 class
```

```java
class Sun {

    // properties
    private final int diameter = 40;
    private final int left = 0;
    private final int top = 0;

    public void draw(Graphics g) {

        // draw the Sun
        g.setColor(Color.yellow);
        g.fillOval(left, top, diameter, diameter);
    } // end of draw method

} // end of Sun class
```

These are references to the left and top named constants in the Sun class.

```java
class Cloud {

    // properties
    private final int width = 50;
    private final int height = 25;
    private final int left = 30;
    private final int top = 20;

    public void draw(Graphics g) {

        // draw the cloud
        g. setColor (Color.gray);
        g. fillOval(left, top, width, height);
    } // end of draw method

} // end of Cloud class
```

These are references to the left and top named constants in the Cloud class.

objects, not `Cloud` objects. Likewise, it is clear that `left` and `top` defined in the `Cloud` class are properties of `Cloud` objects.

Java allows the scopes of an instance variable and a local or parameter variable to overlap. When they do, the local or parameter variable is *visible* and the instance variable is *hidden*. However, having local or parameter variables with the same names as instance variables is not recommended because it makes the code hard to understand. In fact, it is a common mistake to accidentally define a local variable with the same name as an instance variable. The compiler won't give you an error message because it is legal to do so, but your program probably won't work correctly if you do. The example in Code 5.15 illustrates how this can happen.

CODE 5.15

```
public class Scene {

    private int size;

    public void startup() {
        int size = Animator.readInt();
    } // end of startup method

} // end of Scene class
```

> You wrote `int` by mistake, so this is a new local variable called `size`, and the instance variable `size` is not set as intended.

Assuming the purpose of the `startup` method is to give the instance variable `size` an initial value, the mistaken use of `int` winds up creating a new local variable called `size` that hides the use of the instance variable. Hence the local variable `size` gets set to `newvalue`, and the (different) instance variable `size` remains unchanged.

{Good Ideas}

Be careful that you do not accidentally create a new local variable with the same name as an instance variable.

Written Exercises

1. What is meant by the term *scope?*

2. Why is it possible to use the same local or parameter variable name in two different methods without confusion?

3. Find the scope-related errors in the following methods. Assume there are no instance variables.

   a.
   ```
   public void draw(int x, int y, Graphics g) {
       temp = 7;
       ...
   } // end of draw method
   ```

b.
```
public void draw(int x, int y, Graphics g) {
    x = 17;
    int y = 19;
    . . .
    } // end of draw method
```

c.
```
public void draw(int x, int y, Graphics g) {
    int sum = x + y;
    . . .
    int sum = sum + 1;
    . . .
```

4. Why must a call to a method be preceded by the name of a variable that is a reference to an object?

Programming Exercises

1. Modify your solution to problem 1 of the programming exercises in Section 5.2 to use the same names for as many variables, named constants, and methods as is appropriate (e.g., Graphics g, public void draw).

2. Do the same thing as in the previous problem to problem 2 of the programming exercises in Section 5.2.

3. Do the same thing as in the previous problem to problem 3 of the programming exercises in Section 5.2.

5.4 AN OBJECT DESIGN EXAMPLE

I will now design a program that will draw the simple rolling cart pictured in Figure 5.5. I will assume in this example that the wheels have diameter 40, that they will be centered 25 units on either side of the middle of the cart, that the

FIGURE 5.5

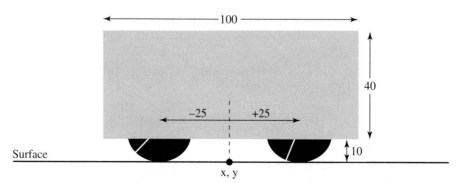

cart itself will be 100 units long and 40 units high, and that the bottom of the cart will be 10 units above the surface.

The first step of the design will be to decide what objects I'll need. Since the cart consists of two wheels and a box, I'll have two `Wheel` objects (defined by a slightly modified version of the `Wheel` class from Chapter 4) and a `Box` object, each of which will draw the appropriate shape in the scene. I'll use a `Cart` object to create the `Wheel` and `Box` objects and then to call their `draw` methods.

Now consider the two wheels. They look completely identical except for their position. Since the `draw` method in the `Wheel` class has parameters that specify where to draw the wheel, all I'll need to do in the `draw` method of `Cart` is to send one `Wheel` object's `draw` method the position of the left wheel and the other `Wheel` object's `draw` method the position of the right wheel. The code for the `draw` method for both `Wheel` objects will be exactly the same, and in fact the entire `Wheel` class that defines the `Wheel` objects will be identical. This means that we won't need two separate but identical class definitions for the two wheels!

Each `Wheel` object will have a named constant to specify the radius of the wheel (20), and the `Box` object will have two named constants to specify the length and height of the box (100 and 40, respectively). The `Cart` object will have three instance variables, two of them references to the two `Wheel` objects and one a reference to the `Box` object. Figure 5.6 pictures the objects, their contents, and their relationships.

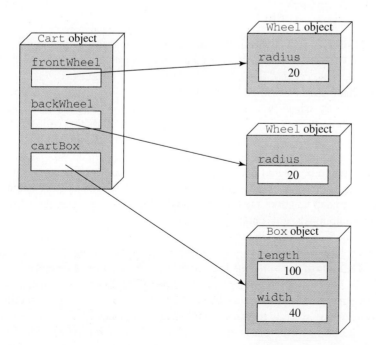

FIGURE 5.6

CODE 5.16

```
class Wheel {                                      No public or extends
    private final int radius = 20;                Animator.

    // x and y are the coordinates of the          radius is made a
    // bottom middle of the wheel                   named constant.
    public void draw(int x, int y, Graphics g) {
        int diameter = 2*radius;

        // draw a black circle
        g.setColor(Color.black);
        g.fillOval(x-radius,y-diameter,diameter,diameter);

        // draw rotating spokes
        g.setColor(Color.white);
        int xc = x;
        int yc = y-radius;
        double angle = 1.0*x/radius;
        int dx = (int)Math.rint(radius*Math.cos(angle));
        int dy = (int)Math.rint(radius*Math.sin(angle));
        g.drawLine(xc-dx,yc-dy,xc+dx,yc+dy);
        angle = angle + Math.toRadians(90.0);
        dx = (int)Math.rint(radius*Math.cos(angle));
        dy = (int)Math.rint(radius*Math.sin(angle));
        g.drawLine(xc-dx,yc-dy,xc+dx,yc+dy);
    } // end of draw method

} // end of Wheel class
```

Code 5.16 is the definition of the Wheel class. It is identical to the definition in Chapter 4, except that I used a named constant, and since it isn't the main class (Cart is), it isn't public and doesn't extend Animator. Note that the draw method expects parameters x and y to specify the bottom middle of the wheel (where it touches the surface). This is an important fact that we'll need when we write the code in the Cart class that calls the draw method and sends values for x and y. These facts are so important that I put a comment to that effect at the beginning of the draw method, so that the facts don't have to be figured out by reading the code (i.e., good documentation!).

The Box class is pretty simple (Code 5.17). It has two named constants for the length and height of the box and simply draws a gray rectangle. Also note the assumptions about x and y.

Code 5.18 is a first cut of the Cart class. So far it only has instance variables that refer to newly created Wheel and Box objects, and an empty draw method.

The calls of the draw methods of the two Wheel objects and the Box object are similar to those in previous examples. The difference is that we must be sure to pass the proper coordinate values to the draw methods in order to get the objects to draw their shapes in the correct places.

The draw method in the Wheel class expects to receive the coordinates of the bottom middle of where it is supposed to draw the wheel. But the

```
class Box {
    private final int length = 100;
    private final int height = 40;

    // x and y are the coordinates of
    // the bottom middle of the box
    public void draw(int x, int y, Graphics g) {
        // draw a gray rectangle
        g.setColor(Color.gray);
        int left = x-length/2;
        int top = y-height;
        g.fillrect(left,top,length,height);
    } // end of draw method

} // end of Box class
```

CODE 5.17

```
public class Cart extends Animator {
    // properties
    Wheel leftWheel = new Wheel();
    Wheel rightWheel = new Wheel();
    Box cartBox = new Box();

    // x and y are coordinates of the
    // bottom middle of the cart
    public void draw(int x, int y, Graphics g) {
        // draw the cart (to be added)
    } // end of draw method

} // end of Cart class
```

CODE 5.18

coordinates sent to the draw method of Cart by the Animator are those of the bottom middle of the cart. In the case of the left wheel, the bottom of the cart is the same as the bottom of the wheel, so we can just send y. But the middle of the left wheel is 25 pixels to the left (less) than the middle of the cart, so we must send the value x-25. Hence the command to call the draw method of the leftWheel object is

```
leftWheel.draw(x-25,y,g);
```

The right wheel is similar, except it is 25 pixels to the right, so the command to call the draw method of the rightWheel object is

```
rightWheel.draw(x+25,y,g);
```

Note that in both cases the reference to the Graphics object that the draw methods will use is passed also.

Drawing the box is similar, except while the middle of the box is the same as the middle of the cart, the bottom of the box is 10 pixels above the bottom of the cart. Hence the command to call the `draw` method of the Box object is

Cart
Draws a two-wheeled cart.

```
cartBox.draw(x,y-10,g);
```

Code 5.19 is the complete program.

CODE 5.19

```java
import java.awt.*;

public class Cart extends Animator {
    // properties
    Wheel leftWheel = new Wheel();
    Wheel rightWheel = new Wheel();
    Box cartBox = new Box();

    // x and y are coordinates of the
    // bottom middle of the cart
    // public void draw(int x, int y, Graphics g) {
        leftWheel.draw(x-25,y,g);
        rightWheel.draw(x+25,y,g);
        cartBox.draw(x,y-10,g);
        } // end of draw method

    } // end of Cart class

class Wheel {
    private final int radius = 20;

    // x and y are the coordinates of the
    // bottom middle of the wheel
    public void draw(int x, int y, Graphics g) {
        int diameter = 2*radius;
        // draw a black circle
        g.setColor(Color.black);
        g.fillOval(x-radius,y-diameter,diameter,diameter);

        // draw rotating spokes
        g.setColor(Color.white);
        int xc = x;
        int yc = y-radius;
        double angle = 1.0*x/radius;
        int dx = (int)Math.rint(radius*Math.cos(angle));
        int dy = (int)Math.rint(radius*Math.sin(angle));
        g.drawLine(xc-dx,yc-dy,xc+dx,yc+dy);
        angle = angle + Math.toRadians(90.0);
        dx = (int)Math.rint(radius*Math.cos(angle));
        dy = (int)Math.rint(radius*Math.sin(angle));
        g.drawLine(xc-dx,yc-dy,xc+dx,yc+dy);
        } // end of draw method

    } // end of Wheel class
```

```
class Box {
    private final int length = 100;
    private final int height = 40;

    // x and y are the coordinates of
    // the bottom middle of the box
    public void draw(int x, int y, Graphics g) {
        // draw a gray rectangle
        g.setColor(Color.gray);
        int left = x-length/2;
        int top = y-height;
        g.fillRect(left,top,length,height);
    } // end of draw method

} // end of Box class
```

This is a good time to review the concept of different methods having distinct parameter variables, even if they have the same name. In this example, each draw method has separate and distinct parameter variables x and y. Even though they have the same names in all three methods, more than one x and y variable will exist at the same time, and they may have different values even though they have the same name. For example, suppose the draw method in the Cart class has just called the draw method in the Box class. Assume the value of x in the draw method in the Cart class is 100 and the value of y is 50. Then Figure 5.7 is a picture of the variables of the two draw methods at that time.

As you can see, the value of the parameter variable y in the draw method of the Cart class is 50, which is what was sent to it by the Animator. However, the value of the (distinct) parameter variable y in the draw method of the Box class is 40, which is what was sent to it from the draw method of Cart (i.e., y-10).

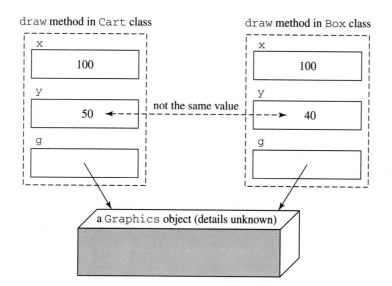

draw method in Cart class   draw method in Box class   **FIGURE 5.7**

Programming Exercises

1. Modify the `Cart` class to display three wheels, one in the center and the others centered 30 units in front of and behind the center wheel.

2. Add a second version of the `Wheel` class (called `SmallWheel`) that defines an object that draws a red wheel with black spokes and has diameter 15. Modify the `Cart` class to use `SmallWheel` instead of `Wheel` for the front wheel of the cart.

3. Write class definitions called `Scene`, `Sun`, and `Tree`. `Sun` draws a sun in the upper left corner of the animation scene, and `Tree` draws a tree on the right side of the scene. `Scene` creates a `Sun` object and a `Tree` object and calls their `draw` methods to get them displayed.

4. Design a scene consisting of several trees (all the same except for their positions). Write a program consisting of a `Scene` and a (single) `Tree` class, where the `draw` method of the `Scene` class creates several `Tree` objects and calls their `draw` methods with different arguments to get the trees drawn at different places in the scene.

5.5 CONSTRUCTORS

The `TwoClouds` program in Section 5.2 had two almost identical class definitions for the two clouds that were being drawn. It used different names for all the instance, parameter, and local variables and the method names. But we now know, because of the scope rules, that using different names is not necessary. Hence the only remaining difference between the two classes is the value of the named constant that specified the offset of the cloud (either 0 or 200). I alluded at that time that there was something we could do about this, so that we could use a single class definition for both clouds. Now it is time.

We already know that when an object is created, the commands that comprise the instance variables are executed to create those variables and give them initial values. In addition to that, there is a special method that is always "called" (automatically) that can help to create the object. This method is called a *constructor*.

There are two differences between a constructor method and other methods. First, as already indicated, it is called automatically whenever an object of that class is being created. That's why it is called a constructor—it helps *construct* the object. Second, the difference lies in the way it is declared, which I will demonstrate shortly with an example.

> **{Definition of Terms}**
> A **constructor** is a method that is called automatically when an object of the class is created.

Like all methods, a constructor can have parameters. It receives values for those parameter from the command that causes a new object to be created, for example,

```
Cloud secondCloud = new Cloud (200);
```

Assuming there is a `Cloud` class with a constructor that has a single `int` parameter variable, then when the new `Cloud` object is created, the constructor will be called (automatically—you don't call it explicitly) and its parameter variable will be sent the initial value 200.

{New Concepts}

Argument values are sent to a constructor from the new command.

Code 5.20 shows a generic `Cloud` class containing just such a constructor.

CODE 5.20

```
class Cloud {
    // properties
    private final int width = 40;
    private final int height = 20;
    private final int top = 15;
    private final int offset;

    public Cloud(int offsetParam) {
        // set the named constant to the value
        // sent when a Cloud object is created
        offset = offsetParam;
    } // end of constructor

    public void draw(int clock, Graphics g) {
        // draw the cloud
        g.setColor(Color.gray);
        int left = (clock+offset)%
            (Animator.getSceneWidth()+width)-width;
        g.fillOval(left,top,width,height);
    } // end of draw method

} // end of Cloud class
```

A constructor has the same name as the class and does not have `void`.

Named constants can be assigned an initial value in a constructor.

The constructor method has a name that is the same as the name of the class (`Cloud`). It also does not have the reserved word `void`, like all the other methods we've seen so far. This is how the Java compiler knows it is a constructor.

{New Concepts}

A constructor has the same name as the class it is a constructor in.

When a new `Cloud` object is created using the command shown earlier, the following things happen. First, the instance variable declarations (named constants in this case) are executed, creating, in order, `width`, `height`, `top`, and `offset` and giving them their initial values. Then the constructor is called and sent the argument value 200, which becomes the value of the parameter variable `offsetParam`. The single assignment command in the constructor is executed, setting the instance variable (named constant) offset to 200. The constructor finishes, and that's the end of the creation of the new Cloud object.

Note that it is legal in a constructor to assign a value to a named constant. However, the named constant must not have been given an initial value when it was created. For example, in the Cloud class the constructor could not have assigned values to width, height, and top because they were already given initial values when they were created.

It should now be obvious how to create two different Cloud objects that are identical except for the value of the named constant offset. Just send the constructor different argument values (0 and 200) when they are created. Code 5.21 is a complete, new, and simpler version of the TwoClouds program.

TwoClouds2

Uses a constructor to create two similar **Cloud** objects from a single **Cloud** class definition.

CODE 5.21

```java
import java.awt.*;

public class TwoClouds2 extends Animator {
    // properties
    private Cloud firstCloud = new CLoud(0);
    private Cloud secondCloud = new Cloud (200);

    public void draw(int clock, Graphics g) {
        // tell the Cloud objects to draw themselves
        firstCloud.draw(clock, g);
        secondCloud.draw(clock, g);
    } // end of draw method

} // end of TwoClouds2 class

class Cloud {
    // properties
    private final int width = 40;
    private final int height = 20;
    private final int top = 15;
    private final int offset;

    public Cloud (int offsetParam) {
        // set the named constant to the value
        // sent when a Cloud object is created
        offset = offsetParam;
    } // end of constructor

    public void draw(int clock, Graphics g) {
        // draw the cloud
        g.setColor (Color.gray);
        int left = (clock+offset)%
            (Animator.getSceneWidth()+width)-width;
        g.fillOval(left,top,width,height);
    } // end of draw method

} // end of Cloud class
```

Two distinct Cloud objects are created. One will have offset = 0, the other offset = 200.

Written Exercises

1. How is a constructor defined differently from an ordinary method?
2. When is a constructor called?
3. How are parameter values sent to a constructor?

Programming Exercises

1. Define a `Tree` class that has an instance variable for the height and a constructor that is used to give the height an initial value. Then define a `Scene` class that creates four different `Tree` objects of different heights and displays them across the scene.

2. Modify the `Cart` class to display an 80-long by 20-high rectangle with four wheels with radii 5, 10, 10, and 5, evenly spaced across the bottom. Use only three classes,—`Cart`, `Wheel`, and `Box`—and use a constructor to define different-size wheels.

3. Define a `Cloud` class that has four instance variables—`width`, `height`, `offset`, and `altitude`—and a constructor that gives them initial values. `Altitude` is the distance from the top of the scene to the top of the cloud. Then define a `Scene` class that creates five different-sized `Cloud` objects and causes them to be drawn across the screen at different altitudes and offsets.

5.6 EXAMPLES

5.6.1 Saving a Value Between Calls

Suppose we want to draw a simple square that moves across the scene under the control of the left and right buttons, but also display the speed the square is moving. To do so, we need to compute the difference between consecutive x values provided as the parameter to the `draw` method on two consecutive calls. This means we will have to save the value from one call to be used on the next call to compute the difference. A instance variable can be used to save this value since it won't disappear when the `draw` method is finished, as a local variable will.

Code 5.22 shows the entire program. Each time the `draw` method is called, we compute the difference between the parameter variable x and the instance variable `previousX`, and we display this as the speed of the cart. Before the `draw` method finishes, we'll assign x to `previousX` to get ready for the next call to the method.

A small problem arises the first time the `draw` method is called. When the speed is calculated, the value of `previousX` is 0, not an actual previous value since there isn't yet a previous value. As a result, the speed will be incorrectly calculated and displayed the first time. However the Animator calls the draw method 10 times per second, so the incorrect value will not be displayed for

CODE 5.22

```
import java.awt.*;

public class ShowSpeed extends Animator {
    // properties
    private final int size = 100;
    private final int xSpeed = 10;
    private final int ySpeed = 50;
    private int previousX = 0;

    public void draw(int x, int y, Graphics g) {
        g.setColor(Color.black);
        int left = x-size/2;
        int top = y-size;
        g.fillRect(left,top,size,size);
        int speed = x - previousX;
        g.drawString("Speed = " + speed,xSpeed,ySpeed);
        previousX = x;
    } // end of draw method

} // end of ShowSpeed class
```

Compute the speed as the difference between two consecutive x values.

Save the most recent x value for the next call (to become the previous x value).

ShowSpeed
The instance variable **previousX** is used to compute the speed of the square as it moves across the screen.

long (try running it and see if you can see the first incorrect value). At this point we don't know enough Java to fix this minor problem.

5.6.2 More Complex Objects

In this example I'll construct a scene that consists of many objects. I'll use the existing Cloud and Wheel classes (code reuse!) to display several clouds and a wheel. I'll also define a collection of classes that define objects that will draw a fence consisting of four posts and three rails. Figure 5.8 shows the scene.

The length and height of the fence will be requested from the user. In this figure you can see that the user entered 400 for the length and 50 for the height.

The fence will be drawn by four Post objects (one per post) and three Rail objects (one per rail). One class will define all four posts, another all three rails. Rather than have all fence objects created by the main object, I'll define a separate Fence object that will do the work. The main object will simply create the Fence object and let the Fence object create the posts and rails.

The Fence will have one fixed property, the x coordinate of its middle. Other properties are the references to the Post and Rail objects that make up the fence. The Fence object will do no drawing itself, but will call the draw methods of the Post and Rail objects to draw themselves.

A Post will have three properties—the x coordinate of the middle of the post (set by the constructor), the width (fixed at 5), and the height (supplied by the user and set via the constructor). A Rail will have four properties—the x coordinate of the middle of the rail (set by the constructor), the length of the

FIGURE 5.8

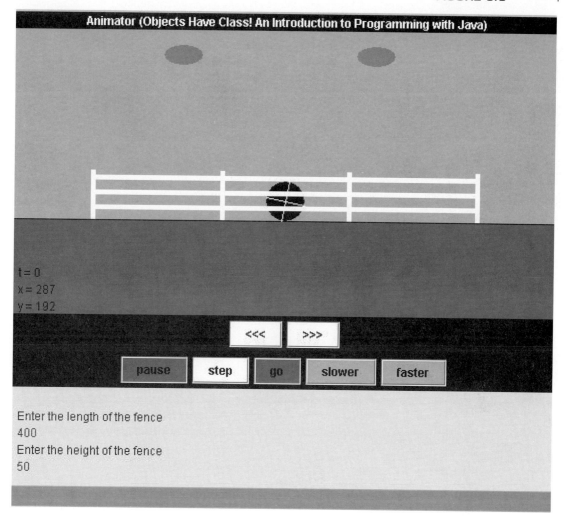

rail (supplied by the user and set via the constructor), the height of the rail (fixed at 5), and the distance above the surface (set by the constructor).

Since the Fence object will create all the Post and Rail objects, it will have to compute the positions of the posts and the distances above the surface of the rails from the length and height supplied by the user. The length and height will be supplied to the Fence object via its constructor. Hence the main class will read the length and height from the user and send the values to the Fence constructor when the Fence is created.

Figure 5.9 pictures the objects and their relationships. Values for instance variables that are computed based on the length and height of the fence or on the width of the scene are not yet shown.

FIGURE 5.9

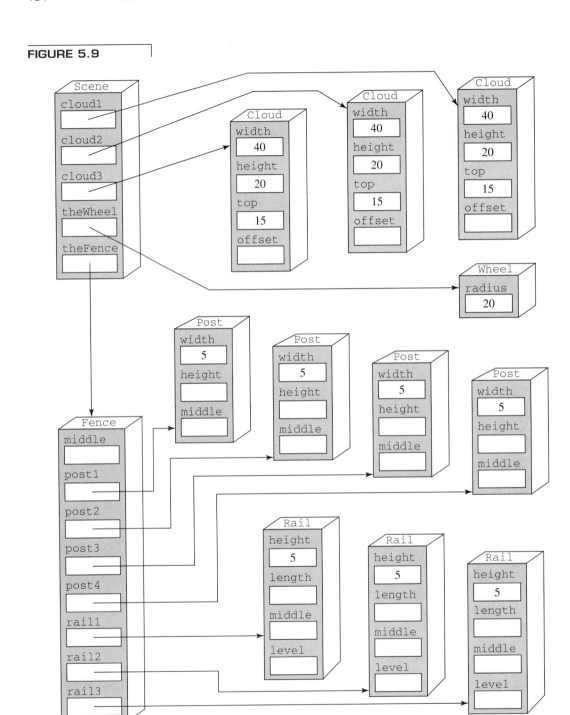

Code 5.23 is the class definition for the `Post` objects.

CODE 5.23

```
class Post {

    // properties
    private final int width = 5;
    private final int height;
    private final int middle;

    public Post(int mid, int hgt) {
        height = hgt;
        middle = mid;
    } // end of constructor

    public void draw(Graphics g) {
        // draw a post
        g.setColor(Color.white);
        int left = middle-width/2;
        int top = Animator.getSurface()-height;
        g.fillRect(left,top,width,height);
    } // end of draw method

} // end of Post class
```

> The creator of a `Post` object (Fence) supplies the values for the x coordinate of the middle of the post and its height.

The constructor plays a key role. It is sent the x coordinate value of the middle of the post and the height of the post when the post is created. It saves these two values in instance variables `height` and `middle` to be used later by the `draw` method to get the post drawn correctly (the dotted line shows how the value for the height of the post flows from the parameter of the constructor `hgt` to the instance variable `height`). Both `height` and `middle` are final because they shouldn't change once the constructor has given them initial values.

Code 5.24 is the class definition for the `Rail` objects.

Again, the constructor plays an important role in giving initial values to the length of the rail, the x coordinate of the middle of the rail, and the distance above the surface of the rail. Note the use of `Animator.getSurface` to determine the y coordinate of the surface of the scene.

Next comes the `Fence` class shown in Code 5.25.

The constructor does the most work. It receives the values for the length and height of the fence, then computes the positions and sizes of the posts and rails, and then creates the posts and rails. Of special note is that the instance variables that refer to the `Post` and `Rail` objects that comprise the fence are assigned their references in the constructor. This is because when a `Post` object is created, it must be sent values for the middle and the height of the post, but these values depend on values received by the `Fence` constructor. Since

CODE 5.24

```
class Rail {

    // properties
    private final int height = 5;
    private final int length;
    private final int middle;
    private final int level;

    public Rail(int len, int mid, int lev) {

        length = len;
        middle = mid;
        level = lev;
    } // end of constructor

    public void draw(Graphics g) {

        // draw a rail
        g.setColor(Color.white);
        int left = middle-length/2;
        int top = Animator.getSurface()-level;
        g.fillRect(left,top,length,height);
    } // end of draw method

} // end of Rail class
```

the constructor is executed after the instance variables are created, the Post objects have to be created in the constructor.

The draw method simply calls the draw method of each Post and Rail object. It sends along the reference to the Graphics object it receives from the main object of the program.

Finally comes the class that defines the main object, shown in Code 5.26.

First, the three Cloud objects and the Wheel object are created, but the Fence object and associated Post and Rail objects are not. Only when the Animator calls the startup method, and after the startup method reads the length and height of the fence, is the Fence object created. The creation of the Fence object also causes the creation of all the Post and Rail objects.

Once the program has begun, the user enters the length and height of the fence (400 and 50, respectively), and all objects have been created, Figure 5.10 shows the objects, their instance variables and values, and the relationship between the objects (assuming the scene is 600 pixels wide).

Now the Animator starts calling the draw method of the FenceScene object, which in turn calls the draw methods of the Cloud objects, the Wheel object, and the Fence object. When the draw method of the Fence object is called, it in turn calls the draw methods of the four Post and three Rail objects. Because the wheel is drawn first and the fence afterward, the wheel will appear behind the fence.

CODE 5.25

```java
class Fence {
    // properties
    private final int middle = Animator.getSceneWidth()/2;
    private Post post1;
    private Post post2;
    private Post post3;
    private Post post4;
    private Rail rail1;
    private Rail rail2;
    private Rail rail3;

    public Fence(int length, int height) {
        // compute the x-coordinate of each post
        int post1middle = middle-length/2;
        int post2middle = middle-length/6;
        int post3middle = middle+length/6;
        int post4middle = middle+length/2;

        // create each post
        post1 = new Post(post1middle,height);
        post2 = new Post(post2middle,height);
        post3 = new Post(post3middle,height);
        post4 = new Post(post4middle,height);

        // compute the y-coordinate of each rail
        height = (int) (height*0.9);
        int rail1level = height/3;
        int rail2level = 2*height/3;
        int rail3level = height;

        // create the rails
        rail1 = new Rail(length,middle,rail1level);
        rail2 = new Rail(length,middle,rail2level);
        rail3 = new Rail(length,middle,rail3level);
    } // end of constructor

    public void draw(Graphics g) {
        // draw the posts and rails
        post1.draw(g);
        post2.draw(g);
        post3.draw(g);
        post4.draw(g);
        rail1.draw(g);
        rail2.draw(g);
        rail3.draw(g);
    } // end of draw method

} // end of Fence class
```

> Each Post and Rail object must be created in the constructor in order to use the length and height values sent to the Fence constructor.

CODE 5.26

```
import java.awt.*;

public class FenceScene extends Animator {
    // properties
    private Cloud cloud1 = new Cloud(0);
    private Cloud cloud2 = new Cloud(200);
    private Cloud cloud3 = new Cloud(400);
    private Wheel theWheel = new Wheel();
    private Fence theFence;

    public void startup() {
        // get the length and height of the fence
        Animator.write("Enter the length of the fence");
        int length = Animator.readInt();
        Animator.write("Enter the height of the fence");
        int height = Animator.readInt();

        // create the fence
        theFence = new Fence(length,height);
    } // end of startup method

    public void draw (int clock, int x, int y, Graphics g) {
        // draw all objects
        cloud1.draw(clock,g);
        cloud2.draw(clock,g);
        cloud3.draw(clock,g);
        theWheel.draw(x,y,g);
        theFence.draw(g);
    } // end of draw method

} // end of FenceScene class

// the Cloud class here

// the Wheel class here

// the Fence class here

// the Post class here

// the Rail class here
```

The Fence object is created here since the values for the length and height of the fence are received from the user here.

Send the appropriate argument values to each draw method when called.

FenceScene

Draws a scene with moving clouds and wheel, and a fence whose size is determined by the user.

FIGURE 5.10

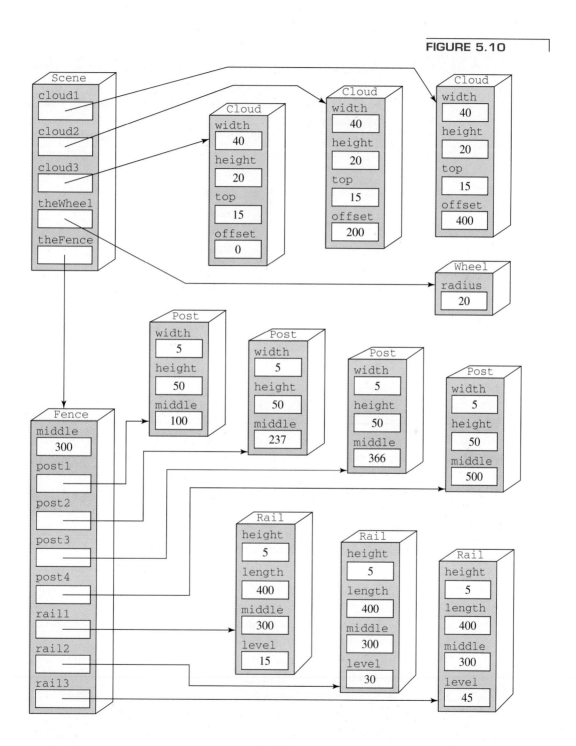

Programming Exercises

1. Modify the `ShowSpeed` program to display the total distance traveled by the rectangle instead of the speed of the rectangle.

2. Write a program consisting of several classes that displays a sun and a large black square (the size given by the user) with a white ladder going up the middle. The ladder should consist of two legs with width 3, and five rungs with width 2 and length one-half the size of the square.

Summary

- An instance of a class is an object defined by that class. A class may have many instances.
- Instance variables are created when an object is created and exist as long as the object exists.
- Named constants are instance variables that cannot be changed once given an initial value.
- New objects are created using the `new` operator.
- A variable defined as an object actually contains a reference to an object, not the object itself.
- When an object is being created, the commands that create its instance variables are executed (in order).
- The scope of a name is the region of the code in which it can be used.
- The scope of a parameter variable name is the method in which it is a parameter.
- The scope of a local variable of a method begins where the variable is created and extends to the end of the method.
- A constructor is a special method that is called automatically when a new object is created.
- Any arguments provided with the `new` operator are passed as parameters to the constructor.
- Initial values of instance variables can be given in the definition itself or by code in a constructor.

- The scope of a private instance variable is anywhere in the class that it appears in, except where the scope of a parameter or local variable of the same name hides it.
- The scope of a public method name is everywhere.
- Two different methods can use the same names for parameters and/or local variables without confusion because their scopes do not overlap.

Glossary

Code Reuse Using previously written classes in a new program rather than writing them from scratch.

Constructor A method that is called when an object of the class it is defined in is created.

Instance (of a Class) An object defined by some class.

Instance Variable A variable that is part of an object, defined in a class but outside of the methods of the class. It is created when an object of the class is created and exists as long as the object does.

Named Constant An instance variable that is given an initial value that cannot be changed.

Reference Variable A variable that stores a reference to an object.

Scope The region of a program in which an identifier that names a class, method, or variable can be used.

Interacting Objects and Events

6.1 HOW OBJECTS INTERACT

Two objects interact by calling each other's methods. In doing so, the calling object can request that the other object exhibit some behavior. It can also send information to the other object in the form of arguments. This is what we have been doing with the various animations, mainly via calls to the `draw` method by the Animator and by our own methods. One object can also request information from another object by calling a method and having the method return that information.

> **{New Concepts}**
>
> Objects interact by calling one another's methods. They send information via arguments and can get information returned.

For one object to be able to call a method in another, it needs a reference to that other object. In all the examples in previous chapters, every object that needed to call a method in a second object created the second object itself. But in many situations this won't be the case. An object has to call a method in a second object, but the first object does not create the second one. The second object was created somewhere else, by yet a third object. So somehow the third object, which has a reference to the second object, must give the first object a reference to the second object.

Figure 6.1 is an animation that demonstrates this concept. It displays three things: a fixed rectangle (representing a person), a circle moving under control of the left/right buttons (representing a balloon), and a line connecting the two (representing the string connecting the person and the balloon). I'll define a main object (called `BalloonScene`) that creates a `Person` object, a `Balloon` object, and a `Line` object and calls the `draw` method of each one to draw the scene. The new wrinkle is

143

FIGURE 6.1

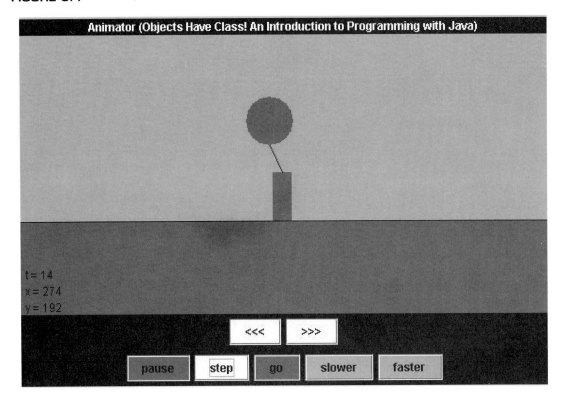

that the `Line` object will not be sent the coordinates of where the person and balloon are drawn. Instead, the `Line` object will ask the `Person` object and the `Balloon` object where they are in the scene, then draw a line connecting them. To do this, the `Line` object will need references to the `Person` and `Balloon` objects even though it didn't create them itself.

To accomplish this, I'll have the `BalloonScene` object send references to the `Person` and `Balloon` objects to the `Line` constructor when it creates the `Line` object. The `Line` object will store these references in instance variables, just as we have done before. The only real difference between this and what we've done before is that the `Line` object is not creating the `Person` and `Balloon` objects itself. It is being told about them by another object.

Figure 6.2 is a picture of the objects, their instance variables, and relationships for this program. For simplicity I'll leave out instance variables and named constants for properties such as the sizes and positions.

Code 6.1 is the beginnings of the class definitions for these objects. All that is done so far is to create the objects and get the `Line` object's two instance variables to refer to the `Balloon` and `Person` objects.

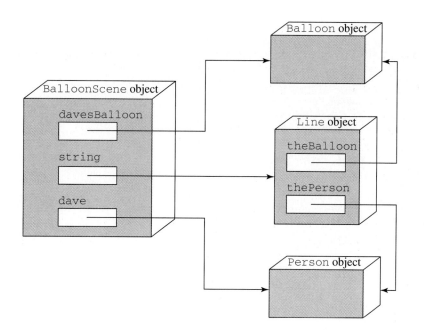

FIGURE 6.2

The key is that when the `Line` object is created, it is sent references to the `Person` and `Balloon` objects that were previously created. Because the `Line` object's constructor receives these references in parameter variables that disappear when the constructor finishes, the references are copied into the instance variables of `Line`, which stay around. Hence the constructor is simply the mechanism by which the `Line` object's instance variables are set to reference the `Person` and `Balloon` objects.

Let's review the sequence of events that take place when this program starts executing. The Animator creates the `BalloonScene` object. As part of creating that object, first the instance variable `dave` is created, then a new `Person` object is created, and a reference to it is stored in `dave`. Second, the instance variable `davesBalloon` is created; then a new `Balloon` object is created, and a reference to it is stored in `davesBalloon`. Third, the instance variable `string` is created, then a new `Line` object is created, and in doing so, the constructor of `Line` is sent references to the `Person` and `Balloon` objects that were just created. Note that the order is important here. The `Person` and `Balloon` objects *must* be created first so that references to them can be sent to the constructor of `Line` when it is created.

As the `Line` object is created, instance variables `thePerson` and `theBalloon` are created. Then the constructor is called, with parameter variable `p` set to reference the `Person` object and parameter variable `b` set to reference the `Balloon` object. The constructor then copies the reference to the `Person` object from `p` to `thePerson` and the reference to the `Balloon` object from `b` to `theBalloon`. The constructor finishes, and that is the end of creating the `Line` object. The `BalloonScene` object also is fully created

CODE 6.1

```
import java.awt.*;

public class BalloonScene extends Animator {
    // properties
    private Person dave = new Person();
    private Balloon davesBalloon = new Balloon();
    private Line string = new Line(dave,davesBalloon);

    public void draw(int x, int y, Graphics g) {
        } // end of draw method

    } // end of BalloonScene class
```

> References to the Person object (dave) and the Balloon object (davesBalloon) are sent to the Line constructor.

```
class Person {

    public void draw(Graphics g) {
        } // end of draw method

    } // end of Person class
```

```
class Balloon {

    public void draw(int x, int y, Graphics g) {
        } // end of draw method

    } // end of Balloon class
```

```
class Line {
    private Person thePerson;
    private Balloon theBalloon;

    public Line(Person p, Balloon b) {
        thePerson = p;
        theBalloon = b;
        } // end of constructor

    public void draw(Graphics g) {
        } // end of draw method

    } // end of Line class
```

> The Line constructor receives references to the Person and Balloon objects via parameters p and b, then saves those references in instance variables thePerson and theBalloon.

once the Line object has been created. At this point the Animator will begin calling the draw method in the BalloonScene object to do the animation.

Code 6.2 shows the code added to the program for named constants and the draw methods of the BalloonScene, Person, and Balloon classes.

We now need to complete the draw method of the Line class. All it does is draw a line from the top of the person to the bottom of the balloon. But to do

CODE 6.2

```
public class BalloonScene extends Animator {
    // properties
    private Person dave = new Person();
    private Balloon davesBalloon = new Balloon();
    private Line string = new Line(dave,davesBalloon);

    public void draw(int x, int y, Graphics g) {
        dave.draw(g);
        davesBalloon.draw(x,y,g);
        string.draw(g);
    } // end of draw method

} // end of BalloonScene class
```

```
class Person {
    private final int width = 20;
    private final int height = 50;
```
The person is a 20 × 50 blue rectangle drawn in the middle of the scene.
```
    public void draw(Graphics g) {
        g.setColor(Color.blue);
        int left = Animator.getSceneWidth()/2 - width/2;
        int top = Animator.getSurface() - height;
        g.fillRect(left,top,width,height);
    } // end of draw method

} // end of Person class
```

```
class Balloon {
    private final int diameter = 50;

    public void draw(int x, int y, Graphics g) {
        g.setColor(Color.red);
        int left = x - diameter/2;
        int top = y/3;
        g.fillOval(left,top,diameter,diameter);
    } // end of draw method

} // end of Balloon class
```

so, it must get the x and y coordinates of the ends of the line from the Person and Balloon objects. As I said at the beginning of this section, to do so it must call methods in the Person and Balloon objects that will return those coordinates.

We've already used methods that return values. They were the math and Animator methods (e.g., Math.sqrt, Animator.getSurface). Now we will write our own methods that will return values.

A method that returns a value is much like any other method. It is public and has a name and parameters. However, instead of writing void in front of the name, we write the type of value returned by the method (e.g., `int`), and we execute a `return` command in the method to cause a particular value to be returned. Note that a method can return only one value.

For the `Line` method to get the x and y coordinates of the top middle of the person, it must call two different methods in the `Person` object. One will return the x coordinate; the other, the y coordinate. Hence we will add two methods to the `Person` class, called `getMiddle` and `getTop` (Code 6.3).

CODE 6.3

```
class Person {
    private final int height = 50;
    private final int width = 20;
    private int top;
    private int middle;

    public void draw(Graphics g) {
        g.setColor(Color.blue);
        int left = Animator.getSceneWidth()/2 - width/2;
        top = Animator.getSurface() - height;
        g.fillRect(left,top,width,height);
        middle = Animator.getSceneWidth()/2;
    } // end of draw method

    public int getMiddle() {
        return middle;
    } // end of getMiddle method

    public int getTop() {
        return top;
    } // end of getTop method

} // end of Person class
```

The `draw` method determines the top, middle of the person, and saves the coordinates in instance variables.

Each method returns the appropriate value to the caller in the `Line` class.

The `return` command in each method simply causes the value of the expression that follows it (a variable value in these cases) to be returned to the place where the method was called from. The `return` command also causes the method to finish immediately, although in these cases the methods would have terminated anyway since `return` is the last command in both methods.

{Definition of Terms}

The `return` command returns the value of the expression that follows it. The command causes the method it is in to finish immediately, even if it is not the last command in that method.

Note that since the coordinates of the top, middle of the person are determined in the `draw` method, but the values are to be returned by the `getMiddle` and `getTop` methods, the coordinate values must be saved in instance variables, hence instance variables `middle` and `top`. Note that `top` used to be a local variable in the `draw` method, but removing the `int` where it was created makes `top` refer to the instance variable instead.

Eventually we will add code to the `draw` method in the `Line` class that will call these two methods every time it needs the coordinates of one end of line. When the `getMiddle` method is called, no arguments are sent (none are expected), then the return command in the `getMiddle` method is executed (in the context of the `Person` object), and the value of `middle` saved by Person's `draw` method will be returned. This is the way one object (the `Line`) asks another (the `Person`) for information.

The `Balloon` object works the same way as the `Person` object except that it returns the coordinates of the bottom, middle of the balloon (Code 6.4).

CODE 6.4

```
class Balloon {
    private final int diameter = 50;
    private int bottom;
    private int middle;

    public void draw(int x, int y, Graphics g) {
        g.setColor(Color.red);
        int left = x - diameter/2;
        int top = y/3;
        g.fillOval(left,top,diameter,diameter);
        bottom = top + diameter;
        middle = x;
    } // end of draw method

    public int getMiddle() {
        return middle;
    } // end of getMiddle method

    public int getBottom() {
        return bottom;
    } // end of getBottom method

} // end of Balloon class
```

Now all the `draw` method of the `Line` class needs to do is to get the coordinates of the top, middle of the person and the bottom, middle of the balloon and draw a line between them (Code 6.5).

CODE 6.5

BalloonScene
Uses object interactions to
draw a scene.

```java
import java.awt.*;

// BalloonScene class here

// Person class here

// Balloon class here

class Line {
    private Person thePerson;
    private Balloon theBalloon;

    public Line(Person p, Balloon b) {
        thePerson = p;
        theBalloon = b;
    } // end of constructor

    public void draw(Graphics g) {
        int x1 = thePerson.getMiddle();
        int y1 = thePerson.getTop();
        int x2 = theBalloon.getMiddle();
        int y2 = theBalloon.getBottom();
        g.setColor(Color.black);
        g.drawLine(x1,y1,x2,y2);
    } // end of draw method

} // end of Line class
```

Written Exercises

1. Why does an object need a reference to another object in order to call a method in that object?

2. Why do you think a method can return only a single value?

Programming Exercises

1. Write an animation that has three objects (not counting the main object that sets everything up). One displays a 50 × 20 cloud that moves on its own across the scene. Another displays a 30 × 30 square that moves according to the left/right buttons. The third displays the distance between the middle of the cloud and the square somewhere in the lower part of the scene. The cloud and square objects should send their coordinates to the third object every time their draw method is called, so it can use those values to compute and display the distance. The distance between two points x_1, y_1 and x_2, y_2 is $\sqrt{(x_1 - x_2)^2 + (y_1 - y_2)^2}$.

2. Write an animation that has two objects (not counting the main object that sets everything up). One draws a wheel (use the Wheel class from

Chapter 4). The other draws a vertical line from the top to the bottom of the scene that represents the farthest right that the right edge of the wheel has gone. The wheel should send the x coordinate of the right edge of the wheel to the line drawing object every time its `draw` method is called. Use the `Math.max` method to determine if the current right edge of the wheel is farther than the old farthest right the wheel has gone. `Math.max` expects two integer values to be sent to it, and it returns the larger of the two.

6.2 EVENTS

It's likely that you have used programs with menus you can pull down to select various options, buttons you can click on to make various things happen, areas you can type text into, etc. These programs all have one thing in common. When you select a menu item, or you click on a button, or type text into an area, the program must react to what you did. The program doesn't know which of all those things you are going to do next, so it must be ready to handle anything.

When you choose a menu item or click on a button, you cause an *event* to occur. An event is simply something happening, usually at an unpredictable time.

{Definition of Terms}

An **event** occurs when something happens during the execution of the program that the program will react to, such as clicking the mouse in the animation scene. Events usually occur at unpredictable times.

The Animator has a facility for you to use to react to the event of the user clicking the mouse somewhere in the animation scene. All you need to do is to tell the Animator that you are prepared to handle an event, and the Animator will call a method called `click` when the event occurs. It will send the x and y coordinates of where in the scene the mouse was when it was clicked to the `click` method. Each mouse click will cause one call of the `click` method.

If you haven't told the Animator you want to handle clicks, then no `click` method need be defined. If you have a `click` method but still haven't told the Animator that you want to handle clicks, then the method won't be called. Hence you must do both things—tell the Animator you want to react to click events and define a `click` method.

The way you tell the Animator that you want to react to click events is by calling the `Animator.addClickListener` method and sending a reference to an object. That object must be defined by a class that has a `click` method in it. This object is called a **listener** because it *listens* for a click event. This object can do other things, too.

Code 6.6 is a simple program that simply writes the x and y coordinates of where the mouse was clicked to the Animator's text output area.

CODE 6.6

```
import java.awt.*;

public class ClickDemo extends Animator {
    private Listener ear = new Listener();

    public void startup() {
        Animator.addClickListener(ear);
    } // end of startup method

    public void draw(Graphics g) {
        // don't draw anything
    } // end of draw method

} // end of ClickDemo class

class Listener implements ClickListener {

    public void click(int x, int y) {
        Animator.write("click at " + x + "," + y);
    } // end of click method

} // end of Listener class
```

> Send the Animator a reference to the object that contains the `click` method.

> Any class that defines an object that will react to events via a `click` method must implement `ClickListener`.

ClickDemo
Displays the coordinates of where the mouse was clicked in the scene.

Remember that two things must be done to react to a click event in the Animator. First, you must have an object with a `click` method in it that is defined by a class that `implements ClickListener`. The name `ClickListener` refers to an *interface,* and by saying that this class *implements* the interface called `ClickListener` we are saying that this class will have a `click` method in it. At this point that's all I'll say about interfaces, but we'll return to them in a later chapter.

Second, you must tell the Animator which object has the `click` method by calling `Animator.addClickListener` and sending a reference to that object. This must be done before a click event occurs. If you forget to tell the Animator about the `Listener` object, then even though you have defined and created one, the Animator won't know about it and hence won't call the `click` method when an event occurs.

{New Concepts}

To react to a click event, you must create an object that `implements ClickListener` and has a `click` method, and you must send the Animator a reference to that object by calling the `Animator.addClickListener` method.

When the animation in Code 6.6 executes, the `draw` method will be called repeatedly (but nothing will be drawn). When the mouse is clicked in the scene somewhere, the Animator will call the `click` method in the `Listener` object, which will display the coordinates of the click. The `draw` method will continue to be called, both before and after a click. Hence you cannot predict when a click will happen during an Animation.

Now let's modify the `ClickDemo` to draw a red circle in the scene, centered at the point where the mouse was clicked. I'll include a `Circle` class that defines an object that draws the circle. To make this work, we will have to save the coordinates of the click as instance variables, so the `draw` method in the `Circle` object can use them to draw the circle every time it is called. I could use the same approach as in the `BalloonDemo` and save them in the `Listener` object, then have the `draw` method in the `Circle` object ask the `Listener` object to send them to it. However, to demonstrate another way of having objects interact, I'm going to save the coordinates in the `Circle` object and have the `Listener` object send the coordinates to it.

The key to this program is that the `click` method in the `Listener` object will call a method in the `Circle` class (I'll call it `setCoordinates`) and send it the coordinates of the click. In order for the click method to call the `setCoordinates` method, it will need a reference to the `Circle` object. Figure 6.3 shows the relationships among the objects.

A `Circle` object will have instance variables to store the coordinates of the click and the `setCoordinates` method to receive those coordinates from the `Listener`. The constructor for the `Listener` will receive a reference to the `Circle` object and save it in its own instance variable so that its `click` method can use it (Code 6.7).

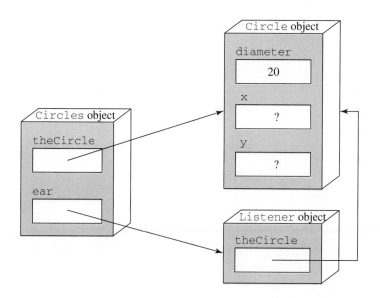

FIGURE 6.3

CODE 6.7

```java
import java.awt.*;

public class Circles extends Animator {
    private Circle theCircle = new Circle();
    private Listener ear = new Listener(theCircle);

    public void startup() {
        Animator.addClickListener(ear);
        } // end of startup method

    public void draw(Graphics g) {
        theCircle.draw(g);
        } // end of draw method

    } // end of Circles class

class Circle {
    private final int diameter = 20;
    private int x = -100;
    private int y = -100;

    public void draw(Graphics g) {
        g.setColor(Color.red);
        int left = x-diameter/2;
        int top = y-diameter/2;
        g.fillOval(left,top,diameter,diameter);
        } // end of draw method

    public void setCoordinates(int newx, int newy) {
        x = newx;
        y = newy;
        } // end of setCoordinates method

    } // end of Circle class

class Listener implements ClickListener {
    private Circle theCircle;

    public Listener(Circle c) {
        theCircle = c;
        } // end of constructor

    public void click(int x, int y) {
        theCircle.setCoordinates(x,y);
        } // end of click method

    } // end of Listener class
```

Send the `Listener` object a reference to the `Circle` object.

Put the latest click coordinates in instance variables x and y.

Save a reference to the `Circle` object.

Send the coordinates of the click to the `Circle` object.

Once the objects are created and the animation begins, the `draw` method in the `Circles` object will be called repeatedly. In turn it will call the `draw` method in the `Circle` object. Until the first click, it will draw a circle centered at −100, −100, which won't be visible in the scene. As soon as the user clicks in the scene, the `click` method in the `Listener` object will be called and sent the x and y coordinates of click. The `click` method in turn will call the `setCoordinates` method of the `Circles` object and send the x and y coordinates to it. The `setCoordinates` method in the `Circles` object will save the new coordinates in instance variables `x` and `y`, so that until the next click the `draw` method in the `Circles` object will draw the circle at the new coordinates.

6.2.1 Another Example

The next program (Code 6.8) draws a line between two consecutive mouse clicks in the scene. In it the listener is also the object that does the drawing. This illustrates that a listener object can also do other things. Or put another way, an object that does other things can also be a listener.

Before any clicks a line from 0, 0 to 0, 0 is drawn. The first click causes a line to be drawn from 0, 0 to the point of the click. From then on, the line is from the previous click to the next.

Written Exercise

1. What must an animation program have in order to respond to click events?

Programming Exercises

1. Write an animation that draws a vertical bar 10 pixels wide from the surface to the point where the mouse is clicked (either above or below the scene). Use a `Bar` object to do the drawing and a `Listener` object to respond to click events.

2. Redo the previous problem with just a single object to do the drawing and react to click events.

3. Write an animation that displays a spaceship (an oval with some colored circles in it representing lights) that moves across the sky under the control of the left/right buttons. When the user clicks somewhere in the scene, draw a red line from the bottom of the spaceship to that point. Use the same object to draw the spaceship and the line, but a separate object to listen for the click event. The listener object should send the coordinates of the click to the spaceship so it can draw the line. The line should continue to emanate from the bottom of the spaceship to the click point until another click is made.

CODE 6.8

Connect

Draws a line between two consecutive clicks in the scene.

```java
import java.awt.*;

public class Connect extends Animator {
    private Connector con = new Connector();

    public void startup() {
        Animator.addClickListener(con);
    } // end of startup method

    public void draw(Graphics g) {
        con.draw(g);
    } // end of draw method

} // end of Connect class

class Connector implements ClickListener {
    private int lastx = 0;
    private int lasty = 0;
    private int thisx = 0;
    private int thisy = 0;

    public void click(int x, int y) {
        // replace previous coordinates
        // with the old latest
        lastx = thisx;
        lasty = thisy;
        // replace the old latest
        // coordinates with the latest
        thisx = x;
        thisy = y;
    } // end of click method

    public void draw(Graphics g) {
        g.setColor(Color.black);
        g.drawLine(lastx,lasty,thisx,thisy);
    } // end of draw method

} // end of Connector class
```

Instance variables keep track of the locations of the previous and most recent points.

4. Write an animation that draws an orange circle initially in the middle of the scene resting on the surface. When the mouse is clicked somewhere on the screen, make the circle move in that direction along the surface 1 pixel per call to the draw method. Use one object to do the drawing and to listen for the click event. *Hint:* If xcircle is the x coordinate of the circle and xclick is the x coordinate of the click, then (xclick-xcircle)/Math.abs(xclick-xcircle) is +1 if the click is to the right of the circle and −1 if it is to the left.

6.3 APPLETS

An *applet* is a program that is usually run as part of an Internet web page.[1] It provides the ability for interaction between the user, the Web page, and even the remote computer from which the Web page was obtained (the *Web server*). Applets always have at least a simple graphical user interface and are defined to react to actions caused by the user such as clicking on a push button or typing text into a box.

In this chapter I'll define a series of increasingly complex applets. These applets will show how objects that interact with each other are used to create interesting and useful programs. Applets use events to react to user actions such as clicking on buttons and entering text into boxes.

{Definition of Terms}

An **applet** is a Java program that has a graphical user interface and runs as part of a Web page.

Applets do not use the Animator. When they are displayed, only a solid gray background will appear unless you put in code to display something else. Hence none of the Animator methods are available with applets. On the other hand, all the concepts we've used to construct interacting objects still apply and will be used.

6.3.1 A Simple Applet

Let's start with a simple applet that displays the message "Merry Christmas" in red letters on a green background (see Figure 6.4).

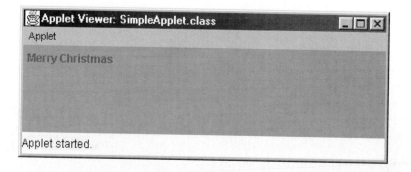

FIGURE 6.4

---

1. Applets can also be run by a program called the Applet Viewer. This is a simple program that simulates a Web page but is much simpler. You will probably use the Applet Viewer to test your applets before you add them to a Web page.

I'll start by making the region the applet occupies on the screen be green (Code 6.9).

CODE 6.9

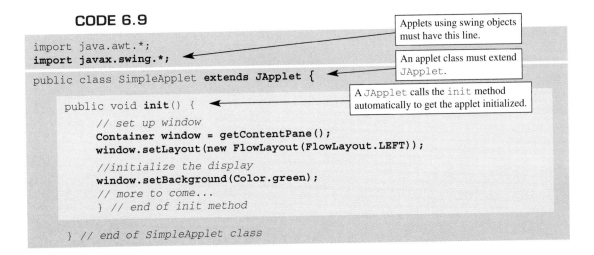

```
import java.awt.*;
import javax.swing.*;

public class SimpleApplet extends JApplet {

    public void init() {
        // set up window
        Container window = getContentPane();
        window.setLayout(new FlowLayout(FlowLayout.LEFT));

        //initialize the display
        window.setBackground(Color.green);
        // more to come...
        } // end of init method

    } // end of SimpleApplet class
```

Callouts:
- Applets using swing objects must have this line.
- An applet class must extend JApplet.
- A JApplet calls the init method automatically to get the applet initialized.

SimpleApplet version 1
The visible region of this applet is made green.

A JApplet calls the init method to get the applet initialized (much like the startup method with the Animator). You can do whatever you like in the init method, but usually you create the user interface for the applet by creating various displayable components (e.g., labels, buttons, boxes to enter text into) and add them to the display.

The first thing you need to do in the init method is to get a reference to the content pane and set its layout manager. The content pane is a **Container** object that represents the applet's visible region on the screen. It is defined by the Container class that is supplied with Java, so you don't have to define it yourself. You will add displayable components to the Container object to get them displayed. The layout manager decides where displayable components will appear on the screen. Other than this simple explanation of the first two commands in the init method, just assume they must be there and I'll explain them in greater detail later.

The Container object referred to by window has many methods. One of them, setBackground, is used to set the color of the region the Container represents on the screen. Hence a simple call to window's setBackground method with Color.green as an argument will cause the visible region to become entirely green.

Now we need to display the text "Merry Christmas." To do so, we must create a new object, using a predefined Java class called JLabel, and add the JLabel object to window. When the JLabel object is added, it will become visible in the region (Code 6.10).

CODE 6.10

```
import java.awt.*;
import javax.swing.*;

public class SimpleApplet2 extends JApplet {
    private JLabel theLabel = new JLabel("Merry Christmas");

    public void init() {
        // set up window
        Container window = getContentPane();
        window.setLayout(new FlowLayout(FlowLayout.LEFT));

        // initialize the display
        window.setBackground(Color.green);
        theLabel.setForeground(Color.red);
        window.add(theLabel);
    } // end of init method

} // end of SimpleApplet2 class
```

Creates a JLabel object, but does not get it displayed.

Makes the text red.

Causes the text in the JLabel object to be displayed.

SimpleApplet 2
Notice particularly the position of the text.

The constructor for a JLabel expects a string as an argument. This string will appear on the screen when the JLabel object is added to window. The color of the text displayed by the JLabel object is set by calling its setForeground method and passing Color.red as an argument. Finally the add method of the Container class is used to add the JLabel object to window, causing it to be displayed.

{New Concepts}

A JLabel object displays a String on the screen, but only after it has been added to the Container object (window) that represents the screen area.

Note that the order in which the three commands in the begin method are executed does not really matter much, mainly because everything appears to the eye to be done instantaneously. The background becomes green, then the label with red letters appears. However, if the commands were in the order

```
window.add(theLabel);
theLabel.setForeground(Color.red);
window.setBackground(Color.green);
```

then a label with gray letters (the default) would appear first, next the letters would become red, then the background green. The final result is the same, and they happen so quickly that you can't tell the difference. The point here is that it is possible to set foreground and background colors (and as we'll see soon, the text of JLabel objects) after objects are added to window. When set, even seconds, minutes, or hours later, the effect becomes visible at that time. We'll use this feature later.

Where on the screen the text of the JLabel object appears is decided by the *layout manager* of window. There are many different layout managers in Java, and I'll describe another later in this chapter. It suffices to say that objects that are added to window will be displayed from left to right across the top until there is no more room, at which time another row will be started. Hence objects will appear from left to right, then top to bottom in the order they are added to window. Each object will have a preferred size, which in the case of a label is high enough and wide enough to display all the characters in the string it contains. Note that if the text that the label displays is changed sometime later, the space taken up by the label on the screen will change if the length of the String being displayed changes.

{New Concepts}

When a displayable object such as a JLabel is added to window, the layout manager decides where to put it partially based on the preferred size of the object.

Written Exercises

1. What happens if you create a JLabel object but don't add it to window?
2. Why doesn't it matter whether a JLabel object is added to window first and then its foreground color set, versus setting the foreground color first and then adding the JLabel object to window?

6.4 PUSH-BUTTON OBJECTS AND REACTING TO USER EVENTS

The simple applet above has no provision for handling any sort of input from the user. It simply displays a message that never changes. The next applet I'll write will display a "push button," which looks like a box with some text in it. However, when the mouse is used to position the cursor over the box and the mouse button is clicked (i.e., pushing the button), the applet will react to this event and change the background color of the push button and the text that labels it (Figure 6.5 shows the applet before the button is pushed).

FIGURE 6.5

Let's first write our main class to display the push button (Code 6.11).

CODE 6.11

```
import java.awt.*;
import javax.swing.*;

public class ButtonApplet extends JApplet {
    private JButton pushMe = new JButton("push here");

    public void init() {
        // set up the display
        Container window = getContentPane();
        window.setLayout(new FlowLayout(FlowLayout.LEFT));
        pushMe.setBackground(Color.green);
        window.add(pushMe);
        // more to come
    } // end of init method

} // end of ButtonApplet class
```

Creates a `JButton` object identified on the screen by "push here."

Change the background color of the button to green.

ButtonApplet version 1
Notice the button, its position and color, but that clicking on it does nothing yet.

Creating an object to represent the push button is very similar to creating a `JLabel` object. The predefined class `JButton` is used instead of `JLabel`, but otherwise it is simply created and then added to `window` just as the `JLabel` is.

Unlike the `SimpleApplet` in the previous section, this time the background color of the push button will be set to green instead of the background color of the entire window (which will remain the default color—gray).

6.4.1 Applet Event Listeners

Reacting to the event of the user clicking on the push button requires a listener object similar to the Animator's click listener. For applets the listener object must contain a method called `actionPerformed`. This method will be called automatically whenever the user clicks on the button. The code in this method then performs whatever actions are necessary to react to the event. In this example, the actions will be to change the color and text of the push button.

```
{New Concepts}
```
A listener object's `actionPerformed` method is called automatically when a button push event occurs.

We need a class that defines the listener object, and that includes code in the `actionPerformed` method that reacts to the event. The class definition has the basic structure shown in Code 6.12.

CODE 6.12

> This must be here if you have code to react to applet events.

```
import java.awt.event.*;

class ButtonListener implements ActionListener {

    public void actionPerformed(ActionEvent event) {
        // react to the button being pushed by changing
        // the color and text of the push button
    } // end of actionPerformed method

} // end of ButtonListener class
```

> A listener object for a JButton must be defined by a class that implements ActionListener.

> A class that implements ActionListener must have an actionPerformed method declared exactly this way.

The class definition for a listener for button push event is like the Animator's click listener definition except that it implements ActionListener. Note that the actionPerformed method has one parameter, a reference to an ActionEvent object called event. An ActionEvent object contains all sorts of information about the event that caused the method to be called, but at this point none of it will be of any interest to us. The fact that the actionPerformed method has been called is all we need to know.

Also note that java.awt.event.* must be imported into any file containing a listener class. It includes definitions of the ActionListener interface and ActionEvent class (among other things). Failure to import it will result in the compiler complaining that these two identifiers are not defined.

Now we need to add commands to the actionPerformed method to change the color and text of the button. To do so, we need a reference to the JButton object so we can call its methods to make the changes. We will do that by passing the reference to the JButton object to the constructor in the ButtonListener class when we create the ButtonListener object (Code 6.13).

When this program runs, it will create all the objects and display the button on the screen. Then the program will wait until the user clicks on the push button. When the user does, an event occurs. The program (code that is part of the applet that you don't see) resumes execution, recognizes the event to be the pushing of the button, and attempts to call the actionPerformed method in the listener object for that button. However, the program doesn't know which object is the listener for the JButton.

The problem is similar to the one with the Animator—we haven't given the applet a reference to the listener object. There is a small difference, however. Instead of telling the applet about the listener, we tell the JButton object. This allows programs with more than one JButton object to have a separate listener object for each one. That way the program can react differently to button push events on different buttons.

The method in the JButton object that we can use to send a reference to its listener object is called addActionListener. The method saves a

CODE 6.13

```
import java.awt.*;
import.java.awt.event.*;
import javax.swing.*;

public class ButtonApplet extends JApplet {
    private JButton pushMe = new JButton("push here");
    private ButtonListener pushListener =
        new ButtonListener(pushMe);

    public void init() {
        // set up the display
        Container window = getContentPane();
        window.setLayout(new FlowLayout(FlowLayout.LEFT));
        pushMe.setBackground(Color.green);
        window.add(pushMe);
        // more to come
        } // end of init method

    } // end of ButtonApplet class

class ButtonListener implements ActionListener {
    private JButton theButton;

    public ButtonListener(JButton b) {
        theButton = b;
        } // end of constructor

    public void actionPerformed(ActionEvent event) {
        theButton.setBackground(Color.red);
        theButton.setText("don't push");
        } // end of actionPerformed method

    } // end of ButtonListener class
```

Creates a listener object and sends its constructor a reference to the `JButton` it listens for (pushMe).

Save the reference to the `JButton` object to change.

ButtonApplet version 2
Clicking on the button still doesn't cause anything to happen.

copy of the reference in some instance variable in the `JButton` object. Code 6.14 shows the completed program.

The commands in the `actionPerformed` method do two things when the method is called: the first one sets the background color of the push button referenced by `theButton` to red, and the second one sets (i.e., changes) the identifying text of the push button to "don't push" by calling the `setText` method defined by the `JButton` class.

At this point we have a collection of objects containing instance variables, as shown in Figure 6.6 (the `ButtonApplet` object that set all this up is not shown). Note that the instance variable names in the `Container` and `JButton` objects are not known to us since we can't see the class definitions. We know, however, that such instance variables must exist for the object to work properly.

CODE 6.14

```java
import java.awt.*;
import java.awt.event.*;
import javax.swing.*;

public class ButtonApplet extends JApplet {
    private JButton pushMe = new JButton("push here");
    private ButtonListener pushListener =
        new ButtonListener(pushMe);

    public void init() {
        Container window = getContentPane();
        window.setLayout(new FlowLayout(FlowLayout.LEFT));
        pushMe.setBackground(Color.green);
        window.add(pushMe);
        pushMe.addActionListener(pushListener);
        } // end of init method

    } // end of ButtonApplet class

class ButtonListener implements ActionListener {
    private JButton theButton;

    public ButtonListener(JButton b) {
        theButton = b;
        } // end of constructor

    public void actionPerformed(ActionEvent event) {
        theButton.setBackground(Color.red);
        theButton.setText("don't push");
        } // end of actionPerformed method

    } // end of ButtonListener class
```

Tell the JButton object which object is its listener.

ButtonApplet version 3
Now clicking on the button causes the text and background color of the button to change.

FIGURE 6.6

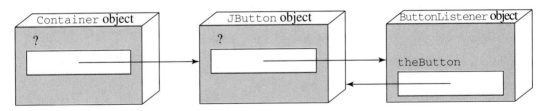

{New Concepts}

The class definition for a listener object for a `JButton` must `implement`
`ActionListener` and contain a method called `actionPerformed`. The listener object
must be created, and the object it listens for must be told about it via the
`addActionListener` method.

Let's trace the execution of the program when the button is clicked on.
First, the program resumes execution and determines that our button was
clicked on. It tells the `JButton` object that it had an event. The `JButton`
object uses its instance variable to find the object that is listening for it, and
calls the `actionPerformed` method in the listener object's class definition.
The `actionPerformed` method executes, changing the color and text of the
`JButton`. The program stops executing again until another event occurs.
Should the button be clicked again, the same thing will happen, but of course
nothing will appear to change on the screen because the button is already red
and identified by "don't push."

6.4.2 A Program Design Note

In the code above, `pushMe` and `pushListener` were made instance variables. This was done to make the code similar to the code written in previous
chapters. However, there really is no need to make them instance variables this
time, because they are only used temporarily to refer to the `JButton` and
`ButtonListener` objects until all the necessary relationships between the
objects could be established. Once the constructor finished, the variables were
never used again. Hence from a readability standpoint, making `pushMe` and
`pushListener` local variables is probably a better idea. Then the creation of
the objects and their use are closer together and hence probably easier to understand. Code 6.15 is a new version of the `ButtonApplet` class definition
using local variables instead of instance variables.

CODE 6.15

```
public class ButtonApplet extends JApplet {

    public void init() {
        // set up button
        JButton pushMe = new JButton("push here");
        pushMe.setBackground(Color.green);
        window.add(pushMe);
        // set up listener
        ButtonListener pushListener = new ButtonListener(pushMe);
        pushMe.addActionListener(pushListener);
    } // end of init method

} // end of ButtonApplet class
```

Remember, local "variables" are discarded when the method they are created in finishes. However, the "objects" they refer to are not discarded, so the `JButton` and `ButtonListener` objects remain after the method finishes.

Because this way of writing the begin method is more readable, I will routinely use it instead of instance variables, but only when appropriate. Note that some variables must be instance variables because they must persist when methods finish—they are true properties of the objects.

Written Exercises

1. Describe in your own words how the listener object in the `ButtonApplet` finds out about and remembers how to refer to the `JButton` object that it modifies.

2. Modify the `ButtonApplet` program by omitting the `addActionListener` call and run it. What happens (or doesn't happen)?

6.4.3 Debugging Applets

If you've been using the `Animator.write` command to print out debugging information when you try to get your animations to work, then you'll have to use a slightly different command to do the same thing with applets. The command that displays the value of an expression is

```
System.out.println(an expression);
```

On most Web browsers and development environments the value of the expression (an `int`, or a `double`, or a `String`) is displayed on what is referred to as "the Java console." This is simply a place where this command puts its output. This is not the window in which the applet is displayed. If you are using the appletviewer to test your programs, the output will appear in the same window in which you type the command to run the appletviewer.

Yet another way to debug an applet is to use the "debugger" supplied with most development environments. It allows you to mark a particular command (the mark is called a *breakpoint*) and have the program pause just before it executes it. At this time you can ask the debugger to show you the values of variables and then continue, pausing again when just before the marked command is executed again. In most debuggers you can also step through the execution of an applet one line of code at a time. Since there are many different development environments, you'll have to consult the documentation that comes with the one you are using to find out how to use it.

6.5 THE NULL POINTER EXCEPTION

We have now reached a point where a certain kind of error is often made by programmers (beginning and experienced alike). This error is not detected by the Java compiler, but is detected when the program executes. The error arises when a variable is created that is supposed to be a reference to some object, but is never actually made to reference any object.

As mentioned earlier, Java will give default values to any int or double instance variable (0 and 0.0, respectively). It will also give a default value to an instance variable that will (hopefully) contain a reference to an object. That value is called *null*. Any use of a reference variable with the value null to reference an object will result in the program causing a *null pointer exception*.[2]

Consider the reference variable theButton in ButtonListener. The variable is created when the ButtonListener object is created, but it does not contain a reference to any object until the constructor is executed. Now suppose that I had forgotten to put the command

```
theButton = b;
```

in the ButtonListener constructor (or perhaps had forgotten the constructor altogether), as shown in Code 6.16.

CODE 6.16

```
class ButtonListener implements ActionListener {
    private JButton theButton;  ←——————  The initial value of
                                          theButton is null.

    public ButtonListener(Button b) {  ←——  Forgot to assign b to theButton.
    } // end of constructor


    public void actionPerformed(ActionEvent event) {  Null pointer exception trying
        theButton.setBackground(Color.red);           to use theButton because
        theButton.setLabel("don't push");             theButton does not refer
    } // end of actionPerformed method               to any object.

} // end of ButtonListener class
```

Then when the actionPerformed method is called in response to a click on the JButton and it tries to change the background color of the button (i.e., tries to execute theButton.setBackground), it won't have a reference to the JButton object. Instead theButton will contain the default value—a *null* reference (or pointer). Trying to use a null reference, instead of an actual

---

2. It should be called a null *reference* exception, but the term *pointer* is carried over from other programming languages such as C and C++.

reference to some object, is what causes the exception (an exception being something abnormal, or exceptional, that happens during the execution of the program).

{Definition of Terms}

A *null pointer exception* is an error that occurs when your program tries to execute a command that uses a variable that is supposed to reference an object, but at the time of the error doesn't reference any object.

When you get a null pointer exception, you will know it because a message to that effect will be printed in the Java console window or the command window where the appletviewer was run from. At that point you should look for a reference variable that you haven't assigned a value to, either initially when the reference variable was created or eventually via an assignment command.

The error message indicating that you had a null pointer exception will help you isolate the particular command that caused the exception. The messages you will see will look something like that shown in Figure 6.7.

Right after the error message is the key piece of information. It tells you that the exception occurred in the `actionPerformed` method in the `ButtonListener` class, at line 33 in the `ButtonApplet.java` file.

FIGURE 6.7

```
java.lang.NullPointerException
    at ButtonListener.actionPerformed(ButtonApplet.java:33)
    at javax.swing.AbstractButton.fireActionPerformed(AbstractButton.java:1066)
    at javax.swing.AbstractButton$ForwardActionEvents.actionPerformed
        (AbstractButton.java:1101)
    at javax.swing.DefaultButtonModel.fireActionPerformed(DefaultButtonModel.java:378)
    at javax.swing.DefaultButtonModel.setPressed(DefaultButtonModel.java:250)
    at javax.swing.plaf.basic.BasicButtonListener.mouseReleased
        (BasicButtonListener.java:204)
    at java.awt.Component.processMouseEvent(Component.java:3160)
    at java.awt.Component.processEvent(Component.java:2999)
    at java.awt.Container.processEvent(Container.java:990)
    at java.awt.Component.dispatchEventImpl(Component.java:2394)
    at java.awt.Container.dispatchEventImpl(Container.java:1035)
    at java.awt.Component.dispatchEvent(Component.java:2307)
    at java.awt.LightweightDispatcher.retargetMouseEvent(Container.java:2043)
    at java.awt.LightweightDispatcher.processMouseEvent(Container.java:1827)
    at java.awt.LightweightDispatcher.dispatchEvent(Container.java:1730)
    at java.awt.Container.dispatchEventImpl(Container.java:1022)
    at java.awt.Component.dispatchEvent(Component.java:2307)
    at java.awt.EventQueue.dispatchEvent(EventQueue.java:287)
    at java.awt.EventDispatchThread.pumpOneEvent(EventDispatchThread.java:101)
    at java.awt.EventDispatchThread.pumpEvents(EventDispatchThread.java:92)
    at java.awt.EventDispatchThread.run(EventDispatchThread.java:83)
```

This directs you right to the line in your program that caused the exception. It does not, unfortunately, tell you what you did wrong, except that you can infer that you didn't give `theButton` a reference to any object. You'll have to look through your code to discover where you forgot to do so.

The rest of the information listed above generally won't be of much use, and you don't have to be concerned with it at this time. However, if you are curious, each line corresponds to a method. The last line is the first method called to run your applet (`run`). It then called the method named in the line above it (`pumpEvents`), which in turn called the method named in the line above it (`pumpOneEvent`), etc., all the way through many more methods until finally our `actionPerformed` method was called that caused the error. Eventually when you write your own methods that call other methods that call other methods, you'll find more of this information useful in figuring out how you got to the point in your program where the exception occurred.

Null pointer exceptions are very common and are usually easy to diagnose. You get enough information to find the offending command, and it isn't that hard in most cases to figure out where you forgot to give the offending variable a reference to some object. In the example above it is clear that the constructor contained the error.

Written Exercise

1. Modify the `ButtonListener` class in the `ButtonApplet` to omit the command in the constructor (as in the example above) and run it. Describe what your development environment does.

6.6 MULTIPLE LISTENERS FROM ONE CLASS DEFINITION

The next applet demonstrates the use of two listeners for two push buttons. It displays two push buttons, one labeled "red" and the other "green," and one label displaying "which one?" in black on a white background (Figure 6.8). Clicking on the "red" push button changes the background color of the label to red, and clicking on the "green" push button changes the background color of

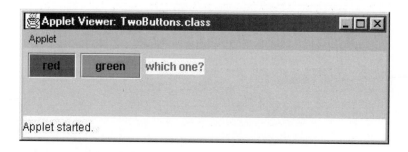

FIGURE 6.8

the label to green. The main points illustrated in this example are the use of a single class definition for both listener objects and the use of instance variables in the listener objects to record which one listens for the red push button and which one listens for the green.

This applet is structured much like the last one. The main class defines an object whose sole responsibility is to create the required objects and add them to `window`. As in the previous example, each `JButton` object will have an associated listener object, with each `JButton` being told about its listener via the `addActionListener` method. In addition, each listener will have a reference to the `JLabel` object so that it can use the `setBackground` methods of the `JLabel` class to change the color of the label on the screen. The objects and their relationships are shown in Figure 6.9.

FIGURE 6.9

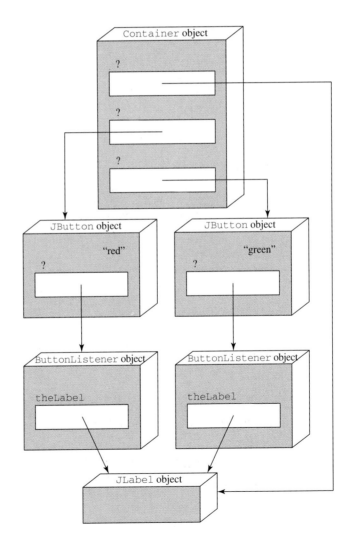

Note the similarity to the previous example. The `Container` object has references to the `JLabel` and `JButton` objects, and each `JButton` object has a reference to its associated `ButtonListener` object. However, instead of each `ButtonListener` object having a reference to the `JButton` object, they both have references to the `JLabel` object. This is because the `actionPerformed` method of `ButtonListener` must call the `JLabel` object's `setBackground` method.

First, Code 6.17 shows the code to create the `JButton` and `JLabel` objects and display them on the screen.

CODE 6.17

```java
import java.awt.*;
import java.awt.event.*;
import javax.swing.*;

public class TwoButtons extends JApplet {

    public void init() {
        Container window = getContentPane();
        window.setLayout(new FlowLayout(FlowLayout.LEFT));

        JButton red = new JButton("red");
        red.setBackground(Color.red);
        window.add(red);

        JButton green = new JButton("green");
        green.setBackground(Color.green);
        window.add(green);

        JLabel which = new JLabel("which one?");
        which.setOpaque(true);
        which.setBackground(Color.white);
        window.add(which);

        // more to come
    } // end of init method

} // end of TwoButtons class
```

TwoButtons version 1
Creates the `JButton` and `JLabel` objects and displays them on the screen. There are no listeners yet, so the buttons won't do anything.

Note that a `JLabel` is defined to let the color of the window show through it, like a clear piece of glass with writing on it. We can change a `JLabel` to be opaque (i.e., not clear) by calling the `setOpaque` method and passing the argument `true` (the reserved word `true` is a literal that means exactly what it says, and there is also a corresponding literal `false`). An opaque `JLabel` will normally have a gray background no matter what the color of the window behind it, but that can be changed by calling the `setBackground` method as in this example. Be sure to remember to make your `JLabel` objects opaque if you want to give them a background color.

> **{New Concepts}**
>
> A `JLabel` by default will have the same background color as the window it is added to. To give it its own background color, you must first make it opaque via the `setOpaque` method.

Now let's consider the listeners. I need two `ButtonListener` objects, but I want to write only a single class definition. The `ButtonListener` objects do almost exactly the same thing—call the `setBackground` method of the `JLabel`. The only difference is that the `ButtonListener` for the red button passes `Color.red` as an argument, and the `ButtonListener` for the green button passes `Color.green`. To accomplish this, the `ButtonListener` objects will have a `Color` instance variable (called `theColor`), which in one `ButtonListener` object will have the value `Color.red`, the other `Color.green`. When the two `ButtonListener` objects are created, we'll send the appropriate `Color` value to their constructor and have the constructor save that value in their respective instance variables. Hence the constructor will have two parameters, one a reference to the `JLabel` object that will have its color changed, the other the actual color (Code 6.18).

The key to this example is that the single class definition of `ButtonListener` is used to create two different objects. Both objects have the same instance variables, `theLabel` and `theColor`, but the value of `theColor` in one of them is set to red when it is created, the other to green. When later the `actionPerformed` method is called as a result of a click on one of the push buttons, say, the red one, then the `setBackground` command will pass the value of `theColor` from the `ButtonListener` object associated with the red push button, which is `Color.red`.

A very important concept to review at this point is that whenever a method executes, it executes in the context of some single object, using the values of the instance variables in *that* object.[3] In this example, the `actionPerformed` method will sometimes be executed in the context of the `ButtonListener` object associated with the red push button, and hence pass `Color.red` when it executes the `setBackground` method; and sometimes it will be executed in the context of the `ButtonListener` object associated with the green push button, and hence pass `Color.green` when it executes the `setBackground` method.

> **{New Concepts}**
>
> A method executes in the context of some object. When it is executing, any reference to an instance variable is a reference to the variable in that object.

---

3. There are exceptions to this. For example, the `Math` methods do not execute in the context of any object.

CODE 6.18

```java
import java.awt.*;
import java.awt.event.*;
import javax.swing.*;

public class TwoButtons extends JApplet {

    public void init() {
        Container window = getContentPane();
        window.setLayout(new FlowLayout(FlowLayout.LEFT));
        JButton red = new JButton("red");
        red.setBackground(Color.red);
        window.add(red);
        JButton green = new JButton("green");
        green.setBackground(Color.green);
        window.add(green);
        JLabel which = new JLabel("which one?");
        which.setOpaque(true);
        which.setBackground(Color.white);
        window.add(which);
        ButtonListener redLstner =
            new ButtonListener(which, Color.red);
        red.addActionListener(redLstner);
        ButtonListener greenLstner =
            new ButtonListener(which, Color.green);
        green.addActionListener(greenLstner);
        } // end of init method

    } // end of TwoButtons class
```

Create a `ButtonListener` object with color property "red."

Create a `ButtonListener` object with color property "green."

```java
class ButtonListener implements ActionListener {
    private JLabel theLabel;
    private Color theColor;

    // constructor
    public ButtonListener(JLabel lbl, Color c) {
        theLabel = lbl;
        theColor = c;
        } // end of constructor

    public void actionPerformed(ActionEvent event) {
        theLabel.setBackground(theColor);
        } // end of actionPerformed method

    } // end of ButtonListener class
```

When executed in the context of the object with color property "red," it will set the background color of the label to red; but when executed in the context of the object with color property "green," it will set the background color of the label to green.

TwoButtons version 2
Note how each listener object gets and uses different values for the instance variable named thecolor.

Written Exercises

1. Using the `TwoButtons` applet, draw a picture of the objects and their relationships just after the `JLabel` which was added to `window` but before either listener object was created.

2. Suppose you were going to modify the `TwoButtons` applet to eliminate the label and have each button change the background color of the other button (i.e., the red button changes the background of the green button to red, the green button changes the background color of the red button to green). Show the objects such a program would create and their relationships.

3. Why can one class definition describe two different listener objects that do almost, but not quite, the same thing?

Programming Exercises

1. Write an applet with two buttons, one "red" the other "green," such that when one of the buttons is pushed, it changes the background color of the whole window to the indicated color. Before you write any code, draw a picture of the objects and their relationships that the program must create.

2. Write an applet with three buttons, one "red," one "white," and one "blue," such that when one of the buttons is pushed, it changes the background color of the whole window to the indicated color. Before you write any code, draw a picture of the objects and their relationships that the program must create.

3. Write an applet with two buttons, one "me" the other "all," such that when the "me" button is pushed, the background color of that button is changed to yellow; and when the "all" button is pushed the background color of the whole window is changed to yellow. Before writing any code, you should draw a picture of the objects and their relationships that the program must create.

6.7 INPUTTING TEXT

A `JTextField` object displays a rectangle on the screen and allows a user to type into it, then hit the Enter (or Return) key to cause an event to occur. The event is similar to a click on a `JButton`, and it can be acted on by a listener object just as a `JButton` does. The listener object can retrieve the characters typed into the rectangle (as a `String`) and then use it in the program. The `getText` method in the `JTextField` class returns that `String`.

The Java program shown in Code 6.19 creates a `JTextField` and a `JLabel`; then when the user types a number into the box and hits Enter, it

CODE 6.19

```java
import java.awt.*;
import java.awt.event.*;
import javax.swing.*;

public class SqrtApplet extends JApplet {

    public void init() {
        Container window = getContentPane();
        window.setLayout(new FlowLayout(FlowLayout.LEFT));
        JTextField textIn = new JTextField(10);
        window.add(textIn);
        JLabel message = new JLabel("nothing typed yet");
        window.add(message);
        TextListener textListener =
            new TextListener(textIn, message);
        textIn.addActionListener(textListener);
    } // end of init method

} // end of SqrtApplet class

class TextListener implements ActionListener {
    private JTextField theField;
    private JLabel theLabel;

    public TextListener(TextField f, JLabel lbl) {
        theField = f;
        theLabel = lbl;
    } // end of constructor

    public void actionPerformed(ActionEvent event) {
        String num = theField.getText();
        double x = Double.parseDouble(num);
        double sqrtOfX = Math.sqrt(x);
        theLabel.setText("sqrt = "+ sqrtOfX);
    } // end of actionPerformed method

} // end of TextListener class
```

Retrieve the text typed into the `JTextfield` by the user.

changes the text of the `JLabel` to be the square root of the number entered (Figure 6.10).

Most differences between this applet and the previous one are straight-forward. Note the following more significant differences:

1. The constructor for a `JTextField` expects an integer argument that will be the width of the rectangle on the screen (I picked 10 arbitrarily). The user can type more than 10 characters into the rectangle, but only 10 will be visible at any time.

SqrtApplet
Try entering various numbers, and try making corrections to the numbers via the Backspace key and by using the mouse to position the cursor in the middle of the number then deleting or typing in more digits. Notice that until the Enter or Return key is hit, no event occurs.

FIGURE 6.10

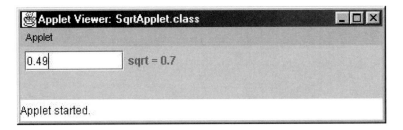

2. The `TextListener` object needs access to the `JTextField` in order to retrieve the characters that were typed. As a result, the constructor in the `TextListener` class has a parameter that is a reference to the `JTextField` object, which is saved in the instance variable `theField`.

3. The `TextListener` object also needs access to the `JLabel` object so it can change it when the user enters some text. This is handled analogously to the `JTextField` reference.

4. The characters that were typed are retrieved by calling the `getText` method of the `JTextField` object and putting into a local `String` variable `theText`.

{New Concepts}

A `JTextField` object displays a box on the screen that the user can type into. The characters entered into it by the user can be retrieved by the `getText` method. A `JTextField` object causes an action event when the user presses the Enter or Return key.

Written Exercises

1. The `SqrtApplet` has a `JTextField` with room for 10 digits. Run the `SqrtApplet` and enter a number 100000000000 (which has 12 digits). What does the `JTextField` do when you enter the extra two digits? Does it still compute the correct square root? (The answer is 1000000.)

2. Run the `SqrtApplet` again, enter a number with several digits, but don't hit Enter or Return, then use the mouse to position the cursor somewhere in the middle of the number and hit the Backspace key. What happens? Without moving the cursor, type in a couple more digits. What happens? Again without moving the cursor, hit Enter or Return. Of what number is the square root taken?

Programming Exercises

1. The text of a `JTextField` can be retrieved even if Enter or Return has not been pushed. Write a program that has a button, two text fields, and a label (initially showing 0). The user types two numbers into the two text

fields, then pushes the button. This causes the two numbers in the text fields to be retrieved and added, and the sum displayed using the label. *Hint:* You only need one listener object, for the button. Be sure to draw the objects and their relationships before you write any code.

2. Modify your answer to the previous problem to have two buttons, one labeled "+" and the other "x." When the "+" button is pushed, the sum of the numbers in the text fields should be displayed; when the "x" button is pushed, the product should be displayed.

3. Write a program with three text fields (let's call them A, B, and C), a button, and a label. When the button is pushed, the following expression should be computed and the result displayed in the label:

$$\frac{-B + \sqrt{B^2 - 4AC}}{2A}$$

4. Write a program with three text fields and a label. Whenever the user enters text into one of the text fields and hits Enter or Return, change the label to display the text in that text field.

6.8 A VERY SIMPLE CALCULATOR

The next example will be a very simple calculator, or actually, adding machine (Figure 6.11). It will have 10 push buttons, labeled 0 through 9, and a label in which clicks on the digit push buttons will be accumulated into a number. It will also have another push button labeled "+" and another label. When the "+" is clicked on, the number accumulated in the first label will be added to the number in the second and the number in the first label changed back to 0. Both labels will be 0 to begin with.

Let's first consider the objects needed for this applet. Clearly there will be 10 JButton objects for the digit push buttons, and another JButton object for the "+". Every JButton object will need an associated listener object, with the listeners for the digit JButton objects being very similar (so I'll use a single class to describe them).

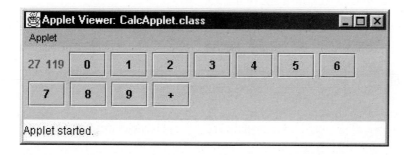

FIGURE 6.11

The new issue of concern is how to keep track of the digits entered so far, and how to keep track of the sum. One way is to let the `JLabel` objects keep track. Whenever a new digit is entered, the `getText` method (which works for `JLabel` objects just as it does for `JTextField` objects) can be called to get the current number being displayed by the `JLabel` (which will be a `String`); and then the `String` that is the concatenation of the old `String` and the new digit can be put back into the `JLabel` via the `setText` method. As for the sum `JLabel`, the `getText` method can be called to get the `Strings` from both `JLabel` objects, both `Strings` converted to ints, the sum computed, and the result put back into the sum `JLabel` via `setText`. This way of doing things is fairly straightforward and is a simple extension of the applets we've seen so far in this chapter. It needs no new objects and uses techniques already demonstrated. However, it does have the disadvantage of making the listeners have two roles: listening and computing. From an object-oriented point of view, this might not be the best approach. Consider the following alternative.

Another way of doing things is to use a completely different object with two `int` instance variables—one to accumulate the number in, the other to keep track of the sum. This object will have a method for adding in each new digit (called by the digit listeners) and another method for computing the sum (called by the listener for the "+" push button). Each method will update the text being displayed by the `JLabel` objects whenever either (or both) of them change. Let's call this a `Calculator` object.

From an object-oriented perspective, this is probably better. Now the listener objects just call the appropriate method in the `Calculator` object to do the computing, so they now have just one function—listening. All keeping track of values and all calculation and display of results are done by the `Calculator` object. Let's implement this version.

Figure 6.12 shows the objects and their relationships. The `Container` object has references to the 10 digit `JButton` objects, the plus `JButton` object, and the two `JLabel` objects so they can be displayed on the screen. Each digit `JButton` object has a reference to its listener object (a `DigitListener`), and the plus `JButton` object has a reference to its listener object (a `PlusListener`). All 11 listeners have a reference to the `Calculator` object so they can call the appropriate method in the `Calculator` class to update the accumulator or add to the sum.

Let's write the code for the `Calculator` object first. In the discussion above I indicated that it would have two `int` instance variables that keep track of the current values of the accumulator and the sum. We also know that it will have two methods, one for updating the accumulator and one for adding to the sum. From Figure 6.12 it is clear that it will also need two instance variables that reference the two `JLabel` objects that are displayed on the screen, and a constructor that the main class can use to set up those references when the `Calculator` object is created. The `accumulate` method has a single

FIGURE 6.12

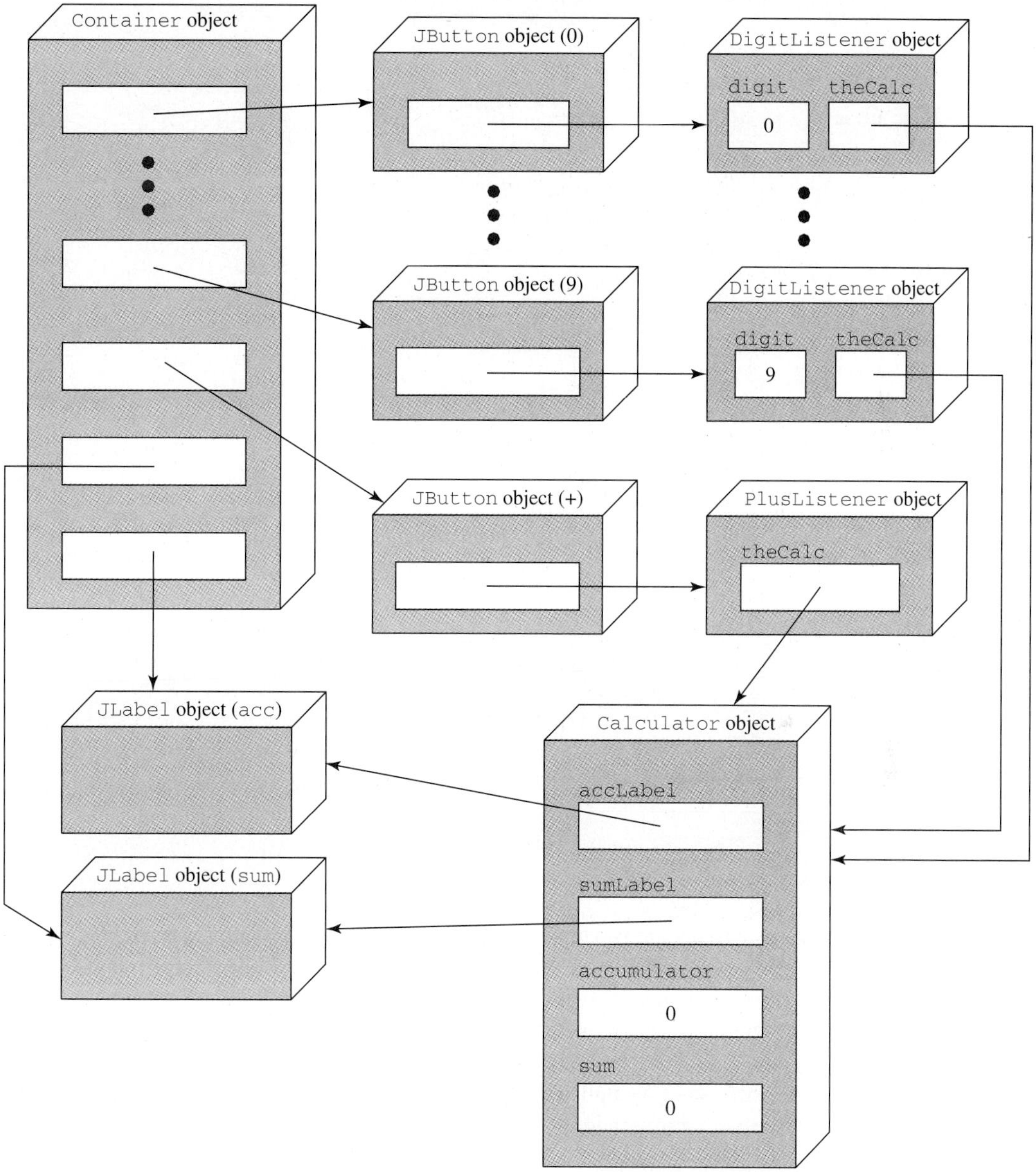
Container object
JButton object (0)
DigitListener object
digit
theCalc
0
JButton object (9)
DigitListener object
digit
theCalc
9
JButton object (+)
PlusListener object
theCalc
JLabel object (acc)
JLabel object (sum)
Calculator object
accLabel
sumLabel
accumulator
0
sum
0

parameter which will be the integer value of the digit that should be appended
to the accumulator (Code 6.20).

CODE 6.20

```
class Calculator {
    private int accumulator = 0;
    private int sum = 0;
    private JLabel accLabel;
    private JLabel sumLabel;

    public Calculator(JLabel a, JLabel s) {
        accLabel = a;
        sumLabel = s;
    } // end of constructor

    public void accumulate(int digit) {
        // code to update accumulator
        // and display the new value
    } // end of accumulate method

    public void add() {
        // code to update the sum,
        // zero the accumulator,
        // and display the new values
    } // end of add method

} // end of Calculator class
```

To update `accumulator`, consider the following example. If `accumu-
lator` contains the number 748 and the next digit to be appended is 5, then
the new value of `accumulator` should be 748 times 10, plus 5, or 7485. In
general, to update `accumulator` we can just multiply its current value by 10
and add the new `digit` value. Then the `JLabel` object referred to by
`accLabel` is updated via `setText` to display the new value. The `add`
method simply adds `accumulator` to `sum`, sets `accumulator` to 0, and
displays the new values of both (Code 6.21).

The 10 listeners for the digits are virtually identical except for the value
that they send to the `accumulate` method. I'll define a single class and give
them each an `int` instance variable that will contain the value they send. The
instance variables will be set by the constructor from a parameter sent to it
when the listener object is created (Code 6.22).

CODE 6.21

```
class Calculator {
    private int accumulator = 0;
    private int sum = 0;
    private JLabel accLabel;
    private JLabel sumLabel;

    public Calculator(JLabel a, JLabel s) {
        accLabel = a;
        sumLabel = s;
        } // end of constructor

    public void accumulate(int digit) {
        accumulator = accumulator*10+digit;
        accLabel.setText(accumulator+"");
        } // end of accumulate method

    public void add() {
        sum = sum + accumulator;
        accumulator = 0;
        accLabel.setText("0");
        sumLabel.setText(sum+"");
        } // end of add method

} // end of Calculator class
```

CODE 6.22

```
class DigitListener implements ActionListener {
    private int digit;
    private Calculator theCalc;

    public DigitListener(Calculator c, int d) {
        theCalc = c;
        digit = d;
        } // end of constructor

    public void actionPerformed(ActionEvent event) {
        theCalc.accumulate(digit);
        } // end of actionPerformed method

} // end of DigitListener class
```

The listener for the plus button is straightforward (Code 6.23).

CODE 6.23

```
class PlusListener implements ActionListener {
    private Calculator theCalc;

    public PlusListener (Calculator c) {
        theCalc = c;
        } // end of constructor

    public void actionPerformed(ActionEvent event) {
        theCalc.add();
        } // end of actionPerformed method

    } // end of PlusListener class
```

Finally the main class creates all the objects, adds the JButton and JLabel objects to the Container, and tells all the JButton objects about their listeners (Code 6.24).

Notice that the order in which objects were created is important since references must be passed to other objects when those others are created. Since the Calculator object must reference the two JLabel objects, the JLabel objects were created first, then the Calculator object. The listener objects were created after the Calculator object so they could be sent references to the Calculator object.

The order in which the objects were added to window was somewhat arbitrary, however. You've probably noticed when you try running this applet that the positions of the labels and push buttons are not very nice. We'll fix that by using a different layout manager in which we can force the objects to be displayed in a more pleasing arrangement.

Programming Exercises

1. Modify the CalcApplet to include a Clear button. When it is pushed, the sum should be changed to 0.

2. Modify your solution to the previous problem to add a Clear Entry button. When this button is pushed, the number being entered should be reset to 0.

3. Modify the CalcApplet to include a subtract button. When pushed, it subtracts the number being entered from the total. Then add multiply and divide buttons that do the obvious things.

4. Write an applet with four buttons and a label. The buttons are labeled 1, 2, 4, and 8. The label initially displays 0. When one of the buttons is pushed, the label has that value added to what it currently displays.

CODE 6.24

```java
import java.awt.*;
import java.awt.event.*;
import javax.swing.*;

public class CalcApplet extends JApplet {

    public void init() {
        // create labels to display results
        Container window = getContentPane();
        window.setLayout(new FlowLayout(FlowLayout.LEFT));
        JLabel accum = new JLabel("0");
        window.add(accum);
        JLabel sum = new JLabel("0");
        window.add(sum);

        // create the object to do the calculating
        Calculator calc = new Calculator(accum, sum);

        // create a listener for the 0 button
        JButton zero = new JButton("0");
        window.add(zero);
        DigitListener zeroList = new DigitListener(calc,0);
        zero.addActionListener(zeroList);

        // similar code for the remaining 9 digit buttons

        // create the plus button
        JButton plus = new JButton("+");
        window.add(plus);
        PlusListener plusList = new PlusListener(calc);
        plus.addActionListener(plusList);

    } // end of init method

} // end of CalcApplet class

// DigitListener class here

// PlusListener class here

// Calculator class here
```

CalcApplet version 1
Enter a number by clicking on the digit buttons, then add the number to the sum by clicking on the plus button. The horrible arrangement of buttons will be fixed in the next version.

6.9 LAYOUT MANAGERS

You have probably already noticed by now that the `JButton`, `JTextField`, and `JLabel` objects you have added to `window` usually aren't arranged nicely. This is because when a new object is added to the `Container`, it is put on the screen to the right of the previous one, unless there is no more room for it, in which case it begins a new row of objects. If this layout is what you desire, then you are all set. But often this default layout leaves something to be desired.

Every `Container` object has associated with it another object that is responsible for deciding where within its region of the screen newly added objects will appear. This object, called a **layout manager,** by default positions objects as described above—left to right until there is no more room, then starting a new row of objects. This is called a **flow layout manager** because it flows objects across the region much as text flows across and then down the page.

{New Concepts}

A layout manager object decides where displayable objects will appear on the screen.

If a flow layout is not what you desire, then you can use one of several other layout managers that Java supplies. At this point I'll only describe one of them, the **grid layout manager.**

The grid layout manager gives you greater control over where your objects appear in the `Container` object's display region. It works much as the flow layout manager does, except that you can tell it how many objects to display in each row. This essentially gives you a two-dimensional grid in which objects will appear in the region since every row will have the same number of objects.

To use this layout manager, you need to create one and then tell the `Container` to use it. Since a grid layout manager is just an object, it is created as any other object, via the new operator. The name of the class that describes a grid layout manager is `GridLayout`. When a grid layout manager is created, it expects to be given two arguments—the number of rows and the number of objects in every row (i.e., the number of columns). Hence to create a new `GridLayout` object that will position objects added to a `Container` in 5 rows of 2 objects each, you write the command

```
GridLayout myManager = new GridLayout(5,2);
```

To make this new layout manager replace the default flow layout manager for the `Container` window, you write the command

```
window.setLayout(myManager);
```

The two commands are usually combined into one to save a little typing:

```
window.setLayout(new GridLayout(5,2));
```

Now you can start adding objects to `window` as before, remembering that objects will be added from left to right in the first row until the row is full, then further objects will be added to the next row. In the example above, the first two objects added to `window` will be in the first row, the next two objects will be in the second row, etc.

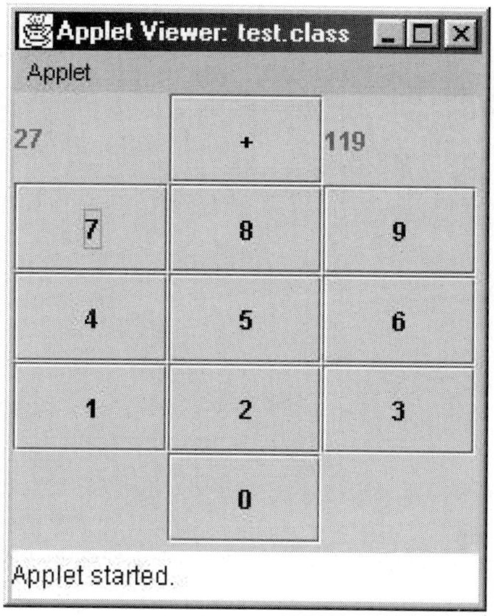

FIGURE 6.13

Let's modify the `Calculator` applet from the previous section to make a more pleasing display, looking somewhat like a standard calculator keypad and display (Figure 6.13).

The grid layout manager is perfectly designed to handle this arrangement since there are five rows of three objects each. The only minor complication is that there are two entries on the last row of the grid that don't have anything in them. However, the grid layout manager adds objects left to right, top to bottom, so we must put something in at least the lower left empty spot, so that the 0 button is in the lower center. This is easily accomplished by creating an extra `JLabel` object that displays an empty `String` (Code 6.25).

Written Exercise

1. Modify the `SimpleApplet` to center and right-justify objects added to the window, and add enough new `JLabel` objects so that a second row is needed to display them. Run the different version and describe what you see.

Programming Exercises

1. Redo the problems in the previous section, using a grid layout manager to improve the appearance.

2. Write an applet with 16 buttons arranged in a 4 × 4 grid. Each button should have a white background initially. When a button is pushed, it and every button in the same row and column should be changed to have a green background.

3. Write a calculator applet that has addition, subtraction, multiplication, division, square root, 1/x, Clear(C), and Clear Entry (CE) buttons. It should look like Figure 6.14.

CODE 6.25

```
import java.awt.*;
import java awt.event.*;
import javax.swing.*;

class CalcApplet extends JApplet {

    public void init() {
        Container window = getContentPane();
        window.setLayout(new GridLayout(5,3));

        JLabel accum = new JLabel("0");
        JLabel sum = new JLabel("0");
        Calculator calc = new Calculator(accum, sum);

        JButton zero = new JButton("0");
        DigitListener zeroList = new DigitListener(calc,0);
        zero.addActionListener(zeroList);

        // similar code for the remaining 9 digits

        JButton plus = new JButton("+");
        PlusListener plusList = new PlusListener(calc);
        plus.addActionListener(plusList);

        // add things in the proper order
        window.add(accum);
        window.add(plus);
        window.add(sum);
        window.add(seven);
        window.add(eight);
        window.add(nine);
        window.add(four);
        window.add(five);
        window.add(six);
        window.add(one);
        window.add(two);
        window.add(three);
        JLabel blank = new JLabel("");
        window.add(blank);
        window.add(zero);
        } // end of init method

    } // end of CalcApplet class

// DigitListener class here

// PlusListener class here

// Calculator class here
```

Give window a grid layout with 5 rows and 3 columns.

Add displayable objects so that they will look right given that they will be added to the grid from left to right, row by row.

CalcApplet version 2
Hopefully you will find the layout much better this time.

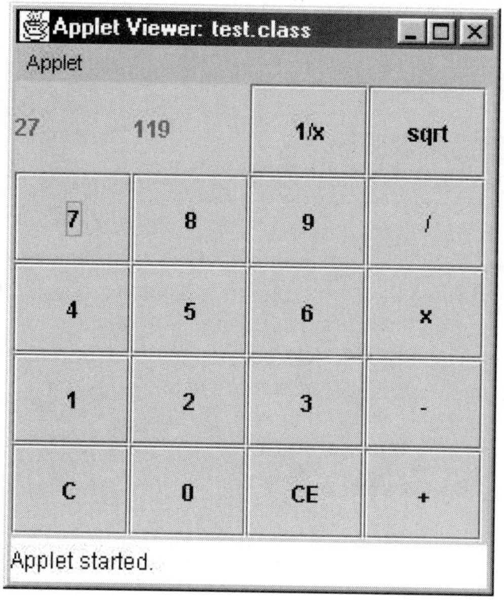

FIGURE 6.14

4. Modify the `SqrtApplet` to display the input `JTextField` and result `JLabel` with identifying information as shown below.

input: | JTextField |

output: **JLabel**

5. When you create a `JLabel` object, you can pass its constructor two arguments. The first is the text to be displayed (as when you just pass a single argument), and the second is `JLabel.LEFT`, `JLabel.CENTER`, or `JLabel.RIGHT`. Using the second argument will cause the text to be left-justified, centered, or right-justified in the area of the window where the layout manager puts the text. Modify your code for the previous problem to make it appear as shown below.

input: | JTextField |

output: **JLabel**

6.10 PASSING PRIMITIVE TYPES VERSUS OBJECTS TO METHODS

We've seen examples in which integers, doubles, and references to objects have been passed to methods. It is important at this point to look carefully at what happens when each type is passed. We'll see that there is a subtle difference.

First, `int`, `double`, and `char` are called *primitive types*. They are called that largely because they are not composed of other things as objects are. They have no class definitions. They are simple, basic, primitive. Java has other primitive types that we haven't discussed yet, most of which aren't used except in unusual circumstances.

{New Concepts}

Primitive types, such as `int`, `double`, and `char`, are not described by class definitions.

When a parameter variable of a method is a primitive type, the parameter variable is created when the method is called, and the initial value comes from the argument in the calling command. If the argument in the call is simply a variable, then the value of the parameter variable is initially set to the same value as the argument variable has. For example, consider the following code segment (Code 6.26):

CODE 6.26

```
public void callingMethod() {
    int a = 5;
    obj.calledMethod(a);
    } // end of callingMethod
...
public void calledMethod(int p) {
    p = p + 5;
    }
```

a remains unchanged after the call to `calledMethod`.

The value 5 is passed to this method, which has no idea that it came from a. *The initial value for* p *is 5.*

The value of p *becomes 10, but* a *is not changed!*

Notice that when `meth` is called, a new variable named p is created and given the initial value 5 (since that was the value of the local variable a when `meth` was called). It is very important to understand that p is a new variable that has no relationship to a except that its initial value is the same as the value of a at the time `meth` was called. Remember, only *values* are passed from method to method.

Now consider what happens if p is changed inside `meth`. Because a value was passed, changing p has absolutely no effect on the value of a. The previous example illustrates this. The parameter variable p was changed to 10 inside `meth` by adding 5 to it. However, when `meth` finishes and execution continues after the call, the local variable a will still have the value 5.

This manner of passing an integer to a method when it is called is referred to as **passing by value.** This is because a *value* is passed to the method (5 in this case). Java passes all primitive types *by value*. A very important point to remember about passing by value is that there is *no* way for a method to change any variable that is used as an argument when the method is called. In the example above, this means that there is *no* way for `meth` to change a.

> **{New Concepts}**
>
> All arguments are sent to a method as values. Primitive types are passed by value.

Now consider passing variables that are references to objects. Just as with primitive types, Java passes the *value* of any variable to the method being called. If the variable is a reference to an object, the value of the variable is the *reference* (you can think of this as the arrow in the pictures) and *not* the object itself. Hence the *reference* is passed. This means that the method that the reference is passed to will now have a parameter variable that refers to the *same* object as the variable used as an argument in the call.

> **{New Concepts}**
>
> Object references are passed by value, but that allows a method receiving such a reference to access the original object.

Consider the example shown in Code 6.27.

CODE 6.27

```
public void callingMethod() {
    JLabel message = new JLabel("initial value");
    obj.calledMethod(message);
    } // end of callingMethod method
...
public void calledMethod(JLabel lbl) {
    lbl.setText("new value");
    } // end of meth method
```

The JLabel object created by this method is changed to display "new value." The reference variable message is not changed—it still is a reference to the same object.

lbl is a reference to the *same* JLabel object that message references.

This command changes the value displayed by the JLabel object created in the callingMethod.

The calling method creates a JLabel object and a local variable message to refer to it. The String that is stored in the JLabel object is "initial value". When calledMethod is called, the *reference* to the JLabel object is passed by value, so the initial value of parameter variable lbl is a *reference* to the *same* JLabel object. Then calledMethod calls the JLabel object's setText method to change the String that is stored in that JLabel object to "new value."

Hence the *object* that was created in the calling method *can be changed* by the method that is called. This is unlike primitive types, which are created by the calling method but *cannot* be changed by the method that is called. While this may appear somewhat confusing, if you simply remember that

- Java passes everything *by value*.
- Java passes *references* to objects (and not the objects themselves).

then you will see that a method can change the object that is referred to by one of its parameter variables but not an argument variable from which a parameter variable got its initial value.

Written Exercises

1. Why is it impossible in Java to write a method (say, called `swap`) that when called as `swap(x,y)`, where x and y are `int` variables, exchanges the values in x and y?

2. Is it possible in Java to write a method (say, called `swap`) that when called as `swap(x,y)`, where x and y are references to two different objects of the same class, makes the object referenced by x become referenced by y and the object referenced by y become the one referenced by x? Explain your answer.

6.11 "this"

Now that you've become familiar with creating objects and connecting them so they can work together to do interesting things, I'm going to show you a slightly different way to do things that is often simpler. The key to this new way of doing things is to realize that Java doesn't care which object is a listener for a `JButton` or `JTextField`. In particular, it doesn't have to be a separate object whose only role is to listen. It can be any object, including objects that do other things, too.

> **{New Concepts}**
> Any object can be a listener, including objects that do other things.

Consider the `ButtonApplet` from the beginning of this chapter. Instead of creating a whole new listener object, I'm going to make the `ButtonApplet` object itself be the listener object for the `JButton`. To do so, I will say that the `ButtonApplet` implements `ActionListener`, and I will put the `actionPerformed` method in the `ButtonApplet` class definition (Code 6.28).

As you can see, the code is a lot simpler. Instead of creating a whole new class for a separate listener object, we just make the `ButtonApplet` object do the work. This object will both set up the display and listener for button pushes.

There is one small problem. For the `JButton` object to be able to react to a button push event, it must be told which object is the listener. This was easy in our original version, because the reference variable `pushListener` had a reference to the listener object. But we don't have this variable in this version because there is no separate listener object. In fact, we don't have any reference variable that refers to the listener object.

Java solves this problem via the reserved word `this`. It means *this* object, which is exactly what we need. We need to tell the `JButton` that *this* object, the one that is setting up the display, is also the object that is the listener. So we can put this in place of the question mark, resulting in the new, complete, and simple version of the `ButtonApplet` (Code 6.29).

CODE 6.28

```
import java.awt.*;
import java.awt.event.*;
import java.swing.*;

public class ButtonApplet extends JApplet
                    implements ActionListener {
    private JButton pushMe = new JButton("push here")

    public void init() {
        Container window = getContentPane();
        window.setLayout(new FlowLayout(FlowLayout.LEFT));
        pushMe.setBackground(Color.green);
        window.add(pushMe);
        pushMe.addActionListener( ? );
        } // end of init method

    public void actionPerformed(ActionEvent event) {
        pushMe.setBackground(Color.red);
        pushMe.setLabel("don't push");
        } // end of actionPerformed method

    } // end of ButtonApplet class
```

The `ButtonApplet` object will be the `JButton` object's listener.

We need to send a reference to the listener object, but we don't have a reference to it as before.

We can access `pushMe` here because we are in the same class.

CODE 6.29

```
import java.awt.*;
import java.awt.event.*;
import javax.swing.*;

public class ButtonApplet extends JApplet
                    implements ActionListener {
    private JButton pushMe = new JButton("push here");

    public void init() {
        Container window = getContentPane();
        window.setLayout(new FlowLayout(FlowLayout1.LEFT));
        pushMe.setBackground(Color.green);
        window.add(pushMe);
        pushMe.addActionListener(this);
        } // end of init method

    public void actionPerformed(ActionEvent event) {
        pushMe.setBackground(Color.red);
        pushMe.setLabel("don't push");
        } // end of actionPerformed method

    } // end of ButtonApplet class
```

`this` object is the listener.

Button Applet version 4
A simpler version, using `this`.

The use of `this` is a very important concept, and you'll see it again and again. It is important that you understand exactly what is going on when you use it. The key is to remember that whenever a method is executing, it is executing in the *context* of some object. When the `begin` method in the `ButtonApplet` class is executing, it is executing in the context of the `ButtonApplet` object that was created by the appletviewer or Web browser. That's why the method can access the instance variables particular to that object and no other. Using `this` simply means that you need a reference to that *same* object, even though there is no variable that you can use that has such a reference.

{Definition of Terms}

The reserved word **this** is a variable that references the same object the method is already executing in the context of.

Now although we have a simpler program, combining the code to set up the display and to react to the button push event isn't necessarily the right thing to do. One aspect of object-oriented design is that you should avoid mixing unrelated behavior in a single object. In some ways, setting up the display and reacting to button pushes are unrelated things. Doing so usually makes a program easier to understand.

On the other hand, I think you will agree that this version is a lot easier to understand than the original version. As a result, I would argue that in this case ease of understanding makes this simpler version preferable. It doesn't make the other version wrong, and I won't argue that you should always have separate listener objects or that you should always combine listening with other behaviors in a single object. Just make clarity your goal, and choose whichever is better in the particular situation.

Written Exercises

1. Explain why `this` is needed in the last version of the `ButtonApplet`.
2. Why can't the `TwoButtons` applet put the listener in the `TwoButtons` object?

Programming Exercise

1. Write a program that has a button, two text fields, and a label (initially showing 0). The user types two numbers into the two text fields, then pushes the button. This causes the two numbers in the text fields to be retrieved and added, and the sum displayed using the label. Do not define a separate listener class/object.

Summary

- Objects interact by calling one another's methods, sending argument values when they do, and returning values when those methods finish.

- Objects must have references to the other objects they interact with. These references are often passed to an object when it is created.

- An event is something that happens at an unpredictable time that should be reacted to.

- Events are handled by a listener object that implements a listener interface (e.g, `ClickListener` or `ActionListener`) by including a method of a specific name (e.g., `click` or `actionPerformed`).

- A reference to the listener object must be sent to the object that causes the event (e.g., the Animator, a `JButton`, or a `JTextField`).

- An applet is a Java program designed to be run by a Web browser.

- An applet uses a region of the screen to display various components such as text, push buttons, and boxes into which text can be typed.

- The region is associated with a browser-created `Container` object which has methods for adding objects representing text (`JLabel`), push buttons (`JButton`), and input text (`JTextField`).

- Events such as mouse clicks and text being entered cause a method called `actionPerformed` in a listener object to be called by the Web browser, giving the program the opportunity to act on them.

- Each object that can generate an event (`JButton` and `JTextField` objects) must be associated with a listener object containing an `actionPerformed` method that will act on the event.

- Displayable objects are positioned in the display region by a layout manager object.

- A flow layout manager positions displayable objects from left to right, top to bottom, much as text flows across the screen, starting a new row of objects when the next object to be added won't fit in the current row.

- A grid layout manager object positions displayable objects in a fixed number of rows and columns that are specified when the layout manager object is created. The objects are laid out from left to right as they are added to the `Container`, but the number of displayable objects in each row is fixed.

- Information is passed from one method to another when the first method calls the second.

- The information passed is always a value that may be an integer value, a double value, or a reference to an object.

- The method being called cannot change any variable appearing in the argument list of the call, but it can use and change any object whose reference is passed as an argument.

Glossary

Applet A Java program executed by a Web browser or the appletviewer.

Container An object that represents a region of the screen in which displayable objects can be laid out and made visible.

Event Something that happens at an unpredictable time that should be reacted to, for example, an `ActionEvent`.

Flow Layout Manager A particular layout manager that lays out displayable objects from left to right, then top to bottom, similar to text flowing across and down a page, fitting as many objects as possible on each row.

Grid Layout Manager A particular layout manager that lays out displayable objects in a fixed number of rows and columns.

Layout Manager An object that positions displayable objects (`JButton`, `JLabel`, `JTextField`) within the region of the screen corresponding to a `Container`.

Listener An object containing a method that is called by the Web browser (or appletviewer) when an event occurs.

Pass by Value A manner of passing information from a calling method to a called method in which a value (not a variable or an object) is transmitted.

Primitive Type A type built into Java, and not a class. Int and double are primitive types.

this A reference to the same object that the current method is executing in the context of.

## CHAPTER 7

Making Decisions

- To understand how an if-command works and how to use it.
- To be able to evaluate boolean expressions involving equality, relational, and logical operators.
- To be able to write boolean expressions that test for complex situations.
- To understand that comparing real number approximations (doubles) for equality often doesn't work as expected.
- To understand the primitive type boolean and use it in programs.
- To understand the difference between comparing objects and comparing object references.
- To understand and use the selection structure to choose among several mutually exclusive cases.
- To appreciate the value of indentation to show program structure.

7.1 CHOOSING ALTERNATIVES

The computer gets much of its power from its ability to make simple decisions, doing one thing under some circumstances, something else in others. In Java you can write a command that will decide whether something is true or false, then execute one segment of code if it is true, another if it is false.

As an example, Code 7.1 is a simple animation that displays a circle that moves under the direction of the left/right buttons and in the upper left corner displays whether the circle is moving to the left or the right.

Displaying the correct direction requires the execution of one of two different `drawString` commands depending on whether the variable `speed` is positive (going to the right) or negative (going to the left). If `speed` is zero, it would be nice to display a third message ("not moving"), but to keep things simple at first let's just assume that a speed of zero will cause "going right" to be displayed.

The new code illustrates the use of an *if-command*. The command starts with the reserved word `if` and is followed by an expression enclosed in parentheses, a first set of commands enclosed in matching braces, the reserved word `else`, and a second set of commands enclosed in braces.[1]

---

1. If the true- or false-part consists of just a single command, the braces { and } that enclose it can be omitted. However, this can lead to subtle errors if later you go back and add one or more commands to the true- or false-part and forget to put in the braces. I'll always use braces even when there is only one command.

195

CODE 7.1

```java
import java.awt.*;

public class Direction extends Animator {
    private final int diameter = 40;
    private int previousX = 0; // x coordinate of previous call

    public void draw(int x, int y, Graphics g) {
        // draw the circle
        g.setColor(Color.white);
        int left = x-diameter/2;
        int top = y-diameter;
        g.fillOval(left,top,diameter,diameter);

        // compute the speed
        int speed = x - previousX;

        // display appropriate direction
        g.setColor(Color.black);
        if (speed < 0) {
            g.drawString("moving left",10,30);
        }
        else {
            g.drawString("moving right",10,30);
        }
        // save the x coordinate for the next call
        previousX = x;
    } // end of draw method

} // end of Direction class
```

> Compare the value of speed with 0.

> Do this command if speed is less than 0.

> Do this command if speed is not less than 0.

Direction
Uses an if-command to display a message indicating the direction in which a circle is moving.

It has the following structure:

```java
if ( expression ) {
    // commands done if expression evaluates to true
    // (called the true-part, or then-part)
}
else {
    // commands done if expression evaluates to false
    // (called the false-part, or else-part)
}
// continue here after one part or the other is executed
```

When evaluated, the expression must produce a result that is either true or false. If the result of evaluating the expression is true, then the first set of commands is executed. If the result of evaluating the expression is false, then the second set is executed. One set of commands or the other is executed, but never both. The expression may evaluate to a different value each time the if-command is executed, so sometimes the first set of commands will be executed, sometimes the second set. Once one set of commands or the other is executed, execution continues *after* the second set of commands.

The commands executed when the expression is true are referred to by some as the *then-part* of the if-command, and by others as the **true-part** of the if-command. Likewise the commands executed when the expression is false are referred to as either the *else-part* or the **false-part.** I'll use the terms *true-* and *false-part,* but either is acceptable. Notice that the commands that comprise the true-part and the false-part are indented. This makes it very easy to identify which commands belong to one set or the other, and which commands don't belong to either (those that are not indented, either prior to or following the true-part and false-part).

{Definition of Terms}

An **if-command** executes one set of commands (the true-part) if an expression evaluates to true, another set of commands (the false-part) otherwise.

The false-part of the if-command is optional (the true-part is not). For example, suppose we want to modify the Direction class to simply display the word "stopped" when the circle is not moving. When it is moving, nothing will be displayed. Code 7.2 implements this change.

CODE 7.2

```java
import java.awt.*;

public class Stopped extends Animator {
    private final int diameter = 40;
    private int previousX = 0; // x coordinate of previous call

    public void draw(int x, int y, Graphics g) {
        // draw the circle
        g.setColor(Color.white);
        int left = x-diameter/2;
        int top = y-diameter;
        g.fillOval(left,top,diameter,diameter);
        // compute the speed
        int speed = x - previousX;
        // display appropriate situation
        g.setColor(Color.black);
        if (speed == 0) {
            g.drawString("stopped",10,30);
        }
        // save the x coordinate for the next call
        previousX = x;
    } // end of draw method

} // end of Stopped class
```

No false-part needed if there is nothing to do when the expression is false.

Stopped
Displays the message "stopped" when the circle is not moving.

Note the use of two consecutive equal signs to test for equality. This will be discussed in the next section.

{New Concepts}

The false-part of an if-command is optional.

Now let's modify the class to display all three possibilities: moving left, moving right, or stopped (Code 7.3).

CODE 7.3

```java
import java.awt.*;

public class Movement extends Animator {
    private final int diameter = 40;
    private int previousX = 0; // x coordinate of previous call

    public void draw(int x, int y, Graphics g) {
        // draw the circle
        g.setColor(Color.white);
        int left = x-diameter/2;
        int top = y-diameter;
        g.fillOval(left,top,diameter,diameter);
        // compute the speed
        int speed = x - previousX;
        // display appropriate direction, or stopped
        g.setColor(Color.black);
        if (speed == 0) {
            g.drawString("stopped",10,30);
        }
        else {
            If (speed < 0) {
                g.drawString("moving left",10,30);
            }
            else {
                g.drawString("moving right",10,30);
            }
        }
        // save the x coordinate for the next call
        previousX = x;
    } // end of draw method

} // end of Movement class
```

> Do this command if speed is equal to 0.

> Do this if-command if speed is not equal to 0.

> Do this command if speed is less than 0.

> Do this command if speed is not equal to 0 and it is not less than 0, i.e., if speed is greater than 0.

Movement
Displays the direction in which the circle is moving, displays "stopped" when it is not moving.

The new version contains a second if-command that is in the false-part of the first if-command. This is perfectly acceptable and is referred to as a **nested if** because one `if` is nested inside another. The code will execute as follows. If `speed` is equal to zero, the true-part of the first if-command will be executed, and the false-part (i.e., the entire second if-command) will not be executed. Hence the string "stopped" will be displayed, and execution will continue with the drawing of the front wheel. If speed is not equal to zero, the true-part of the first if-command will be skipped and the false-part executed. The false-part of the first if-command consists of the entire second if-command. If speed, which is not zero, is also less than 0, then "moving left" will be displayed. If speed, which is not zero, is also greater than 0, then "moving right" will be displayed.

Indentation is important in making nested if-commands easy to read. Notice that the first line of the second if-command is indented four spaces because it is the false-part of the first if-command. The true- and false-parts of the second if-command are indented eight spaces—four because they are part of the first false-part, and four more because they are the true- and false-parts of the second.

You should get in the habit of indenting properly *as you write code,* not afterward. Doing so makes it easier to write correct code. Compare the version of the draw method from Movement in Code 7.4 with the properly indented version. I think you'll agree that the indented version is easier to read.

Experience shows that indenting your code as you write it and keeping it indented properly when you make changes eliminate many errors. For example, a very common error that can be difficult to track down is a missing right

CODE 7.4

```
public void draw(int x, int y, Graphics g) {
    // draw the circle
    g.setColor(Color.white);
    int left = x-diameter/2;
    int top = y-diameter;
    g.fillOval(left,top,diameter,diameter);
    // compute the speed
    int speed = x - previousX;
    // display appropriate direction, or stopped
    g.setColor(Color.black);
    if (speed == 0) {
    g.drawString("stopped",10,30);
    }
    else {
    if (speed < 0) {
    g.drawString("moving left",10,30);
    }
    else {
    g.drawString("moving right",10,30);
    }
    }
    // save the x coordinate for the next call
    previousX = x;
} // end of draw method
```

brace. These are easy to forget when you are writing the true- or false-parts of if-commands and don't indent them. This is especially true when writing nested if-commands. If, as in the `Movement` example, both if-commands end at the same place, then it is very easy to forget to put in both right braces. The compiler eventually will detect the missing brace, but will not give you a very useful error message.

For example, if there is only one right brace at the end of the nested if instead of two, then the line

```
previousX = x;
```

will become part of the false-part of the first if-command and the compiler will think that the right brace that is supposed to end the `draw` method actually ends the false-part of the first if-command (despite the comment to the contrary), and then think that the next right brace that is supposed to end the class definition actually ends the method, then finally discover an error when there isn't one more right brace to really end the class definition. The compiler will tell you that you have an error on the last line of your program, and that the error is a missing right brace at the end of the class, when in fact the error is the missing right brace that ends the false-part of the first if-command six lines up in the program.

Written Exercise

1. Remove the right brace just before the command

```
previousX = x;
```

    in the `Movement` class and compile it. What error message do you get? Does it make sense?

Programming Exercises

1. Modify the `Direction` class to display a yellow circle if it is either stopped or moving right and to display a magenta circle if it is going to the left.

2. Modify the `Direction` class to display an arrow that points in the direction in which the circle is traveling.

3. Modify the `Direction` class to display the circle normally as long as x is less than 200. If x is greater than or equal to 200, then display the circle at 200. In effect, this will keep the circle from going farther to the right than 200.

4. Modify the `Sun` class from Chapter 3 to use the time version of the `draw` method to draw a yellow sun for 100 ticks of the time parameter, then a cyan sun (`Color.cyan`) for 100 ticks, then yellow for 100 ticks, etc.

(*Hint:* Use the % operator.) Also display the `String` "day" near the top middle of the scene when the sun is yellow and display the `String` "night" when it is cyan. Note that the sky in the scene is cyan so when the sun is also cyan, it will effectively disappear.

7.2 EXPRESSIONS INVOLVING COMPARISONS

The expressions found in the if-commands above contain some new operators. The < (less than) operator compares the value of its left and right operands and results in the value *true* if the one on the left is less than the one on the right, or results in the value *false* otherwise. The == (equals) operator results in true if the two values are equal, false otherwise. Java has a complete set of *equality operators* and **relational operators,** shown in Table 7.1.

Table 7.1

Operator	Meaning	Kind
==	Equal to	Equality
!=	Not equal to	Equality
<	Less than	Relational
<=	Less than or equal to	Relational
>	Greater than	Relational
>=	Greater than or equal to	Relational

Note that some of these operators consist of two symbols that must *not* have a space between them. For example, if you put a space between the < and = of the less-than-or-equal-to operator, then you will get an error message from the compiler because it will think you mean a less-than operator followed by an assignment operator.

{New Concepts}

Operators consisting of two characters must not have any space between the two characters.

Take special notice that the equality operator consists of *two* consecutive equals signs. It is a *very* common mistake, made by both beginning and experienced programmers, to write an expression in an if-command and use only one equals sign. Recall that a *single* equals sign is used to assign a value to a variable, and not to compare two values and give a result that is true or false. Fortunately the compiler will give you an error message if you use a single equals sign instead of two consecutive ones in the expression beginning an if-command.

> **{Definition of Terms}**
>
> The **equality operator** is two consecutive equals signs.

True and false are new kinds of values, called **boolean values.** The if-command expects an expression that evaluates to a boolean value. If you write an expression that evaluates to some other type of value (`int`, `double`, `String`, etc.), then you will get an error. Expressions that produce boolean results when evaluated are called *boolean expressions* (sometimes also referred to as *conditional expressions*).

> **{Definition of Terms}**
>
> A **boolean expression** evaluates to the boolean value true or false.

Java permits fairly complex boolean expressions that involve equality, relational, and arithmetic operators. For example, you could write the expression

```
x+y < 2+3*a
```

It is evaluated by first adding the values of x and y, then multiplying the value of a by 3 and adding 2, and finally comparing the two values that result. If the value of x is 8, the value of y is 2, and the value of a is 3, then $x+y$ evaluates to 10, $2+3*a$ evaluates to 11, and the comparison evaluates to true since 10 is less than 11.

The order of evaluation seen above occurs because the less-than operator has lower **precedence** than *any* arithmetic operator. The concept of precedence is already familiar to you because you know that you always do multiplications before additions (as in the subexpression $2+3*a$ above). This is because multiplication has higher precedence than addition (i.e., multiplication takes precedence over addition).

The precedence rule for evaluating expressions is that whenever faced with the choice of doing two operations, always do the one with the higher precedence first. If they both have the same precedence, then do the left one first. In the expression above, the addition of x and y was done first because addition has higher precedence than less-than. The multiplication of 3 and a was done next because multiplication has higher precedence than addition. Of course, parentheses can be used to override any precedence rule. Table 7.2 summarizes the precedence relationships among the operators presented so far.

Table 7.2

$*, /, \%$	Highest
$+, -$	
$<, <=, >, >=$	
$==, !=$	Lowest

Comparisons when one operand is an int and the other is a double follow the same pattern as do the arithmetic operators. The int is first converted to a double, and the comparison is then done between two doubles.

{New Concepts}

The conversion of ints to doubles is performed with equality and relational operators exactly the same as with arithmetic operators.

7.2.1 Comparing Doubles

You must be careful when doing equality comparisons between two doubles. In particular, since a double value is just an approximation to a real value, often an equals or not-equals comparison will not work the way you expect it to. For example, consider the following expression:

```
10.0*x == 1.0
```

Suppose just prior to evaluating this expression the value 0.1 was assigned to x. As I pointed out in Chapter 4, 0.1 can't be expressed exactly in the computer. That is, 10.0 times something that is close to, but not exactly, 0.1 will not result in the exact value 1.0. Hence the computer will not find that 10.0*0.1 is equal to 1.0, even though to a human it clearly is.

Because of the approximations used when representing real numbers as doubles, it is recommended that you never compare two doubles using the equals or not-equals operators. Instead you should decide how close to each other two double values should be to be considered "close enough." For example, you might decide that if the value of x is within 0.0001 of 0.0, then it should be considered close enough, and as a result do what should be done if it were in fact exactly 0. The expression you can write to test for "close enough" is

```
Math.abs(x) <= 0.00001
```

Whenever x is greater than or equal to −0.0001 and less than or equal to 0.0001, this expression will evaluate to true, which is "close enough." In general, if you want to know if two variables x and y are close enough to *each other,* where "close enough" is the value of double variable epsilon, then the expression below will suffice:

```
Math.abs(x-y) <= epsilon
```

{Good Ideas}

Double variables/literals should never be compared for equality.

7.2.2 An Example

Here's an example of an animation consisting of a small rectangle, representing a person, and a large rectangle, representing a building. The person moves according to the left/right buttons whereas the building is stationary in the middle of the scene. When the person is halfway into the building (his middle is even with the side of the building), a red circle will be displayed in the middle of the building. Otherwise the circle will be white.

The program uses if-commands to decide when the person is in the building. A main object creates `Person` and `Building` objects, and the `Building` object asks the `Person` object for the x coordinate of its middle. The `Building` object will then decide whether to make the circle red or white (Code 7.5).

CODE 7.5

```java
import java.awt.*;

public class InsideOutside extends Animator {
    private Person waqas = new Person();
    private Building home = new Building(waqas);

    public void draw(int x, int y, Graphics g) {
        // draw the person and the building
        waqas.draw(x,y,g);
        home.draw(g);
        } // end of draw method


    } // end of InsideOutside class

class Person {
    private final int width = 15;
    private final int height = 50;
    private int middle;

    public void draw(int x, int y, Graphics g) {
        // draw the person
        int left = x-width/2;
        int top = y-height;
        g.setColor(Color.blue);
        g.fillRect(left,top,width,height);

        // save coordinate of the person
        middle = x;
        } // end of draw method

    public int getPosition() {
        return middle;
        } // end of getPosition method

    } // end of Person class
```

Create `Person` and `Building` objects and send the `Building` object a reference to the `Person` object.

Save the coordinate of the middle of the person so it can be sent when requested via `getPosition`.

```
class Building {

    private final int width = 100;
    private final int height = 60;
    private final int diameter = 20;
    private Person owner;

    public Building(Person p) {

        owner = p;
        } // end of constructor

    public void draw(Graphics g) {
        // draw the building
        int left = Animator.getSceneWidth()/2 - width/2;
        int right = left + width;
        int top = Animator.getSurface()-height;
        g.setColor(Color.black);
        g.fillRect(left,top,width,height);

        // draw the light
        if (owner.getPosition() < left) {
            g.setColor(Color.white);
        }
        else {
            if (owner.getPosition() > right) {
                g.setColor(Color.white);
            }
            else {
                g.setColor(Color.red);
            }
        }
        int lightLeft = Animator.getSceneWidth()/2 - diameter/2;
        g.fillOval(lightLeft,top,diameter,diameter);

        } // end of draw method

} // end of Building class
```

If the person is left of the building, make the light white.

If the person is right of the building, make the light white.

If neither left nor right of the building, make the light red.

A nested if is used to make the decision. If the middle of the person is to the left of the left side of the building, then the person cannot be in the building. Likewise if the middle of the person is to the right of the right side of the building, then the person also cannot be in the building. If neither of these two things is true, the person must be in the building.

InsideOutside
Displays a different colored circle depending on whether the object overlaps another.

Written Exercises

1. Assume i, j, and k are integer variables and x and y are double variables. Which of the following are valid boolean expressions? If not, explain why.

    a. i + j < 2   *b.* x != 1 + y   *c.* k = 10

2. Evaluate the following boolean expressions. Assume i, j, and k are integer variables with values 7, 3, and −4, respectively, and x and y are double variables with values 7.1 and 4.2, respectively. Remember, boolean expressions always evaluate to true or false.

a. i < j	*b.* i+k == j	*c.* (i+k) == j
d. j < y	*e.* i/2 != j	*f.* x > 0.0

7.3 LOGICAL OPERATORS

One often needs to be able to decide whether a value of a variable is one of several possibilities. For example, let's modify the Movement class to print "moving right slowly" if speed is equal to 1 or 2. One way to do this is to write a nested if structure (Code 7.6).

CODE 7.6

```java
import java.awt.*;

public class Slowly extends Animator {
    private final int diameter = 40;
    private int previousX = 0; // x-coordinate of previous call

    public void draw(int x, int y, Graphics g) {
        // draw the circle
        g.setColor(Color.white);
        int left = x-diameter/2;
        int top = y-diameter;
        g.fillOval(left,top,diameter,diameter);

        // compute the speed
        int speed = x - previousX;

        // print the message if appropriate
        g.setColor(Color.black);
        if (speed == 1) {
            g.drawString("moving right slowly",10,30);
        }
        else {
            if (speed == 2) {
                g.drawString("moving right slowly",30,10);
            }
        }
        // save x for the next call
        previousX = x;
    } // end of draw method

} // end of Slowly class
```

Slowly
Displays "moving right slowly" when the circle is moving to the right 1 or 2 pixels per call of the draw method.

Although this will work correctly, it is not very elegant and it is prone to error (e.g., by not typing the `drawString` calls the same both times—look carefully at the code above because the two calls are not the same but should be). A much better way to do this, with less typing, greater clarity, and less chance of error, is to use *logical* **operators.**

In English, a single expression that tests for both cases above would be stated; "speed equals one or speed equals two." As a Java expression, this is written as

```
If (speed == 1 || speed == 2){
    g.drawString("moving right slowly",10,30);
    }
```

The operator || (two consecutive vertical bar characters, called the **conditional-or** operator) stands for the logical operation or, which has even lower precedence than ==. The expression will evaluate to true if either (or both) of the equality comparisons was (were) true, but false if both were false. I think you'll agree that this version of the code is simpler than the previous version with two if-commands.

You might be tempted to write the even simpler but incorrect expression

```
If (speed == 1 || 2) ...
```

This would read "if speed equals 1 or 2, then . . . " which sounds fine in English. However, in Java the conditional-or operator has lower precedence than ==, so the comparison between the value of `speed` and 1 will be done *first*, resulting in either true or false. Then true or false will be or'ed with 2, which makes no sense. (Is "true or 2" true or false?) In fact, the compiler will detect the problem and give you an error message.

Now suppose the values for which we want to print the message "moving right slowly" are not just 1 or 2, but any integer from 1 to 4. The conditional expression used above could be modified to

```
If (speed == 1 || speed == 2 || speed == 3 || speed == 4 ...
```

But what if the range of values is from 1 to 50? Clearly this would lead to a very large expression. What we are really looking for is when the value of `speed` is greater than or equal to 1 *and* less than or equal to 50. This can be written as a Java expression as

```
If (speed >= 1 && speed <= 50) ...
```

In this case, `speed` is compared with 1 and, if it is greater than or equal to it, results in true. Then `speed` is compared with 50 and if it is less than or equal to 50, it results in true. Then the two boolean values are and'ed to produce true if the results of both comparisons were true and false otherwise. The two consecutive ampersands comprise a symbol called the **conditional-and** operator, which produces a result of true only if both its operands are true.

Again, it might be tempting to mimic mathematics and write the following expression to test whether speed is between 1 and 50:

```
If (1 <= speed <= 50) ...
```

This is incorrect since the first operation performed is `1 <= speed`, which results in true or false, and then the resulting boolean value is compared with 50 (e.g., false $<=$ 50), which is meaningless. Again, the compiler will detect the problem and give you an error message.

The operation of the two conditional operators $||$ and && can be summarized as follows. Each expects that both of its operands are boolean values and produces a boolean value as a result. The conditional-or operator produces true if either or both of its operands are true, false otherwise. The conditional-and operator produces true only if both of its operands are true, false otherwise.

{New Concepts}

The conditional operators | | and && expect both of their operands to be boolean values and produce a boolean result.

The precedence of the conditional operators is lower than any arithmetic, equality, or relational operator. The precedence of conditional-or is lower than that of the conditional-and. The precedence of all the operators presented so far is summarized in Table 7.3.

Table 7.3

*, /, %	Highest
+, −	
<, <=, >, >=	
==, !=	
&&	
||	Lowest

{New Concepts}

The conditional operators have lower precedence than the arithmetic, relational, and equality operators; && has higher precedence than | |.

7.3.1 Using Extra Parentheses in Boolean Expressions

There are now so many operators that it may be difficult to remember the precedence order of all of them. Even experienced programmers often forget the order and have to look it up when they write complex boolean expressions. This is especially difficult for people who know more than one programming language since different langauges have different precedence orders for some of the operators.

A simple technique that will solve this problem is to use extra parentheses to force the boolean expression to come out the way you want it to. For example, it doesn't hurt, and probably helps, to write the boolean expression

```
(speed == 1) || (speed == 2)
```

even though the parentheses around each comparison are not needed.

7.3.2 Short-Circuit Evaluation

Consider the following expression:

```
a < b || c > d
```

Now if a is less than b, then the comparison on the left is true. But then the entire expression is also true regardless of whether c is greater than d.

Java takes advantage of this property of the || operator by performing what is called *short-circuit evaluation*. When an expression is being evaluated and the left operand of the || is true, the right operand, no matter how complex, is not evaluated *at all*. Java essentially is trying to save some time since evaluating the right operand is a waste of time in this case. Of course if the left operand is false, then the right operand must evaluated.

Short-circuit evaluation also will be performed in expressions with the && operator. In this case if the left operand of the && operator is false, then the result of the && operation will be false no matter what the value of the right operand is, so it isn't evaluated.

Short-circuit evaluation, in addition to saving time, can be useful in other ways. For example, consider the following if-command:

```
if (x >= 0.0 && Math.sqrt(x) < 1.0) { ...
```

If x is less than 0, then calling the square root function will result in an error, but this expression avoids calling the square root function when this is the case. Be careful not to write

```
if (Math.sqrt(x) < 1.0 && x >= 0.0) { ...
```

because then short-circuit evaluation will not help you. Remember, the left operand is always evaluated, but the right one may not be.

{New Concepts}

Short-circuit evaluation avoids evaluating the right operand of || and && operators when the result can be determined from the value of the left operand alone.

7.3.3 An Example

The program in Code 7.7 is a modification of the Movement class that displays one of the following:

"stopped" if the speed is 0

"barely moving left" if the speed is −1 or −2

"barely moving right" if the speed is 1 or 2

"moving left normally" if the speed is −3, −4, or −5

"moving right normally" if the speed is 3, 4, or 5

"moving left quickly" if the speed is less than −5

"moving right quickly" if the speed is greater than 5

Each if-command tests a successive case and displays the appropriate message if it applies. If not, the next case is tested. Finally if none of the first six cases is true, the only thing left is the last case. Hence it isn't tested for explicitly.

CODE 7.7

```java
import java.awt.*;

public class HowFast extends Animator {
    private final int diameter = 40;
    private int previousX = 0; // x-coordinate of previous call

    public void draw(int x, int y, Graphics g) {
        // draw the circle
        g.setColor(Color.white);
        int left = x-diameter/2;
        int top = y-diameter;
        g.fillOval(left,top,diameter,diameter);
        // compute the speed
        int speed = x - previousX;
        // print the appropriate message
        g.setColor(Color.black);
        if (speed == 0) {
            g.drawString("stopped",10,30);
            }
        else {
            if (speed == -1 || speed == -2) {
                g.drawString("moving left slowly",10,30);
                }
            else {
                if (speed == 1 || speed == 2) {
                    g.drawString("moving right slowly",10,30);
                    }
                else {
```

HowFast

Uses a huge nested if with boolean expressions using logical operators to interpret how fast the circle is moving.

```
                    if (-5 <= speed && speed <= -3) {
                        g.drawString(
                            "moving left normally",10,30);
                    }
                else {
                    if (3 <= speed && speed <= 5) {
                        g.drawString(
                            "moving right normally",
                            10,30);
                    }
                    else {
                        if (speed < -5) {
                            g.drawString(
                                "moving left quickly",
                                10,30);
                        }
                        else {
                            g.drawString(
                                "moving right quickly",
                                10,30);
                        }
                    }
                }
            }
        }
    }
    // save x for the next call
    previousX = x;
} // end of draw method

} // end of HowFast class
```

7.3.4 Selections

The nested if-command in this program tests for seven mutually exclusive cases and does one of the actions depending on which case is true. This kind of nested if-command structure is so common that there is a different style of writing the code that makes it a little easier to read. Code 7.8 shows the nested if-commands written in this different style.

This style of writing nested if-commands is termed a **selection.** In a selection the if-commands test for various cases of some relationship between variables. A selection *requires* that the cases be mutually exclusive; that is, only one of the cases can be true for particular values of the variables being compared.

This style of writing if-commands that implement a selection makes it clear that there is a set of mutually exclusive cases that are being tested. This way of writing the nested if-commands is, however, purely a style issue and not something new in Java. It is highly recommended that you use this style when you write if-commands that test a set of mutually exclusive cases because it makes it easier to read and understand. Be careful *not* to use this style if the cases are not mutually exclusive. If you do, other people reading

CODE 7.8

```
if (speed == 0) {
    g.drawString("stopped",10,30);
    }
else if (speed == -1 || speed == -2) {
    g.drawString("moving left slowly",10,30);
    }
else if (speed == 1 || speed == 2) {
    g.drawString("moving right slowly",10,30);
    }
else if (-5 <= speed && speed <= -3) {
    g.drawString("moving left normally",10,30);
    }
else if (3 <= speed && speed <= 5) {
    g.drawString("moving right normally",10,30);
    }
else if (speed < -5) {
    g.drawString("moving left quickly",10,30);
    }
else {
    g.drawString("moving right quickly",10,30);
    }
```

your code who are familiar with the selection style will think you have mutually exclusive cases when you really don't, and this can lead to confusion.

Pay particular attention to where the { and } are. In particular, notice that there are fewer of them than in the original structure, which is partly why this is easier to write and understand. Note also the way the code is indented. I think you'll probably agree that the selection style, when used correctly (i.e., for mutually exclusive cases), is much easier to understand.

Often a selection will cover every possible case, as in the example above. When this happens, it is not necessary to write an expression that tests one of the cases. Once all but one case have been tested for and if none are true, then only one case is left and it is not necessary to have an if-command to test for it. The choice of which one is left untested is usually the one that is the hardest to write a test for, although sometimes there is no clear choice. However, when there is one, you are much less likely to make a mistake if you write expressions for the easiest ones.

{Good Ideas}

A selection structure should be used when testing for mutually exclusive cases. It is much easier to read and avoids excessive indentation.

Written Exercises

1. Which of the following are valid boolean expressions? If not, why?

   a. $a < b$ && $c < d$

   b. $0 < x < 1$

c. $0 < x$ && $x < 1$

d. $i == 7$ || 8

e. $z > 4$ && < 7

f. b || $c < 0$

g. $i < j$ && $x < y$ || $k != z$

h. $(i != k)$ || $(x == y)$

2. Write a boolean expression that is true if x and y are both between (and not equal to) 0 and 1.

3. Write a boolean expression that is true when x is no more than 5 greater than y or no less than 5 less than y.

4. Write a boolean expression that is true if x is an even integer between 2 and 20 (including 2 and 20).

5. Write a boolean expression that is true if $x, y,$ and z all have the same value.

6. Write a boolean expression that is false if $x, y,$ and z all have the same value.

7. Given the boolean expression $a < 6$ && $b > 6$, write another boolean expression that is true when this one is false.

8. Assume a and b are integer variables. Is the following a valid selection? Why or why not?

```
if (a < b) {
    // do something
    }
else if (a == b) {
    // do something else
    }
else if (a >= b) {
    // do a third thing
    }
```

9. Why is it not necessary to test for every possible mutually exclusive case in a selection?

Programming Exercises

1. Modify the `Stopped` class to display one of the following strings depending on the x coordinate of the circle when the circle is stopped:
   - "Stopped at the left" if x is 0.
   - "Stopped close to the left" if x is from 1 to 100.
   - "Stopped far away" if x is greater than 100.

2. Modify whichever circle movement class you like to display one of the following strings depending on the speed and x coordinate of the circle:
   - Nothing if `speed` is 0.
   - "Moving left" if `speed` is less than 0.

- "Moving right" if `speed` is greater than 0 and distance to the right edge of the scene is greater than 100.
- "Getting close to the right edge" if `speed` is greater than 0 and the distance to the right edge of the scene is less than or equal to 100.

3. Modify whichever circle movement class you like to keep track of the largest and smallest x coordinates seen so far and to display one of the following messages:
   - "Been here before" if the current value of x is between the largest and smallest x coordinates seen so far.
   - "New territory" if x is greater than the largest or less than the smallest x coordinate seen so far.
   - "On the edge" if x is equal to the largest or smallest x coordinate seen so far.

7.4 THE BOOLEAN PRIMITIVE TYPE

We've seen that a boolean expression evaluates to the boolean value true or false. These values are treated like any other integer or double value in Java. Just as the integer value 7 can be stored in an `int` variable, and the double value 2.75 can be stored in a `double` variable, the boolean value true (or false) can be stored in a **boolean variable.** The **boolean literals** `true` and `false` can be used anywhere a boolean value is needed (we've already seen `true` used in the `setOpaque` method in Chapter 6).

The computation of the speed in some of the animations in this chapter, which is based on `ShowSpeed` animation in Chapter 5, is not done correctly the first time. This is because the instance variable `previousX` is initialized to 0 and not to the previous value of x (because there is no previous value until the `draw` method is called). We can use a boolean variable and an if-command to fix this problem. Code 7.9 shows a new version of the `ShowSpeed` animation that has an instance variable `firstTime` that is initially `true`, but is immediately set to `false` when the `draw` method is called the first time. From then on every time the `draw` method is called, `speed` will be computed correctly and then displayed.

Now consider this. The if-command

```
if (firstTime == true) {
```

in the program can be replaced with the simpler

```
if (firstTime) {
```

This is because the if-command expects an expression that evaluates to a boolean value. But the variable `firstTime` all by itself is an expression. If

CODE 7.9

```
import java.awt.*;

public class ShowSpeed extends Animator {
    // properties
    private final int size = 100;
    private final int xSpeed = 10;
    private final int ySpeed = 50;
    private int previousX = 0;
    private boolean firstTime = true;

    public void draw(int x, int y, Graphics g) {
        g.setColor(Color.black);
        int left = x-size/2;
        int top = y-size;
        g.fillRect(left,top,size,size);
        int speed = x - previousX;
        if (firstTime == true) {
            firstTime = false;
        }
        else {
            g.drawString("Speed = " + speed,xSpeed,ySpeed);
        }
        previousX = x;
    } // end of draw method

} // end of ShowSpeed class
```

> If this is the first time draw is called, set firstTime to false for the next time draw is called.

> Otherwise draw the string.

firstTime is true, the expression evaluates to true; if firstTime is false, it evaluates to false.

Every place in a program that you need a boolean value you can write an expression that evaluates to a boolean value. This includes inside expressions, such as

```
firstTime && x<10
```

which will be true if the value of the boolean variable firstTime is true *and* the value of x is less than 10.

7.5 EXAMPLES

7.5.1 Guess-the-Number Applet

Code 7.10 is a simple numeric guessing game, asking the user to guess the integer 17 that is built into the program (I assume the user does not have access to the code and so can't cheat).

CODE 7.10

```
import java.awt.*;
import java.awt.event.*;
import javax.swing.*;
```

```
public class GuessApplet extends JApplet{

    public void init() {
        Container window = getContentPane();
        window.setLayout(new FlowLayout(FlowLayout.LEFT));
        JLabel msg = new JLabel("guess an integer");
        window.add(msg);
        JTextField input = new JTextField(10);
        window.add(input);
        Listener inputListener = new Listener(msg, input);
        input.addActionListener(inputListener);
        } // end of init method

    } // end of GuessApplet class
```

```
class Listener implements ActionListener {
    private JLabel theMsg;
    private JTextField theInput;
    private int hiddenValue = 17;

    public Listener(JLabel msg, JTextField input) {
        theMsg = msg;
        theInput = input;
        } // end of constructor

    public void actionPerformed(ActionEvent event) {
        int guess = Integer.parseInt(theInput.getText());
        if (guess == hiddenValue) {
            theMsg.setText("Right!");
            }
        else if (guess < hiddenValue) {
            theMsg.setText("Too small, try again");
            theInput.setText("");
            }
        else {
            theMsg.setText("Too big, try again");
            theInput.setText("");
            }
        } // end of actionPerformed method

    } // end of Listener class
```

GuessApplet
The user tries to guess the hidden number by typing into the JTextField. The response indicates whether the guess was too high or too low.

As was the case with the `TextApplet` in the previous chapter, there is one class that defines an applet object and another class that defines a `Listener` object for a `JTextField` that is used to enter each guess. The `GuessApplet` class creates a `JLabel` object (initially displaying "guess an integer," but to be changed later) and the `JTextField` object, and adds them to the window. It then creates the `Listener` object for the `Textfield` and tells the `Textfield` about it.

The constructor in the `Listener` class saves references to the `JLabel` and `JTextField` objects in instance variables so that they can be used later in the `actionPerformed` method. The value to be guessed (17) is also made an instance variable so that it can be easily changed.

The `actionPerformed` method does all the work when the user enters a guess. First, the number that is entered must be converted from a `String` (the return value of `theInput.getText()`) to an `int`. Then come the if-commands in a selection structure that check for `guess` being equal to, less than, or greater than `hiddenValue` 17.

If `guess` is equal to `hiddenValue`, then the `setText` method of the `JLabel` object `theMsg` is called to change what is displayed on the screen to "Right!". If `guess` is not equal to `hiddenValue`, then if it is less, the `setText` method is called to change what is displayed to "Too small, try again." If `guess` is neither equal to nor less than `hiddenValue`, then it must be greater than, so the message "Too big, try again" is displayed. In either of the last two cases, the number that was typed into the `JTextField` by the user is erased from the `JTextField` by calling the `setText` method of the `JTextField` object and passing it a `String`.

7.5.2 A Small Improvement

The `GuessApplet` is only slightly useful. Once the user guesses 17, there is no reason for him or her to ever run it again. Let's fix it so that as soon as the user guesses the hidden value, a new hidden value is chosen and the user is asked to try to guess it. Each new hidden value will be chosen randomly by using the `Math.random` method. This method returns a different randomly chosen double value between 0.0 and 1.0 every time it is called. I'll use this method to generate a new integer hidden value in the range 0 to 100, by multiplying the value returned from the function by 100 and then converting it to an integer.

All that is necessary to improve the applet is to change the code in the true-part of the first if-command. Whenever the user guesses the hidden value, we'll display the message "Right! Try another" and then assign a new value to `hiddenValue`. The new code is shown below in bold:

```
if (guess == value) {
    theMsg.setText("Right! Try another");
    hiddenValue = (int) (Math.random()*100);
    }
```

We might as well choose the first hidden value randomly, too. To do so, just change the definition of the instance variable `hiddenValue` to

```
int hiddenValue = (int) (Math.random()*100);
```

7.5.3 A Product Pricing Example

Here's a program that requires a somewhat more complex if-command structure. It is an applet that determines the price of two products based on the kind of customer doing the buying and the quantity purchased. I'll assume there are three types of customers: existing good customers, existing not-so-good customers, and new customers; and for simplicity I'll designate them types 1, 2, and 3, respectively. I'll assume there are two types of products, 1 and 2, and price them according to Table 7.4.

Table 7.4

Customer Type	Product Number	Price
1	1	$3 for the first 100, $2 for each additional
1	2	$5 for the first 100, $4 for each additional
2	1	$3.50 for the first 200, $3 for each additional
2	2	$6 for the first 200, $5 for each additional
3	1	$2.75 each
3	2	$4.75 each

The applet will display labeled text fields for the user to enter the customer type, the product number, and the quantity, and a button to push to compute and display the total price (Code 7.11).

7.5.4 A Randomly Moving Object

This next example is an animation of an orange rectangle that slides along the surface of the scene. However, its movement is random in that it goes in one direction for a random distance, then in another. Whenever it hits the left or right edge of the scene, it heads back into the scene (Code 7.12).

The instance variable `distance` is the key to the operation of the animation. It is a counter that keeps track of how many more times the shape should move in the current direction it is moving. If `direction` is negative, then the shape is moving left; if it is positive, the shape is moving right. Each time the `draw` method is called, the x coordinate of the shape is either incremented or decremented by 1 depending on the direction in which the

CODE 7.11

```
import java.awt.*;
import java.awt.event.*;
import javax.swing.*;

public class Pricer extends JApplet implements ActionListener {
    private JTextField cType = new JTextField(3);
    private JTextField product = new JTextField(3);
    private JTextField quantity = new JTextField(5);
    private JButton compute = new JButton("compute price");
    private JLabel price = new JLabel("");

    public void init() {
        Container window = getContentPane();
        window.setLayout(new GridLayout(4,2));
        window.add(new JLabel("Customer Type:"));
        window.add(cType);
        window.add(new JLabel("Product Code:"));
        window.add(product);
        window.add(new JLabel("Quantity:"));
        window.add(quantity);
        window.add(compute);
        window.add(price);
        compute.addActionListener(this);
        } // end of init method

    public void actionPerformed(ActionEvent event) {
        int cust = Integer.parseInt(cType.getText());
        int prod = Integer.parseInt(product.getText());
        int quant = Integer.parseInt(quantity.getText());
        if (prod != 1 && prod != 2) {
            price.setText("invalid product code");
            }
        else {
            if (cust == 1) {
                if (prod == 1) {
                    if (quant <= 100) {
                        price.setText(quant*3.00+"");
                        }
                    else {
                        price.setText(
                            100*3.00+(quant-100)*2.00 + "");
                        }
                    }
                else {
                    if (quant <= 100) {
                        price.setText(quant*5.00 + "");
                        }
                    else {
```

Check for a valid product code once here instead of for each customer.

Pricer
An applet that determines the price of a product based on quantity and type of customer.

```
                            price.setText(
                                    100*5.00 + (quant-100)*4.00 + "");
                    }
                }
            }
        else if (cust == 2) {
            if (prod == 1) {
                if (quant <= 200) {
                    price.setText(quant*3.50 + "");
                }
                else {
                    price.setText(
                            200*3.50 + (quant-200)*3.00 + "");
                }
            }
            else {
                if (quant <= 200) {
                    price.setText(200*6.00 + "");
                }
                else {
                    price.setText(
                            200*6.00 + (quant-200)*5.00 + "");
                }
            }
        }
        else if (cust == 3) {
            if (prod == 1) {
                price.setText(quant*2.75 + "");
            }
            else {
                price.setText(quant*4.75 + "");
            }
        }
        else {
            price.setText("invalid customer");
        }
    }
} // end of actionPerformed method

} // end of Pricer class
```

shape is moving. Also each time the draw method is called, direction is modified to be 1 closer to 0 (1 is added if direction is negative, 1 is subtracted if direction is positive). Whenever direction becomes 0 (including initially), a new random value is chosen for direction.

The named constant variation controls how far the shape will move before it randomly chooses another movement direction and distance. Since the direction is chosen randomly each time, it is possible that the shape may finish moving in one direction and then choose to go in the same direction again.

CODE 7.12

```java
import java.awt.*;

public class RandomShape extends Animator {
    private final int width = 30;
    private final int height = 30;
    private final int variation = 200; // maximum distance
    private int xPosition = 200; // current position
    private int direction = 0; // and direction

    public void draw(Graphics g) {
        // draw the shape
        g.setColor(Color.orange);
        int left = xPosition - width/2;
        int top = Animator.getSurface()-height;
        g.fillRect(left,top,width,height);
        // if it has hit the edge, start it
        // off in the other direction
        if (xPosition <= 0) {
            direction = (int) (Math.random()*variation);
            }
        if (xPosition >= Animator.getSceneWidth()) {
            direction = 0 - (int) (Math.random()*variation);
            }
        // if moving left, decrement position and direction
        if (direction < 0) {
            xPosition = xPosition-1;
            direction = direction+1;
            }
        // if moving right, increment position and
        // decrement direction
        else if (direction > 0) {
            xPosition = xPosition+1;
            direction = direction-1;
            }
        // if not moving, start it off in a random direction
        else {
            direction = (int)
                (Math.random()*2*variation)-variation;
            }
        } // end of draw method

    } // end of Shape class
```

Programming Exercises

1. Write an applet that contains three JButton objects and one JLabel object. The JButton objects should be identified as "LEFT," "MIDDLE," and "RIGHT" according to their placement on the screen. The JLabel should display "no button has yet been clicked" initially. When one of the

JButton objects is clicked on, change the JLabel to display which JButton was clicked on (e.g., "the LEFT button was clicked" if the left button was clicked). Use a single Listener object that compares object references to decide which JButton generated the event.

2. Write an applet that contains three JTextField objects and one JLabel object. The JLabel should display "insufficient data" until the integer values in all three JTextField objects are nonzero. Once all three JTextField objects have nonzero integer values typed into them, the JLabel should display "in order" if the value in the first JText-Field is less than the value in the second JTextField and the value in the second JTextField is less than the value in the third JText-Field; but it should display "not in order" if not.

7.6 COMPARING OBJECTS

Consider the definition of a Box class shown in Code 7.13.

CODE 7.13

```
class Box {
    private final int width;
    private final int height;

    public Box(int w, int h) {
        width = w;
        height = h;
    } // end of constructor

    public void draw(int x, int y, Graphics g) {
        g.setColor(Color.black);
        int left = x - width/2;
        int top = y - height;
        g.fillRect(left,top,width,height);
    } // end of draw method

} // end of Box class
```

Suppose we create two Box objects as shown in the following segment of code:

```
Box one = new Box(10,20);
Box two = new Box(10,20);
if (one == two) {
    // do something...
    }
```

The question is, Will the true-part of the if-command be executed or not? You might think it would, since the Box objects were created in the same way (having length 10 and height 20), which would make them look the same when drawn in the scene. But the true-part is *not* executed. Here's why.

When you compare two variables that are *references* to objects, it is the *references* that are compared, not the objects that they refer to. Remember, the value stored in a variable that is a reference to an object is the *reference,* not the object itself. That's why I've always put arrows inside the rectangles picturing Box object reference variables, as shown in Figure 7.1.

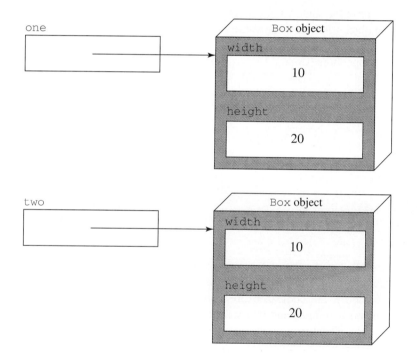

FIGURE 7.1

The equality and relational operators compare the values of variables. Hence when variables are references to objects, it is the references that are compared because the references are the values of the variables. The objects they refer to are *not* compared. As a result, the comparison in the code above will compare the reference (arrow) in one with the reference (arrow) in two and discover that they are not references to the same Box object. As a result, the true-part of the if-command will not be executed because the expression evaluates to false.

Now suppose you want to compare the two Box objects themselves for equality. This can be done, but not by using the equality or relational operators directly. Instead *you* must write a method, usually called equals, to do the comparison. This method is called in the following way:

```
if (one.equals(two)) ...
```

{New Concepts}

Use an equals method to compare two objects for equality. The == operator will only compare references to two objects and will be true if they refer to the exact same object.

Because the definition of the `equals` method is up to you, you can decide what equality means. Usually it means that all the instance variables in both objects have the same values. In the `Box` example, it would mean that height in both objects has the same value and that width in both objects has the same value. These can easily be tested using ordinary if-commands and ordinary equality operators (Code 7.14).

CODE 7.14

```
public boolean equals(Box other) {
    if (this.height != other.height) {
        return false;
        }
    if (this.width != other.width) {
        return false;
        }
    return true;
    }
```

Recall that the `return` command causes the method to finish immediately; so once it is executed, *nothing* else in the method will be executed. In this method if the boolean expression in the first if-command is true, then the method will finish and return false to the place where it was called from. The second if-command will not be executed in this case. If the first expression is false but the expression in the second if-command is true, the method will also finish and return false. However, if neither expression is true, then the last command will execute, which will cause the method to finish and return true.

Now let's consider the boolean expression in the first if-command:

```
this height != other.height
```

This says that `height` in *this* object is being compared with `height` in another object, evaluating to true if they are not equal and to false otherwise. Now here is the code where the `equals` method is called:

```
if (one.equals(two)) ...
```

When the `equals` method in the `Box` class is called, the method is executing in the context of the `Box` object referred to by `one`. Hence `this.height` is the value of the `height` instance variable in `Box` object `one`. The `equals` method is also sent a reference to the `Box` object `two`. The `equals` method uses the parameter variable `other` to hold this reference, which means that `other.height` refers to the instance variable `height` in `Box` object `two`.

Putting this all together, you can see that the expression compares the instance variable `height` in `Box` object `one` (on the left) with the instance variable `height` in the `Box` object `two` (on the right). If their values are not equal, then the expression will evaluate to true; and if they are not, it will evaluate to false. The expression in the second if-command works similarly to compare the two `width` instance variables.

As a result, the `equals` method first compares the `height` instance variables in the two objects and, if they are not equal, returns false. If they are equal, it compares the two `width` instance variables in the two objects and, if they are not equal, returns false. If both instance variables are equal (and neither true-part got executed), the method returns true.

It is important to remember that you must write your own `equals` method when you want to compare two objects and not just references to them. You don't have to call it `equals`, but doing so is accepted practice and is a good idea. You also can write other methods that do other comparisons. For example, you might want to write a method that compares two `Box` objects and returns true if one is smaller than the other, using the product of `height` and `width` (i.e., the area) to represent the size of each. Feel free to write such methods if you need them. I recommend that you very carefully document exactly what the method compares. For example, you could define a method that compares two `Box` objects and returns true if one is smaller than the other, where smaller means that both the `height` of the first is less than the `height` of the second *and* the `width` of the first is less than the `width` of the second. This is a different meaning of smaller than the previous one, so you better make sure your documentation makes it clear what the method actually does.

By the way, the use of the keyword `this` in the code above was entirely unnecessary. The following is a completely equivalent version of the `equals` method. I used `this` in the code above to make it very clear which instance variable in which object was being referenced at each point.

```
public boolean equals(Box other) {
    if (height != other.height) {
        return false;
        }
    if (width != other.width) {
        return false;
        }
    return true;
    } // end of equals method
```

7.6.1 An Object Comparison Example

Consider the modified (but incomplete) version of the `TwoButtons` applet from Chapter 6 shown in Code 7.15.

CODE 7.15

```java
import java.awt.event.*;
import java.awt.*;
import javax.swing.*;

public class TwoButtons extends JApplet implements ActionListener {

    public void init() {
        Container window = getContentPane();
        window.setLayout(new FlowLayout(FlowLayout.LEFT));
        JButton red = new JButton("red");
        red.setBackground(Color.red);
        window.add(red);
        JButton green = new JButton("green");
        green.setBackground(Color.green);
        window.add(green);
        JLabel which = new JLabel("which one?");
        which.setBackground(Color.white);
        window.add(which);

        red.addActionListener(this);      ◄──── this object is the listener
        green.addActionListener(this);    ◄──── for both JButton objects.
    } // end of begin method

    public void actionPerformed(ActionEvent event) {
        ?    ◄──────────────────────    We need to set the label's color
                                        depending on which button was
    } // end of actionPerformed method  pushed, but we get here in either case.

} // end of TwoButtons class
```

This version uses the `TwoButtons` object as the listener for both `JButton` objects, so somehow in the `actionPerformed` method we must decide which button was pushed and set the color of the label appropriately. Fortunately, the parameter event is a reference to an object that has just the information we need to figure out which button was pushed. The `ActionEvent` class has a method called `getSource` that returns a reference to the object that caused the event (i.e., a reference to the appropriate `JButton` object). All we need to do is to compare that reference with the instance variables `red` and `green` to see which `JButton` was pushed and then set the color appropriately. Code 7.16 is the complete version.

CODE 7.16

```
import java.awt.event.*;
import java.awt.*;
import javax.swing.*;

public class TwoButtons extends JApplet implements ActionListener {
    private JButton red = new JButton("red");      ◄──────── red, green, and which
    private JButton green = new JButton("green");  ◄──────── are made instance variables
    JLabel which = new JLabel("which one?");       ◄──────── because both methods need
                                                             access to them.

    public void init() {
        Container window = getContentPane();
        window.setLayout(new FlowLayout(FlowLayout.LEFT));
        red.setBackground(Color.red);
        window.add(red);
        green.setBackground(Color.green);
        window.add(green);
        which.setOpaque(true);
        which.setBackground(Color.white);
        window.add(which);

        red.addActionListener(this);
        green.addActionListener(this);
    } // end of init method

    public void actionPerformed(ActionEvent event) {
        if (event.getSource() == red) {      ◄──────  See which JButton object
            which.setBackground(Color.red);  ◄──────  caused the event, then change
        }                                             the color accordingly.
        else { // must be the green one
            which.setBackground(Color.green);
        }
    } // end of actionPerformed method

} // end of TwoButtons class
```

Written Exercise

1. Why isn't an equals method used to compare `event.getSource` with an object?

Programming Exercise

1. Write an applet with two buttons, one labeled 0 and the other labeled 1, and a label. The applet has an integer instance variable called `baseTen` that is displayed in the label whenever it changes. When the 0 button is pushed, `baseTen` is multiplied by 2 (and displayed). When the 1 button is pushed, `baseTen` is multiplied by 2 and has 1 added to it. Use a single listener.

7.7 THE COMPLETE LOCAL VARIABLE SCOPE RULE

In Chapter 5 it was stated that the scope of a local variable began at the command that created it and ended at the end of the method it was created in. This is not quite true. A more accurate statement of the scope rule for a local variable is that it ends at the end of the *block* that it is created in.

A **block** is all the code that appears between matching { and } symbols. In a simple method with no if-commands, this usually winds up being the entire method. However, with if-commands, the true- and false-parts are also enclosed in matching { and } symbols. That means that the true-part of an if-command is a block and the false-part of an if-command is a (different) block. As a result, any local variable created in the true- or false-part of an if-command has scope that ends at the end of that true- or false-part. No local variable created in a true- or false-part of an if-command can be used outside that part. For example, the following code segment is in error:

```
if (some expression) {
    int a = 5;
    }
int b = a-6; // a's scope does not extend this far
```

This is because the scope of local variable a ends at the end of the true-part of the if-command. The compiler will give you an error message on the last line indicating that a is not defined.

Because the scope of a local variable ends at the end of the block it is defined in, it is possible to use the same name in different blocks. For example,

```
int result;
if (a < b) {
    int temp = a - x/2;
    result = temp*result + temp/2;
    }
else {
    int temp = b + x/2;
    result = temp*result - temp/2;
    }
// use result here
```

The local variable temp is created twice, once in the true-part and once in the false-part. Because their scopes do not overlap, this is perfectly legal. They are different variables and will occupy different places in memory, even though they have the same name. The compiler knows which one to use at the appropriate place.

A scope of a variable defined outside the true- or false-part of an if-command (e.g., in a command prior to the if-command, or as an instance variable) extends *into* the true- and false-parts of the if-command, and it is perfectly legal to use such variables in those parts, as we have done many times already. However, it is not legal to do the following:

```
int x = 5;
if (some expression) {
     double x = 6; // this x clashes with the other one
     }
```

The scope of the first local variable x extends into the true-part of the if-command; hence trying to create another local variable x causes a conflict, and the compiler will inform you of the error.

To summarize, the scope of a local variable begins at the command in which it is created and ends at the end of the block it is created in. The scope extends into any block nested inside that block. It is legal to create two or more local variables with the same name as long as their scopes do not intersect.

Written Exercises

1. If p and q are references to two Box objects, is the boolean expression p==q true or false? Explain.

2. Why is it necessary to write your own equals method for classes you define?

3. Draw a box around the scope of x in the following code segments.

   a.

   ```
   public void methodA(int x) {
        propVar = x;
        x = x + 1;
        }
   ```

   b.

   ```
   public void methodB() {
        int a = 5;
        int x = 4;
        propVar = propVar + a + x;
        }
   ```

   c.

   ```
   public void methodC(double z) {
        if (z < 10.0) {
             double y = z - 1.0;
             double x = y / 2.5;
             }
        else {
             double x = z / 2.5;
             double y = x = 1.0;
             }
   ```

d.

```
public void methodD(int y) {
      int x = 0;
      if (0 <= y && y <= 10) {
           if (y == 9) {
                x = 7;
                }
           }
      else {
           x = 5;
           }
      propVar = x;
      }
```

Programming Exercises

1. Write an animation that draws a black 40 × 40 box in the middle of the scene. When the user clicks somewhere in the scene, if the click is inside the box, draw the box red. If not, draw it black.

2. Modify your solution to the previous problem to draw the box red for 10 calls to the `draw` method, then draw it black again until the user clicks inside the box.

3. Write an animation with a cloud that continually sweeps across the scene from left to right. When the cloud is in the center of the scene (i.e., x coordinate equal to `Animator.getSceneWidth` over 2), it should drop a single raindrop (blue circle with diameter 5) that falls to the surface. Use a separate object for the raindrop and have the cloud object tell the raindrop when it should start falling by calling a `startDrop` method in the raindrop object and sending the coordinates of where the raindrop should first be drawn. The raindrop object should draw nothing until the cloud tells it to start drawing; then it should draw the raindrop 1 pixel lower on each call of its `draw` method. When the raindrop hits the surface, it should stop being drawn again until the cloud tells it to.

4. Modify your solution to the previous problem to have two raindrops (two objects). The first should start falling when the cloud is one-third of the way across the scene, the second when it is two-thirds of the way across the scene.

5. Write an applet that that has two text fields with a label in between. Use two integer instance variables to keep track of integer values entered into the respective text fields, and make their initial values 0. Then when the user enters a number in one text field or the other, convert it to an integer and change the corresponding instance variable to that value. Finally, compare the two instance variables, and change the label between the two text fields to an arrow (e.g., the string "--->") that points at the text field in which the largest value so far has been entered.

Summary

- A boolean expression is an expression that evaluates to one of the boolean values true or false.

- A boolean expression can contain various equality (==, !=), relational (<, <=, >, >=) and conditional (&&, ||) operators.

- An if-command tests the result of evaluating a boolean expression. If the expression evaluates to true, commands in the code that follows (the true-part) are executed. If it evaluates to false, code that follows the reserved word else (the false-part) is executed (if present).

- A nested if occurs when one if-command is contained in the true- or false-part of another if-command.

- One special nested if structure is a selection. In a selection, the boolean expressions in the collection of if-commands test for mutually exclusive cases.

- Two objects cannot be tested using the equality operators. Only the references are compared, and they are found to be equal if they both refer to the exact same object (not two different objects that happen to have the same instance variable values).

- To test two different objects for equality, an equals method must be written for the class that defines the objects. The code in that method decides what "equals" means for objects defined by that class.

- A block is all the code between the symbol { and the matching symbol }.

- The scope of a local variable begins at the command that creates the local variable and extends to the end of the block it is created in, including inside any blocks contained within that block.

Glossary

Block Code between the symbol { and its matching symbol }.

Boolean Expression An expression that evaluates to a boolean value.

Boolean Literal The reserved word **true** or **false.**

Boolean Value True or false.

Boolean Variable A variable that stores a boolean value.

Conditional-And An operator that evaluates to true if both its operands are true and to false otherwise. Both operands must be boolean values.

Conditional-Or An operator that evaluates to false if both its operands are false and to true otherwise. Both operands must be boolean values.

Equality Operator An operator (== or !=) that evaluates to true or false depending on the equality or inequality of its operands.

False-Part Code that is executed if the boolean expression in an if-command is false.

If-Command A command that tests the result of evaluating a boolean expression and executes one of two code sequences depending on the result of the test.

Logical Operator Either conditional-and (&&) or conditional-or (||).

Nested If An if-command that appears in the true- or false-part of another if-command.

Precedence A hierarchy of operators. Operators with higher precedence are evaluated before those with lower precedence.

Relational Operator An operator ($<$, $<=$, $>$, $>=$) that evaluates to true or false depending on the relative values of its operands.

Selection A sequence of nested if-commands that test mutually exclusive conditions.

Short-Circuit Evaluation Evaluation of the left operand of || or && but not the right operand when the result of the operation can be determined from the value of the left operand alone.

True-Part Code that is executed if the boolean expression in an if-command is true.

CHAPTER 8

Program Testing

OBJECTIVES

- To understand the importance of testing programs for correctness.
- To realize that testing usually cannot guarantee that a program has no errors.
- To understand the concepts of white box and black box testing.
- To understand the concepts of incremental testing, unit testing, and integration testing.
- To know the differences between white and black box testing and how they complement each other.
- To have a basic understanding of the white box testing techniques called statement coverage and path coverage.
- To be able to devise statement coverage and path coverage tests.
- To be able to write incremental and unit test programs.
- To be able to devise black box tests.

8.1 PROGRAM CORRECTNESS

What would you pay for a program that doesn't work correctly? Probably not much. Programs that don't work correctly aren't worth much. However, making sure that programs you write are 100 percent correct is not always easy and, as we'll see, usually not even possible.

Most *real* programs are not 100 percent correct. You probably have found errors (bugs) in software that you have used. This is not uncommon, especially in large, complex programs. However, successful programs don't have very many bugs, and those that exist usually don't show themselves except under unusual circumstances. These programs got to the point of having only a few relatively obscure bugs because of good design, talented programmers, and *extensive testing*.

Testing a program has two purposes. One is to verify that the program works correctly. The other is to uncover bugs that are then fixed via debugging. Programs that have had an error discovered and then fixed must be retested (completely), as it is not uncommon that fixing one bug will introduce a new one. This new bug may have been one that a previous test didn't turn up (because it wasn't there), hence a previously successful test will no longer be successful, and you must redo the test to find this out.

Except for very simple programs, testing will not *prove* that a program is 100 percent correct. The best that can be done is to increase your *confidence* that it is 100 percent correct to an acceptable level. As you can imagine, the more testing you do, the fewer errors you will have (assuming you fix the errors that testing uncovers) and the more confident you will be that the program is 100 percent correct. Unfortunately there may still be errors that your testing, no matter how thorough, will not have discovered.

> **{New Concepts}**
> Testing a program with sample input usually will not prove that a program is correct.

An important goal of testing is to be efficient, that is, to verify as much correctness, or to find the most bugs, with the least effort. To that end we'll look at two different approaches to testing. The first, called *black box testing,* assumes that you only know what the program is supposed to do, and not how it actually does it (i.e., you don't get to look at the code when you test). The other, called *white box testing* (some call it *clear box testing*), is designed directly from the code. Both are useful but approach the problem from slightly different directions. Black box testing makes sure the program does what it is supposed to do; white box testing makes sure that all the code works correctly. These may seem like the same thing, but as we will see, they are different.

Large companies have groups of people designing tests and running tests on their software products. Testing programs is not an easy task. Some find it to be an interesting and challenging job to try to find errors in other people's programs. Others find it boring and tedious. Designing effective and efficient tests is as much an art as a science, and in this chapter I'll barely scratch the surface of how to go about testing programs.

Written Exercise

1. Why do you think testing can never prove a program is 100 percent correct (except for extremely simple programs)?

8.2 WHITE BOX TESTING

A program's code is used to design white box tests. Inputs are given to the program that cause it to execute all its commands in as many ways as possible. There are increasingly complex ways of doing this depending on how thorough the tests should be.

> **{Definition of Terms}**
> **White box testing** is designed by inspecting the actual code of a program.

8.2.1 Statement Coverage

The simplest form of white box testing is to make sure that every command in the program gets executed at least once, a technique called *statement coverage.* Consider the `BasicShape` class definition from Chapter 3. Its `draw` method has no if-commands in it, and hence it only needs to be called once to execute every command in it. Doing so and observing that it works correctly does not ensure that it is correct, however, since the behavior of the method might depend on particular values of the parameters x and y of the method. Consider the following incorrect version of the draw method (the last two arguments in the fillOval call are x,x instead of 40,40):

```
public void draw(int x, int y, Graphics g) {
    g.setColor(Color.black);                    Error—two x's instead
    g.fillOval(x-20,y-40,x,x);                  of two 40s.
    g.setColor(Color.white);
    g.drawLine(x-20,y-20,x+20,y-20);
    } // end of draw method
```

This code will draw a circle whose diameter depends on where on the screen the circle is drawn, getting bigger as the circle is moved to the right, smaller as it is moved to the left. This is clearly wrong. However, there is one value for x for which the circle will be drawn correctly—40. If this happened to be the value of x for which the code was tested, it would be drawn on the screen correctly and the person observing this would conclude that the code was correct.

From this simple example you can see that even testing such a simple piece of code as this is not simple. To adequately test this code, it would have to be tried with many values of x (and y) by having the circle be drawn at every position from the far left to the far right of the window.

Now consider the draw method from the Direction class from Chapter 7, shown in Code 8.1.

It displays a String indicating in which direction the circle is moving. To display the words "moving left" and "moving right" correctly, it contains an if-command. To perform statement coverage, we must ensure that both the

CODE 8.1

```
public void draw(int x, int y, Graphics g) {
    // draw the circle
    g.setColor(Color.white);
    int left = x-diameter/2;
    int top = y-diameter;
    g.fillOval(left,top,diameter,diameter);

    // compute the speed
    int speed = x - previousX;

    // display appropriate direction
    g.setColor(Color.black);
    if (speed < 0) {
        g.drawString("moving left",10,30);
        }
    else {
        g.drawString("moving right",10,30);
        }

    // save the x-coordinate for the next call
    previousX = x;
    } // end of draw method
```

true-part and the false-part of the if-command are executed. That means that we must cause the variable `speed` to have both negative and nonnegative values (negative for the true-part to get executed, nonnegative for the false-part). To do that, we must move the circle in both directions when we run the Animator. Hence two statement coverage tests for this code are (1) move the circle left and expect the message to say that it is moving left, and (2) move the circle right and expect the message to say that it is moving right.

Simple statement coverage gets harder when there are more if-commands in a program. In this code structure

```
if (test1) {
    if (test2) {
        // some commands
    }
    else {
        // more commands
    }
else {
    // even more commands
    }
```

there are three pieces of code that must be executed, requiring inputs that sometimes cause `test1` to be true *and* `test2` to be true, sometimes cause `test1` to be true *and* `test2` to be false, and sometimes cause `test1` to be false.

Not every segment of code in all if-commands may need a separate test, however, as the code below demonstrates:

```
if (x < y) {
    // true-part-1
    }
else {
    // else-part-1
    }
// code that does not change x or y
if (x < y) {
    // true-part-2
    }
else {
    // else part-2
    }
```

In this case a test (values of x and y) that causes `true-part-1` to execute will also cause `true-part-2` to execute, and a test that causes `false-part-1` to execute will also cause `false-part-2` to execute. Hence only two sets of test input are necessary to cause all the code to be executed: a test with x < y and a test with x >= y. However, if the code between the first and second if-commands changes x or y, then this may no longer be true and up to four separate sets of test input may be needed.

{New Concepts}

Statement coverage tests ensure that every command in a program gets executed at least once.

Simple statement coverage testing is the minimum one should consider doing. It at least exposes every piece of code to execution, and while perhaps not foolproof, at least gives you some confidence in the correctness of the program. For greater confidence, a white box testing technique called *path coverage* can be used.

8.2.2 Path Coverage

Path coverage involves designing tests to cover every possible sequence of commands (paths) that can be executed in a program. To demonstrate it, and why it is better than statement coverage, consider the following code segment that happens to have two errors:

```
if (w > x) {
     a = a + 1;        ◄──────── This should be a = a + 2;
     }
else {
     a = a + 3;
     }
if (y < z) {
     a = a + 3;        ◄──────── This should be a = a + 2;
     }
else {
     a = a + 4;
     }
```

Suppose that you use the following two statement coverage tests to test this code:

1. A test with $w > x$ and $y < z$, which tests the true-parts of *both* if-commands.

2. A test with $w <= x$ and $y >= z$, which tests the false parts of both if-commands.

These two tests are sufficient to ensure that every piece of code gets executed. Running the first test will result in a final value for a of 4, which is what the correct value should be, even though there are two errors in the program. The second test gives the correct value for a also, so the code passes both statement coverage tests and is declared correct!

Now consider path coverage. This code segment has four paths:

1. a = a + 1 followed by a = a + 3 (caused by a test case with $w > x$ and $y < z$)

2. a = a + 1 followed by a = a + 4 (caused by a test case with $w > x$ and $y >= z$)

3. $a = a + 3$ followed by $a = a + 3$ (caused by a test case with $w <= x$ and $y < z$)

4. $a = a + 3$ followed by $a = a + 4$ (caused by a test case with $w <= x$ and $y >= z$)

If the code were correct, then the first path should result in a having the value 4, the second 6, the third 5, and the fourth 7. With the incorrect code cases 1 and 4 still get the right answer, but cases 2 and 3 get 5 and 6 instead of 6 and 5. Path coverage finds the errors.

Path coverage will discover many such errors because tests are required to cause the program to execute every possible path (all four in the case above) and hence is much more powerful. Unfortunately, the number of paths through a program can be enormous even for fairly short programs, and constructing tests that take the program through every one is usually not possible. For example, a program with 10 if-commands (not nested) will have $2^{10} = 1024$ different paths, and that is a lot of tests.

> **{New Concepts}**
>
> **Path coverage** tests ensure that every path through a program is executed at least once.

8.2.3 Incremental Testing

There are many testing techniques that are used *during* the development of a program, not after it has been completely written. One goes along with incremental development—*incremental testing*. That is, you write part of your program, test it (and debug it as necessary), then add more code, test (and debug) some more, etc., until you have a complete program. This is clearly a white box technique because you have the code and can look at it, but you can also use black box tests as described in the next section.

> **{New Concepts}**
>
> **Incremental testing** involves testing successively more complete versions of the final program.

One of the nice things about incremental testing is that if you've tested carefully up to a certain point, then add more code and test again, the error is more than likely (but not guaranteed) to be in the new code you just added. This helps you debug your code because you don't have to consider the whole program when there is a problem. You are not guaranteed that the error will be in the new code, however, because your new code may interact with your old code in a way that you didn't expect and either didn't or couldn't test for.

8.2.4 Unit Testing

Another form of testing is called *unit testing* (sometimes called *modular testing*). The concept is that if you do a good object-oriented design, any nontrivial program will consist of several objects defined by several distinct classes.

With unit testing you test each class as independently as you can. For example, in animations you can test each different class that defines objects that do not interact with others (e.g., Clouds) independently. Classes that define objects that interact sometimes have to be tested together, but sometimes you can write a dummy version of one or more of them that doesn't do everything it is supposed to but does enough to test the others.

{New Concepts}

Unit testing tests pieces of your program (usually classes and methods) as independently as possible.

With unit testing you often have to write extra code that will not be part of the final product. This **throwaway code,** as it is often called, is simply there to force the objects you are testing to perform various actions (sometimes called a **test driver**), or to be dummy code (sometimes called a **stub**) that the object needs but hasn't been written yet and is not fully functional. However, the extra work in writing (and testing and debugging!) this code often pays off in the long run.

I'll demonstrate unit testing by doing a unit test of the `Calculator` class defined in Chapter 6 (Code 8.2).

CODE 8.2

```
class Calculator {
    private int accumulator = 0;
    private int sum = 0;
    private JLabel accLabel;
    private JLabel sumLabel;

    public Calculator(JLabel a, JLabel s) {
        accLabel = a;
        sumLabel = s;
        } // end of constructor

    public void accumulate(int digit) {
        accumulator = accumulator*10+digit;
        accLabel.setText(accumulator+"");
        } // end of accumulate method

    public void add() {
        sum = sum + accumulator;
        accumulator = 0;
        accLabel.setText("0");
        sumLabel.setText(sum+"");
        } // end of add method

    } // end of Calculator class
```

The class defines an object that displays values in two `JLabel` objects and has a constructor that saves references to the `JLabel` objects, a method that accumulates digits in `accumulator` as they are clicked in and sent to the method, and a method that adds the accumulated number to a total (`sum`) when the user clicks on an "add" button.

To test it, I will write a test driver class that defines an object that creates a `Calculator` object and calls its methods to see if they work. I want to make the test driver class as simple as possible, so I'll create the two `JLabel` objects the calculator needs and add them to the window as simply as possible (not worrying about colors or layout), and then I'll simply insert calls to the `accumulate` and `add` methods as though a user had clicked in digits and hit the "add" button (Code 8.3).

CODE 8.3

```java
import java.awt.*;
import javax.swing.*;

public class UnitTest extends JApplet {

    public void init() {
        // set up simple window
        Container window = getContentPane();
        window.setLayout(new FlowLayout(FlowLayout.LEFT));
        JLabel acc = new JLabel("acc");
        JLabel sum = new JLabel("sum");
        window.add(acc);
        window.add(sum);

        // create Calculator object to test
        Calculator calc = new Calculator(acc, sum);

        // check accumulate method
        calc.accumulate(1);
        calc.accumulate(9);
        calc.accumulate(5);
        calc.accumulate(1);

        // check add method
        //calc.add();

        // check accumulate and add again
        //calc.accumulate(5);
        //calc.add();

        // check accumulate and add one more time
        //calc.accumulate(2);
        //calc.accumulate(6);
        //calc.add();
    } // end of init method

} // end of UnitTest class

// Calculator class here
```

Set up a simple window with the two labels the `Calculator` object needs, then create a `Calculator` object to test.

Simulate clicking in the digits 1, 9, 5, and 1 and see if the `Calculator` object displays 1951.

Uncomment the `add` call and run again to see if `add` works right.

Uncomment these two lines and simulate a single-digit input and add.

Finally uncomment these three lines and simulate one more input and add.

The key is to test a little bit at a time, then more, then more. I first test the `accumulate` method. Assuming it works, I then add code (or uncomment) to test the `add` method. Assuming that works, I add more code and test some more, then add more and test more, etc.

Clearly this is throwaway code. Very little of it will survive into the final program. However, just because it is called throwaway code, don't throw it away until you are done with the entire program and expect to never have to work on it again. As you write and test other parts of the program, you may find that you have to make a change to the `Calculator` class (perhaps because you forgot something when you designed it, or perhaps it doesn't fit well with other parts of the program). If this happens, you can simply resurrect the unit test driver, perhaps make a few simple modifications, and use it to test the new `Calculator` class all over again. My advice is to never throw away throwaway code.

> **{Good Ideas}**
> Save all unit test drivers and stubs in case you have to retest a part of the program.

Here's another example of a unit test that includes a stub. It tests the `DigitListener` class used in the calculator program. The key here is that the driver also substitutes as the `Calculator` object and has an `accumulate` method of its own. This `accumulate` method does not do what the `accumulate` method of the real `Calculator` class does. Instead it simply displays the value sent to it by the listener (Code 8.4).

To make sure the `DigitListener` class, which defines 10 different objects in the real calculator program, handles different digits properly, run the test at least twice with different digits being sent to the `DigitListener` constructor each time. Simply change the digit in the test code, recompile, and run again to test.

As with incremental testing, unit testing allows you to minimize the amount of code in which to look for errors. Of course, the dummy code has to be inspected, too, but usually it is fairly simple and less likely to have an error than the real code you are testing. This makes debugging easier and more efficient.

> **{Good Ideas}**
> Incremental testing and unit testing help isolate possible errors to small sections of code, thereby making debugging easier and more efficient.

8.2.5 Integration Testing

Going along with unit testing is *integration testing*. Once you've tested many of your objects independently, you must then get them to work together (*integrate* them into a whole program). This doesn't necessarily mean putting *all* the pieces together right away to form the complete program and testing it. Instead it often entails putting several already unit-tested pieces together and testing the group (doing essentially unit testing on the group, with drivers and stubs as necessary). Eventually you keep combining more and more units

CODE 8.4

```
import java.awt.*;
import java.awt.event.*;
import javax.swing.*;
```

```
public class Calculator extends JApplet {
     private JLabel output = new JLabel("output");
```

> Change 0 to at least one other digit, recompile, and retest to make sure the DigitListener class handles different digits properly.

```
     public void init() {
          // set up simple window
          Container window = getContentPane();
          window.setLayout(new FlowLayout(FlowLayout.LEFT));
          JButton test = new JButton("test");
          window.add(test);
          window.add(output);
          // create DigitListener object and
          // hook up with the button
          DigitListener digitList = new DigitListener(this,0);
          test.addActionListener(digitList);
          } // end of init method
```

```
     public void accumulate(int digit) {
          output.setText(digit+"");
          } // end of accumulate stub
```

> This method is a stub for the real accumulate method in the real Calculator class.

```
     } // end of Calculator class
```

```
class DigitListener implements ActionListener {
     private int digit;
     private Calculator theCalc;
```

```
     public DigitListener(Calculator c, int d) {
          theCalc = c;
          digit = d;
          } // end of constructor
```

```
     public void actionPerformed(ActionEvent event) {
          theCalc.accumulate(digit);
          } // end of actionPerformed method
```

```
     } // end of DigitListener class
```

and collections of units until you have the entire program, which you can, and should, continue to test.

> {New Concepts}
>
> **Integration testing** involves putting already tested pieces together and testing the combination. It helps ensure that separately tested parts work correctly when combined.

Written Exercises

1. Describe the characteristics of a method in a class definition that can be fully tested (100 percent confidence that it is correct) with just one test.

2. How many tests are required to give full statement coverage of the code in the draw method of the HowFast class in Chapter 7? How many to give full path coverage?

3. What is the maximum number of paths in a program that has seven unnested if-commands?

4. Is the number of tests required to give full statement coverage of a segment of code in a single method finite or infinite? How about full path coverage?

5. Write statement coverage tests for any of the sample programs in the previous chapters.

6. Write path coverage tests for any of the sample programs in the previous chapters.

Programming Exercises

1. Write and use a unit test driver for the Cloud class defined at the end of Section 5.5.

2. Write and use a unit test driver for the Post class defined in Section 5.6.

3. Write and use a unit test for the final version of the Person class in Section 6.1.

4. Write and use a unit test for the final version of the Line class in Section 6.1. Use stubs to return fixed positions of the other (nonexistent) objects.

5. Integration-test the final versions of the Person and Line classes (but not the Balloon class) in Section 6.1. You'll need to write a test driver, and you'll need stubs for the methods that would be in the Balloon class.

8.3 BLACK BOX TESTING

The term *black box testing* comes from the notion that the program code being tested is in a black box and the person doing the testing cannot see it. The test designer works from a description of what the program is supposed to do, sometimes called the **program specification.**

For example, a program that is supposed to display the square root of a number that is input into a `JTextField` should do exactly that—display the correct square root. If it displays the wrong value, no value, the correct value but somewhere on the screen other than where it is supposed to be, or if it aborts, then it has bugs. With black box testing it doesn't matter *how* the program computes and displays the square root, only that it does so correctly.

{Definition of Terms}

Black box testing is designed completely from the specification of a program.

Writing a black box test involves devising inputs that cause the maximum possible behaviors described in the specification to be demonstrated. For example, the specification of the first version of the `GuessApplet` in Chapter 7 requires that the program respond to every number entered into a `JTextField` by the user by displaying a message indicating whether the number was less than, equal to, or greater than a number built into the program (17). Tests for this program would clearly be, at a minimum, a number less than 17, a number greater than 17, and 17 itself. These tests would make sure the program printed the correct message in each case.

8.3.1 An Example

Consider the `Calculator` applet from Chapter 6. Let's come up with a set of black box tests purely from the following specification of what it is supposed to do.

Specification: The calculator will display two numbers; one is the number being entered, and the other is the sum of all numbers entered so far. It will have 10 buttons, labeled 0 through 9 for inputting digits, and another button labeled + for adding the number entered so far to the sum. Initially the number being entered and the sum are both 0. When a number is added to the sum, the number being entered becomes 0 until more digit buttons are pressed. The layout and colors of the components of the display are not important (to keep this simple) as long as they are readable.

Here's a list of some black box tests that will likely discover many potential errors:

1. Start the applet and make sure that everything is readable, that the two numbers are initially 0, and that the + and 10 digit keys exist and are labeled properly.

2. Push the + button. The sum should not change.

3. Push each digit button once. The input number display should show a new number that reflects that particular digit being entered (e.g., if you push the digit buttons 5, 1, 0, 2, 9, 8, 4, 7, 3, and 6, then the input display should show 5, 51, 510, 5102, 51029, 510298, 5102984, 51029847 and 510298473). Note that there are *lots* of possible orders in which the

buttons can be pushed, so this only tests that each button works (and one particular order).

4. Push the + button. The sum should become equal to the input number, and the input number should become 0.

5. Input another number (different from the one entered above). Make sure that the input display is correct.

6. Push the + button. The sum display should show the sum of the input number and the old sum, and the input number should become 0.

7. Push the + button again. Nothing should change.

You can continue inputting more numbers and adding them to the sum, checking that the input display is always correct and the sum is computed correctly, too. The more you do, the more confidence you will have that the calculator is working. But you'll never prove that the program was correct. There may be some subtle error in the code that only shows itself when a certain sequence of digit buttons is pushed or when certain values are added. It may be unlikely, but unless you actually see the code, you will never know.

Written Exercise

1. Write black box tests for any of the sample programs in the previous chapters.

8.4 WHITE BOX VERSUS BLACK BOX TESTING

The two approaches to testing programs complement each other. Each has strengths and weaknesses, and there are things that can be done with one and not the other.

White box testing may give you confidence that every part of the code is working, but it won't convince you that the program does everything it is supposed to. For example, suppose code to compute a square root is being tested, but suppose the programmer did not insert a special check for trying to take the square root of a negative number. All the code that is there to compute the square root of positive numbers may be perfect, but the program isn't correct if it is supposed to do something with negative numbers. In general, white box testing will not discover that the code is missing.

White box testing can also be used to test programs as they are being written. Small pieces of a larger program can be tested independently, then assembled and tested further. As we will see, the technique of writing *and testing* parts of the program as you develop it is a very powerful and effective way of producing large, highly correct programs.

Black box testing is more likely to discover that code is missing, but often doesn't ensure that all code that was written is tested. There may be very unusual combinations of inputs that cause a specific section of code to be executed, but the black box tests do not include it. White box statement coverage testing will cause that combination to be tried.

Both white box and black box testing should be used when high confidence in the correctness of a program is desired. Of course, any white box test can be used as though it were a black box test since it tests whether the program does what is expected.

Written Exercises

1. What are two advantages of black box over white box testing?
2. What are two advantages of white box over black box testing?
3. Why are both white and black box tests important in gaining confidence in the correctness of a program?

Summary

- Testing is required to gain confidence that a program works as it is supposed to. However, testing usually cannot prove that a program is correct.
- White box testing uses the program's code to derive test inputs.
- Statement coverage is one technique that ensures that every piece of code is executed by at least one test.
- Path coverage is another technique that ensures that every possible sequence of commands through the code is executed.
- Path coverage is better than statement coverage, but the number of tests needed usually makes it difficult to use.
- Incremental testing is used during incremental development to test increasingly complete versions of the program.
- Unit tests test single units (classes) or small subsets of units independently. They usually depend, at least in part, on throwaway code (test drivers and/or stubs).
- Both incremental testing and unit testing help focus attention on yet untested but small pieces of code, thereby making it easier to find errors should the code not work correctly.
- Integration testing combines pieces of already tested code and makes sure they work together.
- Black box testing uses the specification of what the program is supposed to do to derive test inputs. The code is not used, so black box tests can be designed before or while the program is being written.

- Black box tests are good for verifying that the program does what it is supposed to do, while white box tests are good for verifying that all the code that is written works correctly.
- Good testing involves the use of both white and black box tests.

Glossary

Black Box Testing Testing using inputs that are derived from a statement of what the program is supposed to do.

Incremental Testing Testing of increasingly more complete versions of a program.

Integration Testing Testing combinations of several separately unit-tested parts of a program.

Path Coverage A white box testing technique that ensures that every unique sequence of commands through a program is executed.

Program Specification A description of what a program is supposed to do.

Statement Coverage A white box testing technique that ensures that every piece of code gets executed at least once.

Stub Partially functional code that is used by another piece of code that is being unit-tested.

Test Driver Code written specifically for the purpose of unit testing another piece of code and not usually part of the final program.

Throwaway Code Code written expressly for the purposes of testing actual parts of a program but then is discarded.

Unit Testing Testing pieces of a program (usually classes) independently using test drivers and/or stubs.

White Box Testing Testing using inputs that are derived by inspection of the code of the program.

CHAPTER 9

Simple Class Extension

OBJECTIVES

- To understand the concept of creating a new class as an extension and not a rewrite of an existing one.
- To know the subclass-superclass relationship.
- To understand what inheriting a method is.
- To understand what overriding a method is.
- To be able to extend the `JPanel` class to draw things.
- To be able to extend the `MouseAdapter` class to react to mouse events in a `JPanel`.

9.1 MAKING NEW CLASSES BY MODIFYING EXISTING ONES

As you have seen, Java includes many class definitions for all sorts of interesting and useful objects. We have created objects from these class definitions and then manipulated the objects via their methods. By doing so we have used one aspect of object-oriented programming.

Java also includes many class definitions that are, in a sense, not complete. You can define a new class by taking one of Java's existing classes and adding things to it or replacing things that are already in it. This is called **extending a class** and is another aspect of object-oriented programming.

Let's go back to the analogy of a ball object and a ball class definition written on a piece of paper. One way to create a modification of the ball class is to make a photocopy of the piece of paper the definition is written on, then write new properties and behaviors on that photocopy, and cross out old properties and behaviors, and write in replacements. The piece of paper will now have a complete class definition on it. This new class definition will probably still have some of the properties and behaviors of a ball, but it will also have some new ones and some replacements for old ones. The new class defines objects that are something like a ball but different in some ways.

Extending a class in Java works similarly, but there is a small difference. A slightly better analogy for the way that Java class extension works is to take a new piece of paper, make a note on it that is an extension of the ball class, then write the new and modified properties and behaviors on it. When a property or method defined in the new class is used, you first check the new piece of paper for the property or behavior. If it is there, then you use it.

If it isn't, you use the note that tells you that this class is an extension of the ball class, then look for the property or behavior on the piece of paper that describes the ball class.

In Java, a new class that is an extension of an existing class is defined in much the same way. If I were going to define a new class called `AutographedBall` that is an extension of the existing class `Ball`, I would begin the class definition by writing

```
class AutographedBall extends Ball {
    ...
```

Simply adding the reserved word `extends` followed by the name of the class that is being extended causes `AutographedBall` to have all the instance variables and methods of the `Ball` class. After that, any instance variables and methods that appear in this class definition either replace instance variables or methods in the `Ball` class that have the same name or are new ones with different names. For example, I might add a new `String` instance variable called `autograph`, and a new method `sign(String name)`, which when called sets `autograph` to `name`. This new class defines `Ball` objects that still have the color property `color` and the bounce behavior, but neither appears explicitly in this new class definition. If you need to see them, you have to look at the `Ball` class definition.

We've already been extending classes in the previous chapters. The animation classes extended `Animator`, which is a class that has the ability to do an animation, but doesn't contain any code that describes what will be seen on the screen other than the background. The `Animator` class is incomplete, and by extending it you give it the ability to draw specific things on the screen.

The ability to extend classes is very convenient. It permits a set of general-purpose classes to be defined and later extended to provide more specific properties or behaviors without having to rewrite a complete class. This saves time and is less prone to error. Just as there are lots of math functions that you can use without having to rewrite them, you can have lots of general-purpose classes that you can extend. Both concepts are extremely useful.

{New Concepts}

Class extension gives you a convenient way to create a modified version of an existing class without having to copy anything from the existing class.

9.2 EXTENDING THE JPANEL CLASS

A simple example of an existing Java class that you can extend is called a `JPanel`. A `JPanel` class defines an object that represents an area on the screen that you can draw on and can receive events from. It already has a set of methods that do useful things, such as `setBackground`. It also has a method called `paintComponent` that gets called by any program that uses a `JPanel` object and wants something to be drawn. The `JPanel` class is much like the various animation classes defined in earlier chapters, except that there is no animation, and instead of a draw method, a `JPanel` class has `paintComponent`. Like the `draw` method, it has a `Graphics` object reference as a parameter, and you can use `setColor`, `fillOval`, `drawRect`, and other drawing methods to create an interesting picture on the screen.

The `paintComponent` method defined in the `JPanel` class doesn't draw anything. Hence if a `JPanel` object is created and added to the window, and then its `paintComponent` method is called, nothing will be drawn. Other methods in the class can be used (e.g., to specify the size of the `JPanel` or to set its background color), but you cannot draw anything on the `JPanel` except by writing your own `paintComponent` method and putting in some drawing code.

Code 9.1 is a simple class that extends a `JPanel` and includes a `paintComponent` method that draws a red circle on the screen.

CODE 9.1

```
class SimpleJPanel extends JPanel {

    public void paintComponent(Graphics g) {
        super.paintComponent(g);   ◄─── Be sure to include this command first in any paintComponent method you write.
        // draw a red circle
        g.setColor(Color.red);
        g.fillOval(25,25,50,50);

    } // end of paintComponent method

} // end of SimpleJPanel class
```

I'll postpone explaining the first command in this method until a future chapter, but for now just make sure it is the first command in any `paintComponent` method you write. If you forget it, your program will still execute and display things, but they may or may not look right. If you get really odd results when using a `JPanel`, make sure you haven't forgotten this command!

Now let's define an applet that uses this new class definition to create a `SimpleJPanel` object (Code 9.2).

Unlike other predefined Java classes such as `JButton`, `JLabel`, or `JTextField`, the `JPanel` class does not define how big the drawing area should be. For those other classes the size is determined by the text that identifies the `JButton` or `JLabel`, or the number of characters you specify for the `JTextField`. But the `JPanel` class does not have such information, so we must tell it by calling the `setPreferredSize` method and passing a reference to a `Dimension` object to it. A `Dimension` object is a very simple object with two integer instance variables representing length and height.

CODE 9.2

```java
import java.awt.*;
import javax.swing.*;

public class JPanelApplet extends JApplet {

    public void init() {
        // set up the window
        Container window = getContentPane();
        window.setLayout(new FlowLayout(FlowLayout.LEFT));

        // create a SimpleJPanel object
        SimpleJPanel simple = new SimpleJPanel();

        // give it a size and background color
        simple.setPreferredSize(new Dimension(100,100));
        simple.setBackground(Color.blue);

        // add it to the window
        window.add(simple);
    } // end of init method

} // end of JPanelApplet class


class SimpleJPanel extends JPanel {

    public void paintComponent(Graphics g) {
        super.paintComponent(g);
        // draw a red circle
        g.setColor(Color.red);
        g.fillOval(25,25,50,50);
    } // end of paintComponent method

} // end of SimpleJPanel class
```

It is necessary to give a size to the `SimpleJPanel`.

JPanelApplet
Draws a red circle on a blue background.

Calling `setPreferredSize` is our first use of a method that does not appear explicitly in the class definition code of the `SimpleJPanel` class. This method is part of the `JPanel` class, though, so that is where it is found since the `SimpleJPanel` class extends the `JPanel` class.

The next command in the `init` method also calls the `setBackground` method from the `JPanel` class to set the background color of the drawing area to blue. Finally the `SimpleJPanel` object is added to the window, which causes it to be displayed on the screen. When displayed, the `paintComponent` method is called, and a red circle will appear against a blue background. The red circle will appear even though we never explicitly called the `SimpleJPanel` object's `paintComponent` method.

Now it may appear strange to you that we didn't have to call the `paintComponent` method to get it to draw the circle on the screen. We don't have to because when `simple` is added to `window`, a call to `paintComponent` is made *automatically*. In fact, a call to `paintComponent` can occur at other times, too. For example, if on your

computer you cover up all or part of what `SimpleJPanel` displays with another application (e.g., you get tired of looking at it and decide to play a game
for a while), and then uncover it again when the application finishes, a call to
`paintComponent` is done automatically to redraw what had been covered
by the application.

Because `paintComponent` can be called at any time, all the information
it needs to draw a correct and complete scene must be included in instance variables of the corresponding object. This should be fairly obvious, especially since
the `paintComponent` method has only a `Graphics` object as a parameter.

{New Concepts}

All information needed by the `paintComponent` method must be included in instance
variables of the corresponding object.

Written Exercise

1. Put the command `System.out.println("paintComponent
   called")` in the `paintComponent` method of the example above,
   and run the new version. Run it. Cover the applet window with another
   window, then uncover it. Cover it partially, then uncover it. Cover it partially, then cover a different part, then uncover it. Iconify the applet window, then un-iconify it again. Describe all circumstances under which
   `paintComponent` is called that you can find.

Programming Exercise

1. Modify the `JPanelApplet` to define two different extended `JPanel`
   classes, one that draws a 50 × 50 green square in a 100 × 100 region with
   a red background, and another that draws a red circle with diameter
   50 centered in a 100 × 100 region with a green background. Create two
   objects of each class, and display them in the order of green square, red
   circle, green square, red circle.

9.3 REPAINT

Let's write an applet that displays a button and a region defined by an extended
`JPanel` object. Initially the region will be black, but when the button is
pushed, a white circle will be drawn in the middle of the region. The key to
writing this is to tell the `JPanel` when to start drawing the circle. Remember,
the `paintComponent` method in the `JPanel` must be prepared to be called
at any time, and it may be called several times before the button is pushed and
several times afterward. The other key is to force the `paintComponent` to
be called so that it immediately draws the white circle when the button *is*
pushed (Code 9.3).

CODE 9.3

```java
import java.awt.*;
import java.awt.event.*;
import javax.swing.*;

public class CircApplet extends JApplet implements ActionListener {
    private CirclePanel cirPan = new CirclePanel();

    public void init() {
        // set up display
        Container window = getContentPane();
        window.setLayout(new FlowLayout(FlowLayout.LEFT));
        JButton drawButton = new JButton("draw a circle");
        window.add(drawButton);
        window.add(cirPan);
        drawButton.addActionListener(this);
    } // end of init method

    public void actionPerformed(ActionEvent event) {
        cirPan.drawCircle();
    } // end of actionPerformed method

} // end of CircApplet class
```

Call the `drawCircle` method in the extended `JPanel` to tell it to start drawing the circle.

```java
class CirclePanel extends JPanel {
    private boolean drawit = false;
```

`drawit` keeps track of whether a circle should be drawn yet.

```java
    public CirclePanel() {
        setPreferredSize(new Dimension(200,200));
        setBackground(Color.black);
    } // end of constructor
```

These commands are now part of the constructor. The `CirclePanel` is now self-contained.

```java
    public void drawCircle() {
        drawit = true;
        repaint();
    } // end of drawCircle method
```

Change `drawit` to indicate a circle should be drawn from now on, and then force a call of `paintComponent`.

```java
    public void paintComponent(Graphics g) {
        super.paintComponent(g);
        if (drawit) {
            g.setColor(Color.white);
            g.fillOval(50,50,100,100);
        }
    } // end of paintComponent method

} // end of CirclePanel class
```

Draw the circle only after `drawCircle` has been called and `drawit` set to true.

Notice first that a `CirclePanel` object has a boolean instance variable `drawit`. The `paintComponent` method checks `drawit` to see if it should draw the white circle. The variable is initially false, but is set to true once the `drawCircle` method is called. Consequently when the button is pushed, the `drawCircle` method should be called. That is exactly what is done in the `actionPerformed` method in the `CircApplet` class. As a result, no circle will be drawn by `paintComponent` until the button is pushed. Once the button is pushed, every call to `paintComponent` will draw the circle.

Of critical importance is the call to `repaint` in the `drawCircle` method. When `repaint` is called, it forces the extended `JPanel` (`CirclePanel`) to be redrawn. This involves redrawing the background and then calling `paintComponent`. This is the way to force an immediate redraw of the region. Clearly we want the circle to appear as soon as the button is pushed, so since `drawCircle` is called when the button is pushed, this is the appropriate place to put the call to `repaint`.

Note that you should *never* call `paintComponent` directly. It is legal, but you almost always want the complete region drawn again, and calling `paintComponent` will not necessarily do that. In particular, you usually want to erase whatever was drawn in the region first, before calling `paintComponent`, and that is effectively what a call to `repaint` will do.

{New Concepts}

Never call `paintComponent` directly. Call `repaint` instead, which will eventually call `paintComponent` for you.

One other point I want to make about this example is that I moved the code that sets the size and background color of the `CirclePanel` into its constructor. This makes the `CirclePanel` class more self-contained, which is usually a good idea. Now everything you want to know about a `CirclePanel` object, including its size and background color, is in the class definition and not scattered throughout the program.

Written Exercise

1. Remove the call to `repaint` from the `drawCircle` method in the `CircApplet` example and run it. Does the circle appear when you push the button? What can you do to make the circle appear?

Programming Exercises

1. Write an applet that has a two buttons and a drawing region defined by an extended `JPanel`. The buttons are labeled "circle" and "square." When the "circle" button is pushed, the extended `JPanel` should display a black circle centered in the drawing region. When the "square" button is pushed, the extended `JPanel` should display a black square centered in the drawing region. Either the circle or the square should appear at any given time, but never both.

2. Write an applet with four `JButton` objects ("up," "down," "left," "right") and a drawing region (extended `JPanel`) that initially contains a yellow circle centered against a blue background. When one of the buttons is pushed, move the circle 5 units in the indicated direction.

9.4 THE MOUSEADAPTER CLASS

A `JPanel` object reacts to mouse clicks somewhat like a `JButton` object does. When a button is clicked on, an action event occurs and the `actionPerformed` method in the associated listener object is called. A similar thing happens when you click anywhere in the area of the screen represented by a `JPanel`. The difference is that a mouse event occurs instead of an action event, and the `mouseClicked` method in an associated listener object is called.

There are other mouse events that the `JPanel` can react to, including the event of a mouse button being pushed down, the event of a mouse button being let back up (which together comprise a click), the event of the mouse moving the cursor into the `JPanel` area on the screen, and the event of the mouse moving the cursor out of the `JPanel` area on the screen. Because there are so many different events, Java defines a new type of listener, called a `MouseListener`, to deal with them all.

Just as with `ActionListener`, any object can be a `MouseListener` by adding `implements MouseListener` to the beginning of its class definition. If a class implements `MouseListener`, it *must* have five methods in it, one for each type of mouse-caused event described above. The methods are

```
public void mousePushed(MouseEvent event) { ...
public void mouseReleased(MouseEvent event) { ...
public void mouseClicked(MouseEvent event) { ...
public void mouseEntered(MouseEvent event) { ...
public void mouseExited(MouseEvent event) { ...
```

Just as the `actionPerformed` method is called when a `JButton` is clicked on, the appropriate method above is called whenever a given type of mouse event occurs with the screen area the `JPanel` is displayed in. And, just as a `JButton` must be told which object is its listener via the `addActionListener` method, the `JPanel` must be told which object is its listener via the `addMouseListener` method.

As stated above, every class that implements `MouseListener` must have code for all five methods. If any one is missing, you will get an error message from the compiler. However, often an applet will not need to react to all five events. In such a situation some of the methods, which still *must* be present, will have *no* commands in them. The developers of Java found that this was the case so often that they have provided a special class, called a `MouseAdapter`, which implements `MouseListener` and has all five

methods, with no commands in them, defined. In fact, Code 9.4 shows the
entire `MouseAdapter` class definition.

CODE 9.4

```
class MouseAdapter implements MouseListener {

    public void mousePushed(MouseEvent event) { }

    public void mouseReleased(MouseEvent event) { }

    public void mouseClicked(MouseEvent event) { }

    public void mouseEntered(MouseEvent event) { }

    public void mouseExited(MouseEvent event) { }

} // end of MouseAdapter class
```

What is really convenient about this class is that it was designed to be
extended. In fact, it isn't of much use if it isn't. For example, if you want to
define a listener object that only reacts to mouse click events, then you can
define a class that extends `MouseAdapter` and only has code for the
`mouseClicked` method (Code 9.5).

CODE 9.5

```
class MyListener extends MouseAdapter {
    // instance variables, constructor, other methods, etc.

    public void mouseClicked(MouseEvent event) {
        // code to do something when the mouse is clicked
    } // end of mouseClicked method

} // end of MyListener class
```

When an event occurs, if it is the mouse clicked event, then *your*
`mouseClicked` method will be called. If it is one of the other events, then
the (empty) method in the `MouseAdapter` class is called.

Now let's modify the `SimpleJPanel` applet to do something a little
more useful and extend the `MouseAdapter` class to handle mouse events.
The new applet will generate and display a red rectangle somewhere in the
`JPanel`. It will have a listener for the `JPanel` that will react to the event of
the user pointing the mouse somewhere in the `JPanel` and clicking the mouse
button. The code in the listener will decide whether the click was inside or outside the rectangle and display an appropriate message.

I'll approach writing this applet by starting with a simpler applet that
displays just a blue background and responds to the event of a mouse click
somewhere on that background. Then I'll add code to draw the rectangle, and
finally code to check whether the click was inside or outside the rectangle. Not

CODE 9.6

```java
import java.awt.*;
import java.awt.event.*;
import javax.swing.*;

class JPanelApplet2 extends JApplet {

    public void init() {
        Container window = getContentPane();
        window.setLayout(new FlowLayout(FlowLayout.LEFT));
        JLabel message = new JLabel("no click yet");
        window.add(message);
        DisplayJPanel display = new DisplayJPanel();
        display.setPreferredSize(new Dimension(100,100));
        display.setBackground(Color.blue);
        window.add(display);
        // create the listener and attach to the JPanel
        Listener displayListener = new Listener(message);
        display.addMouseListener(displayListener);
        } // end of init method

    } // end of JPanelApplet class
```

Inform the `DisplayJPanel` object that `displayListener` is its listener object.

```java
class DisplayJPanel extends JPanel {

    public void paintComponent(Graphics g) {
        super.paintComponent(g);
        // more to come
        } // end of paintComponent method

    } // end of DisplayJPanel class
```

```java
class Listener extends MouseAdapter {
    private JLabel theMessage;

    public Listener(JLabel msg) {
        theMessage = msg;
        } // end of constructor

    public void mouseClicked(MouseEvent event) {
        theMessage.setText("click!");
        } // end of mouseClicked method

    } // end of Listener class
```

This command is here temporarily to test whether the listener is working at all.

JPanelApplet2
Displays the message "click" when the mouse is clicked in the blue area.

only will this illustrate each concept separately, but also it is a good example of incremental development.

The first version (Code 9.6) is very similar to the `ButtonApplet` in Chapter 6. Instead of creating a `JButton` object and attaching a listener to it, we'll extend the `JPanel` class, create an object of that class, and give it a listener.

The `JPanelApplet` class creates a `JLabel` object and a `DisplayJPanel` object and adds them to the window. It also creates a `Listener` object and attaches it to the `DisplayJPanel` object. The `DisplayJPanel` class at this point doesn't do anything. We'll add code in the next version to draw a rectangle. The listener simple displays the message "click!" in the `JLabel` when the mouse is clicked. This is done just for now to make sure that the listener is reacting to the mouse click event. This first (incomplete) version of the program should be tested and fixed until it works (incremental testing).

Now let's make a small modification that will display the x and y co-ordinates of where the mouse was pointing when it was clicked. The `MouseEvent` object (the parameter to the `mouseClicked` method) has methods `getX` and `getY` that return the x and y coordinates of where on the `JPanel` the mouse was clicked. (with 0,0 being the upper left corner of the `JPanel`, not the entire applet display). Code 9.7 is a new version of the `Listener` class that implements this change.

CODE 9.7

```
class Listener extends MouseAdapter {
    private JLabel theMessage;

    public Listener(JLabel msg) {
        theMessage = msg;
        } // end of constructor

    public void mouseClicked(MouseEvent event) {
        int x = event.getX();          ←───────────
        int y = event.getY();          ←───────────     Get the x and y
        theMessage.setText(x + "," + y);  ←──           coordinates of the
        } // end of mouseClicked method                 mouse click and
                                                        display them.

    } // end of Listener class
```

Eventually the final version of this applet will use the x and y coordinates of the mouse click to test whether the mouse was pointed inside or outside the rectangle. Putting in code to display x and y and testing it to make sure it works correctly, however, is time well spent. If the last version with the test for inside/outside doesn't work, and we didn't write this intermediate version and test it, then we might have a hard time finding the error. In particular, we wouldn't know if the error was where we got the x and y coordinates, or in the if-commands that will do the tests, or even somewhere else (more incremental testing).

The next version of the `DisplayJPanel` class will draw the rectangle. The placement and size of the rectangle are not really important in this example, so I'll simply make its upper left corner have x and y coordinates 10 and 20, respectively, and have length and height of 50 and 70, respectively. Code 9.8 is the new version of the `DisplayJPanel` class:

CODE 9.8

```
class DisplayJPanel extends JPanel {
    private int xcoord = 10;
    private int ycoord = 20;          These values are chosen
    private int length = 50;          arbitrarily.
    private int height = 70;

    public void paintComponent(Graphics g) {
        super.paintComponent(g);
        g.setColor(Color.red);
        g.fillRect(xcoord, ycoord, length, height);
        } // end of paintComponent method

    } // end of DisplayJPanel class
```

In the final, complete version of the program, we'll compare the x and y coordinates of where the mouse was clicked with the information about the position and size of the rectangle, to see if the click was inside or outside. The problem is that the `DisplayJPanel` object contains the information about the rectangle but the `Listener` object has the information about where the click was. Somehow this information needs to come together so that the proper comparisons can be made.

A simple way to do this is to define a method in one of the classes and call it from the other. The call passes the needed information as arguments. Since most of the information is already in the `DisplayJPanel` class, I'll define a method there and call it from the `Listener` class. Code 9.9 is a new version of the `DisplayJPanel` class that does the comparison and sets the `JLabel` to "inside" or "outside."

The code for the `mouseClicked` method in the `Listener` class must have a call to the `check` method in the `DisplayJPanel` object, and to do so it needs a reference to the `DisplayJPanel`, which is provided to it via the constructor by the `JPanelApplet` when it creates the `Listener` (Code 9.10).

Finally the `JPanelApplet` class must be modified to pass a reference to the `DisplayJPanel` when it creates the `Listener` object. Code 9.11 is the applet in its entirety.

CODE 9.9

```
class DisplayJPanel extends JPanel {
    private int xcoord = 10;
    private int ycoord = 20;
    private int length = 50;
    private int height = 70;

    public void paintComponent(Graphics g) {
        super.paintComponent(g);
        g.setColor(Color.red);
        g.fillRect(xcoord, ycoord, length, height);
    } // end of paintComponent method

    public void check(int x, int y, JLabel msg) {
        if (x >= xcoord && x <= xcoord+length &&
                y >= ycoord && y <= ycoord+height) {
            msg.setText("inside");
        }
        else {
            msg.setText("outside");
        }
    } // end of check method

} // end of DisplayJPanel class
```

A reference to the JLabel object is sent to this method.

This method will be called from the mouseClicked method to display the correct message.

CODE 9.10

```
class Listener extends MouseAdapter {
    private JLabel theMessage;
    Private DisplayJPanel theJPanel;

    public Listener(JLabel msg, DisplayJPanel c) {
        theMessage = msg;
        theJPanel = c;
    } // end of constructor

    public void mouseClicked(MouseEvent event) {
        int x = event.getX();
        int y = event.getY();
        theJPanel.check(x, y, theMessage);
    } // end of mouseClicked method

} // end of Listener class
```

This object needs a reference to the DisplayJPanel so it can call its check method.

CODE 9.11

```java
import java.awt.*;
import java.awt.event.*;
import javax.swing.*;

class JPanelApplet3 extends JApplet {

    public void init() {
        Container window = getContentPane();
        window.setLayout(new FlowLayout(FlowLayout.LEFT));
        JLabel message = new JLabel("no click yet");
        window.add(message);
        DisplayJPanel display = new DisplayJPanel();
        display.setPreferredSize(new Dimension(100,100));
        display.setBackground(Color.yellow);
        window.add(display);

        // create the listener and attach to the JPanel
        Listener displayListener = new Listener(message,display);
        display.addMouseListener(displayListener);
        } // end of init method

    } // end of JPanelApplet3 class

class DisplayJPanel extends JPanel {
    private int xcoord = 10;
    private int ycoord = 20;
    private int length = 50;
    private int height = 70;

    public void paintComponent(Graphics g) {
        super.paintComponent(g);
        g.setColor(Color.red);
        g.fillRect(xcoord, ycoord, length, height);
        } // end of paintComponent method

    public void check(int x, int y, JLabel msg) {
        if (x >= xcoord && x <= xcoord+length &&
            y >= ycoord && y <= ycoord+height) {
            msg.setText("inside");
            }
        else {
            msg.setText("outside");
            }
        } // end of check method

    } // end of DisplayJPanel class
```

```
class Listener extends MouseAdapter {
    private JLabel theMessage;
    private DisplayJPanel theJPanel;

    public Listener(JLabel msg, DisplayJPanel c) {
        theMessage = msg;
        theJPanel = c;
        } // end of constructor

    public void mouseClicked(MouseEvent event) {
        int x = event.getX();
        int y = event.getY();
        theJPanel.check(x,y,theMessage);
        } // end of mouseClicked method

    } // end of Listener class
```

Written Exercises

1. Modify the `Listener` class above by misspelling `mouseClicked`. Compile the program. Do you get an error? Run the program. What happens?

2. Why is it easier to extend the `MouseAdapter` class than to implement the `MouseListener` interface?

Programming Exercises

1. Write an applet that extends a `JPanel` to define a region that responds to mouse clicks. When the mouse is clicked in the region the first time, save the x and y coordinates in instance variables. When it is clicked in the region a second time, draw a line from the saved coordinates of the first click to the coordinates of the second click.

2. Modify your solution to the previous problem so that the x and y coordinates are saved when the mouse button is pressed, then draw the line when the mouse button is released. The idea is that a user will position the cursor at the beginning point of a line, press the mouse button, drag the cursor to the end-point of the line while holding the button down, then release the button. The line should be drawn from the point where the mouse button was pressed to the point where the mouse button was released. Use the `mousePressed` and `mouseReleased` methods of the `MouseAdapter` class.

3. Write an applet that defines a region with a gray background. When the cursor is moved into the region, change the background to orange. When the cursor leaves, change the background to gray again. Use the `mouseEntered` and `mouseExited` methods of the `MouseAdapter` class.

9.5 BE CAREFUL WHEN EXTENDING A CLASS

Here's a word of warning. When you are extending a class and want to replace an existing method, be very careful to use the exact same name (same spelling, same capitalization) and the same number and type of parameters (you can use different parameter names, however). It is easy to make a mistake, but often very difficult to debug your code and find the mistake. Make a mental note right now to take special care to get the name right as soon as you type it in.

This is especially true when you are extending an adapter class like the `MouseAdapter`. If you don't get the name `mouseClicked` exactly right, or if you forget to put in the `MouseEvent` parameter, then instead of replacing the existing method that does nothing, you will define an entirely new method. Unfortunately when an event occurs, the existing do-nothing method will be called instead of your incorrect replacement, and your program will not react to the event. This kind of mistake can be very hard to find (I spent two days looking for just such an error once).

9.6 CLASS EXTENSION TERMINOLOGY

The term *subclass* is used to refer to the new class that is an extension of another. In the example above, the class `DisplayJPanel` is a subclass of the class `JPanel`. Likewise, the class that is being extended is called the *superclass*. `JPanel` is the superclass of `DisplayJPanel`. A class may have several subclasses, but it may have only one superclass. That is, a class can be an extension of only one class.

> **{Definition of Terms}**
> If class B extends class A, then A is the **superclass** of B and B is a **subclass** of A.

When a class is extended, the new subclass *inherits* instance variables and methods of the superclass. That means that any method in the superclass can be called for an object defined by the subclass. We called the `setBackground` method for the `SimpleJPanel` object because the `SimpleJPanel` class inherited them from the `JPanel` class. It worked just as if it had been part of the `SimpleJPanel` class, which, in effect, it was. You just can't see the code.

A method in the subclass that replaces a method in the superclass is said to *override* the superclass's method. When a method defined in both the superclass and the subclass is called, the subclass's version is called. When the `paintComponent` method is called for a `SimpleJPanel` object, the one we wrote in the `SimpleJPanel` class is called and not the empty one in the `JPanel` class.

> ```
> {Definition of Terms}
> ```
> A method in a subclass that has the same name as one in the superclass **overrides** the one in the superclass. A method in a superclass that is not overridden in a subclass is **inherited** by the subclass.

The ability to extend a class, inheriting methods that work properly already and overriding methods we want to change, is very powerful and very convenient. You probably noticed that I've already been using it throughout the text, extending `Animator` and `JApplet` to make things simpler for you to write your code. You inherited all the code needed to set up and run the Animator and overrode the `draw` method(s). Similarly you inherited the code needed to make an applet work from the `JApplet` and overrode the `init` method.

There are many more things you can do with class extension that we'll cover in Chapter 15, including writing your own superclasses. Class extension is another powerful mechanism that is part of object-oriented programming.

Summary

- New class definitions can be constructed as modifications of existing ones without having to copy all the code from the old to the new and then changing and adding new code.

- Extending a class lets you avoid copying, along with all the risk of making mistakes when you do. It also eliminates two copies of the same code, thereby making the code easier to modify should the need arise.

- An existing class (called a superclass) is extended through the use of the reserved word `extends`.

- The new class (called a subclass) inherits methods from the superclass.

- Any methods in the subclass that have the same name as those in the superclass override the ones in the superclass.

- When a method that has been overridden is called, the one in the subclass is called and not the one in the superclass.

Glossary

Extending a Class Creating a new class by replacing or adding new instance variables and methods of an existing class.

Inherit Make methods of a superclass part of a subclass.

Override Replacing a method in a superclass by one in a subclass.

Subclass A class that extends another class.

Superclass A class that has been extended.

## CHAPTER 10

Repetition

OBJECTIVES

- To understand the concept of repeating code as expressed by the Java looping commands.
- To write code that uses for-, while-, and do-while-loops.
- To use nested loops and helper methods effectively.
- To be able to test looping code efficiently and with high confidence of correctness.
- To be able to debug looping code efficiently and effectively.
- To be able to use manual execution to check the correctness of loop code.
- To understand and be able to use the primitive type char.
- To be able to manipulate characters strings via selected `String` functions.

10.1 THE FOR-COMMAND

Consider again the `Wheel` class defined in Chapter 5. Suppose instead of just 2 white lines we want to have 10. One approach would be to duplicate the code that draws the second line eight more times, each time incrementing the angle by 180°/10 instead of 180°/2 = 90°. This would give us a class definition something like that shown in Code 10.1 (using the comment instead of eight copies of the code to save space):

CODE 10.1

```
import java.awt.*;

class SpokedWheel extends Animator {
    private final int radius = 20;

    public void draw(int x, int y, Graphics g) {
        int diameter = 2*radius;
        g.setColor(Color.black);
        g.fillOval(x-radius,y-diameter, diameter,diameter);
        int xc = x;
        int yc = y-radius;
        double angle = 1.0*x/radius;
        int dx = (int)(radius*Math.cos(angle));
        int dy = (int)(radius*Math.sin(angle));
        g.setColor(Color.white);
        g.drawLine(xc-dx,yc-dy,xc+dx,yc+dy);
        // code in this box duplicated 9 times
        angle = angle + Math.toRadians(180/10);
        dx = (int)(radius*Math.cos(angle));
        dy = (int)(radius*Math.sin(angle));
        g.drawLine(xc-dx,yc-dy,xc+dx,yc+dy);
    } // end of draw method

} // end of SpokedWheel class
```

I think you'll agree that this doesn't seem to be a very good way to draw the 10 lines. What is needed is some way to execute the code in the box nine times without having to write nine copies of it in the class definition. Java provides just such a mechanism, called a *loop*.

A **loop** is a section of code that is executed repeatedly some number of times. The code below replaces the code in the box above:

```
for (int i=1; i<=9; i=i+1) {
    angle = angle + 3.1416/10;          ◄─────────  These four
    dx = (int)(radius*Math.cos(angle)); ◄─────────  commands
    dy = (int)(radius*Math.sin(angle)); ◄─────────  are the
    g.drawLine(x-dx,y-radius-dy,x+dx,y-radius+dy); ◄─ body of the
}                                                    loop.
```

The command starting with the reserved word `for` is a *for-command*. It causes the code enclosed between the braces { and } to be executed repeatedly, as though it were actually written several times. The code between the braces is called the *body* of the loop.

The for-command causes the several commands to be executed repeatedly. The repeated commands are called the **body of the loop.**

A for-command has the following structure

```
for ( expression₁ ; boolean-expression ; expression₂ ) {
    // commands executed repeatedly
    // (the body of the loop)
    }
// continue here after the body has executed
// the appropriate number of times
```

The first expression (essentially a command) is executed *once* before the body of the loop is executed at all. In the example above, the command creates an integer variable i and gives it the initial value 1. Before every execution of the body of the loop the boolean expression is evaluated. If it is true, then the body of the loop is executed. If it is not, then the body of the loop is skipped and execution continues with the code that follows the body. In the example the body of the loop will be executed if the value of i is less than or equal to 9. The third item is an expression (essentially a command) that is executed just after the body of the loop has executed. In the example it is a command that adds 1 to i.

Let's step through the execution of the code above.

i is created and given initial value 1.

$i<=9$ is evaluated and comes out true, so the body of the loop executes one time. Inside the body of the loop angle is incremented, dx and dy are computed, and a line is drawn.

$i=i+1$ is executed, causing i to be set to 2.

$i<=9$ is evaluated again and comes out true again, so the body of the loop executes once more, incrementing angle again and drawing a second line.

$i=i+1$ is executed, setting i to 3, and $i<=9$ is evaluated again.

This sequence is repeated until the time $i=i+1$ is executed and i is set to 10. Then when $i<=9$ is evaluated, it comes out false, and the body of the loop is not executed. Since there is no other code in the method, the method finishes.

To verify that the loop body executes nine times, notice that i has the value 1 when the body executed the first time, 2 the second time, 3 the third time, up to 9 the ninth time. When the value of i becomes 10, the conditional expression evaluates to false and the body does not execute again. Hence the loop body executes nine times. Just a note of terminology—each execution of the body of the loop is often called an *iteration*. There were nine iterations of the body of this loop.

> ```
> {Definition of Terms}
> ```
> One execution of the commands in the body of a loop is called an **iteration.**

This kind of loop, one that executes its body a fixed number of times no matter what is done in the body, is often called a *counting loop*. The term is derived from the fact that variable i counts the number of times the body executes. When you have a counting loop, you can always tell just by looking at the first line how many times it will execute.

> ```
> {Definition of Terms}
> ```
> A loop that executes a number of times that is not dependent on what is done in the body of the loop is called a **counting loop.**

10.1.1 A Small Scope Exception

The for-command in the previous example created a new local variable i in the first item inside the parentheses. The scope of a variable such as i that is created in a for-command does not follow the rule normally used by local variables. Instead, the scope of a such a variable is the remainder of the for-command, which includes the items between the parentheses and the entire body of the loop. Hence i cannot be used in the code that precedes the for-command or the code after it.

> ```
> {New Concepts}
> ```
> The scope of a variable created in any of the three expressions in a for-command includes the body of the loop.

If you need variable i in code following the loop, then simply create i before the for-command in a structure like this:

```
int i;  ←─────────────────────        Create i here so its scope
for (i=1; i<=9; i=i+1) {                extends past the loop code.

    // the body of the loop

    }
// i can be used here                  Just use i here, don't
                                        create it.
```

Programming Exercise

1. Modify the SpokedWheel class to draw a wheel with six lines (12 spokes).

10.2 FOR-LOOP EXAMPLES

The for-command can be used in many useful ways. I'll illustrate a couple in the following animation and applets.

CODE 10.2

```
import java.awt.*;

public class Rocks extends Animator {
    private final int diameter = 10;
    private int rocks;

    public void startup() {
        Animator.write("Enter the number of rocks");
        rocks = Animator.readInt();
    } // end of startup method

    public void draw(Graphics g) {
        g.setColor(Color.black);
        int spaceBetween = Animator.getSceneWidth()/(rocks+1);
        int xMiddle = spaceBetween;
        int yBottom = Animator.getSurface();
        for (int rock=1; rock<=rocks; rock=rock+1) {
            int left = xMiddle-diameter/2;
            int top = yBottom-diameter;
            g.fillOval(left,top,diameter,diameter);
            xMiddle = xMiddle + spaceBetween;
        }
    } // end of draw method

} // end of Rocks class
```

xMiddle is increased on each iteration.

10.2.1 Rocks

> **Rocks**
> Displays evenly spaced rocks along the surface. The number of rocks is provided by the user.

The animation in Code 10.2 displays a number of rocks (black circles) evenly spaced across the surface of the scene. The number of rocks to display is given by the user when the animation is begun.

The variable rock is used to keep count of the number of rocks displayed so far. The variable spaceBetween is the distance between the centers of the rocks (and the edges of the scene). The x coordinate of the middle of each rock is kept track of by xMiddle, which starts out at the position of the first rock on the left and is increased on each iteration by the distance between the rocks.

10.2.2 Compound Interest

Here's an applet that can be used to compute the balance in a savings account in a bank. Most banks pay interest on savings accounts that is compounded on some regular basis, say, monthly, which simply means that the interest on the amount in the bank is computed for a month, added to that amount, and then the interest the next month is computed on the total. For example, if $1000 is in the account and the interest rate is 6 percent per year (or 0.5 percent per month), then the interest for the first month is $1000 \times 0.005 = 5, which is added to the $1000 to make the balance of the account $1005. The next month the interest is computed on the $1005, which comes to $1005 \times 0.005 = \$5.025$ and is again added to the total to make the balance $1010.025.

The applet will have two `JTextField` objects for inputting the initial balance and number of months, a button to push to compute the final balance, and a `JLabel` to display the result. Although it would be more useful to include a third field for entering the interest rate, to keep things simple I'll assume that the interest rate is 6 percent per year (Code 10.3).

CODE 10.3

```java
import java.awt.*;
import java.awt.event.*;
import javax.swing.*;

public class ComputeInterest extends JApplet
                implements ActionListener {
    private final double rate = 0.06; // yearly interest rate
    private JTextField init = new JTextField(10);
    private JTextField time = new JTextField(10);
    private JLabel result = new JLabel("no result yet");

    public void init() {
        Container window = getContentPane();
        window.setLayout(new GridLayout(3,2));
        window.add(new JLabel("Initial Balance:"));
        window.add(init);
        window.add(new JLabel("Number of Months:"));
        window.add(time);
        JButton go = new JButton("Compute");
        window.add(go);
        go.addActionListener(this);
        window.add(result);
    } // end of init method

    public void actionPerformed(ActionEvent event) {
        double balance = Double.parseDouble(init.getText());
        int months = Integer.parseInt(time.getText());
        for (int i=1; i<=months; i=i+1) {
            balance = balance + balance*(rate/12);
        }
        result.setText(balance + "");
    } // end of actionPerformed method

} // end of ComputeInterest class
```

Add the monthly interest rate times balance to balance each time.

ComputeInterest

Inputs an initial balance and number of months, displays the final balance after compounding 6 percent interest for that number of months.

The body of the loop simply computes the monthly interest and adds it to balance, which the counting loop structure causes to be executed months times. The new local variable balance is used to keep track of the amount in the account rather than use the instance variable init, which I didn't want to allow the method to modify.

10.2.3 The Op-Equals Operators

The previous example has two commands in which the value stored by some variable is increased by a particular amount. The third item in the for-command adds 1 to `i`, and the body of the for-command adds the interest to `balance`. Assignment commands like this almost always have the form

```
variable = variable + expression
```

for some `variable` and `expression` (the same `variable` appears in both places). Because this form is very common, Java provides a simpler and shorter way to accomplish the same thing. You can write

```
variable += expression
```

to mean exactly the same thing as the form above. This is purely a convenience, but is quite handy as it reduces the amount of typing and also makes it less likely to make a mistake if you accidentally type the variable name differently.

Java also has the operators $-=$, $*=$, $/=$, and $\%=$ that have meanings analogous to $+=$. For example,

```
variable /= expression
```

is equivalent to

```
variable = variable / expression
```

Using these new forms in the `actionPerformed` method above gives us the code

```
for (int i=1; i<=months; i+=1) {
    balance += balance*(0.06/12);
    }
```

{Good Ideas}
Use op-equals operators when possible to reduce typing and the chance of making mistakes.

10.2.4 Sum of Even Integers

The applet in Code 10.4 demonstrates another variation of the for-command. It is a simple modification of the `TextApplet` in Chapter 6 that expects the user to type an integer in a `JTextField` and then displays the sum of the even integers from 2 up to but not exceeding that number. For example, if the user types 9, then the applet will display the result 20 (i.e., 2 + 4 + 6 + 8).

CODE 10.4

```
import java.awt.*;
import java.awt.event.*;
import javaw.swing.*;
```

```
public class SumOfEvens extends JApplet
                    implements ActionListener {
    private JTextField maximum = new JTextField(10);
    private JLabel result = new JLabel("no result yet");

    public void init() {
        Container window = getContentPane();
        window.setLayout(new FlowLayout(FlowLayout.LEFT));
        window.add(count);
        count.addActionListener(this);
        window.add(result);
        } // end of init method

    public void actionPerformed(ActionEvent event) {
        int max = Integer.parseInt(maximum.getText());
        int sum = 0;
        for (int i=2; i<=max; i+=2) {
            sum += i;
        }
        result.setText(sum + "");
        } // end of actionPerformed method

} // end of SumOfEvens class
```

> The loop starts at 2 and increases by 2 each time.

SumOfEvens
Displays the sum of the even integers from 2 through a maximum entered by the user.

Notice that the initial value for i was 2 (the first positive even integer); and each time the body of the loop finished, i was incremented by 2. Hence i had values 2, 4, 6, 8, ... on successive iterations. Notice also that if the value 9 were input by the user, the body would be executed for i = 8, since i is less than or equal to 9, but not for i=10, since 10 is not less than or equal to 9.

Written Exercises

1. How many times will the body of the loop defined by the following for-commands execute?

   a. `for (i=0; i<10; i+=1) {...`

   b. `for (j=1; j<20; j+=3) {...`

   c. `for (k=10; k>0; k-=1) {...`

   d. `for (m=5; m<0; m+=1) {...`

   e. `for (n=1; n<10; n+=0) {...`

2. What different values will be assigned to i during the execution of the following command?

```
for (i=1; i<1024; i*=2)
```

3. Run the Rock animation and enter a negative number for the number of rocks when prompted. How many rocks are drawn? Enter 0. How many rocks are drawn?

Programming Exercises

1. Write a cart animation class that depicts the speed of the cart by drawing as many vertical red lines as the speed. The first vertical line is centered in the box and 5 units high. Successive ones are 3 units apart, to the left or right (depending on the direction of the cart). For example, if the speed is 4 to the right, then the box part of the cart should look like the following:

2. Write an applet that displays a JTextField and a JLabel. When the user enters a positive integer into the JTextfield, the applet changes the JLabel to be the value resulting from taking 2 to the power of the integer entered. For example, if the user enters 10, the JLabel should be changed to display $2^{10} = 1024$. Use a loop to compute the result. If the user enters a negative number, the JLabel should display "invalid input, try again."

3. Write an animation that displays a red 40×40 box that moves under the control of the left/right buttons, and put 10 evenly spaced black posts (10 wide by 30 high) between the left edge of the scene and the left edge of the box. Keep redrawing the posts evenly spaced between the edge and the box even when the box moves to the left or right. Hence as the box moves to the left, the posts should get closer together; as it moves to the right, they should get farther apart.

4. Write an applet that displays a JTextField and a JLabel. When the user enters a positive integer into the JTextField, display a string in the JLabel that consists of that many copies of the letter z. For example, if the user enters 7, then you should display zzzzzzz. If the user enters a negative number or zero, display nothing.

10.3 USING FOR-LOOPS TO MANIPULATE STRINGS

So far all we've done with strings is to create them, display them, convert numbers to strings and strings to numbers, and create new strings by concatenating other strings together. In this section I will show you some examples of how to use for-loops to perform some interesting and useful manipulations of strings.

10.3.1 The char Type

Before doing so, we'll need to know about a new primitive type, the `char`. A `char` variable stores a single character. A `char` literal consists of a single character enclosed in *single* quote marks. For example, 'B' is a `char` literal. So is '"', which is the double-quote character. A `char` literal that is a single quote is '\'' (a backslash and a single quote, inside single quotes). Here's an example of the creation of a char variable `letter` with initial value '%':

```
char letter = '%';
```

Note that the literals 's' and "s" are different. The first is a `char` literal, the second a `String` literal that happens to be just a single character. So are '7' and 7 different. The first is a `char` literal, the second an `int` literal. *Do not* use a `char` literal where you need a `String` or `int` literal.

Note also that a `char` is a primitive type, like `int` and `double`, whereas a `String` is an object. The `char` values are passed to methods in the same way as `int` and `double` values are—by value.

You can concatenate a `String` and a `char` to get a new `String`. For example, if `str` is a `String` variable with value "hi ther" and c is a `char` variable with value 'e', then the expression

```
str + c
```

evaluates to the `String` "hi there".

10.3.2 String Functions

We'll also need to know about the `String` functions shown in Table 10.1.

Table 10.1

Name	Return Type	Argument Type	Description
length	int	None	Returns the number of characters in the String
charAt	char	int	Returns the character at the specified position
indexOf	int	char	Returns the index of the first occurrence of the specified character

These functions are simply methods that return values and are defined for all `String` objects. To call one, you just use the standard method calling approach that you would for any method defined for an object. For example, if `str` is a variable that is a reference to a `String` object, then `str.length()` is a call of the `length` method that will operate in the context of the `String` object referred to by `str`. Hence it will return the length of the `String` object referred to by `str`.

The `charAt` and `indexOf` functions use the notion of position of characters in the `String`. They assume that the first character is in position 0, not 1. Hence if a `String` consists of the four characters "abcd", then the `charAt` position 0 is 'a', the `charAt` position 3 is 'd', and there is no `charAt` position 4 or higher. You will get a run-time error if you ask for a character at any position except 0, 1, 2, or 3. The `indexOf` the character 'c' is 2. The `indexOf` the character 'f' is -1, which is how the `indexOf` function tells you that the character 'f' is not in the `String`.

This is but a small sample of the functions defined for `String` objects. See the Java documentation Web pages (in the java.lang section) for a complete list.

10.3.3 Counting Spaces

The first example, Code 10.5, is an applet that inputs a sentence from the user and counts the number of spaces in the text. It uses the length function to determine the length of the `String` retrieved from the `JTextField`, and then it uses that length to determine the number of iterations of a for-loop that will inspect each character in the `String`. The `charAt` function is used to get the character stored at each position in the `String` (Code 10.5).

CODE 10.5

```
import java.awt.*;
import java.awt.event.*;
import javax.swing.*;

public class CountSpaces extends JApplet
                   implements ActionListener {
    private JTextField input = new JTextField(100);
    private JLabel output = new JLabel("enter a sentence");

    public void init() {
        // set up display
        Container window = getContentPane();
        window.setLayout(new FlowLayout(FlowLayout.LEFT));
        window.add(input);
        window.add(output);
        input.addActionListener(this);
    } // end of init method
```

```
public void actionPerformed(ActionEvent event) {
    // get the sentence and initialize a counter to 0
    String message = input.getText();
    int count = 0;

    // look at each character in the sentence, and
    // increment the counter if it is a space
    for (int pos=0; pos<message.length(); pos+=1) {
        if (message.charAt(pos) == ' ') {
            count += 1;
        }
    }

    // output the resulting count and clear the input
    output.setText(count +" spaces, enter another sentence");
    input.setText("");
} // end of actionPerformed method

} // end of CountSpaces class
```

pos will vary over the legal positions of characters in the String.

CountSpaces
Displays the number of spaces in text entered by the user.

10.3.4 Extract Part of a String

This example is similar to the previous one, except instead of counting spaces it looks for a left parenthesis and a right parenthesis in the String. If there are both and the left one comes before the right one, then it extracts and displays the part of the String between, but not including, the parentheses (Code 10.6).

Once we retrieve the positions of the first left parenthesis and the first right parenthesis, we check to make sure that both parentheses are present

CODE 10.6

```
import java.awt.*;
import java.awt.event.*;
import java.swing.*;

public class Extract extends JApplet
                implements ActionListener {
    private JTextField input = new JTextField(100);
    private JLabel output = new JLabel("enter a sentence");

    public void init() {
        // set up display
        Container window = getContentPane();
        window.setLayout(new FlowLayout(FlowLayout.LEFT));
        window.add(input);
        window.add(output);
        input.addActionListener(this);
    } // end of init method
```

```
public void actionPerformed(ActionEvent event) {
    // get the message and find parens
    String message = input.getText();
    int left = message.indexOf('(');
    int right = message.indexOf(')');
    // the parens exist and are in the right order
    if (left != -1 && right != -1 && left < right) {
        // copy characters from String
        // one by one and display
        String inside = "";
        for (int pos=left+1; pos<=right-1; pos+=1) {
            inside = inside + message.charAt(pos);
            }
        output.setText("<"+inside+">, enter another string");
        }
    // otherwise display an error message
    else {
        output.setText("bad input, enter another string");
        }
    input.setText("");
    } // end of actionPerformed method

} // end of Extract class
```

> indexOf returns −1 if the indicated character is not in the String.

> pos varies from the position of the first character to the position of the last.

(indexOf didn't return −1 for both positions), and that the left parenthesis comes before the right one (left < right). If everything is ok, then the loop begins at the position of the first character after the left parenthesis and ends at the position of the last character before the right parenthesis, extracting each character and adding it to the end of the growing String inside.

Extract
Displays the characters between left and right parentheses in text entered by the user.

10.4 THE WHILE-LOOP

You will often encounter situations where a segment of code must be executed several times (and hence a loop is needed), but the number of times it will execute is not a constant value, nor does it depend on some variable whose value was determined prior to the loop code. Instead, the number of times the loop should execute depends on what happens inside the body of the loop. In other words, something happens inside the body of the loop that finally dictates that the loop should no longer be repeated. What causes this cannot be predicted in advance and only can be discovered during one of the iterations.

Here's a simple example. Suppose you want to determine the minimum number of terms (fractions) of the sum

$$\frac{1}{2} + \frac{1}{3} + \frac{1}{4} + \frac{1}{5} + \cdots$$

that will result in a total that is greater than some positive number (say, 2.0). For example, adding the fractions up to $\frac{1}{12}$ gives a sum that is approximately 1.977, while adding the fractions up to $\frac{1}{13}$ gives a sum that is approximately 2.054. Hence the minimum number of terms needed to produce a sum that is greater than 2.0 is 13.

There is no way to figure this out except to start adding up terms, adding each one as you go, until the sum finally exceeds 2. A loop that does this will have to be accumulating the sum and testing it as it goes.

Java provides a command that makes writing such a loop straightforward. It is called the *while-command,* and here is a piece of code that uses it. Given a variable max whose value you want the sum to just exceed, this code will set the variable terms to the minimum number of fractions that must be added.

```
double sum = 0;
int terms = 0;
int denominator = 2;
while (sum <= max) {
    sum += 1.0/denominator;
    terms += 1;
    denominator += 1;
    }
```

The operation of the while-command is very simple. The item between the parentheses is a boolean expression. It is evaluated before the body of the loop is executed. If it is true, the body is executed and then the boolean expression reevaluated. If it is false, the body is skipped and execution continues with the first command after the body. The while-command can be thought of as a special case of a for-command that has no first or third items.

{Definition of Terms}

A *while-command* executes the body of the loop as long as the boolean expression remains true.

This example code works as follows. First consider the variable sum. It is initially given the value 0 before the while-command; then in each iteration of the loop it gets the next fraction added to it. As long as sum is less than or equal to max, the summation continues by repeated executions of the body of the loop. As soon as sum becomes greater than max, the boolean expression will evaluate to false and the while-command will complete.

The variable denominator is given the value 2 initially, then used to compute the next fraction to be added to sum on each iteration of the loop. It is incremented by 1 after it is used in preparation for the next iteration.

The variable terms is used to count the number of terms (fractions) added to sum. It is given the value 0 initially and incremented by 1 on each iteration. When the while-command completes, it will have counted the number of iterations of the loop, which will be equal to the number of fractions summed to get the first value greater than max.

10.5 AN APPROACH TO WRITING LOOPS

There are four components of every loop that must work properly together for the loop to execute correctly:

1. Code that gives initial values to variables.
2. A boolean expression that tests whether the body should be executed.
3. The code in the body of the loop.
4. Code that changes one or more variables in such a way that the loop eventually finishes (in a while-command this is part of the body of the loop).

These four components do not have to be written in the order they are listed above, although many beginning students attempt to write them that way. A better approach is to do a little planning and to work on all four somewhat simultaneously. I'll demonstrate what I mean by this with an example.

Suppose I want to write a segment of code that starts with an arbitrary value in the integer variable n and counts the number of times it must be divided by 2 in order to become 0. For example, if the initial value of n is 11, then it can be divided by 2 once to get 5 (remember—integer division), then again to get 2, then again to get 1, then again to get 0, so the answer is 4. Let's assume that the value initially in n will no longer be needed.

I'll start by recognizing that I'll need a loop, and not a counting loop since I don't know in advance how many iterations there will be. Hence I'll write the following to get started:

```
leave space for some code here to initialize things
while (              ) {
      leave space here for the body of the loop
   }
```

From the statement of the problem I know that I will be repeatedly dividing n by 2. This clearly is something that must be done in the body of the loop, so I'll add a command to do it:

```
leave space for some code here to initialize things
while (            ) {
    n /= 2;                    // i.e., n = n / 2;
   }
```

I also know that the loop must stop when n becomes 0, so I'll need a boolean expression that is true when n is not 0 in order to keep repeating the body.

```
leave space for some code here to initialize things
while (n != 0) {
    n /= 2;
    }
```

I now have code that will repeatedly divide n by 2 until it becomes 0. The problem statement was to count the number of times the division was done, so I'll need a new variable that is incremented by 1 on each iteration, so I add a command to do that to the body:

```
leave space for some code here to initialize things
while (n != 0) {
    n /= 2;
    count += 1:
    }
```

And finally I better not forget to create the variable count and give it initial value 0. The final result is

```
int count = 0;
while (n != 0) {
    n /= 2;
    count += 1;
    }
```

Now let's check to make sure I have the four components of a good loop.

1. Are all the variables given appropriate initial values? Yes, count is initialized properly, and I assume that n was set prior to this segment of code.

2. Does the boolean expression stop the loop at the appropriate time? Yes, the boolean expression becomes false when n becomes 0.

3. Does the body of the loop do the right thing? Yes, n is divided by 2 and count is incremented by 1.

4. Is there a command that changes some variable that makes the boolean expression become false eventually? Yes, dividing n by 2 over and over (using integer division) will eventually make it become 0.

{Good Ideas}

Make sure all four components of a good loop are present.

The key to this process lies in recognizing that the four parts of the loop *do not* have to be written starting with the first line of code and ending with the last. Even experienced programmers can't do it in that order except for the simplest loops, so you shouldn't expect to be able to either. There also is no particular reason to write the code in exactly the order I did. Write it in whatever order makes sense to you.

10.6 WHILE-LOOP EXAMPLES

Here are a few examples of the use of while-loops. The best way to learn to write programs with loops is to understand the examples and then get lots of practice by doing lots of exercises.

10.6.1 Find Second Period

Code 10.7 is an applet that displays the position of the second period in text entered by the user. It displays an error message if there aren't at least two periods in the text. The loop is controlled by two variables, pos and count. The variable pos is used to select the next character to inspect. The variable count is used to keep track of the number of periods found so far. As long as count is less than 2, the loop will continue, except that the loop must terminate if it runs out of text to look at before it finds the second period. Hence the while-command also checks that pos is less than the length of the string.

A simple modification of this program will make it find the position of any period, the third, fourth, fifth, etc. Just change the 2 in the boolean expression to 3, 4, 5, etc. Similarly a different character can be searched for by changing the '.' in the if-command.

In fact, making these both be named constants rather than embedding them in the middle of the method would be a good programming practice. As a general rule, you should consider making any literal that is tested for in an if-command or loop a named constant, just in case you might want to change it later. Giving it a name also helps give a meaning to the value, which makes your program easier to read.

However, do not make every literal a named constant. For example, incrementing count or pos by 1 is not likely ever to be changed. Replacing those 1s by a named constant (e.g., one) is not a good idea.

{Good Ideas}
Use named constants instead of literals for values that are tested for in if-commands or loops.

10.6.2 Pattern Matching

In this example applet (Code 10.8) the user will enter two strings into two JTextField objects. It is likely, but not necessary, that the first is longer than the second. The user also will enter a position (an integer) into a third JTextField. Once all three things have been entered, the program will display whether the second string matches the first string, starting at the given

CODE 10.7

```java
import java.awt.*;
import java.awt.event.*;
import java.swing.*;

public class Find2ndPeriod extends JApplet
                    implements ActionListener {
    private JTextField input = new JTextField(100);
    private JLabel output = new JLabel("enter a string");

    public void init() {
        // set up display
        Container window = getContentPane();
        window.setLayout(new FlowLayout(FlowLayout.LEFT));
        window.add(input);
        window.add(output);
        input.addActionListener(this);
        } // end of init method

    public void actionPerformed(ActionEvent event) {
        // get the message
        String message = input.getText();

        // initialize
        int pos = 0;
        int count = 0;

        // loop until second period found or end of String
        while (pos < message.length() && count < 2) {
            if (message.charAt(pos) == '.') {
                count += 1;
                }
            pos += 1;
            }
        // if two periods found show position, else display error
        if (count == 2) {
            output.setText(
                "the second period is at position "+(pos-1));
            }
        else {
            output.setText("there aren't two periods");
            }
        input.setText("");
        } // end of actionPerformed method

    } // end of Find2ndPeriod class
```

> Make 2 and '.' named constants to make the code easier to modify if needed someday.

Find2ndPeriod
Displays the position of the
second period in text
entered by the user.

CODE 10.8

```
import java.awt.*;
import java.awt.event.*;
import javax.swing.*;

public class Patternmatch extends JApplet
                          implements ActionListener {
    private JTextField inputField = new JTextField(100);
    private JTextField patternField = new JTextField(20);
    private JTextField positionField = new JTextField(5);
    private JLabel output = new JLabel("enter data");
    private boolean gotInput = false;
    private boolean gotPattern = false;
    private boolean gotPosition = false;

    public void init() {
        // set up display
        Container window = getContentPane();
        window.setLayout(new FlowLayout(FlowLayout.LEFT));
        window.add(inputField);
        window.add(patternField);
        window.add(positionField);
        window.add(output);

        // attach listeners
        inputField.addActionListener(this);
        patternField.addActionListener(this);
        positionField.addActionListener(this);
    } // end of init method

    public void actionPerformed(ActionEvent event) {
        // record which input was supplied
        if (event.getSource() == inputField) {
            gotInput = true;
            }
        else if (event.getSource() == patternField) {
            gotPattern = true;
            }
        else {
            gotPosition = true;
            }
        // if all three inputs available, try matching
        if (gotInput && gotPattern && gotPosition) {
            // get inputs
            String input = inputField.getText();
            String ptrn = patternField.getText();
            int iPos = Integer.parseInt(positionField.getText());

            // get lengths and set initial pattern position
            int iLength = input.length();
            int pLength = ptrn.length();
            int pPos = 0;
```

```
                // check character pairs until done
                while (pPos < pLength &&
                       iPos >= 0 &&
                       iPos < iLength &&
                       input.charAt(iPos) == ptrn.charAt(pPos)) {
                    iPos += 1;
                    pPos += 1;
                }
                // if loop terminated because we got to the end of
                // the pattern, display success, otherwise failure
                if (pPos == pLength) {
                    output.setText("match");
                }
                else {
                    output.setText("no match");
                }
            }
        // if not all three inputs yet, request more
        else {
            output.setText("enter remaining data");
        }
    } // end of actionPerformed method
```

```
} // end of PatternMatch class
```

Note the multiple-line boolean expression and how it is indented.

PatternMatch
Inputs two strings and a position, then displays whether the second string matches the characters in the first string starting at the indicated position.

position for as many characters as there are in the second string. For example, if the user enters "Rufus T. Firefly" as the first string and "ire" as the second, and gives 10 as the position, then the program will display that there is a match (the "ire" in the first string starts at position 10). If any other position is input, the program will display that there is no match. The program should be able to handle any possible position value the user can enter, even if it is negative or larger than the largest position in the string (in either case there will be no match).

The program uses three boolean instance variables to keep track of which inputs have been entered. Only when all three have been entered will it see if there is a match. Until all three have been input, it displays a message asking the user to enter the missing ones.

The loop's task is to check corresponding characters in each string one by one. The variables iPos and pPos keep track of the positions of the next pair of characters to compare, iPos in the input (first string), pPos in the pattern (second string). Initially pPos is the position given by the user and iPos is 0. These variables are incremented each time through the loop so that the next pair of characters is compared on the next iteration.

The conditions under which the loop should continue executing are:

- The pattern position is a valid position (not too large).
- The input position is a valid position (neither negative nor too large).
- The characters at the current pattern and input positions match.

As soon as any of these conditions becomes false, the loop will terminate. In only one case does the loop terminate because there was a complete match, however, and that is when the pattern position becomes too large. In this case every corresponding character will have matched, and all pattern characters will have been checked. Hence by checking to see if that is the reason for the loop terminating, the if-command after the loop can display correctly whether the pattern matched the input.

10.7 TESTING AND DEBUGGING LOOPS

It is easy to write code with subtle errors that will result in loops that do not work correctly. Even experienced programmers make such mistakes, and good programmers know that they must test code with loops very thoroughly to gain confidence in its correctness.

Using statement coverage tests for-loops usually isn't sufficient to gain much confidence. Simply using a test that causes the body of the loop to execute (at least) once won't discover subtle errors since many loops will work for many, if not most, values of the applicable variables. The subtlest errors often occur in only a few situations.

Unfortunately path coverage is generally impossible to achieve. The number of paths grows quickly as the number of iterations of the loop grows, and even figuring out what the paths are for complex loops with embedded if-commands can be daunting.

But testing is still important, and there are techniques that will minimize the effort but maximize the confidence you have in your code. Shortly I'll demonstrate such testing techniques for the example programs in the previous sections. But let's first discuss a couple of different kinds of problems that can arise in incorrectly written loops.

10.7.1 Infinite Loops and Off-by-One Errors

A common problem with writing loop code is that it is not hard to make a mistake that keeps the loop from ever terminating. For example, when writing a while-command you must make sure that one or more variables are changed in the body in such a way that eventually the boolean expression becomes false. A common error is to forget this, or somehow to make a mistake in the command that changes a variable that is tested, or to have an error in the boolean expression itself. If the boolean expression never becomes false, the body of the loop will be executed over and over, and the while-command will never finish. This is called an *infinite loop,* and it is something you probably don't want to have happen. You can also get an infinite loop when you write an incorrect for-command, but it is less likely.

{Definition of Terms}

An **infinite loop** occurs when nothing happens in the code that executes to cause the loop to stop.

If an infinite loop does occur when you test your program, you will most likely notice that the program is taking a very long time to do something such as to display a result, to finish, or to respond to some new input. After you wait a while, it will start to dawn on you that you probably have an infinite loop. You will have to stop your program manually (every development system has a way of doing this) and then debug your program.

Another common loop error occurs when the loop executes once too many times or once two few times. This kind of error is often called an *off-by-one* error. It is caused by many things. A common error is created by not giving the proper initial value to a variable. An even more common error occurs when the boolean expression that is tested to see if the loop should iterate again used < where it should have used <= (or > instead of >=). Such errors are not always easy to find.

{Definition of Terms}

Off-by-one errors, which cause a loop to execute one time too few or too many, are common.

10.7.2 Examples of Testing Loops

Consider the `CountSpaces` program in the previous section. The only input we can give it is text, so what text should we try? Since the program simply counts spaces, some obvious inputs are sentences with spaces in it. Some sentences should have just a few spaces, others a lot. If we get the right answers, we will have reasonable confidence that it can at least count correctly. We should also try a sentence with two or more consecutive spaces.

Important inputs that should always be considered are those with no spaces, just one space, a space in the first position, and a space in the last position. Other important inputs consist of an empty sentence (no characters at all), exactly one space character (and nothing else), and several spaces (and nothing else). These types of inputs are called *boundary test cases* because the input checks the code at its boundaries.

There is no exact definition of what comprises a boundary case. Included, however, are cases that cause a loop to do no iterations (i.e., the boolean expression is false the first time) and one iteration. Cases that test that the loop does the right thing on the first iteration (i.e., that the initial values of the relevant variables are set correctly), and that force every termination possibility to be checked are also important. If the body of the loop has if-commands, then simple statement coverage insists that each true- and false-part be checked; but it is also useful to include cases that do only one part every time through the loop (such as the no space and all spaces example above). Testing boundary cases is very useful in finding off-by-one errors and in forcing unexpected infinite loops.

Every experienced programmer will tell you that testing with as many boundary cases as you can is critical in gaining confidence in the correctness of your code. When you are still learning, it may seem hard enough to get a loop

Table 10.2

Input	Pattern	Position	Description
abcdefg	*nothing*	4	Test zero iterations of loop
abcdefg	c	1	Test one iteration of loop, no match
abcdefg	c	2	Test one iteration of loop, match
abcdefg	f	0	Test a match in first position, no match
abcdefg	a	0	Test a match in first position, match
abcdefg	x	6	Test a match in last position, no match
abcdefg	g	6	Test a match in last position, match
abcdefg	abd	0	Test a match that fails in the last pattern character
abcdefg	abcdefg	0	Test a match of the whole input
a	a	0	Test a match of the whole input, but only one character
abc	abcd	0	Test a match of a pattern longer than the input
abcdefg	fgh	5	Test a match of a pattern that goes past the end of the input

to do the right thing in *any* case; but as you gain experience, you'll find that subtle errors still creep in that are usually caught only by testing boundary cases.

{Definition of Terms}

Boundary test cases are test inputs that, among other things, force loops to execute zero and one iteration, that ensure that the first and last iterations do the right things, and that ensure all possible termination conditions are encountered.

Now consider the `PatternMatch` program. Good boundary case tests are shown in Table 10.2.

Before you try it, what is the output of the program in the first case when there is no pattern?

10.7.3 Debugging by Manual Execution

Once testing has turned up a problem, you'll have to find the error. Often the particular test will suggest an obvious problem (e.g., an off-by-one error), and finding and fixing it may be fairly easy. Unfortunately this is not always the case, and you'll have to resort to putting in some effort to find out what's wrong.

It can be extremely useful to trace through the execution of a loop by hand to see what it is doing. This is called **manual execution.** Very often you can find subtle errors that are difficult to detect just by staring at the code. Let's manually execute the code for the loop at the beginning of Section 10.3 that determines the minimum number of terms (fractions) of the sum

$$\frac{1}{2} + \frac{1}{3} + \frac{1}{4} + \frac{1}{5} + \cdots$$

that will result in a total that is greater than some positive number.

The key to manual execution is to carefully keep track of the value of each variable in the code being traced. An easy way to do this is to picture the variables as we did in previous chapters by drawing a box for each, labeling the box with the variable's name, and writing the current value inside. Whenever a new value is assigned to a variable, erase or cross out the old and write in the new.

First I'll manually execute the code for the case that the variable max has the value 0.0. In this case the final value for terms should be 1 since summing zero terms does *not* result in a value greater than max but summing one term (0.5) *does*. Here is a picture of the variables just after the first three commands have been executed (just prior to starting the while-command).

max

| 0.0 |

denominator

| 2 |

sum

| 0.0 |

terms

| 0 |

Next the boolean expression is evaluated. Since 0 (sum) is less than or equal to 0 (max), the expression evaluates to true and the body of the loop will be executed. The values of the variables after executing all three commands in the body once are now

max

| 0.0 |

denominator

| 3 |

sum

| 0.5 |

terms

| 1 |

The boolean expression is evaluated again, using the new value for sum. This time 0.5 (sum) is not less than or equal to 0.0 (max), so the expression evaluates to false. The while-command is now complete, and execution will continue with the code that follows the body. The value of terms at this point is 1, which is correct.

Now let's try manually executing the code again, this time with 1.0 being the value of max. The correct final value for terms is 3 since $\frac{1}{2} + \frac{1}{3} = 0.8333 \cdots$ (less than 1.0) and $\frac{1}{2} + \frac{1}{3} + \frac{1}{4} = 1.08333 \cdots$ (greater than 1.0). The two pictures above will still capture the values before the while-command starts and after one iteration of the loop; but this time after one iteration 0.5 (sum) is less than or equal to 1.0 (max), so the body will be executed again. The values of the variables after a second iteration are

max	denominator
1.0	4

sum	terms
0.8333 · · ·	2

The boolean expression is evaluated again, using the new value for sum. This time 0.8333 · · · (sum) is still less than or equal to 1.0 (max), so the expression evaluates to true and the body will be executed again. The values of the variables after a third iteration are

max	denominator
1.0	5

sum	terms
1.08333 · · ·	3

The boolean expression is evaluated again, using the new value for sum. This time 1.0833 · · · (sum) is not less than or equal to 1.0 (max), and the while-command is complete. The final value for terms, 3, is correct.

{Good Ideas}

Manually executing a loop (or any code) is a good way to find subtle and not-so-subtle errors or to gain confidence that it is correct. Always manually execute a loop until it terminates.

10.7.4 Debugging by Tracing Execution

Another way to debug a loop (or any other code) that isn't working correctly is to display the values of relevant variables during the execution of the code, via either the System.out.println command or the debugger supplied with the development environment you are using. Usually you will discover that one or more variables are not changing the way you expect them to, and that will lead you to focus on the problem.

The only difficulty with this method is that sometimes your loop will execute many, many times before the problem begins to show up. This either results in a lot of debugging output, if you use the System.out.println command, or will take you a long time to get there with a debugger. If this is the case, try to use test inputs that limit the number of iterations of the loop.

Written Exercises

1. How does your development environment stop a program that is in an infinite loop? Write a tiny program that consists only of an infinite loop, and try it.

2. Use manual execution to find the error in the following code. It is supposed to set the variable `sum` to the sum of the first n even integers (that is, $2 + 4 + 6 + \cdots + 2*n$).

```
int sum = 0;
for (int i=1; i<=2*n; i+=1) {
    if (i/2 == 0) {
        sum += i;
    }
}
```

3. Use manual execution to find the error in the following code. It is supposed to print $n/2$, then $n/4$, then $n/8$, etc., all the way down to, and including, 0. For example, if n is 25, it should print 12, 6, 3, 1, 0.

```
while (n >= 0) {
    System.out.println(n/2);
    n /= 2;
}
```

4. Use `System.out.println` or your development environment's debugger to find the errors in the following applet. It is supposed to display the sum $x + x^2/2 + x^3/3 + x^4/4 + \cdots$ as long as successive terms (that is, x^n/n) are greater than 0.01. It computes this sum for $x = 0.5$.

```
import java.awt.*;
import java.swing.*;

public class BadLoop extends JApplet {

    public void init() {
        Container window = getContentPane();
        double x = 0.5;
        int n = 2;
        double sum = 0.0;
        double xToTheNth = x;
        double term = xToTheNth / n;
        while (term > 0.01) {
            n += 1;
            xToTheNth += x;
            sum += term;
        }
        JLabel result = new JLabel("the sum is "+ sum);
        window.add(result);
    } // end of init method

} // end of BadLoop class
```

5. Devise a set of test inputs for the `Find2ndPeriod` program. For each one, describe what it is testing. Be sure to test boundary cases.

6. Devise a set of test inputs for each of the programming exercises below, before you write code for them. For each one describe what it is testing. Then write the code and see if you can come up with more test cases, especially boundary cases.

Programming Exercises

1. Write an applet that displays a `JTextField` and a `JLabel`. When the user enters an integer into the `TextField`, find the largest nonnegative (that is, $>=0$) integer such that 2 to the power of that integer is less than or equal to the number entered by the user; display the result as the `JLabel`. For example, if the user enters 1000, the `JLabel` should display 9 (since $2^9 = 512$ but $2^{10} = 1024$).

2. Write an applet that displays several vertical, parallel lines 200 units high. The empty space between the first and second line should be 100 units, between the second and third 50, between the third and fourth 25, etc. Display only enough lines that the distance between the last two is 1.

3. Write an applet into which the user enters an integer and your program tells the user whether that number is the sum of some number of consecutive integers starting at 1 (and if so, how many). For example, if the user enters 10, then your program should indicate that 10 is the sum of the first four consecutive integers $(1 + 2 + 3 + 4)$. If the user enters 11, your program should indicate that 11 is not the sum of some number of consecutive integers.

4. Modify the `CountSpaces` applet to display a new string that is equivalent to the input string but has every space removed. For example, if the input is "Love is patient, Love is blind." then the string "Loveispatient,Loveisblind." should be displayed.

5. Write an applet that displays the reverse of the string that is input into a `JTextField`. For example, if "Madam, I'm Adam" is input, then "madA m'I ,madaM" should be displayed.

6. Write an applet that inputs two strings from `JTextField` objects and displays the first position in which both strings have identical characters, and that character. For example, if the inputs are "A bird in the hand is worth two in the bush" and "Neither a borrower nor a lender be" then it should display 9 and ' '. If the two strings do not have matching characters at any position, display "no match".

7. Write an applet that inputs a string and finds and displays the first pair of consecutive repeated characters. For example, if the input is "Green eggs and ham" it should display "ee".

8. Write an applet that inputs a string and displays the same string but inserts in front of each character the number of times it appears consecutively,

starting at the first occurrence of each character. For example, if the input is "abccccdeeffffg" then it should display "1a1b4c1d2e4f1g".

10.8 NESTED LOOPS

A *nested loop* occurs when a for- or while-command appears in the body of another for- or while-command. These are quite common, and I'll use them a lot in the next chapter, but at this point I'll do a simple example that demonstrates how they work.

> **{Definition of Terms}**
>
> A **nested loop** is one loop in the body of another.

Let's write a simple animation that draws a box filled with the collection of ovals shown in Figure 10.1, and that moves under the control of the left/right buttons. The width and height of the box will be input from the user.

I will assume that no matter what the length and height of the box, it will always contain four rows with five ovals in each row. Now you could just write 20 calls to the fillOval method with different x and y coordinates in each call, but with nested loops there is a much easier way.

The idea is to have a counting loop that executes four times, once for each row—the **outer loop.** In the body of that loop there will be another counting loop that executes five times—the **inner loop.** The body of the inner loop will contain a single call to fillOval. The inner loop will draw five ovals, one next to the other in a row. The outer loop will cause the inner loop to do this four times, with each row under the previous one, thereby drawing a total of 20 ovals. All we need to do is to get the coordinates right on each call to fillOval, and we'll get the design shown in Figure 10.1.

The length of each oval is one-fifth of the total length of the box. Likewise the height of each oval is one-fourth of the total height of the box. Hence the call to fillOval will have length/5 and height/4 as its last two parameters. The upper left corner of each oval will change each time, of course,

FIGURE 10.1

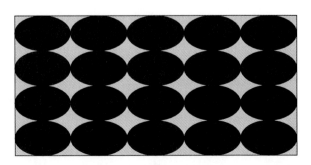

so I'll use local variables `left` and `top` to keep track. The call to `fillOval` will be

```
g.fillOval(left, top, length/5, height/4);
```

As successive ovals are drawn across a row, `left` will increase by the length of an oval, thereby getting each one drawn to the immediate right of the previous one. When each next row is started, `top` will increase by the height of an oval, thereby getting each row drawn immediately below the previous one. Hence the code will have to define `left` and `top`, give them initial values when appropriate, and increase them when necessary. Code 10.9 shows the code.

Consider the outer loop. It is a counting loop that executes its body four times. Its body consists of a command that sets the variable `left` to the

FilledBox
Displays a box that is filled exactly with four rows of five ovals. Uses a nested loop.

CODE 10.9

```java
import java.awt.*;

public class FilledBox extends Animator {
    private int length;
    private int height;

    public void startup() {
        Animator.write("Enter the length of the box");
        length = Animator.readInt();
        Animator.write("Enter the height of the box");
        height = Animator.readInt();
    } // end of startup method

    public void draw(int x, int y, Graphics g) {
        // draw the rectangle
        g.setColor(Color.gray);
        int left = x-length/2;
        int top = y-height;
        g.fillRect(left,top,length,height);

        // draw the ovals
        g.setColor(Color.black);
        for (int row=1; row<=4; row+=1) {
            left = x-length/2;
            for (int col=1; col<=5; col+=1) {
                g.fillOval(left,top,length/5,height/4);
                left += length/5;
            }
            top += height/4;
        }
    } // end of draw method

} // end of FilledBox class
```

coordinate of the left edge of the box, another (nested) counting loop, and a command that increases `top` by `height/4`. Hence each time through the body of the loop, a row of ovals will be drawn, and then `top` will be increased the appropriate amount so that the next row gets drawn at the proper place. Since the top of the first oval is the same as the top of the box, the value set in the command that creates `top` just before drawing the rectangle will be the initial value of `top`.

The inner loop is a counting loop that executes its body five times. Each time the body is executed, one oval is drawn and then `left` is increased by `length/5`, so that the next oval will be drawn just to the right of the previous one. Just before each row is drawn, however, `left` must be reset to the left edge of the rectangle. Hence just before the inner for-command there appears the command that gives `left` the proper initial value to begin drawing each row.

Let's step through the execution of this code. First the rectangle is drawn, and the color of the ovals set. Then the outer for-command begins. The first time through, the body of the outer loop `left` is given the initial value equal to the x coordinate of the left side of the rectangle. Then the inner loop begins. The first oval is drawn in the upper left corner of the box, and `left` is increased by the length of the oval just drawn. Then the second, third, fourth, and fifth ovals are drawn across the first row. The inner loop has now executed five times and is complete. The variable `top` is increased by the height of the ovals in the first row, and then second execution of the outer loop body begins. The variable `left` is again given the initial value equal to the x coordinate of the left side of the rectangle, so that the first oval drawn in the second row is at the left side. The inner loop now executes and draws five ovals across the second row, and `top` is increased again. The third and fourth executions of the body of the outer loop draw the remaining two rows of ovals.

Note that the body of the inner loop was executed five times for each execution of the body of the outer loop. This results in a total of 20 executions of the body of the inner loop and as a result 20 calls to `fillOval`, which results in 20 ovals being drawn.

The choice of five rows of four ovals each was arbitrary on my part and can easily be changed. In fact named constants should be used instead of putting the literals 4 and 5 in the code. Code 10.10 is a better version that uses named constants.

Now simple changes to the values of named constants `rows` and `columns` and a recompile will give us a different-looking box without having to hunt down all the 4s and 5s in the code and change them.

10.8.1 Using Private Helper Methods to Simplify Nested Loop Design

Designing and coding nested loops can be difficult, so here's a technique that makes reasoning about and understanding what is happening quite a bit easier. Although there is a little more coding, it is such a good technique to

CODE 10.10

```java
import java.awt.*;

public class FilledBox2 extends Animator {
    private final int rows = 4;
    private final int columns = 5;
    private int length;
    private int height;

    public void startup() {
        Animator.write("Enter the length of the box");
        length = Animator.readInt();
        Animator.write("Enter the height of the box");
        height = Animator.readInt();
    } // end of startup method

    public void draw(int x, int y, Graphics g) {
        // draw the rectangle
        g.setColor(Color.gray);
        int left = x-length/2;
        int top = y-height;
        g.fillRect(left,top,length,height);
        // draw the ovals
        g.setColor(Color.black);
        for (int row=1; row<=rows; row+=1) {
            left = x-length/2;
            for (int col=1; col<=columns; col+=1) {
                g.fillOval(left,top,length/columns,height/rows);
                left += length/columns;
            }
            top += height/rows;
        }
    } // end of draw method

} // end of FilledBox2 class
```

> **FilledBox2**
> Same as FilledBox but uses named constants for readability and to make it easier to change.

use that often it will *significantly* reduce the time to get correctly working code.

I'll illustrate the idea by redesigning the code for the previous example. Think of the collection of ovals as follows. There are four rows. A row consists of five ovals. These are two concepts, and writing separate code for each is simpler than writing code to fill the whole box. One loop simply draw four rows, whatever a row is. The other loop draws five ovals, and that's it.

Now suppose we add a method to the FilledBox class that simply draws a row of five ovals. Not four rows, just one row. We will have to tell the method where to draw the first oval, but with just that information it can draw the five ovals. Hence the method will have two parameters, the left and top coordinates of the first oval. Code 10.11 shows this method.

CODE 10.11

```
private void drawRow(int left, int top) {
    // left and top are the coordinates of the first oval
    for (int row=1; row<=columns; row+=1) {
        g.fillOval(left,top,length/columns,height/rows);
        left += length/columns;
    }
} // end of drawRow method
```

This method is `private` to ensure that it can be called only from other methods in the same class.

The method can still use the named constants `rows` and `columns` and instance variables `length` and `height` because it is part of the class. As you can see, this code is essentially the inner loop in the original version of the program.

Note that the method is `private` instead of `public`, as we've made every method up to now. A private method can only be called from another method in the same class, whereas a public method can be called from other classes. This method is designed to be used only by the `draw` method, and hence we don't want to let it be called from any other class. Hence it is `private`.

Now all we have to do to draw the entire collection of ovals is to call `drawRow` four times, each time sending it the coordinates of the upper left corner of the first oval in the row. Code 10.12 shows the new version of the `FilledBox` program using this method.

Notice that the call to `drawRow` must be preceded by the name of something that references an object. This is because every method must execute in the context of some object. The object we want `drawRow` to execute in the context of is the same object that `draw` is executing in the context of. Since in this class there is no variable that has such a reference, we can count on `this` to be a reference to the object that `draw` is already executing in the context of. Using `this` in this way is so common that Java permits you to leave it off and simply write

```
drawRow(left,top);
```

Java assumes that if you call a method and there is no reference variable or `this` preceding it, then you are calling a method defined in the same class and executing it in the context of the same object.

The code for each method is now pretty simple. The `draw` method's task is to draw the rectangle, then draw several rows. It doesn't have any code to draw the ovals themselves. It has delegated the details of drawing a row of

CODE 10.12

```java
import java.awt.*;

public class FilledBox3 extends Animator {
    private final int rows = 4;
    private final int columns = 5;
    private int length;
    private int height;

    public void startup() {
        Animator.write("Enter the length of the box");
        length = Animator.readInt();
        Animator.write("Enter the height of the box");
        height = Animator.readInt();
    } // end of startup method

    public void draw(int x, int y, Graphics g) {
        // draw the rectangle
        g.setColor(Color.gray);
        int left = x-length/2;
        int top = y-height;
        g.fillRect(left,top,length,height);

        // draw the ovals
        g.setColor(Color.black);
        for (int row=1; row<=rows; row+=1) {
            left = x-length/2;
            this.drawRow(left,top,g);
            top += height/rows;
        }
    } // end of draw method

    private void drawRow(int left, int top, Graphics g) {
        // left and top are the coordinates of the first oval
        for (int col=1; col<=columns; col+=1) {
            g.fillOval(left,top,length/columns,height/rows);
            left += length/columns;
        }
    } // end of drawRow method

} // end of FilledBox3 class
```

`this` is used here because we want the `drawRow` method to work in the context of the same object as `draw`.

FilledBox3
Same as `FilledBox2` but uses a private helper method to make the code easier to understand.

ovals to drawRow. All it needs to do is to tell drawRow where to start the row. Hence there is a single loop in the draw method, and the nested loop is avoided (actually it is still there in effect). When writing the draw method, you don't have to worry about the details of drawing a row. Just get the one loop that draws the rows designed and written.

The `drawRow` method's task is to draw a row of ovals, given the position of the first one. It doesn't have any code that figures out where the first oval is. Hence there is a single loop in the `drawRow` method, and when you are writing it, you don't have to worry about the details of figuring out where the row starts. Just get the one loop that draws the ovals designed and written.

This technique of using a separate method for the inner loop separates to a large extent the details of each loop. Hence you can concentrate on writing a single loop at a time and not get confused about the details of the other. Even though you wind up with more code, the ability to think about one part at a time will result in making it easier to do and more likely that you will produce correctly working code sooner.

Another advantage of using a separate method for the inner loop is that you can unit-test it. The idea is to write `drawRow`, then instead of writing the loop in the `draw` method that calls it, you can first write a single call of `drawRow` and see if it draws the row correctly. For example, if you first write the `draw` method as shown in Code 10.13, then you can unit-test the `drawRow` method. If it doesn't work, you can focus your debugging attention on `drawRow`. Once you get `drawRow` working, then replace the single call with the final version of the loop that draws all the rows.

CODE 10.13

```
public void draw(int x, int y, Graphics g) {
    // draw the rectangle
    g.setColor(Color.gray);
    int left = x-length/2;
    int top = y-height;
    g.fillRect(left,top,length,height);
    // unit test the drawRow method
    g.setColor(Color.black);
    drawRow(left,top,g);
} // end of draw method
```

Unit test `drawRow` by just calling it once. It should draw the top row of ovals.

Using separate private methods for the inner loop of a nested loop is a special case of using separate private methods to simplify the writing of any complex piece of code. They enable you to focus your attention on one thing at a time, and doing so has been proven to make writing correctly working code easier and quicker. These private methods are referred to as *helper methods* because they help accomplish the task that a method using them needs done.

{New Concepts}

A **helper method** is used to simplify the writing of complex code. It performs some part of a complex task and enables you to focus your attention on one thing a time. It is usually private.

FIGURE 10.2

10.8.2 Another Example

In the previous example, the number of ovals in a row is not dependent in any way on which row is being drawn. Five ovals are drawn no matter whether it is the first row or the last row. The number of ovals in a row is *independent* of which row is drawn.

Suppose we want to draw the box with ovals in it as shown in Figure 10.2. This is easily done by modifying the helper method `drawRow` to have a third parameter, which is the number of ovals to draw, and modifying the call of `drawRow` to send it the number to draw each time (Code 10.14).

Note that the numbers of rows and columns in the box are equal. This means that we don't need both instance variables `rows` and `columns`. The instance variable `columns` is never used and therefore was removed.

10.8.3 More Pattern Matching

As a final example, let's extend the pattern matching applet to search for a match of the pattern anywhere in the input string. This is done by first trying to find a match starting at position 0. If there is no match, then try to find a match starting at position 1. Continue trying to find a match farther and farther along the input string until there aren't enough input characters to match with or a match is found. Once a match is found, display the starting position of the match; otherwise display that there was no match.

For example, if the input is "A stitch in time saves nine." and the pattern is "ti" then the pattern will first be compared with "A ", then " s", then "st", then "ti", at which time it finds a match (at position 3). The first match is reported even though there is another "ti" in "time".

The code for this will contain two loops. One is similar to the one in the original program that checks for a match, starting at a given position. This loop will be put into a helper method, which will have the position to start checking for the match at as a parameter. The method will return true if there is a match at that position, false otherwise. The other loop will call this method repeatedly, sending it increasingly larger starting positions each time. If the method returns true, then the loop will terminate. The loop will also terminate once the starting position gets too large to have a possibility of matching.

CODE 10.14

```java
import java.awt.*;

public class HalfFilled extends Animator {
    private final int rows = 4;
    private int length;
    private int height;

    public void startup() {
        Animator.write("Enter the length of the box");
        length = Animator.readInt();
        Animator.write("Enter the height of the box");
        height = Animator.readInt();
    } // end of startup method

    public void draw(int x, int y, Graphics g) {
        // draw the rectangle
        g.setColor(Color.gray);
        int left = x-length/2;
        int top = y-height;
        g.fillRect(left,top,length,height);

        // draw the ovals
        g.setColor(Color.black);
        for (int row=1; row<=rows; row+=1) {
            left = x-length/2;
            drawRow(left,top,row,g);
            top += height/rows;
        }
    } // end of draw method

    private void drawRow(int left, int top, int howmany, Graphics g) {
        // left and top are the coordinates of the first oval

        for (int col=1; col<=howmany; col+=1) {
            g.fillOval(left,top,length/rows,height/rows);
            left += length/rows;
        }
    } // end of drawRow method

} // end of HalfFilled class
```

> Variable row not only keeps track of which row is being drawn, but also is the number of ovals to draw in that row.

HalfFilled
Fills the lower left half (triangle) of the box with ovals.

Code 10.15 is the beginning of the program, with the helper method defined but no code in it yet.

Notice that since the input strings are local variables to the `actionPerformed` method, they will have to be sent as arguments to the helper method `isMatch` as their scopes do not extend outside `actionPerformed`.

CODE 10.15

```
import java.awt.*;
import java.awt.event.*;
import javax.swing.*;

public class FindMatch extends JApplet
                       implements ActionListener {
    private JTextField inputField = new JTextField(100);
    private JTextField patternField = new JTextField(20);
    private JLabel output = new JLabel("enter data");
    private boolean gotInput = false;
    private boolean gotPattern = false;

    public void init() {
        // set up display
        Container window = getContentPane();
        window.setLayout(new FlowLayout(FlowLayout.LEFT));
        window.add(inputField);
        window.add(patternField);
        window.add(output);

        // attach listeners
        inputField.addActionListener(this);
        patternField.addActionListener(this);
    } // end of init method

    public void actionPerformed(ActionEvent event) {
        // record which input was supplied
        if (event.getSource() == inputField) {
        gotInput = true;
            }
        else {
            gotPattern = true;
            }
        // if both inputs available, try matching
        if (gotInput && gotPattern) {
            // get inputs
            String input = inputField.getText();
            String ptrn = patternField.getText();
            // try matching (to be added)
            // display result (to be added)
            }
    } // end of actionPerformed method

    private boolean isMatch(String input, String ptrn, int iPos) {
        // check if pattern matches input (to be added)
    } // end of isMatch method

} // end of FindMatch class
```

Now let's finish the helper method. The code will be very similar to the code in the original program, but I'm going to assume this time that when this method is called, there will always be enough characters left in the input string to be compared with the pattern. Hence the loop will be simpler because I don't have to check for a negative position or running out of input to check. Code 10.16 shows the new code.

CODE 10.16

```
private boolean isMatch(String input, String ptrn, int iPos) {
    // get length of pattern and set initial
    // pattern position to check
    int pLength = ptrn.length();
    int pPos = 0;

    // check character pairs until done
    while (pPos < pLength &&
            input.charAt(iPos) == ptrn.charAt(pPos)) {
        iPos += 1;
        pPos += 1;
    }
    // if got to end without a mismatch,
    // return true, else false
    if (pPos == pLength) {
        return true;
    }
    else {
        return false;
    }
} // end of isMatch method
```

Keep checking as long as there is more to check and characters match.

Return a boolean value rather than display a message.

Once this method is done, we don't have to worry about how it works any more and can concentrate on the code that finishes the actionPerformed method. All we need to do is to make sure that we pass the input and pattern strings and the initial position of where to start checking for a match to isMatch when we call it.

The loop that calls isMatch is pretty simple, basically calling isMatch with the initial position starting at 0 and increasing. Since isMatch is expecting that the initial position will always be such that there are enough input characters to check, we must stop the loop at the right point. The maximum initial position is simply the difference between the length of the two strings, iLength-pLength. Code 10.17 is the complete version of the actionPerformed method.

The loop basically calls isMatch repeatedly until there is a match or until there is no longer a possibility of a match. If isMatch returns true, stillLooking is set to false and the position of where the match was found is saved in matchStart. Then the loop will terminate. If there is no match when the loop terminates, then stillLooking will still be true, so we

CODE 10.17

```
public void actionPerformed(ActionEvent event) {
    // record which input was supplied
    if (event.getSource() == inputField) {
    gotInput = true;
        }
    else {
        gotPattern = true;
        }
    // if both inputs available, try matching
    if (gotInput && gotPattern) {
        // get inputs
        String input = inputField.getText();
        String ptrn = patternField.getText();
        // get lengths and set stopping position
        int iLength = input.length();
        int pLength = ptrn.length();
        int lastStart = iLength-pLength;
        // look for pattern
        int startPos = 0;
        int matchStart = 0;  ◄─────────────
        boolean stillLooking = true;
        while (stillLooking && startPos<=lastStart) {
            if(isMatch(input,ptrn,startPos)) {
                stillLooking = false;
                matchStart = startPos; ◄──────
                }
            startPos+=1;
            }
        // the pattern, display success, otherwise failure
        if (stillLooking) {
            output.setText("no match");
            }
        else {
            output.setText("match at position " + matchStart);
            }
        }
    // if not both inputs yet, request more
    else {
        output.setText("enter remaining data");
        }
    } // end of actionPerformed method
```

matchStart is used to record the position at which a match is found. It is given an initial value of 0 only to avoid a compiler error.

display that there was no match. If `stillLooking` is false when the loop terminates, then there must have been a match, so we display the position of where it was found.

There is one simplification to the `isMatch` method that is worth seeing (Code 10.18).

CODE 10.18

```
private boolean isMatch(String input, String ptrn, int iPos) {
    int pLength = ptrn.length();
    int pPos = 0;
    // check character pairs
    while (pPos < pLength) {
        if (input.charAt(iPos) != ptrn.charAt(pPos)) {
            return false;
        }
        iPos += 1;
        pPos += 1;
    }
    // if get here, there must have been a match
    return true;
} // end of isMatch method
```

Return `false` immediately if characters don't match.

If the loop ends "normally," then every character matched. Return `true`.

Recall that the `return` command causes the method to terminate immediately when it is executed. Hence as soon as a pair of characters that don't match is encountered, the method finishes and returns false. Otherwise the loop will end when there are no more characters to check, and the command following it will be executed, returning true since every character matched. Code 10.19 is the complete program.

CODE 10.19

```
import java.awt.*;
import java.awt.event.*;
import javax.swing.*;

public class FindMatch extends JApplet
                       implements ActionListener {
    private JTextField inputField = new JTextField(100);
    private JTextField patternField = new JTextField(20);
    private JLabel output = new JLabel("enter data");
    private boolean gotInput = false;
    private boolean gotPattern = false;

    public void init() {
        // set up display
        Container window = getContentPane();
        window.setLayout(new FlowLayout(FlowLayout.LEFT));
        window.add(inputField);
        window.add(patternField);
        window.add(output);

        // attach listeners
        inputField.addActionListener(this);
        patternField.addActionListener(this);
    } // end of init method
```

```
public void actionPerformed(ActionEvent event) {
    // record which input was supplied
    if (event.getSource() == inputField) {
    gotInput = true;
        }
    else {
        gotPattern = true;
        }
    // if both inputs available, try matching
    if (gotInput && gotPattern) {
        // get inputs
        String input = inputField.getText();
        String ptrn = patternField.getText();

        // get lengths and set stopping position
        int iLength = input.length();
        int pLength = ptrn.length();
        int lastStart = iLength-pLength;

        // look for pattern
        int startPos = 0;
        int matchStart = 0;
        boolean stillLooking = true;
        while (stillLooking && startPos<=lastStart) {
            if(isMatch(input,ptrn,startPos)) {
                stillLooking = false;
                matchStart = startPos;
                }
            startPos+=1;
            }
        // the pattern, display success, otherwise failure
        if (stillLooking) {
            output.setText("no match");
            }
        else {
            output.setText("match at position "+matchStart);
            }
        }
    // if not both inputs yet, request more
    else {
        output.setText("enter remaining data");
        }
    } // end of actionPerformed method
```

```
private boolean isMatch(String input, String ptrn, int iPos) {
    int pLength = ptrn.length();
    int pPos = 0;
    // check character pairs
    while (pPos < pLength) {
        if (input.charAt(iPos) != ptrn.charAt(pPos)) {
            return false;
            }
```

```
        iPos += 1;
        pPos += 1;
        }
    // if get here, there must have been a match
    return true;

    } // end of isMatch method

} // end of FindMatch class
```

FindMatch
Searches an input string for a match to a pattern. Displays the position in the input string that the match starts at.

Written Exercises

1. Create a list of input/pattern pairs that will test the boundary cases of the loops in the FindMatch program.

2. Create a list of test cases for the programming problems below. Create the list before you write the code, then write the code and add more cases (if necessary).

3. Manually execute the entire actionPerformed method in the FindMatch program, assuming the user enters "abc" in the input JTextField and "bc" in the pattern JTextField.

Programming Exercises

1. Write animation classes with loops that draw the box as shown in the following diagrams. Use helper methods.

   a.

   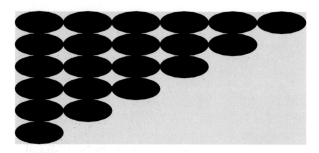

   b.

   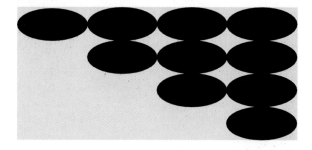

c.

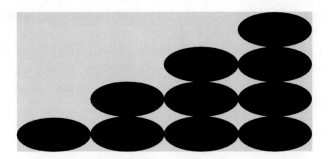

2. Write an applet that computes the sum of the first *N* prime numbers. The user should be able to enter *N* into a `JTextField`, and your applet should display the result in a `JLabel`. Recall that a prime number is an integer that is divisible only by 1 and itself (for example, 2, 3, 5, 7, 11, 13, 17, 19, 23, 29, 31, . . .). You'll need a nested loop.

3. Write an applet that finds and displays the largest prime number less than a positive integer entered by the user. For example, if the user enters 50, your program should print 47. If the user enters a number less than 2, display an error message instead.

4. Write an applet that inputs a string and displays a string that has all second, third, etc., occurrences of each character in the first string removed. For example, if the input is "AABACDGTAFCCX" then it should display "ABCDGTFX". *Hint:* Use a helper method that has a string and a position as parameters and returns a string that is the same as the parameter string, except all duplicates of the character at the indicated position have been removed.

Summary

- Loops provide a mechanism for repeatedly executing segments of code.
- Java has the for-command and the while-command to write loops.
- Both loop commands have a loop body consisting of one or more commands that will be repeated some number of times. Each execution of the loop body is called an iteration.
- Both loop commands evaluate a boolean expression before each iteration, and if true, execute the body again. When the boolean expression evaluates to false, the body is skipped and execution continues with the command after the body.
- The for-command also includes an expression that is executed once before anything else, and another expression that is executed just after the body of the loop finishes an iteration and before the boolean expression is evaluated again.

- A loop that executes a number of iterations that can be determined before the body is executed at all is called a counting loop and is usually written using a for-command.

- A loop in which the number of iterations is determined by something that happens in the body of the loop is usually written using a while-command.

- A loop in which the boolean expression never becomes false is an infinite loop and should be avoided.

- Off-by-one errors, in which loops execute once too many times or once too few times, are common.

- Testing boundary cases of loops will help identify off-by-one and various other errors.

- Manual execution is a technique for gaining confidence that a loop (or any other segment of code) is working correctly. The values of all relevant variables are kept track of by hand as though the computer were executing the code.

- Nested loops occur when the body of one loop contains another. The loop that appears in the body of the other is called the inner loop. The loop that contains the other is called the outer loop.

- If the number of iterations of an inner loop depends on which iteration of the outer loop is being executed, then the inner loop is called a *dependent loop*. Otherwise the inner loop is independent.

Glossary

Body of the Loop The code that is executed repeatedly.

Boundary Test Cases Test inputs that, among other things, force loops to execute zero and one iteration, and that ensure that the first and last iterations do the right things, and that all possible termination conditions are encountered.

Counting Loop A loop that executes a fixed number of times no matter what is done in the body.

Helper Method A method that is written simply to perform one part of a complex task.

Infinite Loop A loop that never terminates.

Inner Loop A loop that appears within the body of another loop.

Iteration One execution of the body of a loop.

Loop A segment of code that is executed repeatedly.

Manual Execution The stepping through of the execution of a segment of code by hand and keeping track of the values of all relevant variables.

Nested Loop A loop contained within the body of another loop.

Off-by-One Error An error that causes a loop to execute one time too few or one time too many.

Outer Loop A loop that contains another loop in its body.

## CHAPTER 11

Arrays

OBJECTIVES

- To understand what arrays are and how to use them.
- To be able to use loop constructs to manipulate array data.
- To be able to search and sort arrays.
- To be able to define and use arrays of two or more dimensions.

11.1 STORING AND MANIPULATING LOTS OF DATA

Up to this point, every variable that you created was given a unique name. This works fine when the number of values and/or objects that a program contains at any given time is small. But when the number of values and objects gets large, creating a unique name for each one becomes an overwhelming task. What is needed is a simple way to refer to a potentially large number of values without having to give each one its own name. One way of doing so is with an object called an *array*.

An array is an object that has a single name but can store a large number of values. The number of values in a particular array object is determined when the object is created. Each value is stored in a unique position in the array, with the positions numbered starting at 0. For example, an array object containing 100 values will have one value at position 0, another at position 1, another at position 2, etc., up to a value at position 99 (and not 100!). Java lets you use the position to refer to a particular value in the array (e.g., the one at position 47). Each position in an array object is called an **element.** Each element of an array object contains *one* value.

> **{Definitions of Terms}**
>
> An **array** is an object consisting of some number of elements, each of which can store a value. An element is identified by a number indicating its position, starting with 0 (0, 1, 2, . . .).

An array of six ints is pictured in Figure 11.1. This picture is much like the picture of any object except that the individual values within the object do not have names. They do have positions, however, which are shown to the right of each box (the position numbers are shown purely

FIGURE 11.1

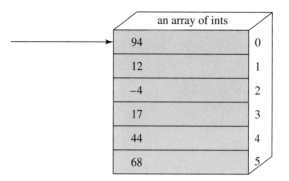

for clarity and are not actually part of the object itself). The box is labeled with "an array of" and then whatever kind of values are stored (in this case, ints). Notice that the positions of this six-element array go from 0 to 5.

> **{New Concepts}**
> The last position in an array of N elements is $N - 1$, not N.

The `new` operator is used to create an array object, but the syntax is a bit different from that used to create objects that are described by class definitions. Here is an example of the code used to create an array object containing 15 doubles, and a variable called `table` to refer to it:

```
double [] table = new double[15];
```

Note the use of square brackets in two places. The first set of square brackets indicates that `table` will be a reference to an array object containing some number of double values. The number of elements in the array object is not specified at this place in the definition. The second set of square brackets encloses an expression that must evaluate to an integer value which indicates the number of elements in the array object (in this case 15). Here is another example of an array object called `inputs` that consists of references to `JTextField` objects:

```
JTextField [] inputs = new JTextField[100];
```

Array objects can be created to hold integers, doubles, or references to objects (e.g., `String` objects or objects described by classes Java defines for you or that you have defined yourself). You cannot have a single array object in which some elements are integers, others are doubles, still others are references to `String` objects, and/or some are references to other kinds of objects. All the elements must be the same type or class.

> **{New Concepts}**
> All elements of an array will be of the same type or class.

It is important to remember that an array is an object, and as a result the command

```
int [] data;
```

creates a reference variable `data` with the initial value null. No array object is created by this command, only a reference variable that at some time will be a reference to an array object. An attempt to use the reference variable `data` before it is made to reference an array object will result in a null pointer exception, just as trying to use any reference variable that currently contains the null reference does.

When an array *object* is created (via `new`), initial values are given to each element. In the case of integers, the values in all the elements are 0. Doubles are initially 0.0, and object references are null (i.e., references to nothing). It is important to realize that when an array of references to objects is created, only the array object itself is created. No objects of the class name used (e.g., `JTextField`) are created. You'll have to create those objects explicitly yourself.

{New Concepts}

Elements of an array of `int` are initialized to 0, an array of `double` to 0.0, and an array of references (to any kind of object) to null.

Given an array object, you need a way to refer to each element, so you can use or change what is stored there. Essentially you need a name for each element. Consider the array object referred to by `table` as defined above. Then

```
table[3]
```

is the element at position 3 in the array object (but it is the fourth element). You can assign the value 37.9 to it by writing

```
table[3] = 37.9;
```

You can test whether it is less than or equal to 100.0 by writing

```
table[3] <= 100.0
```

In fact, you can think of `table[3]` as the name of the element at position 3 in the array object.

The real power of arrays comes from the ability to use an arbitrary expression and not just an integer literal between the brackets when naming an element. An expression between the brackets in an array object reference is often called an **index.** Consider the following command:

```
table[i] = table[i] + 1.0;
```

Assume i is an integer variable that has the value 5. Then when this command is executed, the element at position 5 will be changed to be 1.0 larger than it was. If the next time this command is executed the value of i is 2, then the element at position 2 will be changed to be 1.0 larger that it was. As you can see, by simply giving i a different value each time, this single command can add 1.0 to a different element of the array each time it is executed. By putting this command in a loop, 1.0 can be added to every element of the array object:

```
for (int i=0; i<15; i+=1) {
    table[i] = table[i] + 1.0;
    }
```

The first time through the body of the loop, i will have the value 0, so the element at position 0 of table will have 1.0 added to it. The next time through the body of the loop i will have the value 1, so the element at position 1 will have 1.0 added to it, etc.

Pay special attention to the items in the first line of the for-command. First, the variable i is set to 0 initially because array indices start at 0. Second, the body of the loop will be executed as long as i is *less than* 15. The last time the body is executed i will have the value 14, which corresponds to the index of the last element of the array. A very common mistake is either to start the loop at the wrong value (usually 1 instead of 0) or not to end it properly (usually letting i get up to 15). Both are examples of off-by-one errors.

It is often handy to be able to find out how many elements there are in a given array object. This is especially true if an array object is passed as a parameter to a method and array objects with different numbers of elements are passed at different times. Every array object has an instance variable whose value is the number of elements in that array object. The array object instance variable is called length and is used as shown in the following example:

```
for (int i=0; i<table.length; i+=1) {
    table[i] = table[i] + 1.0;
    }
```

The variable table.length is equal to the number of elements in table.[1] The really nice thing about using an array object's length variable is that the code that does something with the array will always use the correct length. In the original code, if the code that creates the array initially was changed to create an array with 20 elements, the 15 in the for-command will also have to be changed, or else there will be an error. It is easy to forget to

---

1. Don't confuse the length of an array with the length of a String and write table.length(). The parentheses are *not* used to get the length of an array.

change the 15 to 20 in both places, so this is a much safer way to write the code.

Returning to the task of creating an array of 10 JTextField references, *and* 10 JTextField objects for the array to reference, you must do something akin to this:

```
JTextField [] inputs = new JTextField[InputSize];   ◄─── Creates an array object
for (int i=0; i<inputs.length; i+=1) {                    with 10 null references.
    inputs[i] = new JTextField(FieldSize);
    }                              ◄──────── Creates a JTextField object and
                                             saves a reference to it in the array.
```

It is easy to forget that you must create both the array object *and* all the referenced objects, and this is a common error made when first using arrays. As usual, trying to use an element of the array inputs before it is assigned a reference to a JTextField object will give you a null pointer exception, so your program probably won't get very far if you do happen to forget to create all the JTextField objects.

11.1.1 Examples

Code 11.1 is a simple animation that displays as many clouds as the user requests when the animation begins. The left edges of the clouds are evenly spaced from left to right, but the size and altitude are chosen randomly, except that the height is always one-half of the width).

The program creates the array of Cloud references based on the size requested by the user, then creates the same number of Cloud objects and saves a reference to each in successive elements of the array. Then the draw method in the ManyCloud class simply calls the draw method in each of the Cloud objects. Because the Cloud draw method executes in the context of the object being referred to at the time, each Cloud object winds up being drawn in a different location.

As another example, let's incorporate a simple array of doubles into an applet that displays a column of JTextField objects in which the user will enter numbers and displays the sum of the numbers at the bottom of the column using a JLabel. The sum will be updated anytime the user enters a new number in any of the JTextField objects. A single Listener object that will respond to input in any of the 10 JTextField objects, and a calculator object that will compute and display the sum, will do most of the work. The main applet object will create all the other objects, add them to window, and connect the Listener object to all the JTextField objects. An array of doubles will be used to hold the current values in each JTextField object, and an array of references will be used to keep track of the JTextField objects.

Let's consider the calculator object first. It must have access to the array of doubles that contains the values that were entered into the JTextField

CODE 11.1

```java
import java.awt.*;

public class ManyClouds extends Animator {
    private Cloud [] clouds;
    private int numClouds;

    public void startup() {
        Animator.write("how many clouds?");
        numClouds = Animator.readInt();
        clouds = new Cloud[numClouds];
        int offset = Animator.getSceneWidth()/numClouds;
        for (int c=0; c<numClouds; c+=1) {
            clouds[c] = new Cloud(offset*c);
        }
    } // end of startup method
```

> Space the clouds evenly across the scene.

```java
    public void draw(int clock, Graphics g) {
        for (int c=0; c<numClouds; c+=1) {
            clouds[c].draw(clock,g);
        }
    } // end of draw method

} // endof ManyClouds class
```

> Execute the Cloud draw method in the context of each Cloud object.

```java
class Cloud {
    private final int width;
    private final int height;
    private final int altitude;
    private final int offset;

    public Cloud(int off) {
        width = (int) (Math.random()*200);
        height = width/2;
        altitude = (int) (Math.random()*
                    (Animator.getSurface()-height));
        offset = off;
    } // end of constructor
```

> Choose width and altitude randomly.

```java
    public void draw(int clock, Graphics g) {
        g.setColor(Color.gray);
        int left = (clock+offset)%
                    (Animator.getSceneWidth()+width)-width;
        g.fillOval(left,altitude,width,height);
    } // end of draw method

} // end of Cloud class
```

ManyClouds
Displays as many clouds as the user requests.

objects and to the `JLabel` object used to display the sum on the screen. I'll make them instance variables that will be given their values by the constructor (Code 11.2).

CODE 11.2

```
class Calc {

    private double [] info;              The constructor will
    private JLabel total;                make info a reference
                                         to an array object.

    public Calc(double [] vals, JLabel display) {     A reference to an
        // save references to the array of values     array object is
        // and the JLabel                             expected.
        info = vals;                     Make info contain a reference
        total = display;                 to the array object sent to the
    } // end of constructor              constructor.


    public void compute() {
        // compute the sum of the elements of the array
        double sum = 0;
        for (int i=0; i<info.length; i+=1) {
            sum += info[i];
            }
        // display the sum
        total.setText("the sum is " + sum);
    } // end of compute method


} // end of Calc class
```

Note how the array object *reference* appears as a parameter of the constructor, and that the reference is assigned to the instance variable the same as any other object reference. The loop that computes the sum simply creates a variable called `sum` with initial value 0 and then adds the values in each element of the array object to it.

The `Listener` object will convert the text input to a double and store it in the array of values for use by the calculator object. The for-command in the `actionPerformed` method checks each `JTextField` object, looking for the one that caused the event to occur. Note that the event must have been caused by one of the `JTextField` objects, so the if-command in the body of the loop is guaranteed to be true once. After the appropriate element of the array of values is updated, the `doSum` method of the `Adder` object is called (Code 11.3).

Finally the applet object creates all the objects and makes sure they all have the correct information. Notice that the creation of an array object whose elements are references to `JTextField` objects does not create the `JTextField` objects themselves. It only creates an array where references

CODE 11.3

```
class Listener implements ActionListener {
    private double [] info;
    private JTextField [] input;
    private Calc calculator;

    public Listener(double [] vals, JTextField [] in, Calc c) {
        // set up instance variables
        info = vals;
        input = in;
        calculator = c;
    } // end of constructor

    public void actionPerformed(ActionEvent event) {
        // find the JTextField that had the event
        for (int i=0; i<input.length; i+=1) {
            if (event.getSource() == input[i]) {
                info[i] =Double.parseDouble(input[i].getText());
            }
        }
        // calculate and display the sum
        calculator.compute();
    } // end of actionPerformed method

} // end of Listener class
```

> input[i] is a reference to one of the JTextField objects.

can be stored. Later in the constructor each JTextField object is constructed, and each element of the array is set to refer to one (Code 11.4).

11.1.2 Initializing Arrays

We've seen the use of commands to put initial values (other than the defaults) into arrays. When the array is large, this is the best way to do it. However, many situations call for a fairly small array with just a few nondefault initial values. Java supplies a simple mechanism called an *initializer list* for creating and initializing such arrays.

Suppose you are writing part of a program that has three integers representing a day, month, and year (e.g., the 29th day of the third month of 1951), but you want to set a JLabel to a readable date with the month spelled out (e.g., "March 29, 1951"). To do so requires converting the integer month (3) to its String equivalent ("March"). Defining a 12-element array, with each element being the String version of the corresponding month, and then indexing into it will be an easy way to do the conversion. Here's a definition of just such an array:

```
String [] months = {"January","February","March","April","May",
                    "June","July","August","September","October",
                    "November","December"};
```

CODE 11.4

```
import java.awt.*;
import java.awt.event.*;
import javax.swing.*;

public class SumApplet extends JApplet {
    private final int fields = 10;
    private final int fieldSize = 10;
    private double [] values = new double[fields];
    private JTextField [] input = new JTextField[fields];
    private JLabel total = new JLabel("");

    public void init() {
        // create calculator and Listener
        Calc calculator = new Calc(values, total);
        Listener listen = new Listener(values,input,calculator);

        Container window = getContentPane();
        window.setLayout(new GridLayout(fields+1,1));

        for (int i=0; i<fieldSize; i+=1) {
            // initialize value to 0
            values[i] = 0;

            // create and add JTextField
            input[i] = new JTextField(fieldSize);
            window.add(input[i]);

            // make the Listener listen to JTextField
            input[i].addActionListener(listen);
        }
        // add the JLabel for the sum
        window.add(total);
    } // end of init method

} // end of SumApplet class
```

```
// Calc class here
```

```
// Listener class here
```

The collection of strings, one for each month, separated by commas and enclosed in braces is an initializer for an array. Java counts the number of items in the collection (12), creates an array object with 12 elements, and initializes each element with one of the items (in order). It is equivalent, but much easier to write than the following:

> **SumApplet**
> Displays the sum of the numbers entered into 10 JTextFields, using an array.

```
String [] months = new String[12];
months[0] = "January";
months[1] = "February";
months[2] = "March";
months[3] = "April";
months[4] = "May";
```

```
months[5]  = "June";
months[6]  = "July";
months[7]  = "August";
months[8]  = "September";
months[9]  = "October";
months[10] = "November";
months[11] = "December";
```

The code to set a `JLabel` (let's call it `date`) is then

```
date.setText(months[month-1]+" "+day+", "+year);
```

Note that since months are numbered from 1 to 12 but array indices go from 0 to 11, I had to subtract 1 from `month` to use it as an index.

Arrays of integers and doubles have similar-looking initializer lists. For example, here's an array of integers with each element containing the number of days in the corresponding month:

```
int [] daysInMonth = {31,28,31,30,31,30,31,31,30,31,30,31};
```

Arrays of object references can also be initialized with references to new or existing objects. A five-element array of references to `JLabel` objects, and the `JLabel` objects themselves, can be created by writing

```
Jlabel none = new JLabel("none");
JLabel [] response = {new JLabel("left"), new JLabel("right"),
                      new JLabel("up"), new JLabel("down"),
                      none};
```

Note that new objects can be created in an initializer list or existing object references can be used (e.g., `none`).

> **{Good Ideas}**
> Initializer lists are a convenient way to both create an array object and give each element a nondefault initial value.

Written Exercises

1. Consider an array with 1000 elements. What are the indices of the first and last elements?

2. What is wrong with the following code segment?

```
int [] stuff = new int[99];

...

for(n=0; n<=99; n+=1) {
    stuff[n] = n;
    }
```

3. Write a short code segment that creates an array of 100 integers called `squares`, then puts 0 in element 0, 1 in element 1, 4 in element 2, 9 in element 3, 16 in element 4, . . . , n^2 in element n, up to 99^2 in element 99.

Programming Exercises

1. Modify the `SumApplet` to display the average of the values in the array instead of the sum.

2. Modify the `SumApplet` to ignore values that are less than 0 when computing the sum.

11.2 MORE EXAMPLES

11.2.1 Finding the Maximum

Let's modify the previous applet to display the largest number in the collection of `JTextField` objects instead of the sum of the numbers. The maximum is found by picking the value in element 0 of the array as the first guess at the maximum, then checking the rest of the values to see if any is larger. Whenever a larger value is found, it becomes the new maximum (so far). When the loop terminates, the value of `max` will be the largest value in the array (Code 11.5).

A common mistake when you are writing code to find the maximum is to set `max` to some arbitrarily small value (say, 0) and then check every value in the array, replacing the old value of `max` whenever a larger value is found, as shown here:

```
public void calculate() { // incorrect version

    // find the largest value in the array     Don't pick an arbitrary
    double max = 0.0;                          small initial value for
    for (int i=0; i<info.length; i+=1) {       max unless you know
        if (info[i] > max) {                   all values in the array
            max = info[i];                     will be bigger than
        }                                      that value.
    }
    // display the maximum
    maximum.setText("the maximum is " + max);
} // end of calculate method
```

This is a bad idea unless you know that there will be at least one value in the array that is greater than or equal to 0.0. If all the values in the array are negative, then none of them will be greater than 0.0 and the resulting maximum value found by this code incorrectly will be 0.0.

11.2.2 Searching

Suppose an array has been created and every element given a unique value. A common task is to search the array for a given value, with the goal of discovering either its index or that the value isn't in the array at all. If the values are

CODE 11.5

```java
import java.awt.*;
import java.awt.event.*;
import javax.swing.*;

// SumApplet class here (name change to MaxApplet)

// Listener class here

class Calc {
    private double [] info;
    private JLabel maximum;

    public Calc(double [] vals, JLabel display) {
        // save references to the array of values
        // and the JLabel
        info = vals;
        maximum = display;
    } // end of constructor

    public void calculate() {
        // find the largest value in the array
        double max = info[0];
        for (int i=1; i<info.length; i+=1) {
            if (info[i] > max) {
                max = info[i];
            }
        }
        // display the maximum
        maximum.setText("the maximum is " + max);
    } // end of calculate method

} // end of Calc class
```

MaxApplet
Displays the maximum of the numbers entered into 10 JTextField objects, using an array to store the numbers.

in no particular order in the array, then the only way to search for some given value is to begin at the first element and work toward the end, comparing each element with the searched-for value.

The following method assumes an array of ints is being searched for a particular target value, and has the array as a parameter. This makes the method fairly general-purpose, as any array of ints can be searched. It returns the index of the matching element, or −1 if there is no match.

```java
public int find(double [] data, int target) {
    int i = 0;
    while (i < data.length && data[i] != target) {
        i += 1;
    }
```

Keep looping as long as there are more elements and there has not been a match.

```
    if (i < data.length) {
        return i;
    }
    else {
        return -1;
    }
} // end of find method
```

> Check what caused the loop to terminate.

The while-loop moves through elements of the array to look for a match. If a match is found, the loop terminates. The loop also terminates if no match is found because i will become equal to data.length. The if-command after the while-loop is necessary since at this point it is not known why the loop terminated. Hence if i is still less than data.length, it must have terminated because of a match.

Another way to write this method is as follows:

```
public int find(double [] data, int target) {
    int i = 0;
    while (i < data.length) {
        if (data[i] == target) {
            return i;
        }
        i += 1;
    }
    return -1;
} // end of find method
```

> Return immediately when a match is found.

> Can only get here if there was no match.

In this version the while-command ensures only that i doesn't get too big. In the body of the loop the if-command checks for a match and returns immediately from the method (and the loop too!) if found. If the loop terminates normally, then it was because there was no match, so −1 can be returned with no further ado.

There is some debate as to which of the previous two implementations of the search method is better. Some think that the first is better because the loop continuation (and conversely termination) condition is completely contained within the boolean expression in the while-command. Others think that the shorter version without the extra if-command after the loop is simpler and hence easier to understand. Since there is no consensus, either can be used unless someone insists on one or the other.

A third way to write this method is like this:

```
public int find(double [] data, int target) {
    for (int i=0; i<data.length; i+=1) {
        if (data[i] == target) {
            return i;
        }
    }
    return -1;
} // end of find method
```

> This looks like a counting loop, but isn't.

While some may argue that this is even simpler and therefore more desirable that the previous two versions, I would suggest avoiding it. The for-command looks like a counting loop, but yet isn't when there is a match and the number of iterations of the loop body is not equal to the number of elements in the array. Hence without careful inspection of the body of the loop there can be confusion.

11.2.3 The Break Command

Suppose instead of just finding a particular value in an array and returning its index we want a method that will change a given value to some new value. The method will be sent the array, the value to search for, and the new value to change it to. Here's an implementation:

```
public void change(double [] data, double target, double newValue){
    int i = 0;
    while (i < data.length && data[i] != target) {
        i += 1;
    }
    if (i < data.length) {
        data[i] = newValue;
    }
```

This is much like the first version of the `find` method above, but has a complex boolean expression that can be confusing and difficult to get correct. Here's another version that is like the second version of the `find` method above:

```
public void change(double [] data, double target, double newValue){
    int i = 0;
    while (i < data.length) {
        if (data[i] == target) {
            break;
        }
        i += 1;
    }
    if (i < data.length) {
        data[i] = newValue;
    }
```

This version has a new command called `break`. The break command causes the loop to terminate immediately (like `return`) and execution to continue with the command that follows the body (unlike the `return`). Hence when a match is found in the code above, execution will continue with the if-command following the body of the loop.

{New Concepts}

Executing the break command causes a loop body and the entire loop to terminate immediately and execution to continue with the command that follows the body of the loop.

The choice of which version is better again is a matter of some disagreement. Those who don't like a return command in the body of a loop don't like a break command there either. Others see the simplicity of the boolean expressions making it easier to write correct code. My suggestion is to use whatever works best for you unless forced otherwise.

One note about the break command. If it appears in the body of the inside loop of a nested loop, it only causes the inside loop to terminate and *not* the outside loop, too.

{New Concepts}

Executing a break command in the inner loop of a nested loop only causes the inner loop to terminate.

11.2.4 Sorting

A very common task is to take an array of numbers that are in no particular order and put them into order (increasing or decreasing). This is called sorting. Many techniques exist to sort arrays, and each has its advantages and disadvantages. In this section I'll describe one of the simplest techniques, called *selection sorting*.

The **selection sort** works as follows. The entire array is searched first to find the smallest value. The position of that value in the array is also saved. Then the value in position 0 of the array is swapped with the smallest value, thereby putting the smallest value in position 0 of the array and putting the value that was in position 0 in the position where the smallest used to be. The array is now partially sorted because the smallest value is in position 0 (Figure 11.2).

Next, position 0 is ignored, and the rest of the array is searched to find the (next) smallest value. Again its position is saved, and then the value in position 1 of the array is swapped with the (next) smallest value. Position 1 now has the second smallest value (Figure 11.3).

The same process is repeated over and over, each time getting the next smallest value into its proper position in the array. Eventually the process gets the second-to-the-last value in its proper position. No more needs to be done because there is only one value left, it must be the largest value, and it is already in the last position of the array.

Let's implement this algorithm by first defining a helper method. Its task will be to do one step of the sort, that is, to find the smallest value in the remaining part of the array and swap it with the value in the first element of the remaining part of the array. It will only need one parameter—the index of the first element of the remaining part of the array. The helper method will simply be called the appropriate number of times, increasing the index of the first element each time. Code 11.6 shows the helper method setMin.

FIGURE 11.2

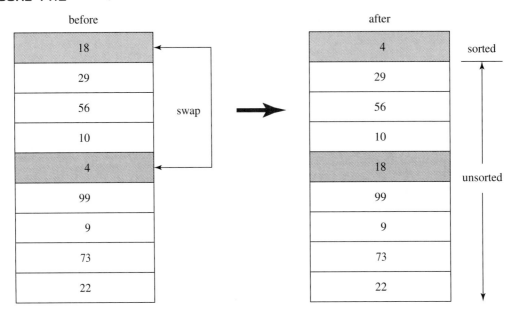

FIGURE 11.3

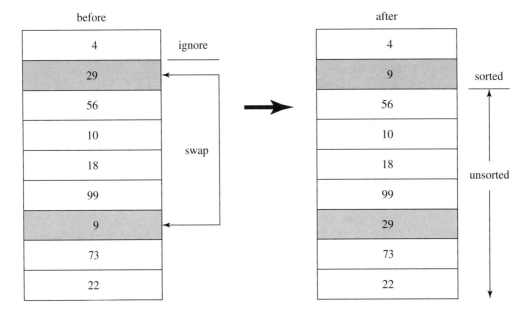

CODE 11.6

```
private void setMin(int firstPos) {
    // find the minimum value and its position
    // in the rest of the array
    double min = info[firstPos];
    int minPos = firstPos;
    for (int j=firstPos+1; j<info.length; j+=1) {
        if (info[j] < min) {
            min = info[j];
            minPos = j;
        }
    }
    // swap the minimum value with
    // the one in position firstPos
    double temp = info[firstPos];
    info[firstPos] = info[minPos];
    info[minPos] = temp;
} // end of setMin method
```

Keep track of the position of the smallest value in `minPos`.

A temporary variable is needed to swap two values.

Notice the following things. First, the variable `minPos` is introduced to keep track of the position of the smallest value so that the value in the first position can be put there later. Second, to swap two values, a third temporary variable `temp` is needed to hold one of the values when the other is copied from one place to the other.

Since most of the work is done in the `setMin` method, the `sort` method simply calls it several times, each time sending the new beginning position of the rest of the array.

```
public void sort() {
    // for each element...
    for (int pos=0; pos<info.length-1; pos+=1) {
        // put the next smallest value in the correct position
        setMin(pos);
    }
} // end of sort method
```

Note that the for-command varies `pos` from 0 to 2 less than the number of elements in the array. For example, if the number of elements in the array is 9, then the last value of `pos` will be 7, which is the position of the next-to-the-last element of the array (remember, positions go from 0 to 8).

Written Exercises

1. Suppose you are writing code to find the maximum (or minimum) value in an array. Why shouldn't you pick an arbitrary maximum (or minimum) value as a first guess and then update it when you find something larger (or smaller)?

2. Why does the outer for-loop in the sort method stop when `i` is 2 less than the length of the array?

3. Why is a temporary variable needed to swap values between two other variables?

Programming Exercises

1. Modify the `SumApplet` to display the minimum value in the array.

2. Modify the `SumApplet` to display the second largest value in the array.

3. Write an applet with two `JTextField` objects and an array of 1000 `String` references (initially null). The first `JTextField` is used to enter strings. Each time a new string is entered, put a reference to it in the next empty array element. When the user enters a string into the other `JTextField`, search for that string in the array and set a `JLabel` indicating whether it was found, showing the index of the string in the array if it is found.

4. Modify the applet in the previous problem to add a third `JTextField`. When a user enters a string into this new `JTextField`, first search for it in the array, and if it is found, remove it by setting the array element to null. Modify your search method to ignore elements that have had their strings deleted (i.e., set to null) when searching.

5. Modify the `sort` method to display the sorted array back in the `JTextField` objects that were used to enter the data originally.

6. Write an applet that displays 10 `JTextField` objects and the minimum value, and has a button that when pushed, changes the contents of the `JTextField` with the minimum value to 0 and recomputes and redisplays the new minimum value (not including the 0 just inserted). Assume that all numbers entered by the user will be greater than 0 and that they will be unique (Figure 11.4).

FIGURE 11.4

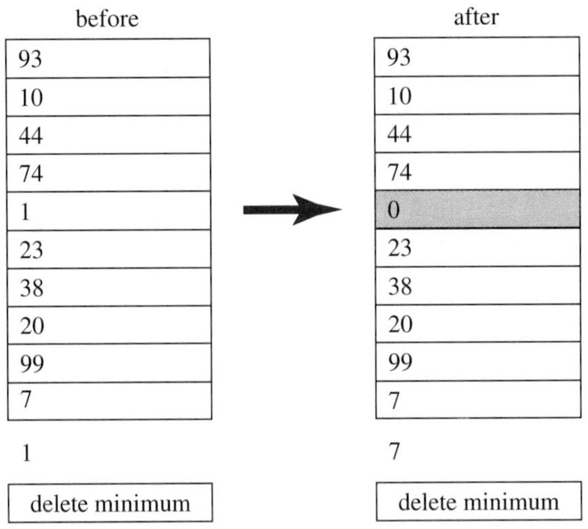

before

| 93 |
| 10 |
| 44 |
| 74 |
| 1 |
| 23 |
| 38 |
| 20 |
| 99 |
| 7 |

1

delete minimum

after

| 93 |
| 10 |
| 44 |
| 74 |
| 0 |
| 23 |
| 38 |
| 20 |
| 99 |
| 7 |

7

delete minimum

11.3 JAVA'S VECTOR CLASS

Probably the biggest problem with arrays is that once you have created one, you cannot change its size. For example, consider an applet that finds the median of several numbers entered by the user. The median is the number such that one-half of the other numbers are less than it, and one-half are greater than it. An easy way to determine the median is to put all the numbers in an array, sort the array, and take the middle value as the median.

Now suppose we don't want to limit how many numbers the user can enter. If so, how big should we make the array that will hold those numbers? You clearly can't choose a size because whatever you choose, the user may enter more numbers than that. Now I suppose in reality you could make the array have a million elements and assume that the user will never be able to enter that many numbers, but for now let's assume that no limit exists.

What would be nice is an array that you could make bigger when necessary. Fortunately, Java provides a class that defines objects that give the appearance of just such arrays—the Vector class.

A Vector object acts a lot like an array. Values are stored in elements at various positions. Values from any position can be retrieved. But there is, in effect, no limit on how many elements there are in the Vector. You can always put a value in a position that is 1 larger than the highest position used so far, and the Vector object will make sure there is space to store it.

There are a few differences between Vector objects and arrays, too. First, only object references can be stored in a Vector. This means that you cannot store primitive-type values directly (there is a way around this, which I'll describe shortly). Second, since a Vector is an object, you cannot use the [ ] syntax to refer to its elements. Instead you must call methods to store and retrieve object references. A Vector object also has a current size that equals the number of object references stored in it. Initially that size is 0, and it increases only when you "add" object references to the Vector. You can also "remove" object references from a Vector, in which case the size decreases by 1.

The Vector class defines the methods shown in Table 11.1 (among others—see the Java documentation). Think of a Vector as a sequence of object references. You can add a new reference anywhere in the sequence, including at the beginning, anywhere in the middle, or at the end. When you add a new reference anywhere but at the end, the positions of all the references that follow it change. For example, if you add a new reference at position 4, then the reference that used to be at position 4 is now at position 5, the reference at position 5 is now at position 6, etc., and the size of the Vector increases by 1. Although you can add a new reference at the end of the Vector, you cannot add one farther past the end. For example, if the Vector currently has 5 references in it (positions 0, 1, 2, 3, and 4), then you can add a new reference at position 5, but not at any position greater than 5.

When you remove a reference at a given position, then just the opposite happens. The positions of all the references that follow it are decreased by 1, and the size of the Vector is also decreased by 1.

Table 11.1

Name	Returns	Parameter Types	Description
add	void	reference, int	Add a new object reference at the indicated position
set	void	reference, int	Change the reference stored at the indicated position
get	reference	int	Return the reference from the indicated position
remove	reference	int	Remove the reference from the indicated position
size	int	none	Return the current size of the `Vector`

Now suppose you want to put values of a primitive type, say `int`, into a `Vector`. Since a `Vector` only stores references to objects, we need to put the `int` value into an object and send a reference to the object to the `add` method of the `Vector`. Fortunately Java provides very simple class definitions for objects that are designed to hold single primitive-type values. For example, the `Integer` class defines an object that stores a single `int` value. There are also `Double`, `Char`, and `Boolean` classes for the other primitive types. To create an `Integer` object containing the value 7, use the command

```
Integer iobj = new Integer(7);
```

To get the `int` value back out of the object, call the method

```
int value = iobj.intValue();
```

The classes `Integer`, `Double`, `Char`, and `Boolean` are called *wrapper classes* because they wrap the primitive value up in an object.

{Definition of Terms}

A **wrapper class** is used to store a primitive value in an object.

Now let's write an applet that has a single `JTextField` where the user can enter as many integer values as she likes, and a `JButton` that she can push when she wants the applet to find the median of the values that have been added so far. We'll simply add each new value (wrapped in an `Integer` object) to a `Vector`; then when the `JButton` is pushed, we'll sort the array and display the middle element. Code 11.7 shows the code.

Note how the `add`, `get`, and `set` methods of the `Vector` class are used instead of the [ ] notation for arrays. Note also how int values are wrapped and unwrapped as they go into are retrieved from the `Vector`. The reason for the

CODE 11.7

```java
import java.awt.*;
import java.awt.event.*;
import javax.swing.*;
import java.util.*;
```

> You must import `java.util.*` if you use the `Vector` class.

```java
public class FindMedian extends JApplet implements ActionListener {
    private JTextField inputField = new JTextField(20);
    private JButton button = new JButton("display median");
    private JLabel result = new JLabel("no median yet");
    private Vector numbers = new Vector();
    private int end = 0;

    public void init() {
        // set up display
        Container window = getContentPane();
        window.setLayout(new FlowLayout());
        window.add(inputField);
        window.add(button);
        window.add(result);
        inputField.addActionListener(this);
        button.addActionListener(this);
    } // end of init method

    public void actionPerformed(ActionEvent event) {
        if (event.getSource() == inputField) {
            int value = Integer.parseInt(inputField.getText());
            Integer iobj = new Integer(value);
            numbers.add(end,iobj);
            end += 1;
            inputField.setText("");
        }
        else {
            sort();
            int middle = numbers.size()/2;
            Integer iobj = (Integer) numbers.get(middle);
            int value = iobj.intValue();
            result.setText("the median is " + value);
        }
    } // end of actionPerformed method
```

> Wrap int value in an `Integer` object and add to the end of the `Vector`.

> Must use a cast to indicate what kind of object is returned.

> Get reference from the middle of the `Vector` and extract the value from the `Integer` wrapper object.

```java
    private void sort() {
        for (int pos=0; pos<numbers.size()-1; pos+=1) {
            setMin(pos);
        }
    } // end of sort method
```

```
private void setMin(int firstPos) {
    // find the minimum value and its position
    // in the rest of the array
    Integer iobj = (Integer) numbers.get(firstPos);
    int min = iobj.intValue();
    int minPos = firstPos;
    for (int j=firstPos+1; j<numbers.size(); j+=1) {
        iobj = (Integer) numbers.get(j);
        int value = iobj.intValue();
        if (value < min) {
            min = value;
            minPos = j;
            }
        }
    // swap the minimum value with
    // the one in position firstPos
    Integer temp = (Integer) numbers.get(firstPos);
    numbers.set(firstPos,numbers.get(minPos));
    numbers.set(minPos,temp);
    } // end of setMin method

} // end of FindMedian class
```

FindMedian
User types in an arbitrary number of integers, then pushes a button to find the median of them.

use of the (Integer) cast when the get method is called will be covered in detail in Chapter 15, so for now just remember that you must tell the Java compiler what kind of object reference is being returned whenever you call the get.

11.3.1 How the Vector Class Works

The Vector class uses an ordinary Java array to store the references to various objects. The get and set methods simply refer to the array elements at the same positions as the Vector positions they are asked to refer to. The add and remove methods, which arrays don't have similar operations to, are interesting.

The remove method is relatively straightforward. When a reference is removed from the Vector, the method actually moves all the references in elements after the removed one down one element position. That's why the positions of all the references after the removed one decrease by 1. They have been moved down one element position in the array.

The add method has to handle the Vector getting larger. It does this by starting out with a small array (10 elements by default, but you can tell it to start with a larger array by passing an int value to its constructor). Then when there is no more room in the array for another reference, it creates a new, larger array that does have room, copies all the existing references from the old array into the new array, and then adds the new reference. Once all this is done, the old array is thrown away. This is how a `Vector` "grows." Technically it doesn't really grow. The array that stores the references is simply replaced with a bigger one when necessary.

The methods that implement the `Vector` class are a good example of array manipulations. The ability to store references to arbitrary objects will be discussed in Chapter 15, so next I'd like to show you the implementation of a class like the `Vector` class that can only store `double` values (primitive, without wrappers). Code 11.8 implements the constructor and the `add`, `set`, `get`, and `size` methods. The `remove` method is left as an exercise.

CODE 11.8

```java
class DoubleVector {
    private final int initialSpace = 10;
    private final int increment = 1;
    private double [] contents = new double[initialSpace];
    private int currentSpace = initialSpace;
    private int currentSize = 0;

    public void add(int position, double value) {
        // if no room, create a new array
        // and copy old one into it
        if (currentSize == currentSpace) {
            currentSpace += increment;
            double [] newArray = new double[currentSpace];
            for (int i=0; i<currentSize; i+=1) {
                newArray[i] = contents[i];
            }
            contents = newArray;
        }
        // make room for new value
        for (int i=currentSpace-2; i>=position; i-=1) {
            contents[i+1] = contents[i];
        }
        // insert new value and increase size
        contents[position] = value;
        currentSize += 1;
    } // end of add method

    public double get(int position) {
        return contents[position];
    } // end of get method

    public void set(int position, double value) {
        contents[position] = value;
    } // end of set method
```

> Replace the old array with the new one. Remember—an array is an object so `contents` is a reference to the array.

```
public int size() {

    return currentSize;
    } // end of size method
```

```
public void remove(int position) {

    // implementation left as an exercise
    } // end of remove method
```

```
} // end of DoubleVector class
```

The variable `contents` is a *reference* to the array that is storing the current contents of the `DoubleVector`. Since it is a reference, we can make it reference the new array once it has been created and the values copied into it from the old one. From then on a reference to `contents`[i] is a reference to an element in the new array, not the old one.

The variable `currentSpace` keeps track of how big the array is. The array that a `DoubleVector` object starts out with has 10 elements, so 10 `add`'s can be done before it must be "grown" (assuming no removes in the mean time). The variable `currentSize` keeps track of how many values are currently in the array, and it is increased by 1 whenever a new value is added and decreased by 1 when a value is removed. Only when `currentSize` equals `currentSpace` is the array full. So if the array is full when `add` is called, then the array must be grown. Otherwise there is still some room to store a new value.

Written Exercises

1. What are the advantages of using the `Vector` class over an array?

2. What are the disadvantages of using the `Vector` class over an array?

3. Why is a wrapper needed when storing primitive types in a `Vector`?

Programming Exercises

1. Complete the implementation of the `remove` method in the `DoubleVector` class; then modify the `FindMedian` program to use the `DoubleVector` class instead of the `Vector` class, and of course to input `double` values instead of `int` values.

2. Write an applet that has a `JTextField` in which the user can enter one string after another, each one being added to a `Vector` of `String` object references. However, no duplicates should be added (use the `.equals` method to compare two `String` objects). The applet should also have a `JButton` and a `JLabel` such that when the user pushes the `JButton`

the first time, it displays the first string in the `Vector`, then each time it is pushed thereafter displays the next string in the `Vector`. Pushing the `JButton` after the last string in the `Vector` has been displayed should display the message "end of `Vector`". If the user enters another string after pushing the `JButton`, then the next `JButton` push should start with the first string in the `Vector` again.

3. Modify the applet above to keep the strings in the `Vector` in ascending order. Two strings can be compared with the `compareTo` method [i.e., `str1.compareTo(str2)`]. It returns an integer that is negative if `str1` is less than `str2`, 0 if `str1` is equal to `str2`, and positive if `str1` is greater than `str2`. Do not sort the `Vector` each time a new string is added. Simply put it in the correct place, and move all the larger strings over to make room for it.

11.4 OVERLOADING METHOD NAMES

The actual implementation of the `Vector` class by default sets the initial size of the array it uses to store things to 10 and increases the size of the array by 1 whenever more space is needed. However, you can send a different size and different increase amount to the `Vector` constructor when you create one, for example,

```
Vector table = new Vector(100,35)
```

This tells the `Vector` object that the array should have 100 elements and that it should grow by 35 elements whenever more space is needed. Being able to provide these two values is very handy because it allows you to avoid having to extend (and copy) the array too often.

But now consider how the `Vector` class must be implemented. Sometimes a `Vector` object is created as in the example above (with two arguments), and sometimes a Vector object is created with

```
Vector table = new Vector();
```

There is no way the `Vector` class can have just one constructor. For example, if all it had was a constructor with two parameters (for the initial size and increase amount), then what would it do if a `Vector` object were created and no arguments were sent? There is no way in Java to know that no arguments were sent.

Instead, the `Vector` class has two different constructors to handle these two situations. One is defined with no parameters, the other with two. When you create a `Vector` object and send no arguments, Java automatically calls the constructor that has no parameters specified. When you create a `Vector` object and you send two arguments, Java automatically calls the constructor that has two parameters. There clearly can be no confusion.

Now let's modify the `DoubleVector` class defined in the previous section to do the same thing. We'll include two different constructors, one with no parameters that creates an array with 10 elements and increases the size by 1, and another that lets the user of the class specify the size and increase amount (Code 11.9).

CODE 11.9

These are now simply the defaults.

```
class DoubleVector {
    private final int defaultInitialSpace = 10;
    private final int defaultIncrement = 1;
    private double [] contents;
    private int currentSpace;
    private int currentSize = 0;
    private final int increment;

    public DoubleVector() {
        contents = new double[defaultInitialSpace];
        currentSpace = defaultInitialSpace;
        increment = defaultIncrement;
    } // end of constructor

    public DoubleVector(int init, int inc) {
        contents = new double[init];
        currentSpace = init;
        increment = inc;
    } // end of constructor

    // all other methods unchanged

} // end of DoubleVector class
```

Constructors must create arrays and give initial values because they depend on which constructor is used.

Notice that the constructors are now responsible for creating the initial array and giving initial values to `currentSpace` and `increment`. These cannot be done as in the original version because the values differ depending on which constructor is used.

This is an example of what is called *overloading,* and it applies not only to constructors but to all methods. The basic idea is that you can have more than one method in a class with the same name, as long as either the number of parameters is different (as shown above) or the types of the parameters are different.

{New Concepts}

A method name is **overloaded** if there are two or more methods in a class with the same name but that differ in the number and/or types of their parameters. Java determines which one to use by the number and/or type of arguments used in the call.

For example, the `Animator.write` method that you called to display debugging or other information when using the Animator is really several methods, all with the name `write`. They all have one parameter, but one has an `int` parameter, one has a `double` parameter, and one has a `String` parameter. They all do pretty much the same thing. In fact the code is almost identical, differing only in that the `int` or `double` must be converted to a `String` before being displayed on the screen.

The name of a method along with the types of its parameters (in order) specifies a *signature* for a method. You cannot have two (or more) methods in a class definition with the same signature.

{Definition of Terms}

A **signature** of a method is the name and the list of parameter types.

The names given to the parameters, the return type, and whether the method is public or private are irrelevant and have nothing to do with the signature. Hence

```
public void doit(int x);
```

and

```
private int doit(int y);
```

both have the same signature (method name `doit` and single `int` parameter) and cannot appear in the same class definition.

Another example of overloading is three methods that we can add to our `DoubleVector` class that search for a particular value in the array and return its index. All three have a `double` parameter that is the value to search for. One version has no additional parameters and simply searches the entire array of current values. Another has a single additional parameter that is the position of the last position to search (i.e., the array will be searched from position 0 to the indicated position, or to the end of the current values if the position is too large), and the third has two additional parameters that specify the starting position and ending position of the search. If the search methods do not find the desired value, they return −1 (Code 11.10).

The third `search` method, with all three parameters, checks for valid starting and ending positions, then does the search. To save writing code, the first two versions simply call the third version and supply the information that they don't get from their own parameters. In a sense the third method is like a private helper method, but it simply isn't private because we *do* want other classes to be able to call it.

Although having each of the first two `search` methods call the third one is a little less efficient, avoiding the duplication of the checking and the searching code makes it easier to write and more likely to be correct. This is commonly done when method names are overloaded because the methods typically have a similar purpose.

CODE 11.10

```
class DoubleVector {

    private final int defaultInitialSpace = 10;
    private final int defaultIncrement = 1;
    private double [] contents;
    private int currentSpace;
    private int currentSize = 0;
    private final int increment;

    public int search(double target) {
    // search over all valid elements
        return search(target,0,currentSize-1);
    } // end of search method
```

Call the most general version and return whatever it returns.

```
    public int search(double target, int endPosition) {
    // search from beginning to endPosition
        return search(target,0,endPosition);
    } // end of search method
```

```
    public int search(double target, int startPosition,
                      int endPosition) {
        // check for invalid positions
        if (startPosition >= currentSize) {
            return -1;
        }
        if (endPosition >= currentSize) {
            endPosition = currentSize-1;
        }
        // check each specified element
        int pos = startPosition;
        while (pos <= endPosition) {
            if (Math.abs(contents[i]-target) < 0.0001) {
                return i;
            }
        }
        return -1;
    } // end of search method
```

The method with all the parameters does the work, and the methods with fewer simply call it.

Remember, never compare doubles for equality.

```
    // all other methods unchanged

} // end of DoubleVector class
```

Written Exercises

1. What are the signatures of the following methods?

   a. `public void f()`

   b. `private void f()`

   c. `private int g(double x)`

d. `private int g(Vector x)`

e. `public void draw(Graphics g)`

f. `public void draw(int x, int y, Graphics g)`

g. `private void sort(int [] table)`

h. `public MyClass()`

i. `public MyClass(int a, double b)`

j. `public MyClass (double a, int b)`

2. Indicate which groups of methods above cannot be in the same class definition.

3. Modify the `DoubleVector` class definition in this section to further overload the search method by adding an optional `double` parameter that specifies the difference between the target value and the array value that is "close enough." Assume the default for this value is 0.0001 if a method that doesn't have it as a parameter is called. In all you should have six `search` methods, the three that are there already plus three new versions with the extra parameter.

11.5 ARRAYS OF TWO (OR MORE) DIMENSIONS

It is quite common for a collection of data items to represent a table or a grid with several rows and several columns. The grid layout manager is an example you've already seen. You may also be familiar with a spreadsheet. It contains a grid of entries in which you can type numbers, text, and formulas. The display screen you use with your computer displays a grid of small colored dots on the screen (each dot is called a pixel). By setting each pixel to a specific color, the screen can display text, graphical shapes, and images.

In Java you can create an array object that has rows and columns—a *two-dimensional array*. Such an array object works much as the simple array objects from the previous section (*one-dimensional arrays*) do except that each element is identified by two positions—the row it is in *and* the column it is in. Two sets of square brackets are used wherever one was before. For example, the following creates a two-dimensional array object with 10 rows and 20 columns and makes the variable `table` refer to it:

```
int [][] table = new int[10][20];
```

Rows and columns are numbered starting at 0 just as before. To refer to the element in the first row and first column, you write

```
table[0][0]
```

Arbitrary expressions that evaluate to integers can be used to specify both the row and column of any element in the array object.

{New Concepts}

A **two-dimensional array** has elements that are indexed by row and column.

Arrays of three, four, and higher dimensions can also be created and used. They are a straightforward extension of the two-dimensional array, using several sets of square brackets when creating them and several indices when referencing them. For example, a 5-by-10-by-4-by-20 array of doubles called `tensor` (four-dimensional) is created by writing

```
double [] [] [] [] tensor = new double [5][10][4][20];
```

11.5.1 A Color Pattern Applet

I'll illustrate the use of two-dimensional array objects via an applet that simply draws a pattern of colors on the screen (Code 11.11). There will be no interaction. The applet will create a two-dimensional array of `JLabel` objects with no text in them. The `JLabel` objects will be added to the window that uses a grid layout manager to make the `JLabel` objects appear in 10 rows of 20 columns. To get color, the background color of each `JLabel` will be set so that those around the border of the grid will be red and those in the middle will be green.

Note the use of a private helper method in place of a nested loop. This is very common when two-dimensional (or more) arrays are used in a program. Note also that the index of the first row and column of the array is 0, the index of the last row is `rows` minus 1, and the index of the last column is `columns` minus 1.

A variation of grid layout manager was used to get a border around each label in the grid. Two extra arguments, both having value 2, were passed to the grid layout manager constructor to indicate that it should leave 2 units of border between each `JLabel` in the grid. The first 2 is for the horizontal border, the second for the vertical. The border is the same color as the background of the window (black), making it possible to distinguish between adjacent `JLabels` that are the same color.

11.5.2 A Simple Spreadsheet

Code 11.12 is another example of using several arrays, both one- and two-dimensional, to present a simple spreadsheet. It displays a grid of `JTextField` objects that the user can enter numbers into. Whenever a number is entered into some `JTextField` and Enter or Return is hit, the applet will compute the sum of all the numbers in the same row and display that sum at the end of that row, and will compute the sum of all the numbers in the same column and display that sum at the bottom of that column.

The display consists of several rows of `JTextField` objects followed by a `JLabel` that displays the row sum, and then one final row of `JLabel` objects for that display column sums, and a blank `JLabel` to fill out the lower

CODE 11.11

```java
import java.awt.*;
import javax.swing.*;

public class ColorApplet extends JApplet {
    private final int rows = 10;
    private final int columns = 20;
    private JLabel [][] display = new JLabel[rows][columns];
    private Container window;

    public void init() {
        window = getContentPane();
        window.setBackground(Color.black);
        window.setLayout(new GridLayout(rows,columns,2,2));
        // create an array of green JLabels (no text)
        for (int row=0; row<rows; row+=1) {
            fillRow(row);
        }
        // change top/bottom border JLabels to red
        for (int col=0; col<columns; col+=1) {
            display[0][col].setBackground(Color.red);
            display[rows-1][col].setBackground(Color.red);
        }
        // change right/left border JLabels to red
        for (int row=0; row<rows; row+=1) {
            display[row][0].setBackground(Color.red);
            display[row][columns-1].setBackground(Color.red);
        }
    } // end of init method

    // fill a row with green JLabels
    private void fillRow(int row) {
        for (int col=0; col<columns; col+=1) {
            display[row][col] = new JLabel("");
            display[row][col].setOpaque(true);
            display[row][col].setBackground(Color.green);
            window.add(display[row][col]);
        }
    } // end of fillrow method

} // end of ColorApplet class
```

ColorApplet
Displays a grid of colors, with the ones around the border red, the inner ones green.

right corner of the grid. Since a grid layout must be filled complete row by complete row, the code uses the setUpRow method to create a row of JTextField objects and a JLabel and add them to the window. This method is called repeatedly to set up all but the last row of the display.

Note that a distinct Listener object is created for every JTextField. Each Listener object records the row and column of its

CODE 11.12

```
import java.awt.*;
import java.awt.event.*;
import javax.swing.*;
```

```
public class SpreadSheet extends JApplet {
    private final int rows = 6;
    private final int columns = 4;
    private JTextField [] [] gridFields =
        new JTextField [rows][columns];
    private double [] [] gridValues = new double [rows][columns];
    private JLabel [] rowSums = new JLabel [rows];
    private JLabel [] columnSums = new JLabel [columns];
    private Container window;
```

> The values, in double form, are kept in the gridValues array.

```
    public void init() {
        // set up window
        window = getContentPane();
        window.setLayout(new GridLayout(rows+1,columns+1));
        // set up all but last row of display
        for (int row=0; row<rows; row+=1) {
            setUpRow(row);
            }
        // set up last row
        for (int col=0; col<columns; col+=1) {
            columnSums[col] = new JLabel("");
            window.add(columnSums[col]);
            }
        window.add(new JLabel(""));
        } // end of init method
```

```
    private void setUpRow(int row) {
        for (int col=0; col<columns; col+=1) {
            gridFields[row][col] = new JTextField(10);
            gridValues[row][col] = 0.0;
            window.add(gridFields[row][col]);
            Listener temp = new Listener(row,col,this);
            gridFields[row][col].addActionListener(temp);
            }
        rowSums[row] = new JLabel("");
        window.add(rowSums[row]);
        } // end of setUpRow method
```

> Each JTextField gets its own Listener object.

```
    public void setValue(int row, int col) {
        String str = gridFields[row][col].getText();
        gridValues[row][col] = Double.parseDouble(str);
        } // end of setValue method
```

```
public void sumRow(int row) {

    double sum = 0.0;
    for (int col=0; col<columns; col+=1) {
        sum += gridValues[row][col];
    }
    rowSums[row].setText(sum+"");
} // end of sumRow method
```

> Each Listener object calls sumRow and sends its row, and calls SumColumn and sends its column.

```
public void sumColumn(int col) {

    double sum = 0.0;
    for (int row=0; row<rows; row+=1) {
        sum += gridValues[row][col];
    }
    columnSums[col].setText(sum+"");
} // end of sumColumn method

} // end of SpreadSheet class
```

```
class Listener implements ActionListener {

    private final int myRow;
    private final int myColumn;
    private SpreadSheet theSheet;

    public Listener(int r, int c, SpreadSheet s) {

        myRow = r;
        myColumn = c;
        theSheet = s;
    } // end of constructor

    public void actionPerformed(ActionEvent event) {

        theSheet.setValue(myRow,myColumn);
        theSheet.sumRow(myRow);
        theSheet.sumColumn(myColumn);
    } // end of actionPerformed method

} // end of Listener class
```

SpreadSheet

Displays a grid of JTextField objects and computes row and column sums of values in the grid.

corresponding JTextField in its instance variables myRow and myColumn, and also has an instance variable for the SpreadSheet object so it can call the setValue, sumRow, and sumColumn methods when its associated JTextField has a new number entered in it. The setValue method extracts the value from the JTextField and puts it in corresponding position of the two-dimensional array of double gridValues. The sumRow method sums the values in the row and displays the result in the JLabel at the end of that row. The sumColumn method sums the values in the column and displays the result in the `JLabel` at the bottom of that column.

Programming Exercises

1. Modify the `ColorApplet` to display an 8-by-8 checkerboard pattern of red and black squares.

2. Modify the `ColorApplet` to display a 10-by-10 pattern of colors, with the boxes along the diagonal from the upper left corner to the lower right corner red and the rest of the boxes white.

3. Modify the `ColorApplet` to display a 19-by-19 bull's-eye pattern of blue and yellow squares. The squares around the border should be blue, those immediately inside them should be yellow, those immediately inside them should be blue, etc.

4. Write an applet that displays a 10-by-10 grid of `JButton` objects, all initially green but with no text displayed, with a 2-pixel-wide white border between them. When the user pushes one of the buttons, make the rest of the buttons in the same row and same column, including the one pushed, become red.

5. Modify the applet in the previous problem to change the color of each button in the same row and column to red if it is green and to green if it is red.

6. Modify the `SpreadSheet` applet to display the sum of all the values in the grid in the lower right corner.

7. Write an applet that displays a 5-by-5 grid of `JTextField` objects, and below it a row of `JButton` objects, all labeled "to top". When the user pushes one of the buttons, find the largest value in the column of `JTextField` objects above it, then exchange the values in the entire row that the largest value is in with the values in the entire first row of the grid. For example, if the grid has the values

11	73	32	26	92
48	74	37	64	31
40	64	65	37	86
33	59	51	70	47
37	53	68	43	89

and the user clicks on the button below the fourth column (position 3), then the program should find the maximum value in that column to be 70 and should swap the first and fourth rows to produce

33	59	51	70	47
48	74	37	64	31
40	64	65	37	86
11	73	32	26	92
37	53	68	43	89

8. Modify your solution to the previous problem so that after a button has been pushed and the grid modified, each value in the first row is subtracted from the value in the same column in each other row. For example, the final result in the example in the previous problem should be

33	59	51	70	47
15	15	−14	6	16
7	5	14	−33	−39
−22	14	−19	−44	45
4	−6	17	27	42

Summary

- A one-dimensional array is an object that stores several values of the same type.
- Each value occupies a position in the array that is identified by an integer value. The first position is numbered 0, and the position of the last value in an array with N values is $N - 1$.
- Each place in the array, commonly called an element, is named by writing an expression enclosed between [and]. The expression, called an index, must evaluate to an integer, which then indicates which position in the array is to be used.
- When an array object is created, its elements are initialized to specific values depending on the type. Elements of arrays of integers are initialized to 0, doubles to 0.0, and object references to null.
- When an array of object references is created, the objects themselves are not. Code must be written to explicitly create the appropriate number of objects and store references to them in elements of the array.

- An initializer list can be used in creating an array to give elements nondefault initial values.
- The number of elements in an array object referred to by some variable can be obtained by writing the variable followed by `.length`.
- Java's `Vector` class defines arraylike objects that are not fixed in size.
- Wrapper classes `Integer`, `Double`, `Boolean`, and `Char` allow values of primitive types `int`, `double`, `boolean`, and `char` to be put into simple objects so they can be used in other classes, such as the `Vector` class, that can only handle objects and not primitive-type values.
- Two-dimensional arrays are indexed by two integer values, a row and a column, and are useful for representing information that has a tabular or grid form. As in one-dimensional arrays, the index of the first row or column is 0.
- Arrays of more than two dimensions can be created and used.
- The `break` command causes a loop to terminate immediately and execution to continue with the command immediately after the body of the loop. Only the innermost loop of a nested loop containing the `break` command is terminated.
- A method's signature is its name and the types of its parameters, in order.
- Overloading allows several methods with the same name but different signatures to exist in the same class. You can always tell which version is called by the number and/or types of the arguments in the call.

Glossary

Array An object that contains several values, all of the same type or class, each of which has a position.

Break A command that causes a loop to terminate immediately.

Element Another name for one position in an array.

Index An expression that when evaluated, specifies a position within an array.

Overloading Having two or more methods with the same name but different signatures in the same class.

Selection Sort A sorting method in which the smallest value is selected and put into the first position, the next smallest into the second position, etc.

Signature The name and parameter types (in order) of a method.

Two-Dimensional Array An array with rows and columns. Elements are identified by two indices (row and column).

Wrapper Class A class that defines an object that stores a primitive-type value. Wrapper classes include `Integer`, `Double`, `Boolean`, and `Char`.

CHAPTER 12

Application Programs

12.1 APPLICATION PROGRAMS VERSUS APPLETS

All the programs shown so far in this book have been applets, designed to run via Web browsers, but also capable of being tested with the Applet Viewer. Such programs are restricted in what they can do, especially when it comes to accessing data on the machine they are being executed on. This restriction exists for security reasons, so that you can trust that when you run an applet written by somebody else, it won't cause you any problems, such as deleting files or accessing private information, either accidentally or intentionally.

You can also write a Java program that is not an applet. Such a program is called an *application program,* and it is just like most other software you probably use on your computer such as a word processor, game, or the tools you use to write, compile, and test your Java programs. Java application programs can read or modify existing files, write new files, access I/O devices, and even be part of a larger program that includes code written in other programming languages such as C and C++.

> **{New Concepts}**
>
> An **application program** can access files and other resources located on the computer it is running on and interact with code written in other programming languages.

347

12.2 A SIMPLE APPLICATION PROGRAM

Every Java application program must have a public method called `main` with a single parameter that is an array of `String` references. An application program is executed by using the name of the class that contains the `main` method (how this is done is dependent on the development environment you are using). When the application program is executed, the Java interpreter will look for the `main` method in the indicated class and automatically call it to get things started. Of course what you do in the method is up to you. The program shown in Code 12.1 simply prints a short message.

CODE 12.1

SimpleApplication
Prints "hello world" in the terminal window.

> An application program must have a `public static void main` method with a parameter that is an array of `String` objects.

```java
public class SimpleApplication {

    public static void main(String [] args) {
        System.out.println("hello world");
    } // end of main method

} // end of SimpleApplication class
```

This is just about the simplest Java application program you can write. Note that nothing is imported and the class does not extend anything. When the program executes, no graphical interface appears. All that happens is that the text "hello world" is output and the program terminates.

> **{New Concepts}**
>
> An application program must have a method declared `public static void main(String [] args)` in the primary class definition (the parameter name does not have to be `args`).

The `main` method in an application program can be sent information via the `String` array parameter `args` when it is executed. Exactly how this is done is very dependent on the development environment you are using to write and run your programs. Since there is no standard for this, you'll have to find out how your environment handles this.

It is important to realize that no objects are created when an application program begins execution. Hence there will be no `SimpleApplication` object unless the program creates one itself, and the example above doesn't. This may seem a bit strange, since up to now I've been saying that it is objects that do things, not classes. Clearly something different is going on here.

The key is that the main method is declared to be `static`. Without going into too many details on the specifics of Java, it suffices to say that a static method is *independent* of any objects. This is unlike nonstatic methods, which have no meaning except when executing in the context of a particular object. A static method can be executed without an object of the class it is in having been created. Hence `main` can be executed even though no `SimpleApplication` object is created.

{New Concepts}

A **static method** exists independently of any objects and can be executed without an object of the class it is in ever having been created. It does not execute in the context of any object.

Since static methods are not associated with any object, they *cannot* directly refer to identifiers that are names of instance variables of any objects, even those that are defined by the same class that the `main` method is in. For example:

```
public class DoesntWork {                 An instance variable of every
      private int instVar;                DoesntWork object.

      public static void main(String [] args) {

           instVar = 17;                  This will give an error
      } // end of main method             message.

   } // end of DoesntWork class
```

The reason you can't do this is because the static method `main` exists independently of any object, and it can be called whether zero, one, or several objects of the class `DoesntWork` exist. If none exist, then there is no variable `instVar` to reference. If there are several, it won't know which one to reference.

{New Concepts}

Static methods cannot access instance variables of objects defined by the class the static method is in.

Written Exercises

1. What objects are created when the application program `SimpleApplication` above is executed? Explain.

2. Why can't an application program's `main` method directly refer to an instance variable in the same class the method is in?

3. How are arguments sent to an application program's `main` method in your development environment?

Programming Exercises

1. Find out how arguments are sent to the `main` method in your development environment, and write a program that prints each one, one per line, using `System.out.println`. Test your program with several different combinations of arguments.

2. Write an application program that prints the first 25 prime numbers, one per line. A number (integer) is prime if it can be evenly divided by only itself and 1 (e.g., 17 is prime, 18 is not because it can be evenly divided by 2, 3, 6, or 9 in addition to 1 and 18).

3. Modify your solution to the previous problem to get an integer, call it N, from the first command line argument. Then print the first N prime numbers, one per line.

12.3 APPLICATION PROGRAMS WITH A GUI

Application programs can also have a graphical user interface just as applets do. As such, they have most of the advantages of applications (file access, etc.) and the advantages of applets (a graphical user interface). Just remember that an application program cannot be run as an applet. Only classes that `extend` `JApplet` can.

Creating a basic GUI is very easy. The swing class `JFrame` defines a very simple, empty window, so simply extending the `JFrame` class (as you would extend a `JApplet` class for an applet) and then creating an object of that class will get things started. After that you add things to the extended `JFrame` just as you would an extended `JApplet`. Code 12.2 is a simple application program example that creates a GUI containing only a `JLabel`.

Once you get things set up, the `MyGUI` class works very much like an applet. It has a content pane, to which other displayable objects can be added. Notice that `JFrame` is extended, not `JApplet`, and that a `JFrame` *does not* expect an `init` method to set things up. Instead you simply use a constructor as you would to set up any other kind of object.

> {New Concepts}
>
> An application can have a GUI by creating a `JFrame` object (via a class that extends `JFrame`). A `JFrame` works much as a `JApplet` except for a small amount of initialization.

By default, a `JFrame` object has no size, and even if it did, it would not be visible on the screen (actually, it does have a size—0 by 0). To give the `JFrame` a size, you call the `setSize` method and pass it two arguments—the width and height, respectively. To make the `JFrame` visible, you call the `setVisible` method and pass the single argument `true`. Be sure that you do both of these calls. If you only set the size, it still won't be visible, and if you only make it visible, it will have size 0 by 0 which is essentially invisible,

CODE 12.2

```
import javax.swing.*;
import java.awt.*;

public class GUIApplication {

    public static void main(String [] args) {
        MyGUI gui = new MyGUI();
    } // end of main method

    } // end of GUIApplication class
class MyGUI extends JFrame {
    private final int frameWidth = 200;
    private final int frameHeight = 150;

    public MyGUI() {
        setSize(frameWidth,frameHeight);
        Container window = getContentPane();
        window.setLayout(new FlowLayout());
        JLabel msg = new JLabel("an application GUI");
        window.add(msg);
        setVisible(true);
    } // end of constructor

    } // end of MyGUI class
```

These are needed for the JFrame and Container classes.

This class looks like an applet, except that the constructor sets everything up, not an init method.

JFrame objects by default are 0 by 0 and invisible. You must give them a size or you won't see anything.

Don't make the JFrame visible until after you have set up the GUI.

GUIApplication
Creates a display window and displays a message in it. It will not terminate itself, you'll have to kill it.

too. Also, don't make the JFrame visible until after you have added everything to window. If you do, then the things you added after making the JFrame visible won't appear.

{New Concepts}

Be sure to give a JFrame object a size *and* make it visible. Failure to do both will result in nothing being displayed on the screen even though the JFrame object was created. Always make the JFrame visible *after* setting up the GUI.

There is one small difference between application programs with a GUI and those without a GUI. Without a GUI, when the execution of the main method ends, the program terminates. However, with a GUI, when the execution of the main method ends, the JFrame is still displayed and continues to execute. To make it terminate, you must execute a call to a special method called System.exit. This method gets rid of the JFrame object and then terminates execution of the program.

The circumstances under which the System.exit is called are up to you when you write your application. Normally it will be in response to some event, such as clicking on a button (a "quit" or "exit" button), or perhaps some error condition that the program detects. Code 12.3 is a modification of the program above that includes a "quit" button.

CODE 12.3

```
import javax.swing.*;
import java.awt.*;
import java.awt.event.*;

public class GUIApplication2 {

    public static void main(String [] args) {
        MyGUI gui = new MyGUI();
    } // end of main method


} // end of GUIApplication2 class
class MyGUI extends JFrame implements ActionListener {

    private final int frameWidth = 100;
    private final int frameHeight = 200;

    public MyGUI() {
        setSize(frameWidth,frameHeight);
        Container window = getContentPane();
        window.setLayout(new FlowLayout());
        JButton quit = new JButton("quit");
        window.add(quit);
        quit.addActionListener(this);
        setVisible(true);
    } // end of constructor


    public void actionPerformed(ActionEvent event) {
        System.exit(0);  ◄─────────────────┐
    } // end of actionPerformed method      │
                                ┌───────────────────────┐
    } // end of MyGUI class     │ This command terminates │
                                │ the application program.│
                                └───────────────────────┘
```

GUIApplication2
Like the original, except has a JButton to push to get it to terminate without having to kill it.

The argument sent to System.exit can be any integer. Generally 0 means that the program terminated normally, any other nonzero value indicates some sort of error occurred that forced termination. Different nonzero values can be used for different error conditions. Development environments use this value in different ways, so check yours to see how it works.

12.3.1 A Simplification

At the beginning of this chapter we saw that a main method can be executed whether or not any objects of the class it is in have been created. Hence, consider the modification in Code 12.4 of the program next page.

When this program is executed, the main method will create a GUIApplication object which constructs and displays the GUI. No other class is needed, especially one that has no other purpose than to contain the

CODE 12.4

```java
import javax.swing.*;
import java.awt.*;
import java.awt.event.*;

public class GUIApplication3 extends JFrame
                      implements ActionListener {
    private final int frameWidth = 100;
    private final int frameHeight = 200;

    public static void main(String [] args) {
        GUIApplication3 gui = new GUIApplication3();
    } // end of main method

    public GUIApplication3() {
        setSize(frameWidth,frameHeight);
        Container window = getContentPane();
        window.setLayout(new FlowLayout(FlowLayout.LEFT));
        JButton quit = new JButton("quit");
        window.add(quit);
        quit.addActionListener(this);
        setVisible(true);
    } // end of constructor

    public void actionPerformed(ActionEvent event) {
        System.exit(0);
    } // end of actionPerformed method

} // end of GUIApplication3 class
```

Putting the main method here doesn't affect anything else in the class.

main method. Having the main method in the same class that defines the GUI is simply a convenience.

> **GUIApplication3**
> Similar to GUIApplication2, except only one class definition.

Written Exercises

1. What Java class defines an object that displays a graphical window?
2. What must be done to make a JFrame visible?
3. What is needed in order to terminate an application program with a GUI?

Programming Exercise

1. Write an application program that has a GUI with four buttons labeled "red," "green," "blue," and "quit." When a given color button is pushed, the background color of the entire window should be set accordingly. The program should terminate when the "quit" button is pushed.

12.4 MULTIPLE JFRAMES

You can use several `JFrames` to create interesting user interfaces that consist of several windows, using the `setVisible` method to make each window appear and disappear as your application dictates. Here is an example that creates a main window with two `JButton` objects, "get info" and "exit". When the "get info" button is pushed, a new window appears that has text fields in which the user can enter the first and last name of a person. When the user pushes the "enter" button on the second window, the second window disappears (this simple application doesn't do anything with the name typed in, but it wouldn't be hard to save it somewhere). Figure 12.1 shows the two windows as they would appear after "get info" was pushed, a first and last name were entered, but before the "enter" button was pushed.

The program that produces this behavior consists of two extended `JFrame` classes, one for the main window (`TwoFrames`), the other for the second window that appears and disappears (`Input`). The main window class contains the `main` method that creates a `TwoFrames` object with the two `JButton` objects, and also creates an `Input` object, but the `Input` object is not made visible yet. Only when the "get info" button is pushed does it become visible. Once data are typed in and the "enter" button is pushed, the `Input` window is made invisible again (Code 12.5).

Notice how the button push events cause the `Input` window to appear and disappear. Note also the use of the `setLocation` method for a `JFrame`. It specifies the location of the upper left corner of the `Input` window relative to the upper left corner of the main window.

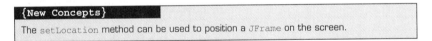

{New Concepts}

The `setLocation` method can be used to position a `JFrame` on the screen.

FIGURE 12.1

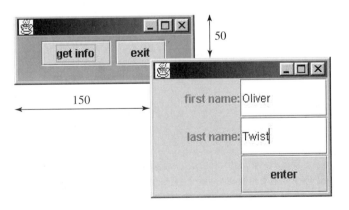

CODE 12.5

```java
import java.awt.*;
import java.awt.event.*;
import javax.swing.*;

class TwoFrames extends JFrame implements ActionListener {

    public static void main(String [] args) {
        TwoFrames me = new TwoFrames();
        } // end of main method

    private final int frameWidth = 200;
    private final int frameHeight = 75;
    private final int inputFrameLeft = 150;
    private final int inputFrameTop = 50;
    private JButton getInfo = new JButton("get info");
    private JButton quit = new JButton("exit");
    private Input info = new Input();

    public TwoFrames() {
        // set up main JFrame
        setSize(200,75);
        Container window = getContentPane();
        window.setLayout(new FlowLayout());
        window.setBackground(Color.green);
        window.add(getInfo);
        window.add(quit);
        getInfo.addActionListener(this);
        quit.addActionListener(this);

        // position the Input JFrame for
        // for when it becomes visible
        info.setLocation(inputFrameLeft,inputFrameTop);
        setVisible(true);
        } // end of constructor

    public void actionPerformed(ActionEvent event) {
        if (event.getSource() == getInfo) {
            // make the Input window visible
            info.setVisible(true);
            }
        else {
            System.exit(0);
            }
        } // end of actionPerformed method

    } // end of TwoFrames class

class Input extends JFrame implements ActionListener {
    private final int frameWidth = 200;
    private final int frameHeight = 150;
    private JTextField first = new JTextField(20);
```

> The TwoFrames constructor does not make the Input object visible, but it does position it relative to the main window.

> Make the Input window visible when the user pushes the "get info" button.

```
private JTextField last = new JTextField(20);
private JButton enter = new JButton("enter");

public Input() {
    // set up GUI for this JFrame
    setSize(frameWidth,frameHeight);
    Container window = getContentPane();
    window.setLayout(new GridLayout(3,2));
    window.add(new JLabel("first name:",
                SwingConstants.RIGHT));
    window.add(first);
    window.add(new JLabel("last name:",
                SwingConstants.RIGHT));
    window.add(last);
    window.add(new JLabel(""));
    window.add(enter);
    enter.addActionListener(this);
} // end of constructor

public void actionPerformed(ActionEvent event) {
    // clear text fields
    first.setText("");
    last.setText("");

    // make this JFrame invisible
    setVisible(false);
} // end of ActionPerformed method

} // end of Input class
```

Set this window's size, but don't make it visible.

Make this window invisible when the user pushes the "enter" button.

TwoFrames
A main `JFrame` creates a second `JFrame` that becomes visible when the user click on a button.

Programming Exercises

1. Write a program with a main window having two text fields and two buttons. The two text fields are for entering x and y coordinates. One of the buttons, when pushed, creates a new visible 100×100 window positioned at the x and y coordinates previously entered into the text fields. Every button push creates a new window. Pushing the other button terminates the program.

2. Write a program that creates three visible, nonoverlapping windows. One of the windows should have a button labeled "Larry," another with a button labeled "Moe," and the third with a button labeled "Curly." Each should have a gray background initially. If any one of the buttons is pushed, the background of the window it is in should be changed to green and the background of the other two windows changed to red. The main window should have a button labeled "exit" that causes the program to terminate when pushed.

12.5 MENUS

JFrame objects are the first we've seen that permit *menus* to be attached. Doing so is fairly easy, and having them will make your application programs more professional-looking.

Menus are defined using three Java classes: JMenuBar, JMenu, and JMenuItem. A JMenuBar defines an object that displays one or more pull-down menus along the top of the JFrame. A JMenu defines an object that displays a single pull-down menu that consists of one or more JMenuItem objects. A JMenuItem object is like a JButton in that it can have an ActionListener that reacts to the corresponding menu item being chosen by the user.

Here is a simple program that demonstrates the construction and use of menus in an application program. The JMenuBar will contain just one pull-down JMenu (you can have as many as you like), and that menu will have four JMenuItem objects, one for turning the background color of the JFrame to red, one to green, and one to blue, and one for causing the application program to terminate. When the user pulls down the JMenu, it will look like Figure 12.2. The code for this simple demonstration program is shown in Code 12.6.

As you can see, JMenuItem objects are added to the JMenu object, which in turn is added to the JMenuBar object. Note in particular that the JMenuBar is *not* added to the JFrame object. Instead the JFrame is told that it should use the JMenuBar object via the setJMenuBar method.

{New Concepts}

Use the setMenuBar method to give a JFrame object a menu bar. Do *not* try to add the JMenuBar object to the JFrame or the content pane.

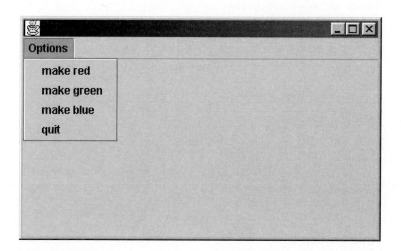

FIGURE 12.2

CODE 12.6

```java
import javax.swing.*;
import java.awt.*;
import java.awt.event.*;

public class MenuDemo extends JFrame
                      implements ActionListener {

    public static void main(String [] args) {
        MenuDemo gui = new MenuDemo();
        } // end of main method

    private final int frameWidth = 200;
    private final int frameHeight = 200;
    private Container window;
    JMenuItem makeRed = new JMenuItem("make red");
    JMenuItem makeGreen = new JMenuItem("make green");
    JMenuItem makeBlue = new JMenuItem("make blue");
    JMenuItem quit = new JMenuItem("quit");

    public MenuDemo() {
        setSize(frameWidth,frameHeight);
        window = getContentPane();

        // set up the menus
        JMenuBar bar = new JMenuBar();
        setJMenuBar(bar);

        JMenu mOptions = new JMenu("Options");
        bar.add(mOptions);

        mOptions.add(makeRed);
        mOptions.add(makeGreen);
        mOptions.add(makeBlue);
        mOptions.add(quit);

        // attach listeners to each JMenuItem
        makeRed.addActionListener(this);
        makeGreen.addActionListener(this);
        makeBlue.addActionListener(this);
        quit.addActionListener(this);
        setVisible(true);
        } // end of constructor

    public void actionPerformed(ActionEvent event) {
        // set the correct window color
        if (event.getSource() == makeRed) {
            window.setBackground(Color.red);
            }
        else if (event.getSource() == makeGreen) {
            window.setBackground(Color.green);
            }
```

Create a `JMenuBar` object and make it part of the `JFrame`. Do not try to add it to `window`!

Create a `JMenu` object and add it to the `JMenuBar`.

Add the four `JMenuItem` objects to the `JMenu`.

`JMenuItem` objects use action listeners just as `JButton` objects do.

```
         else if (event.getSource() == makeBlue) {
             window.setBackground(Color.blue);
             }
     // ... or exit
     else {
             System.exit(0);
             }
     } // end of actionPerformed method
```

Written Exercise

MenuDemo
Demonstrates a pull-down menu with items that cause the color of the window to change.

1. JMenuBar objects cannot be used with applets. Why?

Programming Exercises

1. Modify the MenuDemo menu to include the colors white, gray, black, yellow, and orange.

2. Write a program that has two menus. The first, titled "Program", has two items, "clear" and "quit". "Clear" resets the visible window to all gray. "Quit" terminates the program. The second menu, titled "Colors" has three options: "make red", "make green", and "make blue". Each option sets the background color of the visible window to the corresponding color.

3. Write a program that has a GUI with a single large JTextField. Give it three menus, one for setting the color of the text (the foreground color) to red, orange, yellow, green, blue, white, or black; another for setting the color of the text background to one of the same set of colors; and a third for either resetting the colors to black letters on a gray background or quitting the program. You don't have to do anything with the text other than to display it using the chosen color on the chosen background.

Summary

- An application program executes independently of a Web browser or Applet Viewer.

- An application program can access files on the machine it is running on.

- An application program must have a method declared public static void main(String [] args).

- An application program without a GUI terminates when the main method finishes.

- An application program with a GUI terminates when the System.exit method is called.

- A static method executes independently of any objects in the program.
- A static method (e.g., main) cannot directly reference instance variables of any object.
- A JFrame is used to set up a GUI in an application program.
- A JFrame object must be given a size via the setSize method to be visible.
- A JFrame object is made visible or invisible by using the setVisible method.
- A JFrame object can be positioned on the screen via the setLocation method.
- A JFrame object can have menus.
- Menus are created using JMenuBar, JMenu, and JMenuItem objects.
- A JMenuBar object is added to a JFrame via the setJMenuBar method.
- JMenuItem objects should have action listeners that react to the corresponding item being chosen.

Glossary

Application Program An application program executes independently of a Web browser or the Applet Viewer. Unlike an applet, it has access to all the resources on the machine it is running.

Static Method A method that can be executed independently of any objects in the program.

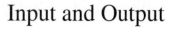

CHAPTER 13

Input and Output

13.1 FILES

A *file* is simply related information saved on one of your computer's permanent memory devices (the hard drive, a CD-ROM, a floppy disk, etc.). You can write programs that read the information in an existing file, create new files with new information, and even modify or add to the information in an existing file.

> {Definition of Terms}
>
> A **file** is information stored on a permanent memory device.

An existing file can be accessed from a Java program in one of two basic ways. Either you can read the information starting with the first thing in the file, followed by the second, etc., all the way to the end (called *sequential access*); or you can jump from place to place in the file and read some information from there (called *random access*). Similarly, you can create (write to) a file from beginning to end (sequentially), or you can write to random places in a file.

> {Definition of Terms}
>
> **Sequential access** occurs when a file is read or written from beginning to end.

Files are used to save information. They are created by programs, and they (usually) continue to exist after the program terminates. Later, another (or the same) program can read the information written earlier. Files are given names when they are created so they can be referred to later by other programs that use them.

By now you are probably familiar with files on the particular computer system you have been using. You should be able to browse around your computer's collection of files, using whatever tools or commands are available.

Notice that there are files for all sorts of things, including files that contain the executable code for programs; files that contain Java code; files that contain documents, pictures, sound (music), movies, etc.

In this chapter I will discuss reading existing files and creating (writing) new ones, and I will only deal with sequential access.

13.1.1 File Structure

Most computers and operating systems make no assumptions about how the information in a file is organized or what it means. A file containing a picture and a file containing a Java program are the same to the system. A program that writes a file may organize the information in a certain way, but once that program finishes and the file is left lying around, the system can't tell much about it except what its name is, where it is, and how much space it takes.[1]

The structure and organization of the file are then reimposed by the program as it reads it. If a program expects a file to have been written a certain way but the file was written a different way, then information in that file will look like gibberish to that program. The program will try to interpret that information in the way it expects it, but it just won't make much sense.

This can be illustrated by considering two files, one containing a picture created by a drawing program and another containing a document produced by a word processor. If you run a program that reads document files and you give it the picture file to read, what the document program will get will not look much like a document. The document program will assume the file has the structure and organization of a document (e.g., an array of characters organized into lines containing words, punctuation, perhaps formatting information) and will try to interpret what it is reading that way. But the picture file was written by a program that gave it the assumed structure and organization of a picture (e.g., an array of colors). What will happen when the word processing program reads this file is anybody's guess.

{New Concepts}

The structure and organization of the information in a file are decided by the programs that write and read it.

Written Exercise

1. Try to read a Java .class file into your editor. Describe what you see.

---

1. Some systems use part of the name of the file to indicate something about its structure and organization, but the name is only a hint and may be wrong. For example, on most systems a file name that ends with ".jpg" implies that the file contains a image represented in a particular way. However, you can change the name to something completely different if you like. The system won't care. The file still contains a picture, and any program that is designed to read image files represented in that particular way will still be able to read and understand it.

13.2 WRITING TEXT TO A FILE

You are already familiar with using the `System.out.println` command to write text to the Java console. Now let's write a simple application program that writes in the same way, but to a file instead.

Java defines classes for several objects that you need to use to write to a file. The first is a `FileOutputStream`. You give this object the name of the file you want to write to when you create the object. Then you call methods of the `FileOutputStream` object and give them the information you want written, and the object takes care of all the details of getting that information into the file.

Unfortunately, a `FileOutputStream` object only has methods to write one or more characters of information to the file, but it doesn't know how to take an integer or double and convert it from the way it is represented inside the memory of your machine to a sequence of readable characters. For that you need another object called a `PrintWriter`.

A **PrintWriter** object can convert the internal representation of integers and doubles to sequences of characters and then send them automatically to the `FileOutputStream` to be written to the file. All you need to do is use the `print` and `println` methods defined for a `PrintWriter` object to write integers, doubles, strings, booleans, etc., to the file. The `println` method is the same as the `print` method, except that it adds a new-line character at the end so that the next thing printed begins at the beginning of the next line.

{New Concepts}

A **FileOutputStream** object writes characters to a file. To write integer, double, and other kinds of values to the text file, a `PrintWriter` object must be used.

Code 13.1 is a very simple application program that creates a `FileOutputStream` object (`out`) and a `PrintWriter` object (`output`), then writes a few different types of values to a file. The file that is written to is created when the `FileOutputStream` object is created, and it will have the name `text.out`.

Creating the `FileOutputStream` object `out` has the side effect of creating the file `text.out`, initially with nothing in it (i.e., empty). This is often referred to as **opening a file.** Corresponding to opening a file, you must also remember to **close a file** when you are done writing to it. Failure to do so will often result in some of the text you think you have written not winding up in the file. This is because a `PrintWriter` object collects many characters and actually transfers a whole bunch at a time (usually referred to as a block) to the file. This is more efficient than writing just a few characters every time you execute a `println` command. Closing the file makes sure that any characters that have been saved up waiting for enough to do a big transfer finally do get transferred to the file.

CODE 13.1

```
import java.io.*;
public class SimpleTextOutput {

    public static void main(String [] args) {
        FileOutputStream out = new FileOutputStream("text.out");
        PrintWriter output = new PrintWriter(out);
        output.print("here is some text output ");
        output.println(1492/2);
        output.println(3.16*4.1);
        output.println(true);
        output.close();
    } // end of main method

} // end of class SimpleTextOutput
```

> This import is required when using file objects.

> The name of the file as known by the system.

> Don't forget to close the file when you are done.

{New Concepts}

Be sure to close a file before your program finishes. Failure to do so may result in some of the last information you thought your program wrote not actually showing up in the file.

Unfortunately, if you compile this program, you will get an error message from the compiler. It will say something to the effect that you do not have code to "catch an exception." To understand why you get this error you need to know what an exception is and what to do about it.

13.2.1 Exceptions

Exceptions are typically abnormal events, such as getting errors when trying to read data from a file, or trying to create a new file but not having permission. Such abnormal conditions usually result in having to terminate the program. However, in some situations termination is not appropriate. If your program asks the user for the name of the file to read and the user types it in wrong, upon discovering that the file doesn't exist (via a file-not-found exception) your program can merely inform the user that there is no such file and ask for the name to be reentered.

Many input and output commands can possibly generate an exception. When one does, Java says that the command **throws** the exception. It is your responsibility to **catch** the exception and do something about it. The way you do it is with Java's try/catch structure.

{New Concepts}

A method will signal the occurrence of an error by throwing an *exception*. You must catch the exception and do something about it.

Whenever you create a `FileOutputStream` object, it is possible that for some reason the new file cannot be created (e.g., there isn't any space left on the disk, or you don't have permission). When this happens, the `FileOutputStream` constructor throws a *file-not-found exception*. To deal with it when it happens, Code 13.2 shows a correct version of the previous program.

CODE 13.2

```java
import java.io.*;
public class SimpleTextOutput {

    public static void main(String [] args) {
        FileOutputStream out;
        try {
            out = new FileOutputStream("text.out");
        }
        catch (FileNotFoundException exception) {
            System.out.println("Can't create text.out");
            return;
        }
        PrintWriter output = new PrintWriter(out);
        output.println("here is some text output");
        output.println(1492/2);
        output.println(3.16*4.1);
        output.println(true);
        output.close();
    } // end of main method

} // end of SimpleTextOutput class
```

The command that might throw an exception must be enclosed in a try block.

This code catches the exception and does something about it.

SimpleTextOutput
Prints a `String`, an `int`, a `double`, and a `boolean` to a text file.

There are two segments of code that are important. The first is the code between the left brace { and right brace } following the reserved word `try` (called a *try block*). It is executed just as any other code as long as no exception occurs. The second segment is the code between the braces following the reserved word `catch` (called a *catch clause*). It is executed *only* if the type of exception indicated between the parentheses following `catch` occurs in the try block, which in this case is a `FileNotFoundException`. If no exception of this type occurs, then this code is completely ignored.

{New Concepts}

Any commands that can cause exceptions must be enclosed in a *try block*. A subsequent *catch clause* must catch an exception and do something about it. Code in the try block is always executed, but code in a catch clause is executed only if the named exception occurs.

Not only is `FileNotFoundException` the type of the exception we want to catch, but also it is the name of a predefined Java class. When the exception occurs, a `FileNotFoundException` object is created and the variable that follows the exception type (`exception`) is made to reference that object. This variable can be used in the catch clause to find out more details about the exception. In particular, the exception class has a method called `getMessage` that returns a `String` containing a somewhat informative message about exactly what happened. Hence you could write

```
System.out.println(exception.getMessage());
```

in the catch clause if you wanted to print that message.

13.2.2 The Resulting Output File

Let's trace the execution of the program. First the `FileOutputStream` object `out` is created. As a side effect of creating this object, the file `text.out` is created, initially with nothing in it. Assuming no exception occurred, the next command executed is the one that creates the `PrintWriter` object `output`. Since we sent `out` as an argument to the `PrintWriter` constructor, `output` knows that it should use the `FileOutputStream` object `out` to actually get information to the file.

Next several `print` and `println` methods in the `output` object were called, each time sending a different type of value (a string, an integer, a double, and a boolean). Each of these data items will be converted by the `PrintWriter` object to a sequence of characters and sent to the `FileOutputStream` object to be written to the file. Finally the `close` method is called to close the file, making sure that any characters not yet transferred to the disk do finally get there.

After executing this program, the file `text.out` contains the following:

```
here is some text output 726
12.956
true
```

Notice that the string was printed by the `print` method, so the integer follows it on the same line. The integer, double, and boolean values were printed with the `println` method, so the next thing printed after each starts on the next line.

Had it been impossible to create the file `text.out`, a `FileNotFoundException` would have been thrown by the `FileOutputStream` constructor, and the catch clause would have been executed. It would have written the message "Can't open text.out" to the Java console and returned from the `main` method, thereby terminating execution of the program.

13.2.3 Another Example

Here is a more involved application program with a GUI. It allows the user to create a text file by entering the file name into a `JTextField` and then

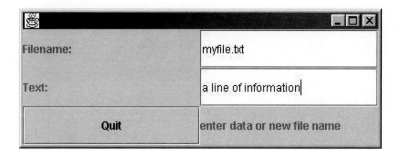

FIGURE 13.1

entering each line of text into another `JTextField`. Each line in the output file will be preceded by a line number. If the user tries to enter text before entering a file name, an error message is displayed. If the user enters a second file name, the first file is closed and a new file is opened, with all text entered after that going into the new file. The GUI also contains a "quit" button that closes an open file and then terminates the program. The GUI is shown in Figure 13.1.

In Figure 13.1, the user has entered the file name `myfile.txt` and has entered some text to put in the file ("a line of information"). Upon hitting of the Enter or Return key, that text will be written to the file, the `JTextField` will be cleared, and the user can enter another line of text (Code 13.3).

CODE 13.3

```java
import java.io.*;
import java.awt.*;
import java.awt.event.*;
import javax.swing.*;
public class FileGenerator extends JFrame
                    implements ActionListener {
    private final int frameWidth = 400;
    private final int frameHeight = 150;
    private JTextField file = new JTextField(20);
    private JTextField data = new JTextField(20);
    private JButton quit = new JButton("Quit");
    private JLabel msg = new JLabel("enter file name");
    private boolean fileOpen = false;
    private FileOutputStream out;
    private PrintWriter output;
    private int lineNumber = 0;

    public static void main(String[] args) {
        FileGenerator gui = new FileGenerator();
    } // end of main method
```

```
public FileGenerator() {
    // set up GUI
    setSize(frameWidth,frameHeight);
    setVisible(true);
    Container window = getContentPane();
    window.setLayout(new GridLayout(3,2));
    window.add(new JLabel("File name:"));
    window.add(file);
    window.add(new JLabel("Text:"));
    window.add(data);
    window.add(quit);
    window.add(msg);
    file.addActionListener(this);
    data.addActionListener(this);
    quit.addActionListener(this);
    } // end of constructor


public void actionPerformed(ActionEvent event) {
    if (event.getSource() == quit) {
        // if a file is open, close it before exiting
        if (fileOpen) {
            output.close();
            }
        System.exit(0);
        }
    else if (event.getSource() == file) {
        // if a file is open, close it before
        // opening another
        if (fileOpen) {
            output.close();
            }
        // open the file
        try {
            out = new FileOutputStream(file.getText());
            }
        catch (FileNotFoundException exception) {
            // print an error message and exit if
            // the file cannot be opened
            System.out.println("Can't open file");
            System.exit(1);
            }
        // open a new file and reset line numbering
        fileOpen = true;
        output = new PrintWriter(out);
        lineNumber = 1;
        msg.setText("enter data or new file name");
        }
```

Always remember to close a file before terminating the program. The boolean variable fileOpen keeps track of whether a file has been opened.

Be sure to close the current file (if one exists) before opening a new one.

```
        else if (event.getSource() == data) {
            // if a file is not open, inform the user
            if (!fileOpen) {
                msg.setText("must enter file name first");
            }
            else {
                // output the line number followed by the input
                output.print(lineNumber + ": ");
                output.println(data.getText());

                // clear the JTextField and
                // increment the line number
                data.setText("");
                lineNumber += 1;
            }
        }
    } // end of actionPerformed method

} // end of FileGenerator class
```

> If the user enters data before entering a file name, don't write to the file.

Written Exercises

FileGenerator
Writes lines of text to one or more text files.

1. Enter and compile the incorrect version of the `SimpleTextOutput` program above (without try/catch). What error message do you get?

2. Find a way to cause a `FileNotFoundException` on your system using the correct version of the `SimpleTextOutput` program. Explain what you did.

3. Modify the correct version of the `SimpleTextOutput` program to print `exception.getMessage()`, then force the exception to occur. What was printed?

Programming Exercises

1. Write a program that creates a file consisting of 100 lines, each with two integers. The first integer in each line should start at 1 and go to 100. The second integer on each line should be the largest positive integer less than the first integer on the line that evenly divides the first integer on that line. For example, the first few lines of the file should contain

    1 1
    2 1
    3 1
    4 2
    5 1
    6 3
    7 1

      8 4
      9 3
     10 5
     . . .

2. Write a program with a simple GUI containing a text area and a button la-
    beled "exit." The user enters text into the text area; then when she pushes
    the button, that text is written to a file named `the.txt` and the program
    terminates.

13.3 TEXT INPUT

The two objects needed to read a text file are very similar to the object used to
write one. Analogous to the `FileOutputStream` object you use a
`FileInputStream` object, and analogous to the `PrintWriter` object
you use an **`InputStreamReader`** object. The commands are as follows:

```
FileInputStream in = new FileInputStream(filename);
InputStreamReader input = new InputStreamReader(in);
```

where *filename* is a `String` containing the name of the file to open. Note that
the `FileInputStream` constructor throws a `FileNotFoundException`,
so you must catch it.

    Unfortunately, the similarity to text output ends here. An
`InputStreamReader` does not have methods to read sequences of characters and convert them to integers, doubles, booleans, strings, etc., similar to the
`print` and `println` methods used for writing. An `InputStreamReader`
object can only read successive characters.

    The `read` method inputs the next single character from the file and re-
turns it as an `int`. The `int` contains the internal representation of the character, which can be easily converted back to a char by casting. For example,

```
char c = (char) input.read();
```

    Now if you know how many characters there are in a file, and your pro-
gram simply needs to read them all, then you can put the `read` call in a counting loop and read the appropriate number of characters. But usually you don't
know how many characters are in a file you are reading, so you need to detect
when there are no more characters to be read. That is, you need to detect the
end-of-file.

    The `read` method will detect the end-of-file by returning the value -1
when you try to read the next character and there is no next character to read.
This is why the `read` method returns an int instead of a char. If it had returned
a char, then every possible return value could be a valid character and hence
there would be no other value that could be used to signal that end-of-file had
been reached.

The read method returns −1 to indicate the end of a file has been reached when a next character after the last one in the file is attempted to be read.

Let's put text input and output together in a simple program that makes a copy of the existing text file input.txt in the new file output.txt (Code 13.4).

Except for the try/catch structures that make the program look a bit messy, the program is fairly straightforward. Both the input and output files are opened, characters are read and written one at a time until the end-of-file is reached, then both files are closed.

Closing an input file is not as important as closing an output file. In fact the program above would work exactly the same even if input.close were not called. However, if you had a program that needed to read the input file more than once, then you would have to close the input file before opening it the second time. A good programming habit to get into is to close all files (input and output) all the time.

It is not essential that an input file be closed. However, closing all files, input or output, is a good habit to get into.

CODE 13.4

```java
import java.io.*;
public class TextFileCopy {

    public static void main(String [] args) {
        // open the input file
        FileInputStream in = null;
        try {
            in = new FileInputStream("input.txt");
        }
        catch (FileNotFoundException exception) {
            System.out.println("Can't open input.txt");
            System.exit(1);
        }
        // open the output file
        FileOutputStream out = null;
        try {
            out = new FileOutputStream("output.txt");
        }
        catch (IOException exception) {
            System.out.println("Can't create output.txt");
            System.exit(2);
        }
        // create reader and writer
        InputStreamReader input = new InputStreamReader(in);
        PrintWriter output = new PrintWriter(out);
```

> Most likely cause for the exception is that the file doesn't exist.

```
        // copy the file one character at time
        try {
            int c = input.read();                    ◄──── Read character into an int so
            while (c != -1) {                              we can check for end-of-file.
                char cc = (char) c;          ◄──
                output.print(cc);                    Convert int to char for
                c = input.read();                    the print method.
            }
            // close both files
            input.close();                   ◄──── Not necessary to close an
            output.close();                          input file, but not a bad habit
        }                                            to get into.
        catch (IOException exception) {
            System.out.println("IOException");
            System.exit(1);
        }
    } // end of main method

} // end of class TextFileCopy
```

TextFileCopy
Makes a copy of `input.txt`
in `output.txt`.

13.3.1 The Stream Tokenizer

Suppose you have a text file containing a collection of numbers, such as

67.78
34
1.0045
−1782.3

. . .

and you want to write a program that computes the sum. You could read each character in the file; collect consecutive digits, decimal points, plus and minus signs into a string for each number; then use the `Double.parseDouble` function to convert each one to a double and add it to a running total. This would be a lot of work, and fortunately Java provides an object that will do everything above except add the double to a running total.

Java's `StreamTokenizer` class defines an object that reads characters from a file and collects them into pieces called tokens. A **token** is one of the following: a sequence of letters and digits beginning with a letter (a word); a sequence of digits with an optional preceding minus sign and an optional decimal point (a number); or any other single character, except space, tab, and new line, which are skipped over and ignored by the `StreamTokenizer`.

A `StreamTokenizer` object has a method called `nextToken` that reads enough characters from a file to form the next token. If the characters turn out to be a word, then it forms a `String` object. If the characters turn out to be a valid number, it will automatically convert them to a double (even if the number looks like an integer like 34 in the example file above).

{New Concepts}

A **StreamTokenizer** object reads text from a file and breaks the text into tokens.

The `StreamTokenizer` constructor expects a reference to an `InputStreamReader` object as its argument. The `read` method returns an integer that is the encoding of a single character, a code indicating whether a word or number was found, or a code indicating that the end-of-file was found. The codes are `StreamTokenizer.TT_WORD` for a word token, `StreamTokenizer.TT_NUMBER` for a number token, and `StreamTokenizer.TT_EOF` for end-of-file. To retrieve the word found by the `StreamTokenizer` object, use the `StreamTokenizer` object's variable, called `sval` (a `String`). To retrieve the number found by the `StreamTokenizer`, use `nval` (a `double`).

Code 13.5 is a program that uses the `StreamTokenizer` to read and sum the numbers in a text file. If anything other than a valid number is found, it prints an error message and exits.

The `nextToken` method can throw an `IOException` so we must catch it. Note that the `StreamTokenizer` object does not have a close

CODE 13.5

```java
import java.io.*;
public class SumFile {

    public static void main(String [] args) {
        // open the input file
        FileInputStream in = null;
        try {
            in = new FileInputStream("input.txt");
        }
        catch (FileNotFoundException exception) {
            System.out.println("Can't open input.txt");
            System.exit(1);
        }
        // create remaining input objects
        InputStreamReader inr = new InputStreamReader(in);
        StreamTokenizer input = new StreamTokenizer(inr);

        try {
            // read and sum the input numbers
            double sum = 0.0;
            int tokenType = input.nextToken();
            while (tokenType != StreamTokenizer.TT_EOF) {
                if (tokenType == StreamTokenizer.TT_NUMBER) {
                    sum += input.nval;
                }
```

The `StreamTokenizer` constructor expects a reference to an `InputStreamReader` object.

Check the return value from `nextToken` for the type of token.

If the token was a number, `nval` (a double) will have the value.

```
            else {
                System.out.println("invalid input");
                System.exit(1);
                }
            tokenType = input.nextToken();
            }
        System.out.println(sum);
        inr.close(); ◄───────────────┐
        }
    catch (IOException exception) {
        System.out.println("IOException");
        System.exit(1);
        }
    } // end of main method

} // end of class SumFile
```

> You can't close a StreamTokenizer, so you have to close the InputStreamReader instead.

SumFile

Prints the sum of the numbers in a text file. If there is anything other than numbers in the file, the program prints an error message and stops.

method. As a result, to close the input file, you must call the close method for the InputStreamReader object instead.

Written Exercises

1. How is the end of a text file detected?

2. What is the purpose of the StreamTokenizer?

3. Find the tokens in the following text.

   Bob said "let's go fishing" after he bought 54 worms. Mary did not want to go fishing. She wanted to go shopping instead.

4. How does the StreamTokenizer indicate that the end-of-file has been reached?

5. Is it necessary to close an input file? Explain.

Programming Exercises

1. Write a program that reads a text file and counts the number of occurrences of each letter of the alphabet, ignoring all other characters. Do not distinguish between capitals and small letters. Write the result to another text file, one line per letter, in the form

   ```
   a: 47
   b: 22
   . . .
   ```

2. Write a program that reads a text file, finding all the numbers, computing their sum, and ignoring everything else in the file (e.g., use the StreamTokenizer). Print the resulting sum to the Java console.

3. Write a program with a GUI containing two text fields and a button. The user types the name of an input file into one text field, the name of an output file in another, and then pushes the button. The program then copies the input file to the output file, changing all lowercase letters to uppercase.

4. Write a program like the one in the previous problem, except that it should replace all contiguous sequences of spaces and/or tabs with a single space.

5. Write a program with a GUI containing a text field for inputting characters representing a token, a label for displaying a value, and a "quit" button. The user enters a token in the text field and hits Enter or Return. The program then opens and reads the file `input.txt`, counts the number of occurrences of that token in the file, closes the file, and displays the count in the label. The user may repeat entering tokens and counting their occurrences in the file. The "quit" button causes the program to terminate.

13.4 READING AND WRITING FILES CONTAINING PRIMITIVE DATA

Text files are not the best way to save information if the information is never going to be viewed directly by people. There are two reasons for this. First, converting boolean, char, int, or double values between the way they are stored internally and a sequence of readable characters is time-consuming. Second, these values generally take more space when stored as sequences of readable characters.[2]

Fortunately, Java permits you to write boolean, char, int, and double values directly to a file. They are stored on the file in the same format they are stored in memory. As a result, no conversions are necessary, and space is almost always saved.

To write to a file this way, you create a `FileOutputStream` object as usual, but then you create a `DataOutputStream` object instead of a `PrintWriter` object. You can then use appropriate methods of the `DataOutputStream`, as shown in Table 13.1, to write specific types of data to the file. Likewise, to read a file created by a `DataOutputStream`,

Table 13.1

Primitive Type	Input Method	Output Method
boolean	readBoolean	writeBoolean
char	readChar	writeChar
int	readInt	writeInt
double	readDouble	writeDouble

---

2. Boolean values will always take more space after conversion to readable characters. Ints and doubles will take more space, and usually considerably more, when the numbers are large (ints or doubles) or have lots of significant digits (doubles).

you create a `FileInputStream` object as usual and then a `DataInputStream` object that uses it.

Files written this way are often referred to as **binary files.**

{New Concepts}

A **DataOutputStream** object writes primitive-type data to a binary file without converting them to readable characters, thereby saving time and space.

13.4.1 Output

Code 13.6 is a simple program that writes a binary file consisting of 100 alternating ints and doubles (the integers from 1 to 100 and their corresponding square roots, as doubles).

Although the `DataOutputStream` constructor throws no exceptions, the write methods for every primitive data type do, so we must put the `writeInt` and `writeDouble` method calls in a try block. To keep the program simple, I put everything in a single try block, since if any of the methods causes an exception, I simply want to print an error message and terminate. Note that when a method throws an exception, all code within the try block that follows that method is skipped, and execution jumps immediately to the code in the catch clause.

WriteDataFile
Writes a binary file consisting of 100 integer/double pairs, where the double is the square root of the corresponding integer.

CODE 13.6

```java
import java.io.*;
public class WriteDataFile {

    public static void main(String [] args) {
        try {
            FileOutputStream out =
                new FileOutputStream("data.bin");
            DataOutputStream output =
                new DataOutputStream(out);
            for (int n=1; n<=100; n++) {
                output.writeInt(n);
                output.writeDouble(Math.sqrt(n));
            }
            output.close();
        }
        catch (IOException exception) {
            System.out.println("IOException");
            System.exit(1);
        }
    } // end of main method

} // end of WriteDataFile class
```

An `ObjectOutputStream` writes primitive data types without converting them to readable characters.

The file will consist of alternating ints and doubles.

Catch an `IOException` from any of the methods.

13.4.2 Input

Reading a binary file is fairly simple, especially if you know how much data is in the file. However, if you do not know how much data there is and must rely on detecting the end of the file, then things get a bit messy. Unlike text files where the read method returns -1 when the end of the file (EOF) is reached, the various read methods defined for a `DataInputStream` throw an `EOFException` instead. Hence the coding structure to handle this is not quite as simple as with text files.

Code 13.7 is a program that reads a file in the same format as written by the program above (alternating ints and doubles). The program prints the maximum of the integers and the maximum of the doubles in the file.

CODE 13.7

```java
import java.io.*;
public class FindMax {

    public static void main(String [] args) {
        // create variables outside of tries
        FileInputStream in = null;
        DataInputStream input = null;
        int maxX = 0;
        double maxY = 0.0;
        // open file and read first values
        try {
            in = new FileInputStream("data.bin");
            input = new DataInputStream(in);
            maxX = input.readInt();
            maxY = input.readDouble();
        }
        catch (IOException exception) {
            System.out.println("IOException");
            System.exit(1);
        }
        // read the remaining values and
        // keep track of maximums
        boolean reading = true;
        while (reading) {
            try {
                int x = input.readInt();
                double y = input.readDouble();
                if (x > maxX) {
                    maxX = x;
                }
                if (y > maxY) {
                    maxY = y;
                }
            }
```

> These variables must be created outside the try block so their scope extends to the end of the method. They are given arbitrary initial values to avoid compiler warnings.

> We'll consider an existing but empty file to be an `IOException` for simplicity. An `EOFException` could be caught and handled separately.

> The boolean `reading` keeps track of whether the end-of-file has been found yet.

```
        catch (EOFException eof) {
            reading = false;
        }
        catch (IOException exception) {
            System.out.println("IOException");
            System.exit(1);
        }
    }
    System.out.println(maxX + " " + maxY);
} // end of main method


} // end of FindMax class
```

The EOFException is caught *inside* the while-loop and causes it to terminate by setting reading to false.

FindMax
Reads a binary file of integer/double pairs and prints the maximum of the integers and the maximum of the doubles.

As with all techniques for finding the maximum, if there are no restrictions on the values, the variable that keeps track of the maximum must be initialized with the first value, then the remaining values compared against it. Hence there are separate reads for the first integer and double value, and the two distinct try blocks.

Since it is possible that a file exists but has no data in it, it is possible to get an EOFException on the first readInt. It turns out in Java that an EOFException is just one of the many types of IOException. Whenever an EOFException is thrown, so is an IOException. Therefore by catching the IOException in the first try/catch structure, we will also catch an EOFException if it occurs. Doing so won't let us distinguish between an error and an empty file, but we'll avoid the problem in this program by considering an empty file to be an error.

Later the program needs to distinguish between an EOFException (which is not an error) and the remaining IOExceptions (which are). Hence the second try/catch structure has two catch clauses. When more than one catch clause exists for a given try block, whichever exception matches will be caught. If, as in this case, both exceptions match (since an EOFException is also an IOException), then the first catch clause that matches will be executed. Hence when an EOFException occurs, the first catch clause is executed, and if an IOException other than EOFException occurs, the second catch clause is executed.

{New Concepts}

A try block is followed by one or more catch clauses. The first exception in the series of catch clauses that matches the exception being thrown will have its associated code executed.

As you can see, the need to catch an exception to detect the end of the file makes the code a little more complex than when reading text. Using the boolean variable reading to control the loop and setting it to false when an EOFException occurs make the code about as simple as it can get.

Written Exercises

1. Reverse the order of the catch clauses in the `FindMax` class and compile it. What happens?
2. Use the `WritePrimitiveDataFile` program to create a file. Then try to edit the file with the text editor you use to write Java programs. What do you see?

Programming Exercise

1. Write a program that reads a file consisting of integer/double pairs (like the file created by `WriteDataFile`) and finds the minimum and maximum of all the integers and the minimum and maximum of all the doubles. Print the four results on the Java console.

13.5 WRITING ENTIRE OBJECTS

Suppose you need to create a file consisting of some number of objects, all of the same class, but with different values for their instance variables, and then be able to read them back later with some other program. An example might be a file of `Student` objects, where the `Student` class is (partially) defined as follows:

```
class Student {
      private String firstName;
      private String lastName;
      private int studentNumber;
      private int credits;
      private double gpa;
      // methods for the class follow...
      } // end of Student class
```

You can't simply write a `Student` object directly to a text file because `print` or `println` can't write objects. You could use a text file and convert each instance variable to the corresponding sequence of readable characters, then convert everything back to their internal form in the program that reads them back in, but the conversions between internal and character form are very inefficient and the file will most likely take a lot more space. You could use a binary file and the `writeInt` and `writeDouble` methods, but then you'd have to write each instance variable in the object separately, and you'd still have to figure out a way to write strings (probably character by character along with some way of marking the length or the end).

Fortunately Java has an **ObjectOutputStream** class that defines an object that you can use to write an *entire* object with just *one* command, and then later read the entire object with *one* command, too. In fact, if one object has instance variables that are references to other objects, then a single write of the first object will cause every object referenced by it to be written also, and every object referenced by those objects will be written, and every object referenced by those objects, etc. In the example above, writing the `Student` object will also cause both `String` objects to be written, along with the two integers and the double in the original object. Hence many related objects can be written with a single command.

{New Concepts}

An entire object, plus every object referenced by it, and every object referenced by them, etc., can be written with one call to the `writeObject` method defined on an `ObjectOutputStream`.

Likewise when you read the originally written object, a single read command will read that object and all the objects it referenced (at the time it was written), and all the objects they referenced, etc. In the example above, a single command will read not only the `Student` object (the two integers and a double) but also the two `String` objects that the `Student` object referred to when it was written. This ability to write and read, with a single command, all the objects referred to by the given object being written or read is a tremendous convenience.

{New Concepts}

The entire collection of objects written by a single call to `writeObject` can be read back in with a single call to `readObject`.

Here's a simple program that demonstrates how this is done. The program has a simple GUI with text fields for entering student information, a button to click on when the information is filled in and ready to put into a `Student` object and written to the file, and "quit" button to close the file and terminate the program. For simplicity I'll assume it will always write to a file called "students" (Figure 13.2).

FIGURE 13.2

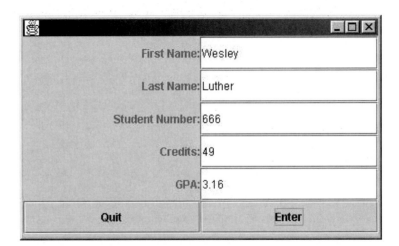

The program is fairly straightforward, simply setting up the GUI and opening the output file, then reacting to pushes of the "enter" button by writing a Student object to the file, and reacting to a push of the "quit" button by closing the file and terminating execution (Code 13.8).

CODE 13.8

```java
import java.io.*;
import java.awt.*;
import java.awt.event.*;
import javax.swing.*;

public class WriteObjects extends JFrame
                    implements ActionListener {

    public static void main(String[] args) {
        WriteObjects gui = new WriteObjects();
    } // end of main method

    private final int frameWidth = 400;
    private final int frameHeight = 240;
    private JTextField first = new JTextField(20);
    private JTextField last = new JTextField(20);
    private JTextField number = new JTextField(20);
    private JTextField credits = new JTextField(20);
    private JTextField gpa = new JTextField(20);
    private JButton quit = new JButton("Quit");
    private JButton enter = new JButton("Enter");
    private FileOutputStream out;
    private ObjectOutputStream output;

    public WriteObjects() {
        // set up the GUI
        setSize(400,240);
        setVisible(true);
        Container window = getContentPane();
        window.setLayout(new GridLayout(6,2));
        window.add(new JLabel("First Name:",
                        SwingConstants.RIGHT));
        window.add(first);
        window.add(new JLabel("Last Name:",
                        SwingConstants.RIGHT));
        window.add(last);
        window.add(new JLabel("Student Number:",
                        SwingConstants.RIGHT));
        window.add(number);
        window.add(new JLabel("Credits:",
                        SwingConstants.RIGHT));
        window.add(credits);
        window.add(new JLabel("GPA:",
                        SwingConstants.RIGHT));
        window.add(gpa);
        window.add(quit);
```

```
        window.add(enter);
        enter.addActionListener(this);
        // open the output file
        try {
            out = new FileOutputStream("students");
            output = new ObjectOutputStream(out);
            }
        catch (FileNotFoundException exception) {
            // print an error message and exit if
            // the file cannot be opened
            System.out.println("Can't open file");
            System.exit(1);
            }
        catch (IOException exception) {
            // print an error message for any IOException
            System.out.println(exception.getMessage());
            System.exit(1);
            }
        } // end of constructor
```

```
public void actionPerformed(ActionEvent event) {
    if (event.getSource() == quit) {
        // close file and exit
        try {
            output.close();
            }
        catch (IOException exception) {
            // print an error message for any IOException
            System.out.println(exception.getMessage());
            System.exit(1);
            }
        System.exit(0);
        }
    else if (event.getSource() == enter) {
        // create a new Student object
        Student student = new Student(first.getText(),
                last.getText(),
                Integer.parseInt(number.getText()),
                Integer.parseInt(credits.getText()),
                Double.parseDouble(gpa.getText()));
        // write the object
        try {
            output.writeObject(student);
            }
        catch (IOException exception) {
            // print an error message for any IOException
            System.out.println(exception.getMessage());
            System.exit(1);
            }
        }
```

> A new `Student` object *must* be created; otherwise `writeObject` won't work properly.

```
    else {
        // standard defensive code
        System.out.println("bad event");
        System.exit(1);
        }
    } // end of actionPerformed method

} // end of WriteObjects class
```

```
class Student implements Serializable {
    private String firstName;
    private String lastName;
    private int studentNumber;
    private int credits;
    private double gpa;

    public Student(String f, String l, int n, int c, double g) {
        firstName = f;
        lastName = l;
        studentNumber = n;
        credits = c;
        gpa = g;
        } // end of constructor

    public void print() {
        System.out.println("----------------------------");
        System.out.print(firstName + " " + lastName);
        System.out.println(" (" + studentNumber + ")");
        System.out.println("credits = " + credits +
                            ", gpa = " + gpa);
        } // end of print method

} // end of Student class
```

> Any object that will be written using `writeObject` must implement `Serializable`.

WriteObjects
Writes a sequence of `Student` objects using `writeObject`.

Please note one rather unusual behavior of the `writeObject` method. If you create a single object, write it once, then change the values of its instance variables and write it again, `writeObject` will write the object with its original values a second time. You can easily avoid this problem by creating a new object each time, as I did in this program.

There is one important thing you must do in order for entire objects to be written using the `writeObject` method. You must make the class that defines those objects implement `Serializable`, as was done with the `Student` class above. Every other kind of object that might be written as a result of writing the `Student` object must also be defined by a class that `implements Serializable`, too (I'll just say that an object is serializable when its class `implements Serializable`), and it is a common error to forget (which will give you an `IOException` when you try to write the object). Fortunately most objects defined by Java classes, such as `String`, are serializable, so you only have to take care of the classes you define yourself.

13.5.1 Serialization

Serialization is the process by which an object is written to a file. To be able to read the object back in, extra information about the object is written along with the current values of the instance variables. This extra information is used when the object is read back in. It identifies the class of the object and any other objects that were written in addition to the main object named in the call to `writeObject`. This will require a little more space in the file than if you had just written all the same information yourself using many `writeInt`, `writeDouble`, etc., calls, but is usually worth it considering how easy it makes writing the code.

Serialization is a very powerful mechanism in Java. But you must be careful that you don't wind up writing a lot more than you think. For example, if one of the objects you write with a `writeObject` call has a reference to an object defined by a class that you do not know much about, that class may wind up referencing a vast number of other objects, all of which will get written by that single call. A typical example of this is a class that has an instance variable that references a Java swing or AWT object like a `JPanel` or `Container`. Writing an object of that class will more than likely wind up writing a huge amount of information to the file, most of which you probably didn't intend.

{Good Ideas}

Be careful when using `writeObject` that you don't wind up writing many unexpected objects.

13.6 READING OBJECTS

Reading objects from a file is almost as easy as writing them. You use an **ObjectInputStream** instead of an `ObjectOutputStream` and call **readObject** instead of `writeObject`. You must use a cast when assigning the reference to the object read by the `readObject` method. For example, if the `ObjectInputStream` is called input, then to read a `Student` object you code

```
Student stRec = (Student) input.readObject();
```

The `readObject` method also throws a new exception, called a `ClassNotFoundException`, so you must catch it. This exception occurs if the program cannot find a class definition for the object that is being read in. This might happen if you accidentally try to read the wrong file, one that has an object in it that your program knows nothing about. It most certainly is an error no matter what the cause.

The readObject method can throw a ClassNotFoundException in addition to an
EOFException and other IOExceptions.

Code 13.9 is a short program that reads a file of Student objects created by the
program in the previous section and prints the information in a readable form.

CODE 13.9

```java
import java.io.*;
public class DisplayFile {

    public static void main(String [] args) {
        FileInputStream in = null;
        ObjectInputStream input = null;
        Student student = null;
        try {
            in = new FileInputStream("students");
            input = new ObjectInputStream(in);
        }
        catch(IOException iox) {
            System.out.println("IOException");
            System.exit(1);
        }
        boolean reading = true;
        while (reading) {
            try {
                student = (Student) input.readObject();
                student.print();
            }
            catch(ClassNotFoundException cnf) {
                System.out.println("Class not found");
                System.exit(1);
            }
            catch(EOFException eof) {
                reading = false;
            }
            catch(IOException iox) {
                System.out.println("IOException");
                System.exit(1);
            }
        }
        try {
            input.close();
        }
        catch(IOException iox) {
            System.out.println("IOException");
            System.exit(1);
        }
    } // end of main method

} // end of DisplayFile class
```

Must cast the reference returned to readObject to Student.

The readObject method throws a ClassNotFoundException, so we must catch it.

```
class Student implements Serializable {

    private String firstName;
    private String lastName;
    private int studentNumber;
    private int credits;
    private double gpa;

    public Student(String f, String l, int n, int c, double g) {
        firstName = f;
        lastName = l;
        studentNumber = n;
        credits = c;
        gpa = g;
    } // end of constructor

    public void print() {
        System.out.println("----------------------------");
        System.out.print(firstName + " " + lastName);
        System.out.println(" (" + studentNumber + ")");
        System.out.println("credits = " + credits +
                           ", gpa = " + gpa);
    } // end of print method

} // end of Student class
```

DisplayFile
Reads the `Student` objects written by the `WriteObject` program and prints them in a readable form.

A final reminder: Be sure to read the objects from a file in the same order in which they were written. It is up to your program to know that order. As I said at the beginning of the chapter, the structure and organization of the file are determined by the program that writes it, so the program that reads it must handle that structure and organization properly.

Written Exercises

1. Invent a way to write a method that will write a `String` object to a file *without* using `writeObject`, so that it can be read back in later by another program. Remember that the length of a `String` object is arbitrary. Describe in words what you would do. Write a letter to Sun Microsystems thanking them for serialization.

2. Remove `implements Serializable` from the `Student` class in the `WriteObjects` program and compile and run it. What happens?

3. Suppose a program has created two objects, and each has an instance variable that contains a reference to the other. If both objects are serializable and one of them is written to a file via `writeObject`, why doesn't the program write the first object, then since it references the other one, it writes the second object, then since it references the first object, it writes the first object, then since . . .? How do you think the `writeObject` method keeps from writing these two objects forever?

Programming Exercises

1. Write a program that creates an object with three integer instance variables, then writes the object to one file but also writes the three integers values (using `writeInt`) to a different file. Compare the sizes of the two files.

2. Write a program that reads a file of `Student` objects into a `Vector`. Then sort the `Student` objects into ascending order by student number and write the `Student` objects (not the `Vector`) to another file. Use the `WriteObjects` program to create a file to test your sort program with, and the `DisplayFile` program to see if the sort worked correctly. Make sure that the `Student` class is defined exactly the same way in all programs.

3. Write a program that reads a file of `Student` objects into a `Vector` (as in the previous problem), then uses a GUI just like the one in the `WriteObjects` program to search the array for a matching student by student number. The user simply needs to type a student number into the student number text field and hit Return; then your program finds a matching record (if there is one) and fills in the remaining text fields with the corresponding information. If there is no match, the remaining text fields should be set to nothing. Make sure that the `Student` class is defined exactly the same way in all programs.

Summary

- A file is a related collection of information stored on a permanent memory device.
- A file can be read or written sequentially (in order from beginning to end) or randomly.
- The structure and organization of a file are determined by the programs that write and read it.
- A file must be opened before it can be used.
- An output file must be closed before the program terminates, or it might not have everything that the program "wrote" in it.
- An input file doesn't have to be closed unless it is opened again in the same program, but closing all files is a good habit to get into.
- A `FileOutputStream` object is used to write data to a file.
- A `FileInputStream` object is used to read data from a file.
- A `PrintWriter` object converts integers, doubles, etc., to sequences of characters and sends them to a `FileOutputStream` object to be written to a text file.
- An `InputStreamReader` object uses a `FileInputStream` object to read characters from a text file.

- A `StreamTokenizer` reads characters from a file and combines sequences of them into tokens.
- Exceptions are unusual or abnormal events.
- A method throws an exception when it detects that one has occurred.
- An exception is caught by enclosing the call to the method throwing it in a try block, which is then followed by a catch clause for that exception.
- Multiple catch clauses can follow a try block. The first matching exception causes the associated catch clause to be executed.
- Most methods associated with input and output objects throw an `IOException`.
- `FileInputStream` objects throw a `FileNotFoundException`.
- `ObjectInputStreams` throw a `ClassNotFoundException`.
- The read method of an `InputStreamReader` returns -1 when the end-of-file is encountered.
- A `StreamTokenizer` returns a special code when end-of-file is encountered.
- All other input methods throw an `EOFException` when end-of-file is encountered.
- A binary file contains data in the same format as they are represented in memory.
- An `ObjectOutputStream` uses a `FileOutputStream` to write primitive data values or objects to a binary file.
- An `ObjectInputStream` uses a `FileInputStream` to read primitive data values or objects from a binary file.
- Objects written via `writeObject` must be defined by classes that implement `Serializable`.
- Serialization occurs when objects are written to a file.
- When an object is written to a file, all objects it refers to are also written, as are the objects they refer to, and so on.
- When an object is read from a file, all objects it referred to when it was written are also read, as are the objects they referred to, and so on.

Glossary

Binary File A file containing data written in the same form as they are represented in memory.

Catch Respond to an exception.

Close a File Action taken to make sure that a file being written to has all the data transferred to it.

DataInputStream A class definition for an object that reads primitive data from a file.

DataOutputStream A class definition for an object that writes primitive data to a file.

Exception An unusual or abnormal condition detected by the program.

File Related information stored on a permanent memory device such as a disk.

FileInputStream A class definition for an object that transfers data from a file to the program.

FileOutputStream A class definition for an object that transfers data from a program to a file.

InputStreamReader A class definition for an object that transfers characters from a `FileInputStream` object.

ObjectInputStream A class definition for an object that transfers objects from a `FileInputStream` object.

ObjectOutputStream A class definition for an object that transfers objects to a `FileOutputStream` object.

Opening a File Associating an object that can transfer data with a file.

PrintWriter A class definition for an object that converts boolean, char, integer, double, and string values to sequences of readable characters and transfers them to a `FileOutputStream`.

Sequential Access Reading or writing of data from the beginning of a file to the end.

Serialization Writing of an object and all the objects it references, and all they reference, etc., to a file.

StreamTokenizer A class definition for an object that combines sequences of characters into tokens.

Throw Cause an exception to be created.

Token A word, a number, or a single character, but not white space.

Graphical User Interface Classes

14.1 THE BORDERLAYOUT MANAGER

When you get the content pane in the init method of a JApplet, it comes with a default layout manager called a BorderLayout manager. Up to now we've been avoiding it and using either a FlowLayout or GridLayout manager instead. Now it's time to learn about the BorderLayout manager and to discover that it can be very useful in creating nicely laid out graphical user interfaces.

The BorderLayout manager divides the displayable area into five regions, appropriately labeled NORTH, SOUTH, EAST, WEST, and CENTER.

{New Concepts}

A **BorderLayout manager** divides the screen into five regions: the top (north), bottom (south), left (west), right (east), and center.

When you add an object such as a JLabel, JButton, or JTextField[1] to a Container (such as the content pane) that has a BorderLayout, you must indicate which region the object is to be added to, for example:

```
window.add(component,BorderLayout.WEST);
```

BorderLayout.WEST indicates that the object referred to by component should appear on the west (left) part of the screen. Code 14.1 is an applet that puts an appropriately identified JLabel in each of the five regions.

---

1. From now on I'll refer to a JLabel, JButton, or JTextField as a **component**.

CODE 14.1

```
import java.awt.*;
import java.awt.event.*;
import javax.swing.*;

public class BorderDemo extends JApplet {

    public void init() {
        Container window = getContentPane();
        // create JLabels
        JLabel north =
            new JLabel("NORTH", SwingConstants.CENTER);
        JLabel south =
            new JLabel("SOUTH", SwingConstants.CENTER);
        JLabel east =
            new JLabel("EAST", SwingConstants.CENTER);
        JLabel west =
            new JLabel("WEST (wide)", SwingConstants.CENTER);
        JLabel center =
            new JLabel("CENTER", SwingConstants.CENTER);
        // give them foreground and background colors
        north.setOpaque(true);
        south.setOpaque(true);
        east.setOpaque(true);
        west.setOpaque(true);
        center.setOpaque(true);
        north.setBackground(Color.red);
        south.setBackground(Color.green);
        east.setBackground(Color.blue);
        west.setBackground(Color.yellow);
        center.setBackground(Color.orange);
        north.setForeground(Color.black);
        south.setForeground(Color.black);
        east.setForeground(Color.black);
        center.setForeground(Color.black);

        // add them to the window
        window.add(north,BorderLayout.NORTH);
        window.add(south,BorderLayout.SOUTH);
        window.add(east,BorderLayout.EAST);
        window.add(west,BorderLayout.WEST);
        window.add(center,BorderLayout.CENTER);
    } // end of init method

} // end of BorderDemo class
```

BorderDemo
Demonstrates the layout
of components in a
`BorderLayout`.

Figure 14.1 shows how this looks when the applet is executed. Notice several things about how these labels are positioned. First, labels in the north and south regions are stretched across the entire window, but are only high enough to contain the label text. Second, the labels in the east and west regions are stretched from the bottom of the north region to the top of the south

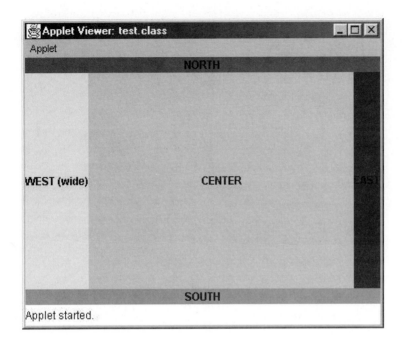

FIGURE 14.1

region, but are just wide enough to contain the label text (I made the west label a little larger to demonstrate how this works). Finally, the label in the center is stretched to fit whatever space remains. Note also that the text in the west, center, and east regions is centered vertically by default.

{New Concepts}

A BorderLayout stretches north and south components horizontally, east and west components vertically, and a center component both ways.

You don't have to put something in each region, so if we deleted the code for the south and east JLabel objects, you'd see the layout in Figure 14.2.

Now suppose we want to design a GUI with a title across the top (a label), a set of buttons down the left side that each pick a color, and a display in the remaining area in which the chosen color is shown. Figure 14.3 shows what it will look like before any of the buttons are pushed.

The BorderLayout is perfect for this, except for one small problem. You can add only *one* component to any given region of a BorderLayout. To get several buttons (or any other components) in a single region, you must put the JButton objects into *another* container object, then add that (single) container object to the appropriate region of the main BorderLayout. The key is that the Container object is itself a single component that may have several other components in it (hence the name *container*). The BorderLayout manager doesn't care how many components are in the container.

FIGURE 14.2

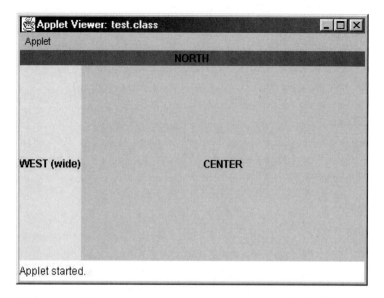

FIGURE 14.3

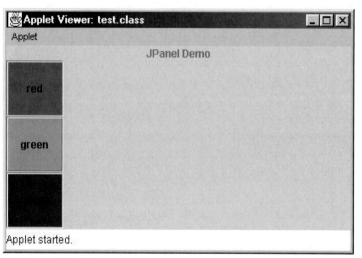

The appropriate container object to use is the `JPanel`.[2] We've seen the `JPanel` before when we extended it and overrode its `paintComponent` method. This time we won't extend the `JPanel`, but just create one, add the buttons to it, and then add it to the west region of `window`. A `JPanel` has a `FlowLayout` manager by default. So to get the three buttons arranged vertically, I'll set the layout manager of the `JPanel` to a `GridLayout` with three rows and one column (Code 14.2).

---

2. A `Container` cannot be used for reasons beyond the scope of this text.

CODE 14.2

```java
import java.awt.*;
import java.awt.event.*;
import javax.swing.*;

public class JPanelDemo extends JApplet implements ActionListener {
    private JButton red = new JButton("red");
    private JButton blue = new JButton("blue");
    private JButton green = new JButton("green");
    private JPanel display = new JPanel();

    public void init() {
        Container window = getContentPane();
        // create and add title
        JLabel title =
            new JLabel("JPanel Demo",SwingConstants.CENTER);
        window.add(title,BorderLayout.NORTH);
        // create buttons, add to JPanel, and add JPanel
        JPanel left = new JPanel();
        left.setLayout(new GridLayout(3,1));
        red.setOpaque(true);
        green.setOpaque(true);
        blue.setOpaque(true);
        red.setBackground(Color.red);
        green.setBackground(Color.green);
        blue.setBackground(Color.blue);
        left.add(red);
        left.add(green);
        left.add(blue);
        window.add(left,BorderLayout.WEST);
        // add display
        window.add(display,BorderLayout.CENTER);

        // add listeners
        red.addActionListener(this);
        green.addActionListener(this);
        blue.addActionListener(this);
    } // end of init method

    public void actionPerformed(ActionEvent event) {
        if (event.getSource() == red) {
            display.setBackground(Color.red);
            }
        else if (event.getSource() == green) {
            display.setBackground(Color.green);
            }
        else if (event.getSource() == blue) {
            display.setBackground(Color.blue);
            }
```

Create a JPanel object to add the JButton objects to.

Give the JPanel a grid layout so the buttons are stacked vertically.

Add the JButton objects to the JPanel object.

Add the JPanel object to the WEST of window.

Use an empty JPanel for the color display area.

Set the background color of the empty JPanel depending on which button is pushed.

```
         else {
            System.out.println("bad event");
            }
         } // end of actionPerformed method

} // end of JPanelDemo class
```

The JPanel class is getting dual use in this applet. It gets used to create an object that groups the three buttons into a single object that can be added to the WEST of the BorderLayout, and an otherwise empty JPanel object is added to the CENTER of the BorderLayout so that we have something to set a background color in (I could have used a JLabel with no message in it instead).

{New Concepts}

Only one component can be added to a given BorderLayout region. Use a JPanel to group subcomponents into a single component that can be added to a region.

14.1.1 Multiple, Nested Containers

The three layout managers (flow, grid, and border) along with the JPanel to group components make it possible to design some really nice-looking GUIs. This is especially true when you consider that a JPanel object can have its own layout manager, as we demonstrated above, and that you can then add a JPanel object with several components in it to part of another JPanel, effectively nesting one inside the other.

To demonstrate what can be done, here's an applet that has four buttons and a display area. The display area (in the center of a BorderLayout) is defined by a JPanel with a paintComponent method. It divides the area into four equal-size quadrants, each of which can be either black or white. The buttons are arranged in a similar way to the quadrants, and when pushed, cause the corresponding quadrant to toggle back and forth between black and white. The buttons are preceded by a label indicating what to do. The label and buttons are in the south of the BorderLayout. Nothing is in any of the other regions. Figure 14.4 shows the way it looks before any buttons are pushed.

The arrangement and nesting of JPanels and components are shown in Figure 14.5. The four JButton objects are in a JPanel with a 2-by-2 grid layout. The JLabel and JPanel with the buttons are in another JPanel with a centered FlowLayout, which is the default layout manager for a JPanel.

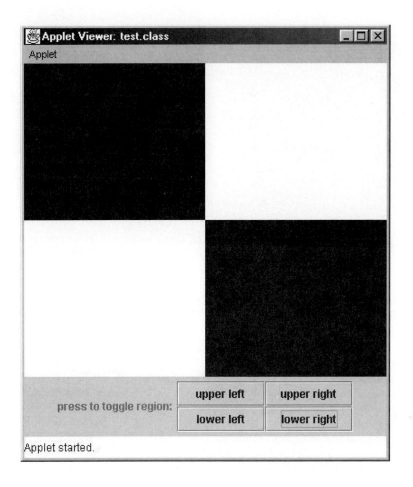

FIGURE 14.4

That `JPanel` is in the south of `window`, which has a `BorderLayout` by default, and the extended `JPanel` is in the center of `window`.

The code to construct this GUI is pretty straightforward. The various components, including `JPanel` objects, are constructed, and the `JPanel` objects are given layout managers. The components are then added to the appropriate containers. Finally the listeners are attached to the `JButton` objects (Code 14.3).

Since the actual size of the extended `JPanel` in the center of the `BorderLayout` is determined by the space remaining in the window, there is no need to give it a size explicitly as we did when putting it in a `FlowLayout`. However, we need to know the size when drawing the pattern. Fortunately the `JPanel` class has methods `getWidth` and `getHeight` that return the width and height, respectively, of the `JPanel` in the window.

FIGURE 14.5

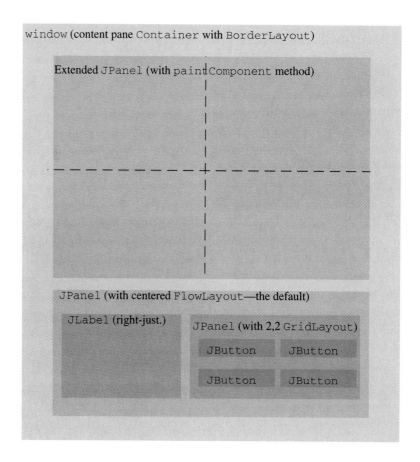

window (content pane `Container` with `BorderLayout`)

Extended `JPanel` (with `paintComponent` method)

`JPanel` (with centered `FlowLayout`—the default)

`JLabel` (right-just.)

`JPanel` (with 2,2 `GridLayout`)

JButton   JButton

JButton   JButton

CODE 14.3

```
import java.awt.*;
import java.awt.event.*;
import javax.swing.*;

public class NestedJPanel extends JApplet
                       implements ActionListener {
    private JButton upperLeft = new JButton("upper left");
    private JButton upperRight = new JButton("upper right");
    private JButton lowerLeft = new JButton("lower left");
    private JButton lowerRight = new JButton("lower right");
    private Display display = new Display();

    public void init() {
        Container window = getContentPane();
        // create JPanels and set layout manager
        JPanel control = new JPanel();
        JPanel buttons = new JPanel();
        buttons.setLayout(new GridLayout(2,2));
```

These components are defined here so both init and `actionPerformed` methods can access them.

```
    // add buttons to JPanel
    buttons.add(upperLeft);
    buttons.add(upperRight);
    buttons.add(lowerLeft);
    buttons.add(lowerRight);

    // add JLabel and button JPanel to another JPanel
    JLabel message = new JLabel("press to toggle region:",
                                SwingConstants.RIGHT);
    control.add(message);
    control.add(buttons);

    // add lower JPanel and Display to window
    window.add(control,BorderLayout.SOUTH);
    window.add(display,BorderLayout.CENTER);

    // attach listeners
    upperLeft.addActionListener(this);
    upperRight.addActionListener(this);
    lowerLeft.addActionListener(this);
    lowerRight.addActionListener(this);
    } // end of init method
```

```
public void actionPerformed(ActionEvent event) {
    if (event.getSource() == upperLeft) {
        display.toggle(0,0);
        }
    else if (event.getSource() == upperRight) {
        display.toggle(0,1);
        }
    else if (event.getSource() == lowerLeft) {
        display.toggle(1,0);
        }
    else if (event.getSource() == lowerRight) {
        display.toggle(1,1);
        }
    else {
        System.out.println("bad event");
        }
    } // end of actionPerformed method

} // end of NestedJPanel class
```

> Send array coordinates of which quadrant to toggle the color in to the extended `JPanel`.

```
class Display extends JPanel {
    private Color [][] quadrant = new Color [2][2];

    public Display() {
        quadrant[0][0] = Color.white;
        quadrant[0][1] = Color.black;
        quadrant[1][0] = Color.black;
        quadrant[1][1] = Color.white;
        } // end of constructor
```

```
public void toggle(int row, int col) {
    if (quadrant[row][col].equals(Color.white)) {
        quadrant[row][col] = Color.black;
        }
    else {
        quadrant[row][col] = Color.white;
        }
    repaint();
    } // end of toggle method
```

```
public void paintComponent(Graphics g) {
    super.paintComponent(g);
    for (int row=0; row<2; row+=1) {
        drawQuadrant(row,g);
        }
    } // end of paintComponent method
```

```
private void drawQuadrant(int row, Graphics g) {
    int width = getWidth()/2;
    int height = getHeight()/2;
    for (int col=0; col<2; col+=1) {
        g.setColor(quadrant[row][col]);
        g.fillRect(col*width,row*height,width,height);
        }
    } // end of drawQuadrant method
```

> getWidth and getHeight return the width and height of the area the JPanel occupies in the center of the BorderLayout after being stretched.

```
} // end of Display class
```

NestedJPanel
Demonstrates the construction of a complex arrangement of components using JPanel objects containing other JPanel objects.

Written Exercise

1. Draw a picture like the one in this section that shows how the following GUI would be constructed from various components and layout managers.

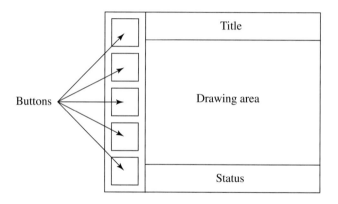

Programming Exercise

1. Write an applet that plays the game called Reversi. The display should look like the following:

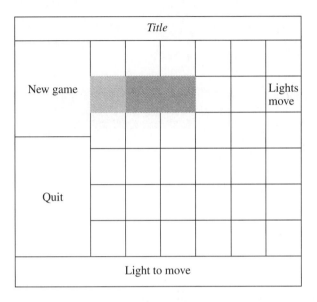

The game is played by two people, each taking a turn. In a turn a player chooses one of the squares not already taken. The square is changed to be the color assigned to that player (pick any two colors you like for the two players). If there is another square of the same color on the same row or column, then all squares between those two are made that color, too, even if they were previously the other player's color (in the diagram if the light color's next move is as shown, then the whole second row becomes light). The object is for a player to get all the squares to be his or her color. Use JButton objects for the squares, changing their background color as appropriate. The "restart" and "quit" buttons on the left do the obvious things. The label at the bottom displays which player's turn it is.

14.2   IMAGES

Java has several facilities for using and manipulating images. I won't go into all of them, but here are a couple of interesting uses.

JLabel and JButton objects can display an image in place of or in addition to text. To use an image in either one, you must first load the image from a file on your computer to an ImageIcon object, then create the JLabel or JButton, and send the ImageIcon object to the constructor instead of (or in addition to) text.

FIGURE 14.6

{New Concepts}

An **ImageIcon** object loads an image from a graphics image file (ending in .jpg, .jpeg, etc.).

Figure 14.6 is the display from a small application program that loads two images, using one for a JLabel and the other for the exit JButton. The Java logo is a JLabel in the center of a BorderLayout, and the exit sign is a JButton in the south. The logo comes from a file called "javalogo52x88.jpg", the exit sign from "exit.jpg" (Code 14.4).

CODE 14.4

```java
import java.awt.*;
import java.awt.event.*;
import javax.swing.*;

public class ImageDemo extends JFrame implements ActionListener {
    private final int frameWidth = 200;
    private final int frameHeight = 200;

    public static void main(String [] args) {
        ImageDemo demo = new ImageDemo();
    } // end of main method

    public ImageDemo() {
        Container window = getContentPane();
        // set up logo in center
        ImageIcon logo = new ImageIcon("javalogo52x88.jpg");
        JLabel logoLabel =
            new JLabel("Java Logo",logo,SwingConstants.CENTER);
        logoLabel.setOpaque(true);
        logoLabel.setBackground(Color.white);
        window.add(logoLabel,BorderLayout.CENTER);
```

Load the logo image.

Create a JLabel object that centers the logo/text.

```
    // set up exit button in south
    ImageIcon exit = new ImageIcon("exit.jpg");
    JButton exitButton = new JButton(exit);
    exitButton.setOpaque(true);
    exitButton.setBackground(Color.gray);
    window.add(exitButton,BorderLayout.SOUTH);
    exitButton.addActionListener(this);
    setSize(frameWidth,frameHeight);
    setVisible(true);
    } // end of constructor

public void actionPerformed(ActionEvent event) {
    System.exit(0);
    } // end of actionPerformed method

} // end of ImageDemo class
```

Load the exit image and create the JButton.

ImageDemo
Demonstrates the use of images to identify labels and buttons.

The constructor of an `ImageIcon` object loads the image into the program from the file name sent to it. A refererence to the `ImageIcon` object is then sent to the constructor of a `JLabel` or `JButton`, in place of or in addition to a string. Note that you must specify the alignment of the image in the `JLabel` constructor. This example centers it, but you can also `LEFT`- or `RIGHT`-justify it.

Programming Exercise

1. Use a drawing program on your computer to create an image; then write a simple Java applet that displays your image as a `JLabel` in the center of a `BorderLayout`.

14.3   OTHER GUI COMPONENTS

There are many useful GUI components, more than I'll cover in this section. You are encouraged to peruse the Java documentation Web pages and various Java texts, online tutorials, etc., to find out more about all the things you can use and how they work.

14.3.1   JCheckBoxes and JRadioButton Groups

A **JCheckBox** looks like a box with a string or image next to it. The box can be checked or not checked, and it is often used to let a user indicate that some item is of interest or not. Here's a simple applet with a `JCheckBox` and an associated label that is used to indicate whether the checkbox is checked. Figure 14.7 shows the applet before and after the box is checked.

The code is shown in Code 14.5.

FIGURE 14.7

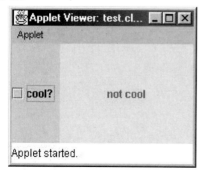
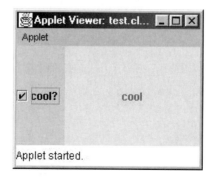

CODE 14.5

```
import java.awt.*;
import java.awt.event.*;
import javax.swing.*;

public class JCheckBoxDemo extends JApplet
                     implements ActionListener {
    JCheckBox cool = new JCheckBox("cool?");
    private JLabel status =
        new JLabel("not cool",SwingConstants.CENTER);

    public void init() {
        Container window = getContentPane();
        window.add(cool,BorderLayout.WEST);
        cool.addActionListener(this);

        status.setOpaque(true);
        status.setBackground(Color.yellow);
        window.add(status,BorderLayout.CENTER);
    } // end of init method


    public void actionPerformed(ActionEvent event) {
        if (cool.isSelected()) {
            status.setText("cool");
            }
        else {
            status.setText("not cool");
            }
    } // end of actionPerformed method

} // end of JCheckBoxDemo class
```

Create a `CheckBox` object, add it to `window`, and give it an `ActionListener`.

`actionPerformed` is called whenever the `CheckBox` is changed.

JCheckBoxDemo

Demonstrates a `JCheckbox`, which is similar to a `JButton` but toggles back and forth between check and not checked every time it is clicked on.

FIGURE 14.8

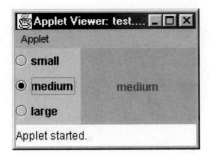

The JCheckBox class defines a checkbox that acts a lot like a JButton. It just looks a little different. A useful method that you can use with a JCheckBox is isSelected. A JCheckBox object keeps track of whether it is selected or not, and isSelected returns the current status.

A variation of the JCheckBox is the JRadioButton. A set of JRadioButton objects is usually grouped so that only one of them can be selected at any one time. This makes them useful for choosing one of several alternatives, as the applet shown in Figure 14.8 illustrates. This applet is like the previous one, except that the radio button currently chosen is displayed on the right.

JRadioButton objects work pretty much the same way as JCheckBox objects. The key to ensuring that only one is selected at a time is to add them to a ButtonGroup object (in addition to adding them to window or a JPanel). The ButtonGroup object detects when one of the JRadioButton objects in its group is selected, then automatically deselects whichever other JRadioButton was selected prior to that (Code 14.6).

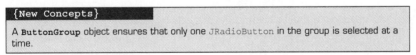

{New Concepts}

A **ButtonGroup** object ensures that only one JRadioButton in the group is selected at a time.

14.3.2 JComboBox

Another interesting component is the JComboBox. A **JComboBox** consists of a collection of items that can be viewed via a pull-down menu, then one is selected. I'll demonstrate it with a program that displays a JComboBox object with three items (U.S. states), a JLabel that indicates what is chosen, and an exit JButton identified by an image. Three views, starting with the initial appearance of the screen, are shown in Figure 14.9.

The JComboBox object is created, then items are added to it. In this example the items are strings, but they can also be images if you like. When an item is selected, it generates a new kind of event called an ItemEvent, and to respond to it we need to implement an **ItemListener** with an itemStateChanged method. Since we also have a JButton (exit), we need an ActionListener to respond to it being pushed (Code 14.7).

CODE 14.6

```java
import java.awt.*;
import java.awt.event.*;
import javax.swing.*;

public class JRadioButtonDemo extends JApplet
                              implements ActionListener {
    private JRadioButton small = new JRadioButton("small");
    private JRadioButton medium = new JRadioButton("medium",true);
    private JRadioButton large = new JRadioButton("large");
    private JLabel status =
        new JLabel("medium",SwingConstants.CENTER);

    public void init() {
        Container window = getContentPane();

        JPanel buttons = new JPanel();
        buttons.setLayout(new GridLayout(3,1));
        buttons.add(small);
        buttons.add(medium);
        buttons.add(large);
        window.add(buttons,BorderLayout.WEST);

        ButtonGroup size = new ButtonGroup();
        size.add(small);
        size.add(medium);
        size.add(large);

        small.addActionListener(this);
        medium.addActionListener(this);
        large.addActionListener(this);

        status.setOpaque(true);
        status.setBackground(Color.cyan);
        window.add(status,BorderLayout.CENTER);
    } // end of init method

    public void actionPerformed(ActionEvent event) {
        if (event.getSource() == small) {
            status.setText("small");
        }
        else if (event.getSource() == medium) {
            status.setText("medium");
        }
        else if (event.getSource() == large) {
            status.setText("large");
        }
        else {
            status.setText("bad event");
        }
    } // end of actionPerformed method

} // end of JRadioButtonDemo class
```

Make the medium button be selected initially.

Add the JRadioButton objects to the JPanel just like any other component.

Also, add the JRadioButton objects to a ButtonGroup object.

JRadioButton objects generate action events just like any other button object.

JRadioButtonDemo
Demonstrates a collection of JRadioButtons grouped into a ButtonGroup to ensure that only one can be selected at a time.

FIGURE 14.9

Initial appearance

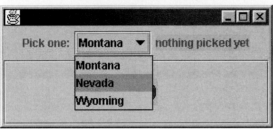

Click on arrow and select Nevada

After Nevada picked

The JComboBox saves the items that are added to it in an arraylike structure. When a new item is selected and the itemStateChanged method is called, we can find out which item was chosen by the user by calling the getSelectedIndex method of the JComboBox object. It returns an integer which is the index of the item that was selected, which we can then send to the getItemAt method to retrieve the item. Since both strings and images can be items, we have to indicate that a String is being returned by casting the return value of getItemAt.

{New Concepts}

A JComboBox objects generates an ItemEvent when a new item is selected. An itemStateChanged method in a class that implements ItemListener must be attached to the JComboBox object to react to the event.

Notice in this example that I used a JPanel object to combine two JLabels and the JComboBox objects, then added the JPanel object to the north of window. I also used the exit image in a JButton to terminate execution of the program.

CODE 14.7

```java
import java.awt.*;
import java.awt.event.*;
import javax.swing.*;

public class JComboBoxDemo extends JFrame
                implements ItemListener, ActionListener {

    private final int frameWidth = 400;
    private final int frameHeight = 100;
    private JLabel status = new JLabel("nothing picked yet");
    private JComboBox choices = new JComboBox();

    public static void main(String [] args) {

        JComboBoxDemo gui = new JComboBoxDemo();
        } // end of main method

    public JComboBoxDemo() {

        Container window = getContentPane();

        JPanel demo = new JPanel();
        demo.setLayout(new FlowLayout());

        JLabel msg = new JLabel("Pick one:", SwingConstants.LEFT);
        demo.add(msg);

        choices.addItem("Montana");
        choices.addItem("Nevada");
        choices.addItem("Wyoming");
        choices.addItemListener(this);
        demo.add(choices);

        status.setOpaque(true);
        status.setBackground(Color.pink);
        demo.add(status);

        window.add(demo,BorderLayout.NORTH);

        ImageIcon exitImage = new ImageIcon("exit.jpg");
        JButton exit = new JButton(exitImage);
        window.add(exit,BorderLayout.CENTER);
        exit.addActionListener(this);
        setSize(frameWidth,frameHeight);
        setVisible(true);
        } // end of constructor

    public void itemStateChanged(ItemEvent event) {
        int which = choices.getSelectedIndex();
        String msg = (String)choices.getItemAt(which)+" picked";
        status.setText(msg);
        } // end of itemStateChanged method

    public void actionPerformed(ActionEvent event) {
        System.exit(0);
        } // end of actionPerformed method

    } // end of JComboBoxdemo class
```

A JComboBox generates ItemEvents, so an ItemListener is needed.

Create an empty JComboBox object.

Add items to the JComboBox, then attach the ItemListener.

Get the index of the selected item, then get that item and display it.

JComboBox objects work the same in application programs and applets. I simply chose an application program and not an applet this time for variety.

JComboBoxDemo
Demonstrates a
JComboBox, which is a
pull-down menu of choices.

Programming Exercises

1. You can add more items to a JComboBox as a program executes. Write an applet that displays a JComboBox (initially with no items), and JTextField for entering new items for the JComboBox. Add a new string item to the JComboBox whenever one is entered into the JTextField, and check to ensure it was added properly by choosing it in the JComboBox.

2. Write an application program with GUI that creates a file of student record objects described by the following partial class definition:

```
class Student {
    private String name;
    private int idNum;
    private int sex; // 0=male, 1=female
    private int major; // 0=CS,1=EE,2=English,3=Business
    private boolean honors;

    // add your methods here
    };
```

Design a GUI that has text fields for inputting the name and id number, two radio buttons for the gender, a JComboBox for the major, and a checkbox for whether the student is an honor student. Include buttons to write a record once the information has been filled in, to clear all the information entered so far for a student and start over, and to quit.

Summary

- A BorderLayout manager defines five regions of the screen: north, south, east, west, and center. A single component can be added to each region.

- A JPanel can be used to group components so that several can be added to a BorderLayout region.

- A JPanel has a flow layout manager by default but can be given any other type.

- An ImageIcon object is used to store an image. Its constructor reads an image from an image file.

- JLabel and JButton objects can display images instead of or in addition to text.

- A JCheckBox displays a box and text. The box can be clicked on to check or uncheck it. An action event is generated when the box is clicked on, and the state of the box can be determined.

- A `JRadioButton` displays a button and text. Several are normally grouped in a `ButtonGroup` to ensure that only one is selected at a time.
- A `JComboBox` displays several strings and/or icons in a pull-down menu. A user can select an item, which generates an `ItemEvent`.
- `ItemEvents` are reacted to by objects defined by classes that implement `ItemListener`.
- The `getSelectedIndex` method returns the index of the selected item in a `JComboBox`.

Glossary

BorderLayout Manager   A layout manager that divides the screen into five regions: north, south, east, west, and center. A single component can be added to each region.

ButtonGroup   A class that defines an object that ensures that only one `JRadioButton` object it contains is selected at any given time.

Component   A displayable object, such as a `JLabel`, `JButton`, `JTextField`, `JPanel`, `JCheckBox`, `JRadioButton`, or `JComboBox`.

ImageIcon   An object that contains an image. Its constructor reads an image from a file.

ItemListener   An interface for reacting to events generated by a `JComboBox`.

JCheckBox   A component that displays a box and a label. The box can be checked or unchecked, either of which generates an action event.

JComboBox   A component that allows a user to choose between several items (which can be strings or images). An `ItemEvent` is generated when a new item is selected.

JRadioButton   A component that displays a circle that can be clicked on and a label. `JRadioButton` objects are grouped in a `ButtonGroup` to ensure that only one is selected at a time.

Class Hierarchies

- To understand the relationship between a class and the class it extends.
- To understand the notion of a hierarchy of classes.
- To understand the IS-A and HAS-A relationships.
- To know the difference between inheriting and overriding instance variables and methods.
- To know the meaning of polymorphism and how it is used in a program.
- To understand what an abstract class is, and when to use one.
- To understand the concept of interfaces, and how they differ from classes and abstract classes.
- To know what final methods and classes are and when to use them.
- To be able to use inheritance, abstract classes, and interfaces effectively.

15.1 INTRODUCTION

Up to this point we have been mostly writing programs that consist of many interacting objects. Doing so is a major aspect of the object-oriented approach to programming.

In Chapter 9, however, we did something different. We wrote new class definitions that were extensions of other classes. We used the class extension mechanism to give greater functionality to an existing class that was part of the Java class library. The writers of the classes in that library designed those classes with every expectation that they would be extended, and we did.

Some of the classes (e.g., the adapter classes) have no purpose other than to be extended. Having a class like the `MouseAdapter` saves us some typing at the very least. The `JPanel` class, on the other hand, has a lot of functionality and is quite usable without ever having to be extended. But it is designed to be extended, too, and we did so by writing our own `paintComponent` methods that drew useful things.

In this chapter we will begin to create our own classes that we will design to be extended.

15.2 SUPERCLASSES

Consider a drawing program in which the user clicks on one of several buttons that represent various shapes, then uses the mouse to click somewhere on a display region to position and then draw the shape. An object-oriented design of this program will include an object for each shape that eventually appears in the display region. The object will have a method (called `draw`) that can be called when the program wants the shape to be displayed on the screen. It will also have a method to set the position at which the shape should be drawn. Each different kind of shape will be defined by a separate class.

Suppose one of the shapes is a red 100 × 100 square. Then Code 15.1 shows a class definition for square objects.

CODE 15.1

```
class Square {
     private int x;
     private int y;

     public void setPosition(int ux, int uy) {
         x = ux;
         y = uy;
         } // end of setPosition method

     public void draw(Graphics g) {
         g.setColor(Color.red);
         g.fillRect(x,y,100,100);
         } // end of draw method

     } // end of Square class
```

The program that uses this class will create a `Square` object, then call `setPosition` to tell it where it should be drawn, and call `draw` to have it displayed. The object itself keeps track of where it will be displayed.

Now let's add another shape—a green circle with diameter of 100 (Code 15.2).

As you can see, these two classes are very much alike. They have different names, of course, and the `draw` methods are a little different, but otherwise they are exactly the same. Consider writing class definitions for more kinds of shapes, and you'll quickly come to the conclusion that you will be writing a lot of duplicate code.

Fortunately there is a better way. In Chapter 9 we saw that we can take an existing class and extend it, inheriting some methods and overriding others. This is similar to what we want to do here. We want the class being extended

CODE 15.2

```
class Circle {
    private int x;
    private int y;

    public void setPosition(int ux, int uy) {
        x = ux;
        y = uy;
        } // end of setPosition method

    public void draw(Graphics g) {
        g.setColor(Color.green);
        g.fillOval(x,y,100,100);
        } // end of draw method

    } // end of Circle class
```

to have code that is common to all the classes that extend it, so those classes can simply inherit it (e.g., the setPosition method). We also want code to put code that is specific to each extension in the extension (e.g., the draw method).

To that end, let's first pull the code that is common to the two class descriptions above and put it into a new class called Shape (Code 15.3).

CODE 15.3

```
class Shape {
    private int x;
    private int y;

    public void setPosition(int ux, int uy) {
        x = ux;
        y = uy;
        } // end of setPosition method

    } // end of Shape class
```

Now the definitions of the Square and Circle classes can extend the Shape class and not have to duplicate this code (Code 15.4).

Except for one small problem, we now have much simpler Square and Circle classes, and we can easily write more classes for other shapes without duplicating several lines of code in each one. This is very convenient, and it also leads to fewer errors since you don't have to type the same code several times. It makes it easy and reliable to change the common code, should the

CODE 15.4

```
class Square extends Shape {

    public void draw (Graphics g) {
        g.setColor(Color.red);
        g.fillRect(x,y,100,100);
        } // end of draw method

    } // end of Square class

class Circle extends Shape {

    public void draw (Graphics g) {
        g.setColor(Color.green);
        g.fillOval(x,y,100,100);
        } // end of draw method

    } // end of Circle class
```

need arise, without having to find every place where it occurs (i.e., all the different shape classes).

The small problem mentioned above is with the private instance variables x and y. Remember, private means that the variables are only accessible in the class they are defined in, period. Therefore, they are not accessible in any subclasses. As a result, when the Square and Circle classes are compiled, we'll get an error message saying that x and y are not defined.

Fortunately Java has a solution to this problem. It has a reserved word protected which, if applied to an instance variable in a class definition, permits that variable to be accessed in the same class *and* any subclass. Therefore if we change the definition of the Shape class as shown in Code 15.5, then the problem is solved and we'll get no error messages. The reserved word protected still works like private in that other classes (non-subclasses) cannot access the variables. Protected also applies to methods, so that protected

CODE 15.5

```
class Shape {
    protected int x;              ←——  Making x and y protected
    protected int y;                    allows them to be used by
                                        classes that extend this one.

    public void setPosition(int ux, int uy) {
        x = ux;
        y = uy;
        } // end of setPosition method

    } // end of Shape class
```

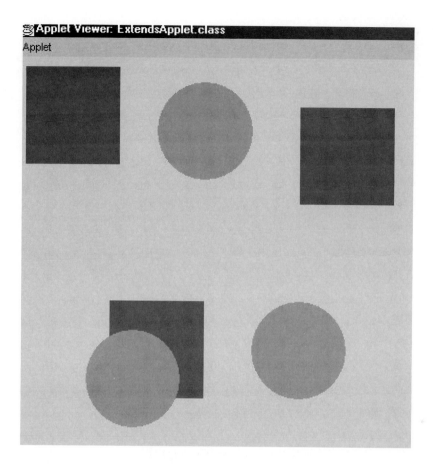

FIGURE 15.1

methods can be called only from the class they are defined in and from any subclasses.[1]

{New Concepts}

Protected instance variables and methods can be accessed only from the class they are defined in and from any subclasses.

15.2.1 Using the Shape Subclasses

Now that we have defined the `Square` and `Circle` classes, let's write a small test program that uses them. All this test program does is to create three `Square` and three `Circle` objects, give them arbitrarily chosen positions on the screen, and display them as shown in Figure 15.1.

---

1. Unfortunately this is not quite true, but the exact details are far beyond what we need to know at this time.

Code 15.6 is the test program.

ExtendsApplet
Displays shapes defined by
extending our own Shapes
class.

```java
import java.awt.*;
import java.awt.event.*;
import javax.swing.*;

public class ExtendsApplet extends JApplet {

    public void init() {
        Container window = getContentPane();
        Display show = new Display();
        window.add(show,BorderLayout.CENTER);
        } // end of init method

    } // end of ExtendsApplet class

class Display extends JPanel {
    private Square [] squares = new Square[3];
    private Circle [] circles = new Circle[3];

    public Display() {
        squares[0] = new Square();
        squares[1] = new Square();
        squares[2] = new Square();
        circles[0] = new Circle();
        circles[1] = new Circle();
        circles[2] = new Circle();

        squares[0].setPosition(10,10);
        squares[1].setPosition(100,250);
        squares[2].setPosition(300,50);
        circles[0].setPosition(150,25);
        circles[1].setPosition(250,250);
        circles[2].setPosition(75,280);
        } // end of constructor

    public void paintComponent(Graphics g) {
        super.paintComponent(g);
        for (int i= 0; i<squares.length; i+=1) {
            squares[i].draw(g);
            }
        for (int i= 0; i<circles.length; i+=1) {
            circles[i].draw(g);
            }
        } // end of paintComponent method

    } // end of Display class

// Shape class here
// Circle class here
// Square class here
```

Written Exercises

1. Describe in words what a superclass of the following classes would look like (e.g., instance variables, methods, and what they would do): full-time salaried employee, full-time hourly employee, part-time hourly employee.

2. Describe in words what a superclass of the following classes would look like: pitcher, catcher, infielder, outfielder.

Programming Exercises

1. Modify Code 15.6 to include three objects of yet another shape. You can design your own shape and pick the positions of the drawings on the screen.

2. Write a superclass description that contains the commonality of the two classes shown in Code 15.7; then rewrite the classes to extend your superclass.

CODE 15.7

```java
class IncreasingArray {
    private final int MAX = 100;
    private int [] values = new int[MAX];
    private int size = 0;

    // add n to the array in increasing order
    public void add(int n) {
        // put the new value at the end
        values[size] = n;
        size += 1;

        // swap it with larger values in front of
        // it until it gets to the right place
        int i = size-2;
        while (i >= 0 && values[i] > values[i+1]) {
            int temp = values[i];
            values[i] = values[i+1];
            values[i+1] = temp;
            i -= 1;
        }
    } // end of add method

    // retrieve the value at position i
    public int valueAt(int i) {
        if (0 < i && i < size) {
            return values[i];
        }
        else {
            return 0;
        }
    } // end of retrieve method

} // end of IncreasingArray class
```

```
class DecreasingArray {
    private final int MAX = 100;
    private int [] values = new int[MAX];
    private int size = 0;

    // add n to the array in decreasing order
    public void add(int n) {
        // put the new value at the end
        values[size] = n;
        size += 1;
        // swap it with smaller values in front of
        // it until it gets to the right place
        int i = size-2;
        while (i >= 0 && values[i] < values[i+1]) {
            int temp = values[i];
            values[i] = values[i+1];
            values[i+1] = temp;
            i -= 1;
        }
    } // end of add method

    // retrieve the value at position i
    public int valueAt(int i) {
        if (0 < i && i < size) {
            return values[i];
        }
        else {
            return 0;
        }
    } // end of retrieve method

} // end of DecreasingArray class
```

15.3 CLASS HIERARCHIES

Suppose we define a class Thing that contains instance variables and methods that describe the general properties and behaviors of all tangible things (e.g., instance variables for mass, position, and velocity and methods to modify the position and velocity, compute a new position after a certain amount of time has elapsed). Then suppose we define a subclass of Thing called LivingThing that adds some instance variables and methods particular to living things. As you would expect, LivingThing inherits variables and methods from Thing. Now suppose we further define a subclass of LivingThing called Animal that adds even more instance variables and methods that are particular to animals (e.g., as opposed to plants). Then Animal inherits variables and methods from LivingThing, including

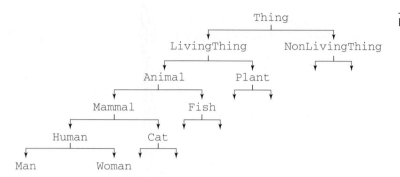

FIGURE 15.2

everything that LivingThing inherited from Thing. In a sense, Animal is a sub-subclass of Thing. We can go further to define subclasses Mammal of Animal, Human of Mammal, Woman of Human, etc. Every subclass inherits instance variables and methods from its superclass, including everything that the superclass inherited from its superclass.

This collection of classes related to one another via the superclass/subclass relationship is called a **class hierarchy.** At the top of the hierarchy in the example above is Thing. Under Thing is LivingThing. Under LivingThing is Animal. This continues all the way down to a class that is not a superclass of anything else. Figure 15.2 shows this hierarchy pictorially.

To make it clear how two classes are related in the hierarchy, we call the class that a given class extends its **direct superclass.** Hence Human is the direct superclass of Man and Woman. Likewise the extended class is called a **direct subclass.** Hence Man and Woman are direct subclasses of Human.

Classes that are part along a path of the hierarchy but are not direct subclasses and superclasses of each other are called *indirect subclasses* and *superclasses.* For example, Mammal, Animal, LivingThing, and Thing are all indirect superclasses of Man and Woman. Similarly, Man and Woman are indirect subclasses of Mammal. For the remainder of this text, when it doesn't matter whether a class is a direct or indirect subclass of another, then I'll just say that one is a subclass of the other. I'll use the analogous terminology for superclass.

Note that two classes may be part of the hierarchy but not direct or indirect subclasses or superclasses of each other. For example, Human is not a subclass or superclass (direct or indirect) of Plant. Hence Human does not inherit anything from Plant and vice versa. Of course, both inherit from LivingThing, so both will have certain instance variables and methods in common.

15.3.1 The Object Class

Java defines a special class called the **Object class.** If a class does not extend any other class, then by default it extends Object, even though it doesn't have extends Object in the definition. For example, the Shape class above is a subclass of Object. So is the Thing class in the hierarchy example. Hence every class hierarchy will have `Object` at the top, and every object is a subclass (direct or indirect) of `Object`.

The `Object` class has no instance variables and a handful of methods, most of which are beyond the scope of this text. However, the `Object` class is extremely handy, as we shall see in the next chapter.

15.3.2 The IS-A Relationship

When an object of the `Square` class is created, we have been saying that a "`Square` object is created." You can turn this wording around a bit and also say that the object that was created "is a" `Square`. However, not only is the object a `Square`, but also it is a `Shape` since it inherits instance variables and methods from the `Shape` class. Hence we can also say that the `Square` object also "is a" `Shape`. This is the basis for the **IS-A relationship**—any object of one class IS-A object of the superclass of that object, too. Note also that every object you can create in Java IS-A `Object`. It is either a direct subclass of `Object` (either by default or because you write `extends Object`) or an indirect one by means of the class hierarchy.

Using the class hierarchy above, we would say that a `Man` IS-A `Human` and a `Woman` IS-A `Human`. A `Human` IS-A `Mammal`, but then we can add that by the hierarchy, a `Man` IS-A `Mammal` and a `Woman` IS-A `Mammal`. In fact, a `Man` IS-A `Animal`, IS-A `LivingThing`, IS-A `Thing`, and IS-A `Object`. Hence a given object IS-A object of the class it is defined by, but it also IS-A object of its direct and indirect superclasses, too, all the way up the hierarchy to `Object`.

> **{New Concepts}**
>
> A given object IS-A object of the class that defines it and of every superclass of that class, including `Object`.

15.3.3 The HAS-A Relationship

The IS-A relationship is contrasted with the **HAS-A relationship.** If you recall the `Cart` class in Chapter 5, then you'll remember that the `Cart` is made up of (has references to) a `Box` object and two `Wheel` objects. You can say that a `Cart` object HAS-A `Box` object and HAS-A `Wheel` object and HAS-A second `Wheel` object (or just that a `Cart` HAS-A `Box` and two `Wheels`). HAS-A is clearly different from IS-A.

> **{New Concepts}**
>
> A given object HAS-A different object if it has an instance variable with a reference to that other object.

It is always easy to distinguish the two just by saying them and seeing if they sound right. If you say, "A `Woman` HAS-A `Human`," it doesn't sound right. "A `Woman` IS-A `Human`" sounds better. Conversely if you say that "a

Cart IS-A Wheel," it also doesn't sound right; but saying "a Cart HAS-A Wheel" does.

Written Exercises

1. Draw a picture of a class hierarchy with a WorldCitizen at the top; DetroitCitizen, SeattleCitizen, MiamiCitizen, Tokyo-Citizen, LondonCitizen, BombayCitizen, HarbinCitizen, etc., at the bottom; and at least two classes in between the top and bottom.

2. Check the Java documentation page for a JTextField. Find and list its direct and indirect superclasses.

3. Write down all the objects defined in the calculator example in Chapter 6, and for each list its HAS-A objects.

4. Explain in your own words why, in the example class hierarchy in this section, it is not the case that Man IS-A Plant.

15.4 POLYMORPHISM

The IS-A relationship gives us a very powerful capability in Java that I'll demonstrate with the Shape example at the beginning of the chapter. First I'll modify the Shape class slightly by adding a draw method to it. This method won't draw anything, but is necessary to take advantage of this new capability (Code 15.8).

CODE 15.8

```
class Shape {
    protected int x;
    protected int y;

    public void setPosition(int ux, int uy) {
        x = ux;
        y = uy;
    } // end of setPosition method

    public void draw(Graphics g) {
        // don't draw anything
    } // end of draw method

} // end of Shape class
```

This method will be overridden in each subclass to draw the appropriate shape.

Now let's modify the test program by replacing the two arrays with a single one and changing all the references to squares and circles to references to shapes instead (Code 15.9).

CODE 15.9

```
import java.awt.*;
import java.awt.event.*;
import javax.swing.*;

public class ExtendsApplet2 extends JApplet {

    public void init() {
        Container window = getContentPane();
        Display show = new Display();
        window.add(show,BorderLayout.CENTER);
        } // end of init method

    } // end of ExtendsApplet2 class
```

```
class Display extends JPanel {
    private Shape [] shapes = new Shape[6];
```
> Just one array is needed to refer to both Square and Circle objects.

```
    public Display() {
        shapes[0] = new Square();
        shapes[1] = new Square();
        shapes[2] = new Square();
        shapes[3] = new Circle();
        shapes[4] = new Circle();
        shapes[5] = new Circle();
```
> A shapes array element can refer to an object of any subclass of Shape.

```
        shapes[0].setPosition(10,10);
        shapes[1].setPosition(100,250);
        shapes[2].setPosition(300,50);
```
> SetPosition in the Shapes class is called because a Square object inherits it.

```
        shapes[3].setPosition(150,25);
        shapes[4].setPosition(250,250);
        shapes[5].setPosition(75,280)
        } // end of constructor
```
> SetPosition in the Shapes class is called because a Circle object inherits it.

```
    public void paintComponent(Graphics g) {
        super.paintComponent(g);
        for (int i= 0; i<shapes.length; i+=1) {
            shapes[i].draw(g);
            }
        } // end of paintComponent method

    } // end of Display class
```
> When shapes[i] refers to a Square object, the draw method in the Square class is called. When it refers to a Circle object, the draw method in the Circle class is called.

```
// new Shape class here
```

```
// original Circle and Square classes here
```

ExtendsApplet2
Modified version of
ExtendsApplet that takes
advantage of polymorphism.

Consider first the line:

```
shapes[0] = new Square();
```

You might think that this would be illegal, since `shapes[0]` is supposed to be a reference to a `Shape` object, not a `Square` one. But a `Square` object IS-A `Shape` object! Hence putting a reference to a `Square` object in a variable that is supposed to contain a reference to a `Shape` object is perfectly legal. It is also legal to put a reference to a `Circle` object in a variable that is supposed to contain a reference to a `Shape` object. A `Circle` IS-A `Shape`, too.

I'll come back to the six commands that call the `setPosition` method a little later, but right now I want to show you the really powerful part. Java *remembers* that each element of `shapes` contains a reference to either a `Square` object or a `Circle` object, and not a `Shape` object. This is extremely important when it comes to the command

```
shapes[i].draw(g);
```

Because Java remembers, for each element of the `shapes` array, what kind of object it references, it calls the correct `draw` method for that kind of object. If `shapes[i]` is a reference to a `Square` object, then it calls the `draw` method in the `Square` class. If instead `shapes[i]` is a reference to a `Circle` object, then it calls the `draw` method in the `Circle` class. In neither case does it call the `draw` method in the `Shapes` class.

This property is called *polymorphism*. It permits us to store a reference to any object that IS-A `Shape` in any element of the `shapes` array, then later have the correct `draw` method called depending on which class of object is currently being referred to. We can even write new classes that extend `Shape`, each with their own `draw` method, but not have to make a single change to the `paintComponent` method in the test program.

{**Definition of Terms**}

Polymorphism permits a reference to a subclass to be stored in a variable defined to be a reference to an object of the superclass. The variable remembers what class of object is referenced so that methods in the subclass are called when appropriate.

Polymorphism is the property that allows us to add `JButton`, `JLabel`, `JTextField`, `JPanel` objects, etc., to a `Container` without the `Container` class having to be written to know exactly which ones are added in which order. `JButton`, `JLabel`, `JTextField`, `JPanel`, etc., are all subclasses of `Component` (e.g., a `JButton` IS-A `Component`). Hence a `Container` object simply stores a reference to whatever object it is given (as long as it IS-A `Component`). Later when the `Container` needs to display the components that were added to it, it simply asks each object defined by a subclass of `Component` to draw itself, and the correct version gets called to get that particular object drawn. When you create a class that extends `JPanel` and write your own paintComponent method, then when the Container needs to draw an object of your class, it calls *your* paintComponent method. This is simply because the object of your class IS-A JPanel and also IS-A Component.

Hence code can be written, as for a Container, that will get the correct version of a method depending on which object is currently being referred to by a reference variable, without knowing when the code is written just what class of object will be referred to. The actual object only has to be a subclass of the correct kind of object.

Written Exercise

1. Modify the correct Shape class in the example above by removing the draw method (that does nothing). Compile the program. What happens? Why?

Programming Exercises

1. Replace the Square class with a new one (your choice of what it draws) in the sample program above. Notice that the only change to the existing code is replacing the creation of a new Square object with the creation of your object.

2. Write an application program with GUI that can be used to create either Faculty objects or Staff objects. Both objects have name (String), social security number (int), and department (String) properties, while Faculty have degree from (String) and tenured (boolean) properties and Staff have full-time (boolean, false means part-time) and union (String) properties. Both have constructors that set the common properties, and each has a setInfo method that sets the distinct properties. The GUI has text fields, buttons, etc., to fill in information for a particular object, and two separate buttons for choosing whether a Faculty or Staff object should be created. Write each object to file (serialized). Then write another simple application program that reads the file and prints out the information in it in a readable form (define print methods for both objects). Define an Employee superclass and use polymorphism whenever possible.

15.5 INSTANCE VARIABLES IN SUBCLASS OBJECTS

As I said earlier, instance variables defined to be private in a superclass cannot be referenced by code in a subclass. However, this does not mean that the instance variables do not exist in subclass *objects*. They do, but you can't access them from subclass code, that's all.

Consider the modification of the `Shape` class shown in Code 15.10.

CODE 15.10

```
class Shape {
    protected int x;
    protected int y;
    private int id;

    public void setPosition(int ux, int uy) {
        x = ux;
        y = uy;
    } // end of setPosition method

    public void setId(int value) {
        id = value;
    } // end of setId method

    public int getId() {
        return id;
    } // end of getId method

    public void draw(Graphics g) {
        // don't draw anything
    } // end of draw method

} // end of Shape class
```

This method will be overridden in the subclasses to draw the appropriate shape.

The instance variable `id` will be assumed to be a unique identifier assigned to each `Shape` object (or subclass of `Shape` object) by the `setId` method and retrieved via the `getId` method. I'll also assume that `id` will not be accessed from any subclass method so it can be made private.

Now assuming the `Square` and `Circle` classes are defined exactly as before, then any object of the `Square` or `Circle` class will have an `id` instance variable. It isn't visible to the code in the `Square` and `Circle` classes, so they can't refer to it directly. The only way to access it is via the `setId` and `getId` methods, which are of course inherited by the subclasses.

This means that if we have the definition

```
Circle ball = new Circle();
```

somewhere in a program that uses the `Circle` (and `Shape`) classes and then later we write

```
ball.setId(69);
```

we will set the `id` instance variable of the `Circle` object referred to by `ball` to 69. Understand what is happening here. The `Circle` *object* has an `id` instance variable, but no method defined in the `Circle` class can refer to it. However, the `Circle` class inherits the `setId` method from the `Shape` class. Because the `setId` method is *defined* in the `Shape` class, it has access to `id`.

{New Concepts}

Private instance variables declared in a superclass exist in any subclass object, but they are not accessible from code appearing in the subclass.

15.6 FINAL AND ABSTRACT METHODS AND CLASSES

15.6.1 Final Methods

Suppose you are implementing a class that you expect will be extended, but you don't want any subclass to be able to override some of its methods. Then all you have to do is to declare those methods *final* by including the reserved word `final` in the declaration of the method. For example, consider the `Shape` class above (with `getId` and `setId` methods). If we want to make sure that the `getId` and `setId` methods cannot be overridden, then Code 15.11 is a class definition that does it.

CODE 15.11

```
class Shape {
    protected int x;
    protected int y;
    private int id;

    public void setPosition(int ux, int uy) {
        x = ux;
        y = uy;
        } // end of setPosition method

    public final void setId(int value) {
        id = value;
        } // end of setId method

    public final int getId() {
        return id;
        } // end of getId method

    public void draw(Graphics g) {
        // don't draw anything
        } // end of draw method

} // end of Shape class
```

These methods cannot be overridden in any subclass of Shape.

Final methods are useful in libraries of classes because you never know who's going to be extending your class. It gives you a level of protection from a user of your class trying to subvert the meaning of one or more of your methods by overriding them with different versions of their own. In fact, you should have a very good reason for a method *not* to be final.

{New Concepts}

A **final method** in a superclass cannot be overridden in any subclass.

15.6.2 Final Classes

Just as a method can be made final to prohibit it from being overridden in a subclass, you can make an entire class final to prohibit it from being extended at all. Again you use the reserved word `final`, but this time in the class declaration. For example, Code 15.12 is a definition of the `Square` class that cannot be extended.

CODE 15.12

```
final class Square extends Shape {          ┌─────────────────┐
   ◀──────────────                          │ The Square class │
                                            │ cannot be extended. │
                                            └─────────────────┘
    public void draw (Graphics g) {
        g.setColor(Color.red);
        g.fillRect(x,y,100,100);
        } // end of draw method


    } // end of Square class
```

{New Concepts}

A **final class** cannot be extended.

15.6.3 Abstract Methods

Consider the `Shape` class with the empty `draw` method. The `draw` method must be there so that polymorphism works properly. However, now suppose you create a `Shape` object (not a `Square` or `Circle`) and then call the `draw` method for that object. Then the `draw` method in the `Shape` class will be called, and *nothing* will be drawn. In fact, when the `Shape` class was defined, its sole purpose was to be extended by `Square`, `Circle`, and perhaps other classes for various shapes and the `draw` method overridden. We never expected to create any `Shape` objects, only `Square` and `Circle` objects.

You can require that a method be overridden in a subclass by declaring it to be an **abstract method** by including the reserved word `abstract` in its definition. This is just the opposite of `final`, which prohibits a method from being overridden. Code 15.13 is a new definition of the original `Shape` class with an abstract `draw` method.

Notice that the abstract method (`draw`) has no implementation, not even an empty one. A semicolon follows the declaration of the method instead of the

CODE 15.13

```
abstract class Shape {
    protected int x;
    protected int y;

    public void setPosition(int ux, int uy) {
        x = ux;
        y = uy;
    } // end of setPosition method

    public abstract void draw(Graphics g);

} // end of Shape class
```

A class with an abstract method must be declared abstract, too.

This method *must* be overridden.

An abstract method has no implementation, not even an empty one.

normal curly braces { }. Notice also that any class that has an abstract method in it *must* itself be declared abstract. A class with one or more abstract methods is called an *abstract class*.

{New Concepts}

An *abstract* method must be overridden in a subclass.

It is not possible to create an object of an abstract class. This new definition of the Shape class therefore will not allow you to create a Shape object at all. The Shape class must be extended, and the draw method overridden, and then only objects of subclasses of the Shape class can be created.

{New Concepts}

A class with one or more abstract methods is an **abstract class.** An object of an abstract class cannot be created.

If you create a subclass of the Shape class and forget to override the draw method, then you cannot create an object of the subclass either. This is because the subclass inherits the abstract draw method and hence it is abstract, too.

One bit of terminology is relevant. A class that is not abstract is called a **concrete class.** You can only create objects of concrete classes.

Written Exercises

1. When should a method be abstract?
2. When should a method be final?

Programming Exercise

1. Modify the Shape class and its subclasses to use abstract methods and final methods where appropriate.

15.7 INTERFACES

Under some circumstances you might find it useful to be able to define a sub-class that extends two or more superclasses. For example, suppose have a class called `Vehicle` that defines various generic properties and behaviors of all kinds of vehicles, and another class called `BlueThings` that describes various generic properties and behaviors of all sorts of blue things. It might make sense to want to create a class `BlueTruck` that extends both `Vehicle` and `BlueThings`. After all a blue truck is a vehicle, and it also is a blue thing. Doing so would be called *multiple inheritance,* since `BlueTruck` would inherit variables and methods from multiple superclasses.

Java does *not* let you define a subclass that extends two (or more) super-classes. Some languages do (e.g., C++), but doing so presents a problem when two or more superclasses define the same protected or public instance variable or method. For example, if both the `Vehicle` and `BlueThing` classes have a protected instance variable `weight`, with one an `int` and the other a `double`, and a command in some method in the `BlueTruck` class says

```
if (weight > 1000) { ...
```

Which `weight` variable is being used, the one defined in `Vehicle` or the one defined in `BlueThing`? There is no obvious answer, so Java simply doesn't allow a subclass to extend more than one superclass. This is called *single inheritance.*

{New Concepts}

A subclass can only extend one superclass (*single inheritance*).

Java does provide another mechanism that allows you to do something similar to multiple inheritance. The two problems with multiple inheritance are two instance variables with the same name and two methods with the same signature but different implementations. However, if a superclass doesn't have any instance variables and it doesn't implement any methods (i.e., they are all abstract), the problems are solved.

Java calls this thing that looks like a class but with all abstract methods and no instance variables an *interface*. An interface is defined just as a class is, but simply requires all abstract methods and no instance variables, and uses the reserved word `interface` in place of `class`.

{New Concepts}

An **interface** has no instance variables, and every method is abstract.

You've already used interfaces that Java provides when you say, for example, a class `implements ActionListener`. `ActionListener` is an interface that is part of the Java library. It is simply

```
interface ActionListener {

    public abstract void actionPerformed(ActionEvent event) ;

} // end of ActionListener interface
```

Now just as an object IS-A object of the class that defines it and any superclasses, it also IS-A object of any interface it implements. For example, suppose a class definition begins with the line

```
class MyFrame extends JFrame implements ActionListener {
```

Then a `MyFrame` object IS-A `JFrame` object, and it also IS-A `ActionListener` object.

Because no multiple-inheritance problems arise with interfaces, you can define a class that implements as many interfaces as you like. For example, you could define a class that extends `JFrame` and implements both `ActionListener` and `MouseListener`.

15.7.1 An Interface Example

Interfaces are useful when you want to ensure that a particular class has implemented certain methods. Interfaces are even more useful when you want to permit that class also to be a subclass of some other. Clearly you can't use an abstract class in this case because then the given class cannot extend both your abstract class and another class because of single inheritance.

As an example, suppose you are working on part of a project that, for debugging purposes, will display graphical information about various objects used in the project. You don't know anything about the objects that will display the information, and in particular you don't know what they will display or how it will look. This will be determined by the objects (and the classes that define them). Your job is simply to get some information about how much space the object needs to display the information, then tell it to display it at a given place on the screen.

To do this, you require that any object that will display such information have methods you can call to get the amount of space needed and to draw the graphical information. Since you don't know, or even want to know, anything else about the objects, and especially whether they are defined by classes that extend other classes, you cannot use an abstract class. Fortunately an interface will work nicely.

The interface merely needs to define the (abstract) methods that any object that will display graphical information about itself will implement. Code 15.14 is one example of just such a simple interface.

Now any object that implements `Displayable` will be guaranteed to have these three methods implemented (hopefully correctly!). So your code can

CODE 15.14

```
interface Displayable {

    public abstract int getWidth();
        // return the width of what will be drawn

    public abstract int getHeight();
        // return the height of what will be drawn

    public abstract void draw(int x, int y, Graphics g);
        // draw the graphical info with upper left corner at x,y

    } // end of Displayable interface
```

simply call `getWidth` and `getHeight` when needed to get the width and height, use that information to decide where on the screen to draw the object, and then call the `draw` method with x and y coordinates of that place to get it drawn.

Note that the interface not only doesn't say how to implement the methods, but also doesn't say what instance variables to use to keep track of all the things necessary to implement them (e.g., the width, the height, and properties of the thing being drawn). Interfaces only say what methods to implement, not how.

Code 15.15 is an example of a partial class definition for a `Something` object that implements `Displayable`. The exact purpose of `Something` objects is not important, and I won't show any instance variables or methods that implement it. I'll just show the implementation of the interface.

The `draw` method is quite simple, drawing a yellow box with a black border and putting the message "I am a Something object" inside. A more sophisticated version might also put the current values of important instance variables in the box, too.

Code 15.16 is a small test program that creates a `Something` object, then uses the interface methods implemented in its class definition to display its message box centered in a 400-by-400 region.

Take special notice of the fact that the only place that this code uses the identifier `Something` is when it creates a `Something` object. After that, it uses polymorphism to do the rest of the work. It all works because an interface is like a superclass in that an object that implements the interface IS-A object of that interface. Hence a `Something` object IS-A `Displayable` object, too, so we can create variables that reference `Displayable` objects and depend on polymorphism to find the right methods.

{New Concepts}

A variable can be declared to be a reference to an object that implements an interface. That variable remembers what kind of object is being referred to and calls the correct method.

Figure 15.3 shows what the screen looks like when the applet is executed.

CODE 15.15

```
class Something extends Whatever implements Displayable {
    private final int width = 150;
    private final int height = 25;
    // instance variables here
    // noninterface methods here
    // interface methods

    public int getWidth() {
        return width;
        } // end of getWidth method

    public int getHeight() {
        return height;
        } // end of getHeight method

    public void draw(int x, int y, Graphics g) {
        // draw an identifying message in a
        // yellow box with a black border
        g.setColor(Color.yellow);
        g.fillRect(x,y,width,height);
        g.setColor(Color.black);
        g.drawRect(x,y,width,height);
        g.drawString("I am a Something object",x+10,y+20);
        } // end of draw method

    } // end of Something class
```

This class both extends (one) class and implements an interface.

These are defined here because they are used more than once below.

CODE 15.16

```
import java.awt.*;
import javax.swing.*;

public class InterfaceApplet extends JApplet {

    public void init() {
        Container window = getContentPane();
        Displayable it = new Something();
        Display disp = new Display(it);
        window.add(disp,BorderLayout.CENTER);
        } // end of init method

    } // end of InterfaceApplet class

class Display extends JPanel {
        private Displayable theThing;

    public Display(Displayable thing) {
        theThing = thing;
        } // end of constructor
```

The variable it is a reference to a Displayable object, and a Something IS-A Displayable object.

```
public void paintComponent(Graphics g) {
    // display in the center of a 400-by-400 region
    int width = theThing.getWidth();
    int height = theThing.getHeight();
    int x = (400-width)/2;
    int y = (400-height)/2;
    theThing.draw(x,y,g);
    } // end of paintComponent method

} // end of Display class
```

```
// interface Displayable here
```

```
// class Something here
```

InterfaceApplet
Demonstrates the use of an interface.

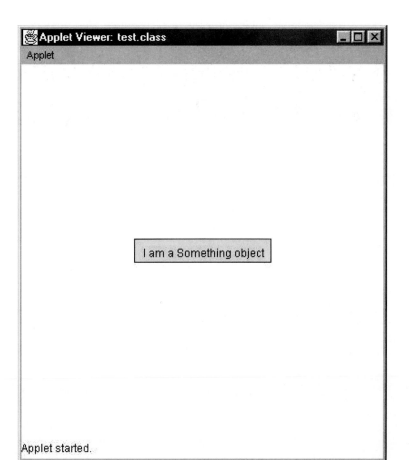

FIGURE 15.3

Written Exercises

1. What is the difference between an abstract class with all abstract methods and no instance variables, and an interface?

2. Why is it possible for a class to extend two different interfaces even if both have the same abstract method in them?

3. Define a class that `implements ActionListener`, but don't include an `actionPerformed` method in it. Compile the class. What happens? Why?

4. Define an interface called `HasIcon` that requires any class that implements it to have a method that draws an icon representing objects of that class. Assume the method has five parameters—the length, height that the icon should be when drawn, the left and top coordinates of the upper left of the icon, and a `Graphics` object to draw with.

Programming Exercise

1. Write two different class definitions similar to the `Something` class above. Have each display something different. Add them to the test program, and modify the test program to show whatever all three objects display stacked one on top of the other, with the first one at the very top of the applet window, the next one right below it, etc., and each centered from left to right.

15.8 THE "SUPER" REFERENCE VARIABLE

Sometimes a superclass will have a method that only partially implements some behavior of an object. It is expected that a subclass will override the method to provide the remaining functionality that is dependent on the particulars of that subclass. What we'd like is for the method in the subclass to be able to call the method of the same name in the superclass and have it supply its part of the behavior while the method in the subclass supplies the rest.

As an example, let's modify the `Shape/Square/Circle` class hierarchy to define different color circles. Every circle will be the same size and will be displayed in the same place. First, Code 15.17 is the `Circle` class modified so that it no longer sets the color (i.e., the `setColor` command has been removed):

CODE 15.17

```
class Circle extends Shape {

    protected void draw (Graphics g) {
        g.fillOval(x,y,100,100);
    } // end of draw method

} // end of Circle class
```

The `setColor` command has been removed.

and Code 15.18 is a class definition for a red circle:

CODE 15.18

```
class RedCircle extends Circle {

    public void draw (Graphics g) {
        g.setColor(Color.red);
        super.draw(g);
        } // end of draw method

    } // end of RedCircle class
```

Set the color here, then call the draw method in the superclass to actually draw the circle.

The key to calling the draw method in the superclass is the reserved word super. Executing super.draw(g) means that the draw method in the superclass is called instead of the draw method in the current class. The net effect in this example is that the draw method in RedCircle first sets the color to draw with, then calls the draw method in Circle, which then draws the circle by calling the fillOval method.

{New Concepts}

The reserved word **super** refers to the superclass.

What is nice about this is that the superclass can have code into a method that is common to all subclass objects (where and what size to draw the circle in this example), then have the subclass override the method to provide functionality peculiar to the subclass (the color of the circle in this example), but then still call the superclass method to get the common functionality.

Defining other color circle objects is simple; for example, a GreenCircle is defined as follows:

```
class GreenCircle extends Circle {

    public void draw (Graphics g) {
        g.setColor(Color.green);
        super.draw(g);
        } // end of draw method

    } // end of GreenCircle class
```

The only difference is the name of the class and the color.

By putting the common code in the superclass method, we avoid having to type it in more than once with the associated risk of not getting it correct every time. Should we ever want to change the position or size of a circle, we only need to change it in one place in the superclass method, thereby saving time and the risks of either missing one of the subclasses or making an incorrect change in one of them.

Now you should understand what was happening when we extended a `JPanel`, provided our own `paintComponent` method, and called `super.paintComponent`. We called the `paintComponent` method in the superclass (`JPanel`) to provide some common functionality (in this case to clear the `JPanel` area on the screen and then fill it with the background color).

15.9 CONSTRUCTORS AND INHERITANCE

When you extend a class, you inherit all public and protected methods of the superclass, but you *do not* inherit the superclass's constructor. However, it is important that the superclass's constructor be called when an object is created. After all, the subclass object IS-A superclass object, too, and the part of the subclass object that is defined by the superclass has to be constructed properly as well.

> **{New Concepts}**
> Constructors are *not* inherited by a subclass.

Fortunately, `super` can also be used in constructors. When an object of the subclass is created and its constructor is called, the subclass constructor *must* call the superclass constructor to take care of its share of the initialization and then proceed to complete the subclass-specific initialization (if any).

Since a constructor method doesn't really have a name, to call the superclass constructor you simply use the reserved word `super`, followed by any arguments you need to send to it. Java requires that the call be the *first* command in the constructor. If you forget to put a call to the superclass constructor in your code, Java inserts

```
super();
```

for you automatically.

> **{New Concepts}**
> Call a superclass constructor by writing `super` followed by any arguments.

Even though constructors are not inherited by subclasses, if you have a superclass with a constructor with no parameters and your subclass has no constructor, then Java will automatically cause the superclass constructor to be called when an object of the subclass is created.

15.10 AN EXAMPLE

Let's put everything together into a single example. First, Code 15.19 defines an abstract class `Thing` that represents various shapes that can be drawn wherever a `Graphics` object exists (i.e., a content pane or a `JPanel`). The `Thing` class provides the instance variables to store the position and size of any particular shape, a constructor that sets the size, and a `setPosition`

CODE 15.19

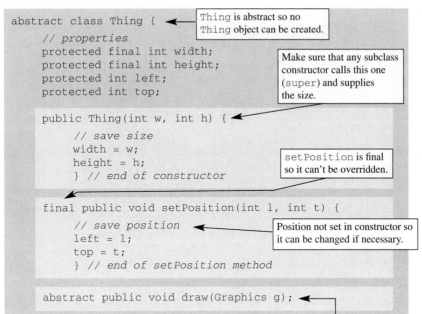

```
abstract class Thing {
```
Thing is abstract so no Thing object can be created.

```
    // properties
    protected final int width;
    protected final int height;
    protected int left;
    protected int top;
```
Make sure that any subclass constructor calls this one (super) and supplies the size.

```
    public Thing(int w, int h) {
        // save size
        width = w;
        height = h;
    } // end of constructor
```
setPosition is final so it can't be overridden.

```
    final public void setPosition(int l, int t) {
        // save position
        left = l;
        top = t;
    } // end of setPosition method
```
Position not set in constructor so it can be changed if necessary.

```
    abstract public void draw(Graphics g);

} // end of Thing class
```
draw must be overridden since it is abstract.

method that can be used to set and, if necessary, change the position of the shape. It also requires that any subclass implement a draw method that draws the particular shape the subclass defines. The instance variables are protected so the draw method implemented in any subclass can access them to draw the correctly sized shape at the correct position. Instance variables width and height are also final since they are only in the constructor and cannot change once set, but left and top are not final since they are set by the setPosition method which might be called more than once (e.g., if the use of the class decides to change the position of the shape at some point). SetPosition is declared to be final so that no subclass can override it and do something else.

Code 15.20 is an example of a subclass RedOval of Thing. It uses the constructor of Thing to save the size of the oval by calling super and passing the size values along to it. It also implements the draw method as required by the superclass.

Now in addition to being able to draw a shape at a given location in a given size, I want some (but not necessarily all) subclass objects to have a method that returns a string indicating what kind of shape it draws, how big it is, and where it is being drawn [e.g., "10 × 20 blue rectangle at (40,90)"]. To do so, I'm going to define an interface that requires any class that implements it to define a getInfo method that returns just such a string (Code 15.21).

Code 15.22 is a class that both extends Thing, and hence can draw itself (a blue rectangle), and implements ShowInfo, and hence has a getInfo

CODE 15.20

```
class RedOval extends Thing {

    public RedOval(int w, int h) {
        // save size
        super(w,h);                              Use the constructor of
        } // end of constructor                  Thing to save the size.

    public void draw(Graphics g) {
        // draw the red oval
        g.setColor(Color.red);
        g.fillOval(left,top,width,height);
        } // end of draw method

    } // end of RedOval class
```

CODE 15.21

```
interface ShowInfo {

    abstract public String getInfo();

    } // end of ShowInfo interface
```

CODE 15.22

```
class BlueRectangle extends Thing implements ShowInfo {
    private final String description;

    public BlueRectangle(int w, int h, String d) {
        // save size and description
        super(w,h);                              Use the superclass constructor
        description = d;                         to save the size, but save the
        } // end of constructor                  description here.

    public void draw(Graphics g) {
        // draw the blue rectangle
        g.setColor(Color.blue);
        g.fillRect(left,top,width,height);
        } // end of draw method

    public String getInfo() {                    ShowInfo interface
        // return info about the blue rectangle  requires this method.
        String size = width + "x" + height;
        String position = "(" + left + "," + top + ")";
        return size + " " + description + " at " + position;
        } // end of getInfo method

    } // end of BlueRectangle class
```

method that can return a string that describes itself. Its constructor has an extra parameter that is used to give BlueRectangle objects a string to use when describing itself.

Code 15.23 is a test program that displays one of each shape, and it has a JButton that can be pushed to get the information about the rectangle.

Looking first at the MyDisplay class, we note that it never uses the name of either subclass of Thing. It only cares about Thing objects. But any object defined by a subclass of Thing is also a Thing object, so everything works fine. This is the beauty of inheritance and polymorphism. You can write a class such as MyDisplay without knowing in advance what subclass objects

CODE 15.23

```java
import java.awt.*;
import java.awt.event.*;
import javax.swing.*;

public class ThingsDemo extends JApplet implements ActionListener {
    // GUI components
    private JButton rectButton =
        new JButton("rectangle information");
    private JLabel description =
        new JLabel("look for information here",
                    SwingConstants.CENTER);
    // Things
    private Thing oval = new RedOval(40,50);
    private Thing rect = new BlueRectangle(100,25,"bar");

    public void init() {
        // set up GUI
        Container window = getContentPane();
        MyDisplay disp = new MyDisplay(oval,rect);
        window.add(disp,BorderLayout.CENTER);
        window.add(rectButton,BorderLayout.NORTH);
        window.add(description,BorderLayout.SOUTH);

        // add listener
        rectButton.addActionListener(this);
    } // end of init method

    public void actionPerformed(ActionEvent event) {
        // return info about the rectangle
        description.setForeground(Color.blue);
        ShowInfo shape = (ShowInfo) rect;
        String info = shape.getInfo();
        description.setText(info);

    } // end of actionPerformed method

} // end of ThingsDemo class
```

The BlueRectangle constructor needs the extra argument because of the way it implements the ShowInfo interface.

A cast is needed to tell the compiler that we know that the object referred to by rect is also a ShowInfo object.

```
class MyDisplay extends JPanel {

    // the Things
    Thing one;
    Thing two;

    public MyDisplay(Thing t1, Thing t2) {

        // save Thing references and make background white
        one = t1;
        two = t2;
        setBackground(Color.white);
    } // end of constructor

    public void paintComponent(Graphics g) {
        super.paintComponent(g);

        // set positions of the Things
        one.setPosition(10,10);
        two.setPosition(getWidth()/2,getHeight()/2);

        // draw the Things
        one.draw(g);
        two.draw(g);
    } // end of paintComponent method

} // end of MyDisplay class
```

> This class only knows about Thing objects, but can handle any object defined by a subclass of Thing.

> Call the setPosition method inherited from the Thing class.

> Call the draw method in the appropriate subclass.

```
// Thing class here
```

```
// ShowInfo interface here
```

```
// RedCircle class here
```

```
// BlueRectangle class here
```

ThingsDemo
Demonstrates several aspects of inheritance, including interfaces and the use of super.

of Thing will be sent to it. As long as those objects are defined by subclasses of Thing, you know they will have a setPosition method that does the right thing (because it was defined in the superclass and was final) and will have a draw method that you assume draws the appropriate shape.

The ThingsDemo class creates a RedCircle object and a BlueRectangle object, then creates a MyDisplay object and sends references to those two objects to its constructor. The MyDisplay object has all it needs to do its job.

All the actionPerformed method needs to know is that the object that it is going to display information about (rect) is defined by a class that implements ShowInfo. It doesn't care that the object is also a Thing object. In fact, it could be any kind of object, just as long as it is defined by a class that implements ShowInfo. That object could be defined by an ordinary class that doesn't extend anything, or one that extends something other than Thing;

and it may implement other interfaces, too. None of that matters in the `actionPerformed` method. The only thing that matters is that the object referred to by `rect` is defined by a class that implements `ShowInfo`, because then the class is guaranteed to have a `getInfo` method.

The line of code

```
ShowInfo shape = (ShowInfo) rect;
```

creates a new variable `shape` that is a reference to a `ShowInfo` object. Since `rect` was defined earlier in the class to be a `Thing` object, we need to let the compiler know that `rect` also IS-A `ShowInfo` object. If we don't, the compiler will give us an error message.

Written Exercises

1. In the example in this section every subclass of `Thing` has access to the size and position instance variables so that it can draw some shape properly. It gets access to them because they are declared to be protected. Unfortunately this also allows a subclass to change those variables, something that you might want to prevent. But if the variables are made private so they can't be modified by a subclass, then they also can't be used by the subclass to draw the shape properly. Can you think of a way to make it possible for the draw method to get the size and position *information* while at the same time not being able to modify the variables?

2. Suppose a class implements two different interfaces, but both interfaces include the exact same abstract method definition. How is this different from the problem of multiple inheritance where both classes being extended define the exact same nonabstract method? Is it a problem? Explain.

Programming Exercises

1. Modify the classes you used in exercise 2 of Section 15.4 to use `super` whenever possible.

2. Define one new class that extends `Thing` and one new class that *both* extends `Thing` and implements `ShowInfo` in the `ThingsDemo` program. Modify the program to use your classes instead of `RedCircle` and `BlueRectangle`.

3. The program in Code 15.24 uses the partially completed `PlusSign` class to define a `JButton`-like component. The `PlusSign` class draws a red plus sign (two red rectangles, one horizontal and one vertical, that overlap) on a white background. The preferred size should be 45 × 45, and the plus sign should extend all the way to the edges of the `JPanel` area. A `PlusSign` object should call the `plusPerformed` method in the object sent to it as a parameter of the `addPlusListener` method.

CODE 15.24

```java
import java.awt.*;
import java.awt.event.*;
import javax.swing.*;
```

```java
public class Test extends JApplet implements PlusListener {
    private JLabel msg = new JLabel("plus not pushed yet");
    private int times = 0;

    public void init() {
        Container window = getContentPane();
        window.setLayout(new FlowLayout());
        PlusSign plus = new PlusSign();
        window.add(plus);
        window.add(msg);
        plus.addPlusListener(this);
        } // end of init method

    public void plusPerformed() {
        times += 1;
        msg.setText("plus pushed " + times + " times");
        } // end of plusPerformed method

    } // end of Test class
```

```java
interface PlusListener {

    abstract public void plusPerformed();

    } // end of PlusListener interface
```

```java
class PlusSign extends JPanel implements MouseListener {

    public PlusSign() {
        // set up object
        } // end of constructor

    public void addPlusListener(PlusListener lstnr) {
        // save reference to PlusListener object
        } // end of addPlusListener method

    public void paintComponent(Graphics g) {
        // draw the plus sign
        } // end of paintComponent method

    public void mouseClicked(MouseEvent event) {
        // inform PlusListener object
        } // end of mouseClicked method

    } // end of PlusSign class
```

Summary

- Class hierarchies are a collection of classes that are related via the subclass/superclass relationship.

- They are useful because they permit instance variables and methods that are common to several subclasses to be combined into a single class superclass.

- The class `Object` is, by default, a superclass of every class and is at the top of every class hierarchy.

- The IS-A relationship is defined between objects of two classes. An object of one class IS-A object of another if the first class is a subclass of the second.

- One object HAS-A second object if the first one has an instance variable that refers to the second.

- Final classes are not extendable and hence are always at the bottom of a class hierarchy.

- Final methods cannot be overridden in any subclass.

- Abstract methods must be overridden in a subclass.

- Object of abstract classes cannot be created, so an abstract class must be extended to produce a concrete subclass with no abstract methods.

- An interface is like a class with all abstract methods and no instance variables.

- A class can extend only one superclass, but can implement several interfaces.

- A method in a superclass with the same name as one in a subclass can be called from a subclass method by using `super`.

- A constructor in a superclass can be called using `super` followed by appropriate arguments.

Glossary

Abstract Class A class that must be extended. Objects of an abstract class cannot be created.

Abstract Method A method that must be overridden in a subclass.

Class Hierarchy A collection of classes related by the subclass/superclass relationship.

Concrete Class A class that is not abstract.

Direct Subclass If A and B are two classes, then B is a direct subclass of A if B extends A.

Direct Superclass If A and B are two classes, then A is a direct superclass of B if B extends A.

Final Class A class that cannot be extended.

Final Method A method that cannot be overridden.

HAS-A Relationship If C and D are two objects, then C HAS-A D if C has an instance variable that contains a reference to D.

Interface A collection of abstract methods.

IS-A Relationship An object IS-A object of the class that defines it, and of any superclass of that class, and of any interface it implements.

Object Class A class provided by Java that every other class is a subclass of.

Polymorphism The ability to call a method based on the class of object that a reference variable refers to and not on the class the variable is defined to be.

Protected A visibility modifier applied to an instance variable or method that permits it to be referenced in the class it is defined in and in any subclass.

Super A reference to the superclass.

CHAPTER 16

Abstract Data Types and Linked Data Structures

OBJECTIVES

- To understand what abstraction is and how important it is to programming.
- To understand information hiding and encapsulation and how to use them.
- To know what an abstract data type is.
- To be able to define abstract data types.
- To be able to implement abstract data types.
- To be able to use linked lists.
- To understand a stack abstraction and various ways of implementing it.
- To understand a queue abstraction and various ways of implementing it.
- To be able to compare different implementations of a given abstraction for suitability in various circumstances.

16.1 ABSTRACTION

An extremely important idea that has evolved in the practice of programming is the distinction between *what* a particular piece of code (a class or a method) does and *how* it does it. For example, the `Math.sqrt` function returns the square root of its argument. This is *what* it does. *How* it does so is irrelevant to anybody who uses the function, just so long as it returns the correct result. In fact, Java makes it possible to use the `Math.sqrt` function without even being able to find out how it works. This simplifies the task of writing a program that needs to compute the square root because the user never needs to learn how the square root is computed and to write code to do it. The details of how the function works are hidden.

Classes, and the objects they describe, are similar. You've been using all sorts of classes from `java.awt`, `javax.swing`, `java.awt.event`, `java.util`, and `java.io`. You've almost certainly never looked at the codes for the classes to see *how* they work; but from the descriptions I've given you in this book and from the documentation you've found on the Web, you know a lot about *what* they do. Again, the details are hidden.

Terms computer scientists use to describe this distinction are *abstraction* and *information hiding*. *Abstraction* is knowledge of *what* something does but not *how*. You have an abstract notion of what a `JButton` is and does. A `JButton` is an abstraction to you. Everything you need to know about what a `JButton` does and how to use one is given to you in the documentation. It describes the abstraction.

{New Concepts}

An **abstraction** specifies *what* an object or method does, but not *how* it does it.

445

The code that makes a `JButton` work is its implementation. You don't need to see the code, or be able to reproduce the code, or even have any concept whatsoever as to how the `JButton` code works. You don't know what instance variables it has, what private methods it has, what other objects it uses, or what variable, method, parameter, and local variable names it uses. Everything about its implementation is hidden. In fact, all the information about how a `JButton` works is hidden, which is where the term *information hiding* comes from.

> **{Definition of Terms}**
>
> **Information hiding** is the placement of implementation details of an abstraction inside a class or method so that they are not visible to the users of the class or method.

Encapsulation is another term used in this context. It means that *all* the details of implementation of a particular abstraction are encapsulated into a single entity (class). Properties of an object of the class are all part of the object and not part of the rest of the program that uses the object. The methods that use and manipulate the properties are also part of the class. Hence code for the abstraction is not strewn all over the program.

> **{Definition of Terms}**
>
> **Encapsulation** is the technique of combining *all* implementation details of an abstraction in one place, like a class or method, and not scattering them throughout a program.

Many of the Java language concepts we have seen so far in this book support these two terms. Classes allow you to group everything about an object into a single entity and provide a clean way of putting together an abstraction and giving it a name. Visibility modifiers such as private and protected make it easy to hide information about the implementation. Scope rules for names help encapsulate the implementation, making it impossible for other classes to access information about the implementation.

> **{New Concepts}**
>
> Java's class concept, visibility modifers, and scope rules make it possible to define and implement abstractions using information hiding and encapsulation.

16.1.1 The Collection Abstraction

Consider an abstract description of an object that stores a collection of strings. These strings can represent anything we like, such as names of our brothers and sisters, the titles of the CDs we own, or the passengers on an airplane. We can add new strings to the collection, remove strings from the collection, and find out if the collection has a particular string in it.

The paragraph above describes, in somewhat imprecise English, what a collection abstraction is. For this to be useful from a programming point of view, I need to be a little more specific. To do so, I'll use partial Java class description, with a few comments, to give just enough information to make the abstraction (class) usable (Code 16.1).

CODE 16.1

```
class Collection {

    public Collection() {
    // construct an empty collection
        } // end of constructor

    public void add(String newValue) {
    // add newValue to the collection
    // duplicates are allowed
        } // end of add method

    public void remove(String what) {
    // remove (one copy of) what from the collection
    // do nothing if what is not present
        } // end of remove method

    public boolean contains(String what) {
    // return true if what is in the collection
    // return false if it is not
        } // end of contains method

    } // end of Collection class
```

Given this information, you should have no trouble creating and using a
`Collection` object in your program. Everything you need to know is there.

Notice what is not there. No private instance variables are there, so we
have no idea how the object keeps track of the strings that have been added. If
there is some order in which they are stored, we don't know what it is. The
code inside each method is also missing, so we don't know how it manipulates
whatever instance variables it uses.

Because none of this information is necessary to design and write a program that uses `Collection` objects, the class can be implemented in many
different ways. In fact, the implementation of the class could be changed without having to make any changes whatsoever to the code that uses it, so long as
the new implementation still satisfies the description shown above.

16.1.2 The Benefits of Abstraction, Information Hiding, and Encapsulation

Being able to use a class without knowing anything about its implementation is one of the really big payoffs of using abstraction and information hiding. If the current implementation isn't acceptable (it's too slow, or the code
is very messy and hard to understand, or simply a better way of doing it suggests itself), then you can simply rewrite it without *any* effect on the code that
uses it.

Another benefit is that the implementation of the class can be tested apart from any program that uses it by writing a simple test driver. This separates the testing of a program that uses the class into two parts: the class itself and the rest of the program. The result will be easier to test and more likely to be error-free than if the class were not tested independently. Abstraction supports incremental development and unit testing.

Further, separating the use and implementation of a class makes it possible to divide a programming project into pieces such that different people can work on it. Because what the class does is clearly specified, the programmer who uses it can write code without any concern for the details of its implementation, thereby reducing the complexity of the portion of the code that programmer writes and hence making that part of the job easier and less error-prone. Likewise, the programmer who implements the abstraction doesn't have to worry about how it will be used, making that part of the job easier and less error-prone, too. The net result will likely be that the complete program will be written much faster and with fewer bugs.

Lastly, separating the use and implementation of a class makes it possible to put the class into a library that can be used by many other programmers in many other programs. All the Java classes you've seen so far have been designed this way.

The bottom line is that using these concepts when coding leads to the production of better programs with less work and in a shorter time.

Written Exercises

1. Modify the `Collection` abstraction to include a method that returns the size of the collection.

2. Modify the `Collection` abstraction to include a method that returns a reference to the *n*th object in the collection, under the assumption that if any new objects are added or existing objects removed, the *n*th object in the `Collection` may not be the same after the addition or removal.

3. Write a definition of an abstraction for a `Set`. A `Set` is like a `Collection` except that duplicates are not allowed.

4. Write a definition of an abstraction for a `Dictionary`. A `Dictionary` stores string pairs. The first string in the pair is a word; the second, its definition. Provide methods for adding and removing entries based on a word (not its definition) and a method for looking up a definition, given a word.

5. Write a definition of an abstraction for an object that draws a colored circle at a given place on the screen. Provide methods for specifying the initial diameter, position, and color; specifying a new diameter, new position, and new color; changing the diameter by a fixed amount (e.g., 5 units larger or smaller), and for changing the position (e.g., move left 7 units, up 3 units).

6. Write a definition of an abstraction for an `OnOffButton`, which is like a `JButton` but displays two halves, one side red (for on), the other green

(for off). Its constructor should have a `String` parameter to label the button, an `addActionListener` method, and a `getState` method that returns a boolean (true means on, false off).

16.2 IMPLEMENTING AN ABSTRACTION

Now let's turn to implementing the `Collection` abstraction (class). I'll show you several implementations and use them in a simple test driver applet. Be sure to note, as the various implementations are presented, that the test driver will never be changed.

The first implementation uses an array to store the references to the `String` objects added to the collection. `String` objects are added to the array, starting at the first element and continuing toward the last. When a `String` object is removed, the `String` objects after it are moved one element toward the beginning of the array to fill in the element vacated by the removed element (Code 16.2).

CODE 16.2

```
class Collection {
    private final int maxSize = 10;
    private String [] element;
    private int size;

    public Collection() {
        // initialize an empty collection
        element = new String [maxSize];
        size = 0;
    } // end of constructor

    public void add(String newValue) {
        // add if there is room
        if (size < maxSize) {
            element[size] = newValue;
            size += 1;
        }
        // otherwise (do nothing?)
    } // end of add method

    public void remove(String what) {
        // first find the desired value
        int where = getIndex(what);
        // if it's not there, return
        if (where < 0) {
            return;
        }
```

> Do nothing for now because the abstraction doesn't specify what to do. This will be fixed in the next version.

> Since both `remove` and `contains` need to do the same thing, use a private helper method to find the value.

```
        // move all values after deleted value down
        for (int i=where; i<size-1; i+=1) {
            element[i] = element[i+1];
            }
        size -= 1;
        } // end of remove method


public boolean contains(String what) {
        // get the index of String
        // if negative, it's not here
        if (getIndex(what) < 0) {
            return false;
            }
        else {
            return true;
            }
        } // end of contains method


private int getIndex(String what) {
        // search the array from front to back
        for (int i=0; i<size; i+=1) {
            if (what.equals(element[i])) {
                // return the index if found
                return i;
                }
            }
        // return -1 if not found
        return -1;
        } // end of getIndex method
} // end of Collection class
```

The size of the array is specified by the named constant maxSize. Unfortunately, once this size is picked, that will be the maximum number of strings that can be stored in the collection unless the constant is changed and the class recompiled. It also means that if the user of a Collection object tries to add too many strings, something must be done; and in this case what was done was to ignore (not add) any strings that were given to it. Unfortunately, the description of a Collection abstraction doesn't say anything about there being a maximum size to the Collection, so we'll have to fix this, which I will do in the next version. It is important to see that this code does *not quite* correctly implement the Collection abstraction!

Note that there is a helper method (getIndex) in the class that is not mentioned in the description. But since it is private, code from other classes cannot call it, and hence it is hidden and clearly should not be mentioned in the description.

At this point it would be useful to use the `Collection` class in a simple program. The one in Code 16.3 creates a GUI with a text field to enter strings into and buttons to push that cause the `Collection` methods to be called (Figure 16.1).

CODE 16.3

```java
import java.awt.*;
import java.awt.event.*;
import javax.swing.*;

public class CollectionDemo extends JApplet
                       implements ActionListener {
    private JTextField input = new JTextField(10);
    private JButton remove = new JButton("remove");
    private JButton find = new JButton("contains?");
    private JLabel result = new JLabel("",
                              SwingConstants.CENTER);
    private Collection things = new Collection();
    private Display display = new Display(things);

    public void init() {
        // set up main window
        Container window = getContentPane();
        window.setLayout(new BorderLayout());

        // set up control panel
        JPanel control = new JPanel();
        control.setLayout(new GridLayout(4,1));
        control.add(input);
        control.add(remove);
        control.add(find);
        result.setOpaque(true);
        result.setBackground(Color.yellow);
        control.add(result);
        JPanel holder = new JPanel();
        holder.add(control);
        window.add(holder, BorderLayout.WEST);

        // set up listeners
        input.addActionListener(this);
        remove.addActionListener(this);
        find.addActionListener(this);

        // set up display
        display = new Display(things);
        display.setBackground(Color.white);
        window.add(display, BorderLayout.CENTER);
        window.validate();
    } // end init method

    public void actionPerformed(ActionEvent event) {
        if (event.getSource() == input) {
            // add String, clear input and result,
            // and redisplay the collection
```

Create an empty `Collection` object.

```
            things.add(input.getText());
            input.setText("");
            result.setText("");
            display.repaint();
            }
        else if (event.getSource() == remove) {
            // remove String, clear input and result,
            // and redisplay the collection
            things.remove(input.getText());
            input.setText("");
            result.setText("");
            display.repaint();
            }
        else if (event.getSource() == find) {
            // see if String is in the collection
            // and display the outcome
            if (things.contains(input.getText())) {
                result.setText("yes");
                }
            else {
                result.setText("no");
                }
            }
        else {
            System.out.println("bad event");
            System.exit(1);
            }
        } // end of actionPerformed method

    } // end of CollectionDemo class
```

```
class Display extends JPanel {
    private Collection stuff;
```

```
    public Display(Collection c) {
        stuff = c;
        } // end of constructor
```

```
    public void paintComponent(Graphics g) {
        super.paintComponent(g);
        stuff.display(g); ◄————
        } // end of paintComponent method
```

Use the temporary debugging method to draw the contents of the Collection.

```
    } // end of Display class
```

```
// Collection class here
```

CollectionDemo
A test driver for the
Collection abstraction.

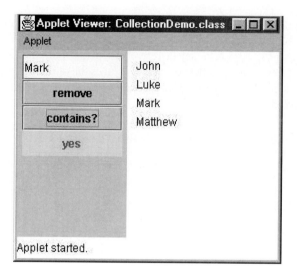

FIGURE 16.1

The add method is called whenever Enter or Return is hit after entering a string in the text field. The remove and contains methods are called when their corresponding buttons are pushed. The outcome of the contains method is displayed in the label with a yellow background. The current contents of the Collection are shown on the right. To make this work, I *temporarily* added a public method called display to the class. The code for it is as follows:

```
public void display(Graphics g) {
    for (int i=0; i<size; i+=1) {
        g.drawString(element[i],10,20*i+20);
    }
} // end of display method
```

> This method is added to the class for debugging purposes and will be removed eventually.

Note that this method is added to the class just for testing, debugging, and illustrative purposes and should be removed eventually.

16.2.1 A Correct Implementation

As indicated earlier, the implementation of the Collection class doesn't quite work according to the way it is described. That is, the description of the Collection abstraction doesn't say that there is a limit on how many strings can be added, or what will be done if the limit is exceeded.

The next implementation modifies some instance variables and the add method to allow any number of strings to be added and is very similar to the

DoubleVector implementation in Chapter 11. It does this by first creating an array of 10 elements. Then whenever the array is full, a new array twice as big is created, the String object references in the old, smaller array are copied to the new array, and the new array replaces the old. This is slightly different from the DoubleVector class that simply increased the size of the array by a fixed amount. Because the remove, contains, and getIndex methods are unchanged, they aren't shown here (Code 16.4).

We now have a properly working implementation for the Collection class. It satisfies the entire definition for the abstraction. Note that both it and the original work just fine with exactly the *same* test applet.

CODE 16.4

```
class Collection {
    private final int initialSize = 10;

    private String [] element;
    private int currentMax;
    private int size;

    public Collection() {
        element = new String[initialSize];
        currentMax = initialSize;
        size = 0;
    } // end of constructor

    public void add(String newValue) {
        // if there isn't room,
        if (size >= currentMax) {
            // make a twice as big array
            currentMax *= 2;
            String [] newArray = new String [currentMax];
            // copy everything from the
            // old array to the new
            for (int i=0; i<size; i+=1) {
                newArray[i] = element[i];
            }
            // replace the old array with the new
            element = newArray;
        }
        // add the new value
        element[size] = newValue;
        size += 1;
    } // end of add method

// no change to other methods
} // end of Collection class
```

Create a new array twice as big, and copy the contents of the old one to it.

Make element reference the new array object. The old array object will disappear.

We could quit right here. But after you write the code above, suppose it occurs to you that the `remove` method can be made more efficient. If instead of moving all the `String` objects after the deleted one toward the beginning of the array, we take the last `String` reference in the array and move it to the empty element. Code 16.5 is a third version of the `Collection` class with a new `remove` method. Note that we still satisfy the definition of the abstraction.

CODE 16.5

```
class Collection {
    // no change to instance variables
    // or other methods

    public void remove(String what) {
        int where = getIndex(what);
        if (where < 0) {
            return;
        }
        element[where] = element[size-1];
        size -= 1;
    } // end of remove method

} // end of Collection class
```

Notice that this new version of the `remove` method will result in the strings in the collection being ordered differently in the array than in the original version. Fortunately the definition of the `Collection` abstraction doesn't say anything about any order of the strings in the collection, so we are free to use this new, faster `remove` method.

This is a simple example of a principle that you should always use when defining an abstraction. Don't overspecify it. If there is no purpose for a property, behavior, feature, or restriction, don't put one in. You'll just limit the freedom of choosing better implementations.

{Good Ideas}

Don't overspecify an abstraction. Define just those properties and behaviors that are necessary and no more. Adding extra information or constraints will only limit choices for implementations.

Of course the user of the `Collection` abstraction must be aware that no "internal" order is implied by the definition of the abstraction. Hence no implementation should try to take advantage of the order that a particular implementation might choose, because if the implementation changes and the order is not the same, the user might find the application of the `Collection` doesn't work as expected any more.

This brings up another principle. Don't take advantage of unspecified properties of a particular implementation of an abstraction. Doing so risks having your program fail to work properly should the implementation ever change. For example, the first implementation of the `Collection` keeps the strings in the same order they were added in. The second one does not. If someone uses the first implementation of the `Collection` and takes advantage of the ordering, then that person's code will likely no longer work if the implementation is changed and the ordering is not preserved.

> {Good Ideas}
>
> When you are using an abstraction, never take advantage of unspecified properties of a particular implementation.

16.2.2 A More General Collection Class

The `Collection` class above was defined to store only references to `String` objects (i.e., a collection of strings). With almost no effort we can convert it to a `Collection` that can store references to *any* kind of objects. All we need to do is to change `String` to `Object` everywhere in the class. Because every class is a subclass of `Object`, and hence every kind of object IS-A `Object`, everything will work properly as long as the objects that are being stored in the collection have an `equals` method that works correctly for those objects.

The `display` method, if present for debugging purposes, won't work properly if `String` is replaced with `Object`. A simple fix, at least for debugging, would be to change the command that prints the string to one that prints `toString` for the object:

```
g.drawString(element[i].toString(),10,20*i+20);
```

The `equals` and `toString` methods are defined in the `Object` class, so every object inherits them. Of course those subclasses can always override them to do the right thing for the particular class. In fact, the subclasses almost certainly will override the `equals` method since the one in the `Object` class works like == (i.e., compares references, not objects) and is not likely to be the way `equals` should be defined for the particular class.

Written Exercises

1. Why doesn't it matter what order the `Collection` implementation stores the objects in?

2. Would there be any advantage to storing the objects in some order?

3. If the objects were to be stored in some order, what kind of method must the objects have? *Hint:* What does "in order" mean?

4. Not counting the temporary display method, is there any way for the user of the `Collection` class to find out what order the objects are stored in? To just find out what the first object is?

Programming Exercises

1. Modify the `Collection` class implementation to increase the size of the array by a fixed amount instead of doubling it. Make the fixed amount 10 and make it a named constant.

2. Modify the `Collection` class implementation to shrink the array by one-half whenever the number of elements used drops below one-fourth of the current array size.

3. Write an application program that uses the `Collection` class to maintain a list of CDs you own (by title). Design a user interface that allows you to enter the name of a new file to create or an old one to edit, to add a CD, to search for a CD, to remove a CD, and to save the file (serialize the `Collection` object). Your application program should not add a CD to the collection if it is already there by using the `contains` method to check.

4. Modify the `Collection` abstraction so that duplicate entries are not allowed. Modify the `Collection` implementation to support it. Modify the CD program from the previous problem to use the new `Collection`.

5. Modify the `Collection` abstraction to include a method that returns the number of objects currently in the `Collection`, and a method that returns a reference to the *n*th object in the `Collection` (see the same problem at the end of Section 16.1). Then modify the `Collection` implementation to include these new methods. Then modify the CD progam from the previous problem to use the new `Collection` and have a button that, when pushed, will cause the CDs in the collection to be displayed.

16.3 USING JAVADOC TO DOCUMENT CLASSES

By now you've seen plenty of Web page documentation for Java classes. It turns out most of it was created directly from the Java source code itself, and not created by hand.

A tool called **javadoc** takes a Java program (a file with a name ending in .java) that has had special comments included and creates a Web page (a file with a name ending in .html) that looks just like the documentation for all the standard Java classes. The special comments are called **doc comments** to distinguish them from the two styles of comments we've seen up to this point. They are similar to comments that are begun with /* and terminated with */, except that they are begun with /** (note two asterisks). They also include special information within the comment itself that is understood and processed specially by the javadoc tool (Code 16.6).

CODE 16.6

```java
/**
 * A Collection object is a set of arbitrary
 * objects that can be compared for equality with the
 * .equals method.
 *
 * @author David A. Poplawski
 */
public class Collection {

    /**
     * Create an empty collection.
     */
    public Collection() {
        } // end of constructor


    /**
    Add an object to the collection. Duplicates are allowed.
     * @param newValue A reference to the object to add.
     */
    public void add(Object newValue) {
        } // end of add method


    /**
     * Remove an object from the collection. Do nothing if not
     * there.
     * @param what The object to remove.
     */
        public void remove(Object what) {
            } // end of remove method


    /**
     * Determine if an object is in the collection.
     * @param what The object to look for.
     * @return True if present, false otherwise.
     */
    public boolean contains(Object what) {
        } // end of contains method


    /**
     * Get the array index of the specified object.
     * @param what The object to look for.
     * @return The index of the object, or -1 if not present.
     */
        private int getIndex(Object what) {
        } // end of getIndex method

    } // end of Collection class
```

From these doc comments and class skeleton code, the javadoc program creates the Web page displayed in Figures 16.2 to 16.5.

Although there are many options for what information gets displayed and how, I'll only focus on the main aspects that are of importance for documenting your classes.

First, a leading asterisk * on a doc comment line is ignored, as are any white-space characters that precede or follow it.

FIGURE 16.2

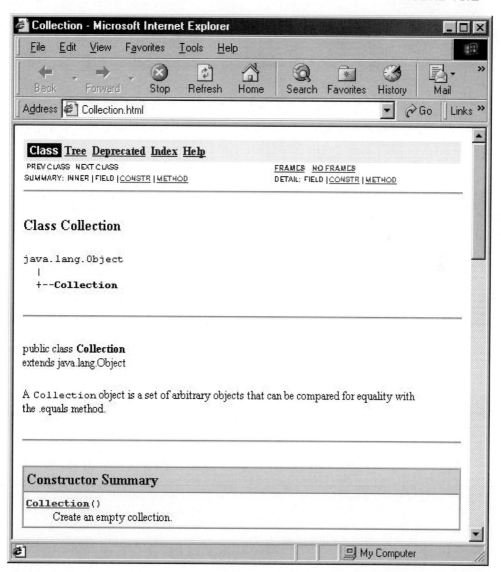

FIGURE 16.3

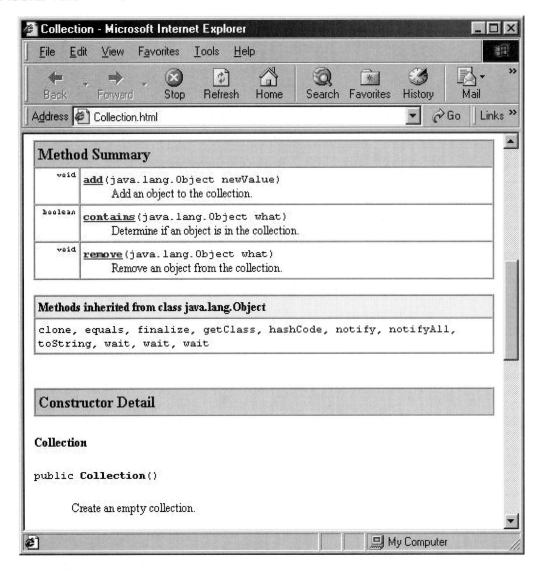

Second, a class and every public method should be preceded by a doc comment. The first sentence in the doc comment is displayed with constructor and method summaries, but everything in the comment is displayed in the full descriptions of the constructor and methods that follow later.

Third, a line with the term @param on it describes a parameter of a method. The information that follows it will be displayed prominently in the

FIGURE 16.4

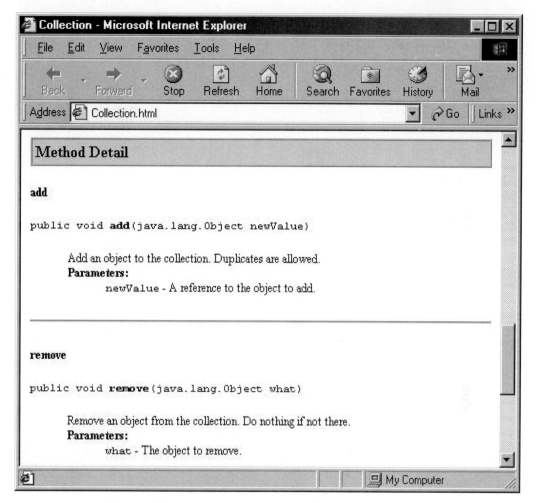

full description, with the first word after `@param` being the parameter name and everything after that being a description of the parameter.

Fourth, a line with the term `@return` on it describes what the method returns. Void methods don't need this line, but methods that return things should. The text following `@return` describes what is returned.

{Good Ideas}

Use doc comments and the javadoc command to generate professional-looking Web page descriptions of your abstractions.

FIGURE 16.5

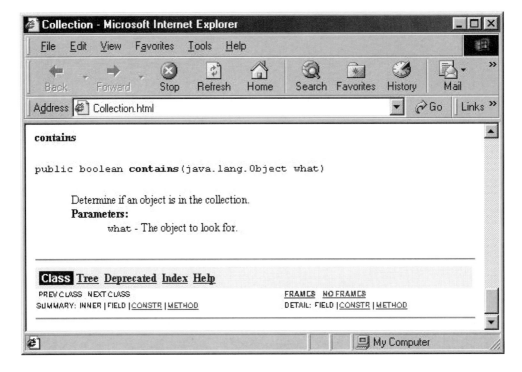

Written Exercises

1. Use doc comments in each of the problems at the end of Section 16.1. Run Javadoc to create the html versions of the documentation.

2. Why doesn't the private method `getIndex` appear in the Web documentation?

16.4 LINKED DATA STRUCTURES

The final implementation of the `Collection` abstraction is a perfectly acceptable one under many circumstances. But suppose a particular collection grows to a very large size and then shrinks considerably. As the collection grows, every time there is no more room in the array for the next object, a new array must be created, which by itself is not very time-consuming. But then every reference to an object must be copied from the old array into the new array, which can be very time-consuming. For example, suppose the collection grows to 1281 objects. Then the numbers of elements in the increasingly larger arrays are 20, 40, 80, 160, 320, 640, 1280, 2560; and the number of `Object` references copied when each new array is created are 10, 20, 40, 80, 160, 320, 640, 1280. Hence the total number of `Object` references copied is

$10 + 20 + 40 + 80 + 160 + 320 + 640 + 1280 = 2550$. There are more `Object` reference copies being made than there are objects in the collection (almost double). This is a big waste of time.

There also is a waste of memory space demonstrated by this example, since the array now has room for 2560 `Object` references but only 1281, or just 1 more than one-half, are used. This, of course, is a worst-case example, but odds are that in any large collection there will be a lot of unused array elements (about one-fourth of them on average). The `Vector` class's approach was to increase the size of the array by a fixed amount instead of doubling it (say, by 10). This would certainly reduce the amount of wasted space (no more than nine elements), but now there would be very many slightly larger new arrays created on the way to having room for 1281 objects (with sizes 20, 30, 40, 50, . . . , 1270, 1280, 1290) and a *lot* of `Object` reference copies ($10 + 20 + 30 + 40 + \cdots + 1260 + 1270 + 1280 = 8256$, or almost four times as many copies as there are objects in the collection).

Hence either you risk the possibility of wasting a lot of space, or you make a lot of `Object` reference copies. There is no solution to this dilemma unless you know in advance the maximum number of `Object` references you expect to have in the collection and create an array of the right size as soon as the `Collection` object is created (i.e., in the constructor, which could have a parameter that tells the object what size array to create—which is a change in the description of the abstraction).

Now suppose a large `Collection` shrinks back down to some small size. Then eventually most of the elements of the large array that was finally created to hold the temporarily large collection go unused, wasting a lot more memory space. Of course, as the collection shrinks, we could always create a new, smaller array, but then we'd have to copy more `Object` references every time we did it, wasting even more time. Then if the `Collection` grew again, more new, larger arrays would be needed. Again the dilemma. Waste space or waste time? It has to be one or the other when you are using an array to store the `Object` references.

Now keep in mind that this dilemma only presents itself if you have a `Collection` whose maximum size is unpredictable and/or has extreme fluctuations in size. If few, if any, new arrays are ever needed, and if the array currently used is kept mostly full, then there is no dilemma. Hence our implementation(s) above is (are) not necessarily faulty. You just need to be aware of what is going on if your particular use for a `Collection` will have a wildly fluctuating size.

So are we doomed to having to waste space or waste time? The answer is no. There is a way to implement the `Collection` abstraction in such a way that wild size fluctuations can be handled without *any* copying of `Object` references. This new implementation does waste some space, however, but the amount wasted is proportional to the number of objects in the collection at any given time and not, like the never-shrinking array implementation, potentially huge.

16.4.1 Implementing a Collection with a Linked Data Structure

The new implementation uses a separate object to keep track of each `Object` reference. When a new `Object` is added to the collection, one of these special objects is created; and when an `Object` is removed, the special object is discarded. These objects are kept (*linked*) together by the use of an instance variable in each one that contains a reference to another one. The entire collection is represented by a sequence of these special objects, with the first containing a reference to the second, the second to the third, etc. Pictorially this looks like Figure 16.6 for a sequence with three objects. Note that the end of the sequence is indicated by a reference variable containing null.

Because this looks somewhat like a chain, with the references from one node to the other being the links, a structure like this is usually referred to as a linked structure. Because there is a first object followed by a second, and a third, etc., it also is like a list of objects. Hence this type of structure is often referred to as a *linked list*.

> **{Definition of Terms}**
>
> A **linked list** is a sequence of objects in which each object contains a reference to the next.

Let's define a class for these new objects that make up the linked list. Clearly two instance variables will be needed in each object, one being an `Object` reference to keep track of the information associated with it, the other a reference to the next one in the list. For historical reasons, these objects have been called **nodes,** so we'll define a `Node` class (Code 16.7).

I'll now modify the entire implementation of the `Collection` class to use this new structure for storing the `Object` references. An instance variable is needed to refer to the first `Node` object in the linked list (from now on I'll just call it a *list* when it is clear that I am talking about a linked list). When the list is empty, this instance variable will contain no reference, that is, `null`. When there are one or more `Node` objects in the list (and therefore one or more objects in the collection), this instance variable will contain a reference to the first `Node` object. Code 16.8 is the beginning of the implementation.

The `add` method of this class must create a new `Node` object and provide a reference to the object being added and a reference to a next node. The question

FIGURE 16.6

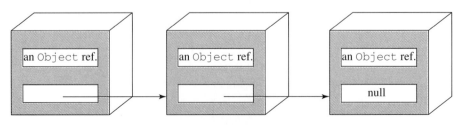

CODE 16.7

```
class Node {
    private Object data;
    private Node next;

    public Node(Object d, Node n) {
        data = d;
        next = n;
        } // end of constructor

    // more methods to come
    } // end of Node class
```

CODE 16.8

```
class Collection {
    private Node first;

    public Collection() {
        first = null;
        } // end of constructor

    // other methods to come
    } // end of Collection class
```

that immediately arises is, "Where to put a new node?" Clearly when the collection is empty, so is the list, so there is only one place to put it. But how about the second, third, and fourth ones? It turns out that it is a lot easier to put them at the beginning of the list than at the end. To put it at the beginning, all that needs to be done is to make the new Node object reference what used to be the first Node object and make first refer to it. To put it at the end, you'd have to find the end of the list by moving along the nodes (**traversing** the list) until there was no next one. Clearly this is harder to write and will execute more slowly.

Figure 16.7 shows how the list is modified when a new first node is inserted.

FIGURE 16.7

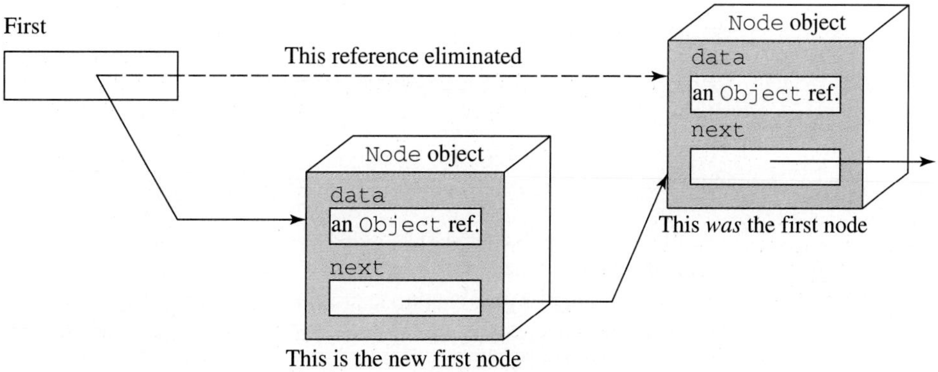

First

This reference eliminated

Node object
data
an Object ref.
next

This *was* the first node

Node object
data
an Object ref.
next

This is the new first node

The code for the `add` method winds up being pretty simple:

```
public void add(Object newValue) {
    first = new Node(newValue,first);
} // end of add method
```

A new `Node` object is created, with a reference to the object being added to the collection and a reference to the (old) first `Node` object in the list being passed to the `Node` constructor. The reference to the new (first) node is then put in `first`. Note that this also works when the collection is empty. In that case `first` will contain null, which will be sent to the `Node` constructor, which will make the first `Node` object have a reference to null stored in its `next` instance variable, which marks the end of the list.

Notice that in the array implementations of a `Collection` new objects were added to the end of the array, while with the linked list implementation they are being added to the beginning of the list. Hence the objects will be in opposite orders in the two implementations. Fortunately, the `Collection` abstraction does not specify that any order need be used, so we are free to implement the `add` method for the linked list in such a way that it puts the objects in the list in the opposite order from the array implementation. This is another case in which defining an abstraction as simply as possible, and not overspecifying irrelevant things, makes for a simpler (and faster) implementation.

Now let's consider the `contains` method. As in the array implementation, the linked list version must search for the desired object from the beginning to the end of the list. A counting loop cannot be used with this linked list implementation because we don't have a size variable that keeps track of how many objects are in the list. Instead we'll simply traverse the list until we get to the last `Node` object, stopping when the `next` instance variable in that `Node` object contains null.

```
public boolean contains(Object what) {
    Node here = first;
    while (here != null) {
        if (what.equals(here.getValue())) {
            return true;
        }
        here = here.getNext();
        return false;
    }
} // end of contains method
```

New methods added to the `Node` class that return the values of the `data` and `next` instance variables.

In this method we need to be able to compare the searched-for object with every object in the list. Hence we need a way to get a reference to the object being kept track of by a given node. To do so, we'll add a `getValue` method to the `Node` class which will simply return the value in the `data` instance variable. Likewise we'll need to find the next node from a given one, so we'll add a `getNext` method to the `Node` class which will simply return the value in the `next` instance variable.

Notice the use of the local variable `here` to keep track of which `Node` object is being checked for a match. A common error is to use `first` to do this, modifying it as the loop moves through the list. Unfortunately if `first` gets changed in the loop, then the reference to the beginning of the list will be lost. If the loop terminates because the matching object is found, then `first` will be left referencing the node that had the reference to the matching object, and unless it was the first `Node` object in the list, some part of the beginning of the list will be lost from the `Collection`. If the loop terminates without a match, `first` will wind up containing null, and the entire list will be lost. So do not change `first` in this method, or any method that uses the list, unless you want to change what comprises the list (as in the `add` method).

Finally, let's consider the `remove` method. To remove an object, we must first find the `Node` object that has the reference to the matching object (if one exists), but that is not enough. To remove that `Node` object from the list, we have to make the `Node` object that precedes it in the list reference the `Node` object that follows it, as shown in Figure 16.8.

To accomplish this, we will need two local reference variables, one referencing the `Node` object being checked for the matching object (`here`), the other referencing the Node `object` just before it in the list (`prev`). To begin the search, `prev` is set to reference the first `Node` object in the list, and `here` the second.

Suppose the list is empty. Then these two variables can't reference the first two nodes because there are none. This is a special case and must be checked for and handled differently than when there are two or more nodes.

Suppose the list has just one node. Again we have a special case that must be handled separately. This time the object the `Node` object refers to must be checked for a match, and if there is one, the single `Node` object removed by making `first` be null.

FIGURE 16.8

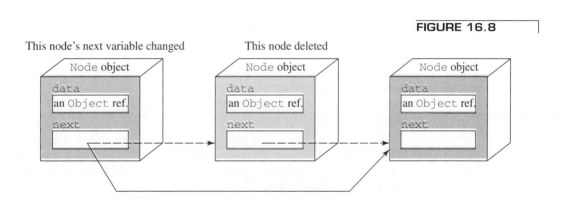

This node's next variable changed   This node deleted

Thus the code for the `remove` method has three cases to check for and handle (Code 16.9).

CODE 16.9

```
public void remove(Object what) {
    // do nothing if the list is empty
    if (first == null) {
        return;
    }
    // check for a match in the first position
    if (what.equals(first.getValue())) {
        first = first.getNext();
        return;
    }
    // handle all other cases
    Node prev = first;
    Node here = first.getNext();
    while (here != null) {
        if (what.equals(here.getValue())) {
            prev.setNext(here.getNext());
            return;
        }
        prev = here;
        here = here.getNext();
    }
} // end of remove method
```

> A reference to the Node object preceeding the one being removed is needed so that the previous Node object can be made to reference the one after the removed one.

Notice that I used another new method in the `Node` class called `setNext`. It simply sets `next` to the value sent to it as an argument.

That completes the linked list implementation of the `Collection` class. However, there is one new concept that I want to introduce at this time that fits in with the notion of information hiding.

Consider the `Node` class. It was defined so that the `Collection` class could be implemented as a linked list. No other classes need to know about the `Node` class, and hence it would be appropriate to try to keep other classes from using it. This can be done by putting the `Node` class definition inside the `Collection` class definition and making it private. Because it is inside the `Collection` class and is private, the scope of the name `Node` is just inside the `Collection` class, just like the scope of private instance variable names. A class defined inside another class is called an **inner class.**

Code 16.10 is the complete `Collection` class definition, including the entire `Node` class within it.

Putting a class definition inside another should always be done when the inner class is used *only* by the outer one. The inner class should always be private since the whole point of putting it inside is to hide it from other classes. This makes it impossible for other classes to know about the implementation of the `Collection` class and therefore to somehow depend on it being a linked list implementation.

CODE 16.10

```
class Collection

    private class Node {
        private Object element;
        private Node next;
```

> Everything inside the dotted lines is an inner class. It is private so it can't be accessed from any code except within the Collection class.

```
    public Node(Object v, Node n) {
        element = v;
        next = n;
        } // end of constructor

    public Object getValue() {
        return element;
        } // end of getValue method

    public Node getNext() {
        return next;
        } // end of getNext method

    public void setNext(Node where) {
        next = where;
        } // end of setNext method

    } // end of Node class

    private Node first;

    public Collection() {
        // initialize an empty collection
        first = null;
        } // end of constructor

    public void add(Object newValue) {
        // add the new value
        first = new Node(newValue, first);
        } // end of add method

    public void remove(Object what) {
        // do nothing if the list is empty
        if (first == null) {
            return;
            }
        // check for a match in the first position
        if (first.getNext() == null) {
            if (what.equals(first.getValue())) {
                first = first.getNext();
                return;
                }
```

```
        // handle all other cases
        Node prev = first;
        Node here = first.getNext();
        while (here != null) {
            if (what.equals(here.getValue())) {
                prev.setNext(here.getNext());
                return;
            }
            prev = here;
            here = here.getNext();
        }
    } // end of remove method

public boolean contains(Object what) {
        Node here = first;
        while (here != null) {
            if (what.equals(here.getValue())) {
                return true;
            }
            here = here.getNext();
        }
        return false;
    } // end of contains method

} // end of Collection class
```

{Definition of Terms}

An *inner class* is a class that is defined inside another class. Use inner clases and make them private when users of the outer class don't need to know about them.

16.4.2 Testing Linked List Code

Both black box testing and white box testing of linked list code are critical, but I'll only consider black box because it tends to find more errors. This is because of special cases that you almost certainly didn't plan for when writing the code. Black box testing gives you another chance to make sure not only that you considered all special cases, but also that they work correctly.

To test linked list code, you almost have to write a temporary display method (a unit test driver), as was done to demonstrate the array implementation of the `Collection` class earlier in this chapter. In fact, since we already have just such a test driver, we can use it.

You always test *adding* objects first because it is hard to test searches or removals until the list has some nodes in it. You will always test adding to an empty list as the first special case because that's the way lists start out—empty. Then test more additions. If everything is added at the beginning, then a couple of tests will be sufficient. If you add things at various places (e.g., an ordered list), then add something in front of everything, just after the first node, after everything, just before the last node, and then a couple in the middle.

Next test searches. Search for the objects that are first and last and for a few in between. Search for something that isn't there. Start with an empty list and do a search. Add one node and do a search both for the node added and for something else that's not there.

Next test removals. Create a list of several nodes, then remove the first node, then the last, then a couple that are neither. In between removals do a complete set of searches (first, last, middle). Eventually remove all the nodes, then do another search. Then just to make sure you got the linked list back to empty correctly, do another add and search.

You might think this is a lot of testing, but I'll guarantee you that it will be well worth it. Writing linked list code can be a little tricky, and it is easy to miss a special case, or to think one of the methods is working, then have another one fail when in fact it was the first one that left the list in an erroneous configuration (e.g., a loop). So take the time to get it right.

{Good Ideas}

Thorough testing of linked list code is essential. Subtle errors often creep in, and special cases are often missed.

16.4.3 Debugging Linked List Code

When writing code to manipulate linked lists, you will almost certainly make mistakes. Even experienced programmers do. The most common manifestation of a mistake is the null pointer exception, which you've almost certainly encountered by now in other programs you've written. If you haven't seen one yet, you probably will with linked lists.

There are two ways to deal with null pointer exceptions in linked list code. First, do your best to avoid them. The best way to do that is to draw lots of pictures of the linked lists you are manipulating with your code. The simple diagrams above can guide you in this. When you have written your code, manually execute it, drawing pictures along the way, to make sure all the references (links) get set right and that you have the correct structure when you are done.

As you saw with the `remove` method, there was one general case that worked almost everywhere in any length of linked list, then a few special cases, such as for an empty list, or a list with one node. Special cases are the norm with linked lists, and as you are writing code, you should be very careful to identify all of them. The two you've already seen—an empty list and a list with one node—are typical special cases.

Other special cases often occur at the end of the list. For example, if you have an abstraction that requires keeping the objects in a linked list in some order, then adding a new object will eventually require that a new node be added at the end of the list. Depending on how you write your code, or on the particular way the linked list is constructed (see below), this may or may not be a special case. But whether it winds up being a special case or not, it is well worth the time and effort to assume that it might be and at the very least think it through.

The second way to deal with null pointer exceptions is to use a good debugging program. Unfortunately IDEs differ in how their debugging environments work, so it is difficult to say exactly how to use them. However, the general idea is to display the contents of the instance variable that refers to the first node in the list, then work down the nodes, looking at each, and especially any reference(s) the node has to other node(s). Draw a picture of what the debugging output indicates, and eventually you'll find a reference what was not set right.

> {Good Ideas}
>
> Null pointer exceptions are common when executing linked list code. Try to avoid them by being very careful when writing your code; but when you get one, a good debugging program can help track down the error.

Another fairly common error is to create a linked list with a loop in it (e.g., node A references node B, which references node C, which references node A). Then later when the list is being traversed, perhaps looking for a particular node, or perhaps looking for the end of the list, the code that is working its way along the list winds up in an infinite loop. When your program gets stuck in an infinite loop, you should always look at the possibility of an unintentional loop having been created in a linked list.

Written Exercises

1. Why not use a linked list implementation of a `Collection` under all circumstances?

2. Why is an inner class usually made private?

3. Put an error in the code for a `Collection` and run it to get a null pointer exception. Use the debugging feature of your development environment to inspect the linked list to find the null pointer that caused the error.

Programming Exercises

1. Add a temporary display method to the `Collection` class and use the test applet from Section 16.3 to test it. Assume in the display method that strings will be the only kind of objects in the `Collection`.

2. Modify the `add` method of the `Collection` class to always add a new object at the end of the list (even though it isn't as efficient). Use the display method and test program from the previous problem.

3. Modify the `add` method of the `Collection` class to keep the strings in alphabetical order (use the `compareTo` method for `String` objects to find out which of two strings comes before the other). Assume that `String` objects will be the only kind of objects in the collection.

4. Redo programming exercise 5 in Section 16.2 with a linked list implementation of the `Collection`.

16.5 LINKED LIST VARIATIONS

There are many variations on the way linked lists are organized. I won't cover all of them there, but it is instructive to see a few that you will likely find useful for various purposes. Two of them are used to simplify the code for adding or removing nodes, being designed to eliminate the special cases. Another is used when a list must be traversed both from front to back and from back to front.

16.5.1 A Header Node

As we saw in the `Collection` implementation above, special cases arose in the `remove` method when there were zero or one `Node` objects in the list. One of them can be eliminated by putting an extra node, called a **header node,** at the front of every list. This node is simply a dummy node, with no information associated with it. An empty list will consist of just this node.

Using a header node requires changes to every method in the `Collection` class. The constructor must create an empty collection by constructing a list with the header node. The other methods must ignore or work around this node as appropriate.

Code 16.11 is a new version of the `Collection` class using a header node. Code that differs from the original implementation is shown in bold.

As you can see, the `remove` method is much simpler than before since there are no special cases to worry about. There will always be at least one `Node` object in the list (the header node), and you never have the special case of changing `first` when the first (real) `Node` object is removed.

The elimination of the special case code from the `remove` method comes at the small price of a very slightly modified constructor and `contains` method, and the very slight waste of memory for the header node. Unless you expect that a very large number of `Collection` objects (and hence a lot of header nodes) will be used, the simplicity of writing, testing, and debugging the `remove` method might well be worth it.

> **{Good Ideas}**
>
> Using a header node in a linked list can remove many special cases from methods than manipulate the list.

16.5.2 Doubly Linked Lists

Suppose you are writing a program to edit text, much like the one you now use to write your Java programs. You'll need a way to store the text so that you can do all sorts of manipulations on it, including inserting and deleting characters, moving the cursor from place to place, and searching for patterns. An abstraction for this implemented as a linked list might be a good approach.

CODE 16.11

```
class Collection {
    // node class not shown to save space (it is unchanged)
    private Node first;

    public Collection() {
        first = new Node(null,null);
    } // end of constructor

    public void add(Object newValue) {
        Node newOne = new Node(newValue, first.getNext());
        first.setNext(newOne);
    } // end of add method

    public void remove(Object what) {
        Node prev = first;
        Node here = first.getNext();
        while (here != null) {
            if (what.equals(here.getValue())) {
                prev.setNext(here.getNext());
                return;
            }
            prev = here;
            here = here.getNext();
        }
    } // end of remove method

    public boolean contains(Object what) {
        Node here = first.getNext();
        while (here != null) {
            if (what.equals(here.getValue())) {
                return true;
            }
            here = here.getNext();
        }
        return false;
    } // end of contains method

} // end of Collection class
```

> Notice how much simpler this code is than the version without a header node.

Let's keep this abstraction simple and assume it must have the ability to store an arbitrary amount of text (characters), must keep track of where the cursor is, must be able to move the cursor to the left or right, and must be able to insert and delete a character. Code 16.12 is a description of this abstraction (class) using doc comments.

Now let's consider the implementation. A linked list is probably appropriate, especially since insertions will be done at arbitrary places in the middle of

CODE 16.12

```
/**
 * A Text object stores a sequence of characters in the
 * order and place they are inserted. It keeps track of
 * a cursor that is positioned between characters.
 */
class Text {

    /**
     * Create an empty Text object.
     */
    public Text() {
        } // end of constructor

    /**
     * Move the cursor one character to the left.
     * If at the left end of the text, do nothing.
     */
    public void moveLeft() {
        } // end of moveLeft method

    /**
     * Move the cursor one character to the right.
     * If at the right end of the text, do nothing.
     */
    public void moveRight() {
        } // end of moveRight method

    /**
     * Insert a character after the cursor.
     * @param newChar The character to insert.
     */
    public void insert(char newChar) {
        } // end of insert method

    /**
     * Delete the character following the cursor.
     * Do nothing if there is no character following
     * the cursor.
     */
    public void remove() {
        } // end of remove method

    } // end of Text class
```

the sequence of characters. An array implementation would require moving characters over one element to make room for the new one—a time-consuming operation. Instead I'll use a linked list with one character per node, which will waste a lot of space, but I'm going to assume it is worth it to avoid moving characters around in an array.

FIGURE 16.9

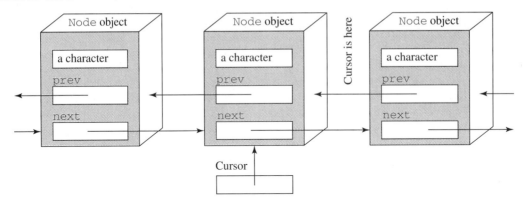

The Text class will have to keep track of a cursor position. Since the abstraction requires that the cursor be "between" characters, we have to make the implementation behave that way. To do so, I'll make the assumption that a cursor reference variable will refer to the previous character (i.e., if the cursor is between A and B, then the cursor variable will refer to the node containing A).

The moveRight method will be easy, as all that needs to be done is to follow the reference to the next node in the sequence. The moveLeft method won't be so easy, however, unless we make the following modification to Node objects. Each Node object in this list not only will refer to the Node object that follows it (i.e., to the right in the text), but also will have a reference to the Node object that precedes it (i.e., to the left in the text), as illustrated in Figure 16.9. Note also how the cursor is implemented.

This structure is called a **doubly linked list** because there are two links, one in the "forward" direction (next), one in the "backward" direction (prev).[1] Moving the cursor to the left uses prev to get a reference to the previous node (i.e., the one to the left).

As with most linked list implementations, there will be special cases to deal with at the beginning (left) and end (right) of the list. To reduce the amount of special case code, I will include a header node at the left and another special node at the right, called a **trailer node.** The trailer node is like the header node. It contains no information, but merely is there to eliminate special case code for dealing with the end of the list.

{Good Ideas}

Use a *trailer node* to eliminate many special case situations at the end of a list.

The header node not only reduces special case code, but also makes it simple to represent the position of the cursor. When there is no text in the Text object, it references the header node. When there is text, but the cursor is positioned at the beginning of the text (i.e., before the first character), it also references the header node. This is simply another good reason to have a header node.

---

1. A linked list using Node objects with just one link is called a **singly linked list.**

Code 16.13 shows the code that implements the Text class using a doubly linked list. Take note of the following points. The constructor creates both
the header and trailer nodes and sets up the cursor. An instance variable
(last) is used to refer to the trailer node, which will be a convenience later.

CODE 16.13

```
public class Text {
    private class Node {
        private char c;
        private Node prev;
        private Node next;

        public Node(char ic, Node p, Node n) {
            c = ic;
            prev = p;
            next = n;
        } // end of constructor

        public void setPrev(Node where) {
            prev = where;
        } // end of setPrev method

        public void setNext(Node where) {
            next = where;
        } // end of setNext method

        public Node getPrev() {
            return prev;
        } // end of getPrev method

        public Node getNext() {
            return next;
        } // end of getNext method

    } // end of Node class

    private Node first;
    private Node last;
    private Node cursor;
```

Notice how straightforward the code is when you don't have many special cases.

```
    public Text() {
        // create header and trailer nodes and set cursor
        last = new Node('>', null, null);
        first = new Node('<', null, last);
        last.setPrev(first);
        cursor = first;
    } // end of constructor
```

```
public void moveLeft() {
    if (cursor != first) {
        cursor = cursor.getPrev();
    }
} // end of moveLeft method
```

```
public void moveRight() {
    if (cursor.getNext() != last) {
        cursor = cursor.getNext();
    }
} // end of moveRight method
```

```
public void insert(char newChar) {
    Node after = cursor.getNext();
    Node newNode = new Node(newChar, cursor, after);
    cursor.setNext(newNode);
    after.setPrev(newNode);
} // end of insert method
```

```
public void remove() {
    if (cursor.getNext() != last) {
        Node deleted = cursor.getNext();
        Node after = deleted.getNext();
        cursor.setNext(after);
        after.setPrev(cursor);
    }
} // end of remove method
```

```
} // end of Text class
```

The moveLeft and moveRight methods are very simple because of the header and trailer nodes, but they do have to check to make sure the cursor doesn't get moved right off either end of the list. The insert method has no special cases! The remove method only has to check that there is a character after the cursor to remove before removing it.

{Good Ideas}
Use a doubly linked list when you must be able to traverse a list both forward and backward.

Written Exercises

1. Are header or trailer nodes ever absolutely necessary?

2. Suppose you had an application that was going to create millions of separate Text objects, each of which would only have at most five characters.

Would you consider implementing the `Text` class without header and/or trailer nodes? Why or why not? What would be the best way to implement the `Text` class for this application? Why?

3. Would there be any advantage in using a doubly linked list in the `Collection` abstraction?

Programming Exercises

1. Write a simple oneline text editor applet using the `Text` class. Draw the text on the screen using `drawString` in a `JPanel`, use left and right buttons to move the cursor, a delete button to erase the character preceding the cursor, and a text field to enter new characters at the cursor position.

2. Modify the implementation of the `Text` class to eliminate the use of header and trailer nodes. Be careful of special cases at the ends of the list!

3. Modify the `Collection` class to use header and trailer nodes and to add new objects to the end of the list instead of at the beginning. Use the test applet to try out your implementation.

4. Modify the `Collection` class to use a doubly linked list, without header or trailer nodes. Use the test applet to try out your implementation.

5. Write a test driver for the `Text` class, and test the implementation as completely as you can.

16.6 THE ARRAY VERSUS THE LINKED LIST IMPLEMENTATIONS

I've compared the various array implementations of the `Collection` class and found that which one was best depended on the use that was going to be made of it. Now let's compare the linked list and array implementations.

The biggest advantage of the linked list implementations is that they don't pay the big price of copying `Object` references as the collection grows (or shrinks if the implementation creates shorter arrays). If the application using the array implementation of the `Collection` class varies the collection's size greatly, this can be a significant problem. For a reasonably stable collection size, however, an array implementation that includes a constructor that can be told approximately how large to make the array might be the best choice.

The disadvantage of the linked list implementations is that you waste space for the extra reference variables used for the links. Compared to an array implementation, this may not be much of a price to pay, especially if the size of the collection varies wildly and the array implementation does not create smaller arrays as the size decreases, and therefore wastes a lot of space as the collection gets smaller and smaller.

The bottom line on choosing an implementation is knowing what use is going to be made of it. There is no way to pick a best implementation without such knowledge. Thinking that either implementation is best in all situations is faulty thinking.

{New Concepts}

The best implementation of an abstraction depends on the use that will be made of the abstraction. Generally no one implemention is best in all circumstances.

On the flip side, if the application creates few collections and you know the collections will be fairly small, then any implementation will do. Neither will be terribly inefficient, and neither will waste much memory. Don't waste your programming, testing, and debugging time in this circumstance. Pick the easiest to implement. Anything else is false economy. Saving a little bit of memory, or very small fraction of a second of execution time, isn't worth the extra effort under these circumstances.

{Good Ideas}

If an abstraction won't be used very much and won't need a lot of space, then pick the easiest to implement.

Written Exercises

1. Suppose a `Collection` class is going to be used in a program in which the collection will be added to but never have anything removed. Which implementation would you pick? Why?

2. What would be the advantage of implementing the `Text` class using a growing/shrinking array instead of a doubly linked list?

16.7 STACKS

A very common abstraction in programs is the **stack.** A stack is like a collection in that objects are added and removed. However, with a stack, the object that is removed must be the most recent one added. So, for example, if A, B, and C are added to a stack (in that order), then C must be removed first, then B, then A. In a sense, the objects are stacked up as they are added, and only the top object can be removed (hence the name). The property of adding and removing in this order is called **last-in, first-out** and often abbreviated **LIFO.**

The commonly accepted method names for a `Stack` abstraction (class) are `push`, to add an object to the `Stack`; and `pop`, to remove the top one. Most `Stack` abstractions also supply a `top` method to acquire a reference to the top object on the stack (but not remove it), and an `isEmpty` method to check whether there are any objects on the stack. In some versions the pop method not only removes the top object, but also returns a reference to it (essentially combining the `top` and the simpler `pop` methods into one).

Code 16.14 is a specification of the `Stack` abstraction in doc comment form.

CODE 16.14

```java
/**
 * A Stack is a last-in, first-out collection of objects.
 */
class Stack {

    /**
     * Create an empty Stack.
     */
    public Stack() {
    } // end of constructor

    /**
     * Push an object onto the Stack.
     * @param thing The object to push on the Stack.
     */
    public void push(Object thing) {
    } // end of push method

    /**
     * Return the top Object on the Stack.
     * @return A reference to the top Object on the Stack,
     * null if the Stack is empty.
     */
    public Object top() {
    } // end of top method

    /**
     * Pop the top Object from the Stack.
     * Does nothing if the Stack is empty.
     */
    public void pop() {
    } // end of pop method

    /**
     * Return whether the Stack is empty or not.
     * @return True if the Stack is empty,
     * false otherwise.
     */
    public boolean isEmpty() {
    } // end of isempty method

} // end of Stack class
```

Stacks have lots of uses. Compilers use them to recognize the structure of a program while it is being translated. When you execute a Java program, every time a method gets called, information about the method doing the calling is pushed on a stack (e.g., where to return to in that method when the called method returns). Even pocket calculators use them to evaluate expressions.

Just as an example of how useful stacks can be, here's an algorithm for evaluating expressions involving integer values and the addition, subtraction, multiplication, and division operators. Two stacks will be used. One will have operators $(+, -, \times, /)$ on it; the other, values. The operator stack is initialized with a special symbol $(\#)$ that is considered to have lower precedence than any other operator. The value stack is initially empty.

The expression is processed from left to right. Let's call the next input token to process X. Pick the item below that applies, do what it says, then pick again, etc., until done.

- If X is a literal, it is simply pushed on the value stack, and the following input token becomes X.

- If X is a left parenthesis, it is pushed on the operator stack, and the following input token becomes X.

- If X is a right parenthesis and the top of the operator stack is a left parenthesis, then the left parenthesis is popped from the operator stack and the following input token becomes X.

- If X is a right parenthesis and the top of the operator stack is not a left parenthesis, then the value stack is popped twice to get two values (let's call them A and B), the operator stack is popped to get an operator (let's call it OP), then A OP B is computed (e.g., if A is 7, B is 3, and OP is $-$, then $7 - 3$ is computed), and the resulting value is pushed onto the value stack. X remains unchanged.

- If X is an arithmetic operator and it has higher precedence than the operator on top of the operator stack, then X is pushed on the operator stack and the following input token becomes X.

- If X is an arithmetic operator and it has lower precedence than the operator on top of the operator stack, then the value stack is popped to get two values (A and B), the operator stack is popped to get an operator (OP), then A OP B is computed, and the resulting value is pushed onto the value stack. X remains unchanged.

- If there are no further input tokens and the top of the value stack is not $\#$, then pop two values and one operator, perform the indicated operation, and push the result on the value stack.

- If there are no further input tokens and the top of the operator stack is $\#$, then the top of the value stack is the value of the entire expression.

Figure 16.10 shows how this works for the expression: $7 \times (12 - 4)/8$.

16.7.1 Stack Implementations

A `Stack` abstraction can be implemented with a fixed-size array if a limit on the maximum number of objects that will ever be in the stack at any given time is known. If not, an implementation that creates larger and larger arrays as the stack grows (and perhaps smaller and smaller ones as it shrinks) can be used, as can a linked list. Code 16.15 is a (singly) linked list implementation.

FIGURE 16.10

X = 7

Action: push 7 on the value stack

#	
operator stack	value stack

X = x

Action: push x on the operator stack

#	7
operator stack	value stack

X = (

Action: push (on the operator stack

| x | |
#	7
operator stack	value stack

X = 12

Action: push 12 on the value stack

| (| |
| x | |
#	7
operator stack	value stack

X = —

Action: push - on the operand stack

| (| |
| x | 12 |
#	7
operator stack	value stack

X = 4

Action: push 4 on the value stack

—	
(	
x	12
#	7
operator stack	value stack

X =)

Action: pop—, 4, and 12; compute 12-4; push 8 on the value stack

—	
(	4
x	12
#	7
operator stack	value stack

X =)

Action: pop (from the operator stack

| (| |
| x | 8 |
#	7
operator stack	value stack

X = /

Action: pop x, 8, and 7; compute 7*8; push 56 on the value stack

#	56
operator stack	value stack

FIGURE 16.10 (CONTINUED)

operator stack	value stack	
/		X = /
#	56	Action: push / on the operand stack

operator stack	value stack	
/	8	X = 8
#	56	Action: push 6 on the value stack

operator stack	value stack	
		X = nothing
#	7	Action: pop /, 8, and 56; compute 65/8; push 7 on the value stack

operator stack	value stack	
		X = nothing
#	7	Action: done, 7 is the answer

CODE 16.15

```
class Stack {
    // Singly linked Node class here
    private Node top = null;

    public void Push(Object thing) {
        top = new Node(thing,top);
        } // end of Push method

    public Object Top() {
        if (top != null) {
            return top.getValue();
            }
        else {
            return null;
            }
        } // end of Top method

    public void Pop() {
        if (top != null) {
            top = top.getNext();
            }
        } // end of Pop method

    public boolean isEmpty() {
        if (top == null) {
            return true;
            }
```

```
        else {
            return false;
            }
        } // end of isEmpty method

    } // end of Stack class
```

16.7.2 Tradeoffs

The decision on whether to use an array, a growing array, a growing/shrinking array, or a linked list implementation of a `Stack` is based on most of the same criteria used to decide which `Collection` implementation to use. Clearly, if a maximum stack size is known and the stack stays reasonably full, a fixed array is probably best. Otherwise the amount of variability in the number of objects on the stack will decide whether a growing/shrinking array or linked list implementation is best. Certainly from a coding point of view it is hard to imagine simpler code than that for the linked list.

Written Exercises

1. Describe a real-world application of the `Stack` abstraction different from those presented above.

2. Modify the description of the `Stack` abstraction to allow an object specified by its distance from the top of the stack to be removed (e.g., remove the fifth object from the top).

3. Modify the description of the `Stack` abstraction to include a method that returns the size of the stack (i.e., the number of objects currently on the stack).

4. Demonstrate the steps used by the expression evaluation method in evaluating.

$$(7 + (7 \times 7 - 4 \times 9 \times 6)) / 2 \times 9)$$

5. Which implementation of the `Stack` abstraction would be best if the maximum size of the stack were known in advance? Why?

6. Which implementation of the `Stack` abstraction would be best if you knew that the stack would initially grow very large, then shrink back down to very small and then stay small for the rest of the program? Why?

Programming Exercises

1. Modify the linked list implementation of the `Stack` abstraction to be able to remove an object specified by its distance from the top of the stack [e.g., `remove(5)` means to remove the fifth object from the top of the stack, `remove(0)` removes the top object].

2. Write a fixed array implementation of the `Stack` abstraction. First modify the description of the abstraction to include a constructor that has a parameter to indicate the maximum size of the stack. Put a check for trying to push too many objects in anyway, and print an error message and exit the program if it occurs.

3. Write a calculatorlike applet in which the user types an expression involving single-digit numbers into a text field, then hits Enter or Return to have the expression evaluated and the result displayed. Use the appropriate implementation of the `Stack` abstraction.

16.8 QUEUES

Another common abstraction programmers use is the **queue.** If you've ever stood in line at the store, then you've been in a queue. Objects are added to one end of a queue and removed from the other. The object that is removed is the one that has been in the queue for the longest time. This is often called **first-in, first-out (FIFO).**

The commonly accepted method names for a `Queue` abstraction (class) are **enqueue,** to add an object to the queue, and **dequeue,** to remove one. Most `Queue` abstractions also supply a `front` method that returns a reference to the object at the front of the `Queue` (but not to remove it), and an `isEmpty` method to check whether there are any objects in the `Queue`.

Code 16.16 is a specification of the `Queue` abstraction in doc comment form:

CODE 16.16

```
/**
 * A Queue is a First-In, First-Out data structure.
 */
class Queue {

    /**
     * Create an empty queue.
     */
    public Queue() {
        } // end of constructor

    /**
     * Add an object to the end of the Queue.
     * @param thing The object to add to the Queue.
     */
    public void enqueue(Object thing) {
        } // end of enqueue method
```

```
/**
 * Remove an object from the front of the Queue.
 * Do nothing if the Queue is empty.
 */
public void dequeue() {
    } // end of dequeue method

/**
 * Return a reference to the object at the front
 * of the queue. The object is not removed.
 * @return A reference to the front object, or null
 * if the Queue is empty.
 */
public Object front() {
    } // end of front method

/**
 * Return whether the Queue is empty or not.
 * @return True if the Queue is empty,
 * false otherwise.
 */
public boolean isEmpty() {
    } // end of isEmpty method

} // end of Queue class
```

16.8.1 Linked Implementation

Both array and linked list implementations can be done for the `Queue` abstraction. I'll do a linked list first since the array implementations have some interesting complications.

When we use a linked list to implement a `Queue`, it is useful to have a reference to both ends of the list. This avoids having to traverse the entire list looking for the end on which to enqueue a new object. Hence I'll use `first` (not `front` since it is used as a method name) and `last` instance variables to keep track of the front and rear of the list (Code 16.17). Note that special case code is needed in the `enqueue` and `dequeue` methods for when the queue is empty.

16.8.2 Array Implementations

There are many ways of using an array to implement the `Queue` abstraction. One is to simply assume that the first element of the array is the front of the queue and that the end of the queue is down into the array some distance (using an instance variable to keep track of its index). When an object is enqueued, it is simply added to the next element after the previous last one (creating a new, bigger array if necessary). When an object is dequeued, however, every object reference must be copied to the previous element in the array to get the second

CODE 16.17

```
class Queue {
    // Singly linked Node class here
    private Node first;
    private Node last;

    public Queue() {
        first = null;
        last = null;
        } // end of constructor

    public void enqueue(Object thing) {
        Node newNode = new Node(thing,null);
        if (last == null) {
            first = newNode;
            }
        else {
            last.setNext(newNode);
            }
        last = newNode
        } // end of enqueue method

    public void dequeue() {
        if (first != null) {
            first = first.getNext();
            if (first == null) {
                last = null;
                }
            }
        } // end of dequeue method

    public Object front() {
        if (first != null) {
            return first.getValue();
            }
        else {
            return null;
            }
        } // end of front method

    public boolean isEmpty() {
        if (first == null) {
            return true;
            }
        else {
            return false;
            }
        } // end of isEmpty method

    } // end of Queue class
```

Must handle an empty queue as a special case.

Must handle removing the last node as a special case.

Must check for an empty Queue as a special case.

FIGURE 16.11

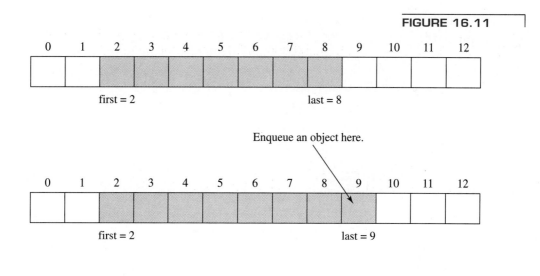

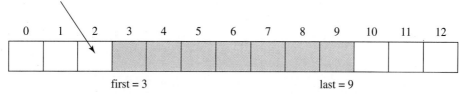

object to be the first, the third be the second, etc. This is very time-consuming if the queue contains many objects and a clear disadvantage compared to a linked list implementation.

There is an alternate array implementation that works extremely well, however. The basic idea is to keep track of two indices, one for the front and the other for the rear. When an object is enqueued, it is put in the next element after the last one, and when an object is dequeued, the index of the first is simply incremented by 1. Figure 16.11 illustrates this, with shaded boxes representing occupied elements of the array.

This way of handling dequeues without having to copy object references works just fine until the rear of the queue reaches the end of the array. Then there is no more room to enqueue another object. What are the options?

First, we could create a new, bigger array and copy everything to it. If we simply copy each object to the same position in the new array as it was in the old, then as further objects are dequeued, more and more of the beginning elements of the array will become unused, thereby wasting more and more space. A better approach would be to copy elements to the beginning of the array, then adjust the first and last indices appropriately, as shown in Figure 16.12.

But is this a good approach? Probably not. A larger array was created, and the overhead of copying object references was taken on even though there was still empty space at the beginning of the array. Worse yet, suppose objects were

FIGURE 16.12

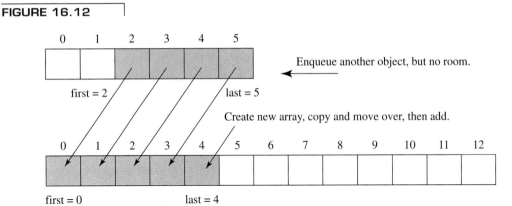

Enqueue another object, but no room.

first = 2

last = 5

Create new array, copy and move over, then add.

first = 0

last = 4

enqueued and dequeued at about the same rate, so that the total number of objects in the queue stayed reasonably constant. Then eventually the occupied part of the array would shift toward the end until there was no more room (at the end), but plenty of room at the beginning. A new, larger array would be created, the object references copied, and normal operation resumed—resumed, that is, until the occupied part of the array shifted to the end of this now larger array, which would again cause a new, even larger array to be created, etc. Larger and larger arrays would be created even though the size of the queue isn't changing much at all.

A fix for this would be to shift elements toward the beginning of the array when there was no more room at the end. If there are no empty elements at the beginning *and* the end, then and only then create a new, larger array. This solves the problem presented in the example above, except that there still will be occasional shifts of elements toward the beginning of the array as the occupied elements drift to the end.

But there is even a way to eliminate all shifting of object references no matter how many enqueues and dequeues are performed. Only when the entire array is full and another enqueue performed does a new, larger array have to be created and object references copied.

The idea is to use empty elements at the front of the array to hold objects enqueued after the rear of the queue reaches the end of the array. Figure 16.13 shows how this is done. Further enqueued objects will occupy elements 1, 2, 3, etc. The first object dequeued will be the one at position 6, then 7, 8, 9, 10, 11, 12, and then 0. You can picture this arrangement as having the queue "wrap around" to the beginning of the array. Some call this a **circular array.**

Now except for one small detail, this technique for storing queue objects in the array will avoid all copying of object references, except when the queue will no longer fit and a new, larger array is created. The small detail is that every element of the array cannot be used to store a reference to an object. Here's why.

First notice that a new object is added to the array element that is 1 larger than the current value of last, subject to wrapping around to the beginning.

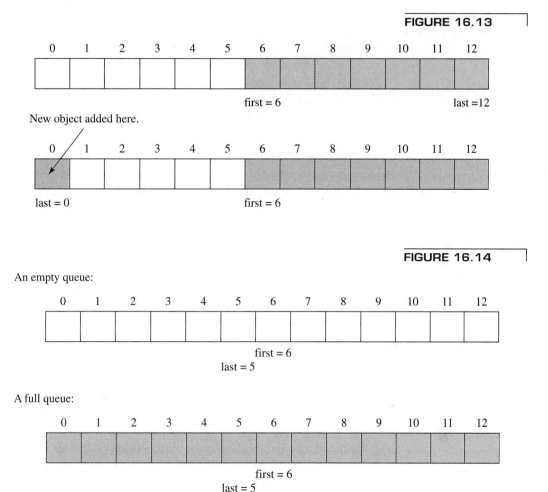

FIGURE 16.13

first = 6   last =12

New object added here.

last = 0   first = 6

FIGURE 16.14

An empty queue:

first = 6
last = 5

A full queue:

first = 6
last = 5

Hence if the queue is empty, `last` will be 1 smaller than `first` (again, subject to wrapping). This makes the test for an empty array to be that `first` is 1 bigger than `last`. Now suppose the queue contains as many objects as there are elements in the array. Then again `last` will be 1 less than `first`, and the empty test will be true! See Figure 16.14.

There are a couple of different ways to fix this, but the easiest is simply to never fill the last array element with an object reference. An empty queue is still defined exactly the same way, but if enqueuing another object would cause `first` to become 1 larger than `last`, consider the array full and create a new, larger array.

Code 16.18 is the implementation code for this wraparound array implementation. The code to create a larger array and copy the object references has been omitted and left as an exercise.

CODE 16.18

```
class Queue {
    private final int initialSize = 10;
    private Object [] data;
    private int first;
    private int last;

    public Queue() {
        data = new Object[initialSize];
        first = 1;
        last = 0;
    } // end of constructor

    public void enqueue(Object thing) {
        if ((last+2)%data.length == first) {
            // array is full, create new array and copy
        }
        else {
            last = (last+1)%data.length;
            data[last] = thing;
        }
    } // end of enqueue method

    public void dequeue() {
        if (isEmpty()) {
            return;
        }
        first = (first+1)%data.length;
    } // end of dequeue method

    public Object front() {
        if (isEmpty()) {
            return null;
        }
        return data[first];
    } // end of front method

    public boolean isEmpty() {
        if ((last+1)%data.length == first) {
            return true;
        }
        else {
            return false;
        }
    } // end of isEmpty method

} // end of Queue class
```

This code left as an exercise.

%data.length causes the index to wrap around to the beginning of the array.

Note the use of the % operator to wrap indices back around to 0. This is yet another handy use for the remainder operator!

16.8.3 Tradeoffs

Again the decision on which implementation is best depends on how the Queue will be used. Quite often a reasonably sized upper bound on the queue size is known, and if so, a circular array implementation would be best. You wouldn't even need to provide code for creating larger arrays if you knew for sure what the maximum number of things in the queue at any one time would be. Otherwise a linked list approach is probably best, as the overhead of copying object references when new arrays are created would be excessive.

Written Exercises

1. If you knew nothing about how a program was going to use a Queue (how large, how variable in length, etc.), what implementation would you choose? Why?

2. Think of a way to use the last remaining array element in a circular array implementation of a Queue. (*Hint:* Use an extra variable.) Explain in English how your technique works.

Programming Exercises

1. Queue data structures are often used in programs that simulate real life queues. Here's a program that simulates a checkout counter at a store. Write a program that reads a text file containing a sequence of integers. A positive integer is the time (in minutes since the store opened) at which a customer gets into line at the checkout counter. A negative integer indicates the time at which a person leaves the checkout counter after being checked out. Use the absolute value of the negative integer as the actual time the person leaves. Assume that the file is set up so that there is always somebody in the line when a negative number is read. Using the linked list Queue implementation, determine the average number of minutes a person spends in line at the checkout counter. *Hint:* Enqueue the arrival time for each person; then when one leaves, subtract the arrival time from the departure time to get the time in the line for that person. For example, if the input file has

   17
   29
   −34
   48
   −50
   −76

then the first person arrives at time 17 and leaves at time 34, spending 17 minutes in the line; the second arrives at time 29 and leaves at time 50, spending 21 minutes in the line; and the third person arrives at time 48 and leaves at time 76 for 28 minutes in the line. The average is $(17 + 21 + 28)/3 = 22$ minutes. Make up other input files to test your program, making sure that the absolute values of the numbers are increasing and that there is always somebody in line when there is a negative number.

2. Redo the previous problem by replacing the linked list implementation with a circular array that grows if need be.

3. Modify the Queue abstraction to add a method that returns the number of objects in the Queue. Then implement the new abstraction using the linked list implementation. Finally, modify the first problem to display the length of the line every time a person gets into the line.

4. Modify the Queue abstraction to add a method that allows an object to be put in the nth position in the queue (1 is the first position). Then add the new method in the linked list implementation. Then modify the previous program to use this new abstraction, modifying the file to include a second integer after each positive one that indicates the position in the queue where the person should be added. Assume that if the second integer is a 0, the person is added to the end of the queue. For example,

   1 0—add at the end

   3 0—add at the end

   5 2—add in the second place

   7 2—add in the second place

   −9

   −11

   −13

   −15

5. Replace the Queue implementation in the previous problem with a circular array implementation.

Summary

- Abstractions are used to specify what an object does, not how it does it.
- Information hiding is used to keep the details of how an abstraction is implemented from the users of the abstraction.
- Encapsulation puts all the information associated with the implementation of an abstraction in one place, usually within a class.
- Java supports abstractions, information hiding and encapsulation via classes, visibility modifers, and scope rules.

- Abstractions should never overspecify what is done, lest it overly restrict possible implementations.

- Users of abstractions should not take advantage of possible implementation properties lest those properties change when a new implementation is used.

- Javadoc is a command that reads a class description with doc comments to produce slick Web pages that describe the class.

- A linked list is a sequence of objects (nodes) connected by references between them. A singly linked list has one reference to the next node in the sequence, while a doubly linked list also has a reference to the previous node in the sequence.

- Header and trailer nodes, which contain no information other than links, are used to eliminate special case code in methods that manipulate linked lists.

- A stack is a last-in, first-out (LIFO) data structure.

- A queue is a first-in, first-out (FIFO) data structure.

- A circular array implementation of a queue allows all (but one) elements of the array to be used to store object references without ever having to copy them.

Glossary

Abstraction A definition of what an object does, but not how it does it.

Circular Array A technique whereby things added to the end of the array start being added at the beginning when there is no more room at the end.

Dequeue Remove something from the front of a queue.

Doc Comments Comments understood and processed by the javadoc command to produce slick Web pages for an abstraction.

Doubly Linked List A linked list in which each node has references to the node before and after it (two links).

Encapsulation Putting everything there is to know about the implementation of an abstraction in one place (usually a class definition).

Enqueue Put something on the rear end of a queue.

FIFO First-in, first-out. A queue.

Header Node An extra noninformation node added to the front of a linked list to reduce the number of special cases in the methods that manipulate the list.

Information Hiding Making the implementation of an abstraction impossible to use from the outside.

Inner Class A class defined inside another class.

Javadoc A command that produces fancy Web pages from special comments included with a class definition.

LIFO Last-in, first-out. A stack.

Linked List A sequence of objects in which each object has a reference to the next.

Node An object used to hold a reference to an information object and one or more references to other nodes.

Queue A structure in which objects are added at one end and removed from the other. Like a waiting line. Also known as a FIFO structure.

Singly Linked List A linked list in which each node has a reference to the next node in sequence.

Stack A structure in which objects are added and removed from the same end. Also known as a LIFO structure.

Trailer Node An extra noninformation node added to the end of a linked list to reduce the number of special cases in the methods that manipulate the list.

Traverse Move from one node of a list to the next, usually looking for a specific node or place.

Introduction to Recursion

17.1 A SLIGHTLY DIFFERENT WAY OF THINKING

Suppose you are going to walk to the store. One "method" for doing it is

```
Take one step after another in the
direction of the store until you get
there.
```

Now consider the following alternative method:

```
If you are at the store, "done".
Otherwise, take one step in the direction
of the store, then walk to the store (from
there).
```

Let's call this "method" (i.e., all three lines above) the walkToTheStore method. Then in Java-like code, we could write

```
public void walkToTheStore() {
    if (at the store) {
        done;
        }
    else {
        take one step in the direction of
          the store;
        walkToTheStore();
        }
    } // end of walkToTheStore method
```

Let's suppose that you are currently three steps away from the store, and from there you decide to walkToTheStore. You first discover you are not at the store yet, so you take one step in the direction of the store (you are now two steps away), and from there you `walkToTheStore`. Again you discover you are not at the store yet, so you take one step in the direction of the store (you are now one step away), and from there you `walkToTheStore`. Again you discover you are not at the store yet, so you take one step in the direction of the store (you are now at the store), and from there you `walkToTheStore`. You now discover that you are at the store, so you are done.

The interesting thing about this method is that it contains a call of itself! This is the essence of a programming technique called *recursion*. Recursion occurs when a method calls itself either directly, as in the example above, or indirectly, as when one method calls another, which calls another, which calls another, etc., until the last one calls the first one.

{Definition of Terms}

Recursion occurs when a method calls itself, either directly or indirectly via a chain of other methods. A method that calls itself is a **recursive method.**

Recursion is a very powerful programming technique. With it you can write some very short pieces of code that do some very complex things. Recursion, however, does not allow you to do anything you couldn't have done without it. Recursion is not necessary. It is very useful, however, and it is a technique that will make writing code to do many common programming tasks much easier than without it.

17.2 THINKING RECURSIVELY

Let's consider solving a few other simple tasks recursively. The key to using recursion is to find a **general case** that can be applied no matter how big the problem, and to assume that we can do that general case. In the example above, the general case was being able to walk to the store no matter where we start. Then take that general case and refine it to first do something simple that gets us nearer the end of the problem, such as taking a single step toward the store, and then doing the general case all over again—going to the store from there.

17.2.1 Summing Integers

Sometimes the order of these two steps is reversed. That is, you do the general case first on a simpler problem, then do a simple step. Consider the task computing the sum of the first n integers (i.e., $1 + 2 + \cdots + n$) for some value of n. A possible general case would be to compute the sum of some arbitrary (smaller) number of integers, and assume we can do that somehow. It is not important to know how, just assume it can be done. The simple step is to be able to add just *two* arbitrary integers. A recursive solution to computing the sum of the first n integers then is to first use the general case for adding up the first $n - 1$ integers, then add the number n to that sum. Clearly if the general case works and gives us the sum of the first $n - 1$ integers, then adding n to that sum will be the sum of the first n integers.

In both of the examples above it is necessary for the general case to have a way of detecting that there is nothing left to do. In the going to the store example, the general case simply checked for being there and said "done." In the sum of the first n integers example, the general case needs to check for when it is being asked to compute the sum of the first 1 integer. Clearly the sum of the first 1 integer is 1. Hence the complete version of the recursive solution to adding the first n integers is as follows: if n is 1, then the sum is 1; otherwise the sum is equal to the sum of the first $n - 1$ integers, plus n. This special case, the one that causes the repeated calling of the general case to eventually stop, is called the **base case.**

Consider what happens when this "program" is "executed" for n equals 4. To compute the sum of the first four integers, we must first compute the sum of the first three integers, then add 4 to that sum. To compute the sum of the first three integers, we must first compute the sum of the first two integers, then add 3 to that sum. To compute the sum of the first two integers, we must first compute the sum of the first one integer, then add 2 to that sum. The sum of the first one integer is 1. Hence the actual calculations proceed as follows. The first sum is 1. To that we add 2 to produce the next sum (3). To that we add 3 to produce the next sum (6). To that we add 4 to produce the final sum (10).

17.2.2 Sorting

Here's another problem that has a nice recursive solution. Suppose you are given a pile of exams and you have to put them in alphabetical order (i.e., sort them alphabetically). Consider the general case of being able to sort some arbitrary number of exams. Then a large number of exams can be sorted by dividing the pile roughly in half, sorting each pile using the general case, then merging the two piles together. Hence if you can sort a small pile of exams, then you can sort a pile roughly twice as large. In fact, if you had a helper, you could sort one half and your helper could sort the other; then you could merge the two piles together.

Since this is a recursive solution, each of the smaller piles is also sorted using the general case. Each small pile is divided roughly in half, each half sorted, then the two halves merged together. So if you start with one big pile, you first divide it in half. Then to sort the two smaller piles you divide both of them in half, and now sort four piles, each roughly one-fourth the size of the original pile. But to sort each of the four small piles, you divide each of them roughly in half and sort each of them (now there are eight even smaller piles to sort). This general case process of dividing a pile in half, sorting it and merging the sorted halves can't go on forever, of course, because eventually the piles will get too small to divide in half (when a pile has exactly one exam in it). But this is precisely the situation that stops the general case. When there is just one exam in a pile to sort, that pile is already sorted. This is the base case.

17.2.3 Searching

Here is yet one more example. Suppose you have a pile of exams in alphabetical order. To find a particular person's exam (for simplicity, assume it is not missing), the general case is to look at the name on an exam roughly in the middle of the pile. If that is the person you are looking for, you are done (the base case). If not, and if the person's name you are looking *for* comes before the one you are looking *at,* then you can ignore the second half of the exams and do the general case on the first half. Otherwise you do the general case on the second half. Each time the number of exams in the remaining pile you are looking in is roughly one-half of the previous time, so if you don't find it along the way, you will eventually get down to only one exam left, which must be the one you are looking for.

This example is very similar to the way you look up a person's phone number in a phone book. You keep dividing the book into smaller and smaller remaining parts to look at, eventually getting down to the exact page. Then you search the page for the name, more or less in the same way, although most people at some point just start scanning down the column for the name.

Written Exercises

1. Define in words (not Java) a recursive method to wash a stack of dishes.

2. Suppose you have a box of marbles. All of them look the same and are the same size, but one is made of gold and the rest are glass painted to look like gold. The gold marble is heavier than the rest. Suppose you have a balance scale with a box on each side in which to put marbles. Define in words a recursive method to find the gold marble by using the scale.

3. Define in words a recursive method to compute *n* factorial, where *n* factorial is defined to be the product of the first *n* integers.

4. Define in words a recursive method to set all elements in an array to 0.

5. Define in words a recursive method to find a particular value in an array. Assume the value is there, but that the values are in random order.

6. Define in words a recursive method to find the smallest value in an array. Assume the values are in random order.

7. Define in words a recursive method to reverse the values in an array. That is, the first becomes the last, the last becomes the first, the second becomes the second to last, the second to last becomes the second, etc.

17.3 RECURSIVE METHODS IN JAVA

Writing a recursive method in Java is not hard once you have a good idea of how the recursion is supposed to work. As an example, Code 17.1 is a Java method that computes and returns the sum of the first *n* integers.

```
public int sumOfFirst(int n) {
    if (n == 1) {                    The base case.
        return 1;
    }                                 Call the general case
    else {                            with a smaller problem.
        int smallSum = sumOfFirst(n-1);
        return smallSum + n;
    }                                 Compute and return
} // end of sumOfFirst method         the next larger sum.
```

Let's use manual execution to see what happens if sumOfFirst is called with a couple different values for n. First, suppose it is called with n having the value 1. Then the method returns the value 1, which is the correct answer.

Suppose instead it is called with the value 4. I'll keep a record of what is happening with the following table, which shows exactly how SumOfFirst was called, what the current value of parameter variable n is at a given time, what the current value of local variable smallSum is at a given time, and what the method returns.

Call	Value of n	Value of smallSum	Returns
sumOfFirst(4)	4	Not created yet	?

First n is compared with 1 and found not to be equal. Hence the variable smallSum is created; but to give it an initial value, sumOfFirst is called again with n-1 (3) as the argument. Notice that the first call of sumOfFirst has not finished yet, so at this point there will be two different sumOfFirst methods in progress.

Call	Value of n	Value of smallSum	Returns
sumOfFirst(4)	4	None yet	?
sumOfFirst(3)	3	Not created yet	?

It is important to recognize at this point that each separate call of sumOfFirst will have a different value for the parameter variable named n because there are two separate variables, both called n, and each can have a different value. In this case the n that belongs to the first call of sumOfFirst has value 4 and the n that belongs to the second call has value 3. The computer always knows which n variable to use because it is only executing one of the calls at a time. Hence at this point the second call of SumOfFirst is executing, so the n that belongs to the second call, the one with value 3, is used.

Again n is compared with 1 and found to be unequal, and another smallSum local variable is created. As with parameter variable n, this is a different variable with the same name, and the computer keeps track of which to use in the same way. To get the initial value for this second smallSum variable, sumOfFirst is called again. The argument value is determined by evaluating the expression n-1, using the second n (the one with value 3).

Call	Value of n	Value of smallSum	Returns
sumOfFirst(4)	4	None yet	?
sumOfFirst(3)	3	None yet	?
sumOfFirst(2)	2	Not created yet	?

Once again the n that belongs to this new call of sumOfFirst (the one with value 2) is not equal to 1. So yet another smallSum variable is created, and yet another call to sumOfFirst is made, this time with argument value 1.

Call	Value of n	Value of smallSum	Returns
sumOfFirst(4)	4	None yet	?
sumOfFirst(3)	3	None yet	?
sumOfFirst(2)	2	None yet	?
sumOfFirst(1)	1	Not created yet	?

Finally the value of n that belongs to this call is 1, and this fourth call of sumOfFirst returns the value 1.

Call	Value of n	Value of smallSum	Returns
sumOfFirst(4)	4	None yet	?
sumOfFirst(3)	3	None yet	?
sumOfFirst(2)	2	None yet	?
sumOfFirst(1)	1	Not created	1

Notice that just before the fourth call of sumOfFirst returns, there are four different parameter variables called n, each with a different value, and three different local variables called smallSum, none of which has a value yet.

When the fourth call returns, the third call picks up where it left off, which is giving an initial value to the smallSum local variable that belongs to it. Since the call returned 1, that will be the initial value of smallSum.

Call	Value of n	Value of smallSum	Returns
sumOfFirst(4)	4	None yet	?
sumOfFirst(3)	3	None yet	?
sumOfFirst(2)	2	1	?

Now the third call of sumOfFirst continues, executing next the command that returns smallSum + n. Since the value of smallSum that belongs to this call of sumOfFirst has value 1 and the value of n that belongs to this call of sumOfFirst has value 2, the value $1 + 2 = 3$ is returned by this (third) call of sumOfFirst.

Call	Value of n	Value of smallSum	Returns
sumOfFirst(4)	4	None yet	?
sumOfFirst(3)	3	None yet	?
sumOfFirst(2)	2	1	3

Now the value of smallSum that belongs to the second call of sumOfFirst is given the initial value 3 that was returned from the third call, and the second call returns 6.

Call	Value of n	Value of smallSum	Returns
sumOfFirst(4)	4	None yet	?
sumOfFirst(3)	3	3	6

Finally the value of smallSum that belongs to the first call of SumOfFirst is given initial value 6, and the first call returns 10.

Call	Value of n	Value of smallSum	Returns
sumOfFirst(4)	4	6	10

Fortunately it worked correctly, as the sum of the first four integers (that is, $1 + 2 + 3 + 4$) is 10.

Using manual execution to trace the execution of a recursive method call and keep track of the various copies of the parameter and local variables and the return value is extremely useful in finding bugs. It takes some patience, and you must be extremely careful to record everything properly, but often it is the best way to figure out what went wrong.

Another debugging technique is to use the computer to help you trace the execution. Putting one or more print commands in your code, as the example in Code 17.2 shows, can save a lot of time.

CODE 17.2

```java
public class ShowRecursion {

    public static void main(String [] args) {
        ShowRecursion sr = new ShowRecursion();
        sr.sumOfFirst(4);
    } // end of main method

    public int sumOfFirst(int n) {
        System.out.println("sumOfFirst called, n = " + n);
        if (n == 1) {
            return 1;
        }
        else {
            int smallSum = sumOfFirst(n-1);
            System.out.print("smallSum = " + smallSum);
            System.out.println(", returning " + (smallSum + n));
            return smallSum + n;
        }
    } // end of sumOfFirst method

} // end of ShowRecursion class
```

ShowRecursion
Prints a trace of the execution of the recursive method for debugging purposes.

The output from the call sumOfFirst(4) is

```
sumOfFirst called, n = 4
sumOfFirst called, n = 3
sumOfFirst called, n = 2
sumOfFirst called, n = 1
smallSum = 1, returning 3
smallSum = 3, returning 6
smallSum = 6, returning 10
```

As you can see, the print command at the beginning of the method shows the sequence of recursive calls along with the parameter value at each call, while the two print commands near the end of the method show the value returned from a previous call and the value to be returned from the current call.

17.3.1 Infinite Recursion

Two things are crucial to making a recursive method work. First, each call must get closer to the base case than the previous one. Second, the base case must eventually become true and stop the succession of recursive calls. If one or the other of these isn't done right, the recursion will continue forever. This is the recursive equivalent to an infinite loop.

{Definition of Terms}

Each recursive call must get closer to the base case, and the base case must eventually execute to avoid *infinite recursion*.

Unlike an infinite loop, however, infinite recursion will eventually stop on its own, for the following reason. Every time the recursive method is called, memory space is used to store new copies of each parameter and local variable, and a little extra space is needed to keep track so that all the returns will work correctly. Since your computer does not have an infinite amount of memory, eventually what is there will get used up and another recursive call will not be able to be made for lack of memory space. You are informed of this via an error message, usually one that alludes to "stack overflow." This is because the information about the call and the parameter and local variables are stored on a stack.

17.3.2 Recursion versus Loops

The recursive method for computing the sum of the first n integers is easily replaced with a loop (Code 17.3). This is probably simpler to write than the recursive version. It is shorter and probably easier to understand, too. The point of doing it recursively was to demonstrate how recursion works with a very simple, easily understood example.

```
public int sumOfFirst(int n) {
    int sum = 1;
    for (int i=2; i<=n; i++) {
        sum += i;
    }
    return sum;
} // end of sumOfFirst method
```

CODE 17.3

Recursive methods have a lot of overhead in terms of extra time to do the calls and to create all the copies of parameter and local variables, and memory space needed to store all the copies and other information, as compared with an equivalent version using a loop. If efficiency is important, then don't use recursion if you can write a nonrecursive version fairly easily.

There are some cases in which there may be an obvious recursive solution, yet recursion should not be used. For example, consider the Fibonacci numbers. The Fibonacci numbers are a sequence of integers such that the next number in the sequence is equal to the sum of the two previous numbers. The first two Fibonacci numbers are 1 and 1. Hence, if F_n is the nth Fibonacci number, then it can be defined mathematically as

$$F_n = F_{n-1} + F_{n-2}$$

This suggests a very simple recursive method (Code 17.4).

CODE 17.4

```
public int f(int n) {
    if (n == 1 || n == 2) {
        return 1;
        }
    else {
        return f(n-1) + f(n-2);
        }
    } // end of f method
```

The problem with this is that for any fairly large n, the number of recursive calls is tremendous. For example, for n = 10, the first call of f(10) results in two recursive calls—f(9) and f(8). Then f(9) results in two more calls—f(8) [a different f(8) than the previous one] and f(7), and the first f(8) results in two more calls—f(7) (again, a different one) and f(6). As you can see, each call of f results in two more calls of f, which for large n winds up being a lot of calls. Not only that, but the same Fibonacci number will be computed recursively several times! This is clearly not a good use of recursion, even though it is pretty easy to write the code. The better solution is the loop version (Code 17.5), which I think you'll agree is not as easy to write or understand, yet is incredibly more efficient.

CODE 17.5

```
public int f(int n) {
    if (n == 1 || n == 2) {
        return 1;
    else {
        int prev = 1;
        int current = 1;
        for (int i=3; i<=n; i++) {
            int next = current + prev;
            prev = current;
            current = next;
            }
        return current;
        }
    } // end of f method
```

As we shall see later in this chapter, there are times when writing and debugging a recursive method for some problem are enormously easier than writing and debugging a nonrecursive version. In fact, later in this chapter I'll show you an example of a problem that has an incredibly simple recursive solution but a fairly complex nonrecursive solution. There isn't much difference in overhead either. Hence recursion should not be avoided at all costs. It is a powerful tool, and one that you should be able to use effectively.

Written Exercises

1. Complete the sequence of tables started below that show the execution of the following method:

```
public int p2(int n) {
    if (n == 0) {
        return 1;
    }
    else {
        int temp = 2 * p2(n-1);
        return temp;
    }
} // end of p2 method
```

Call	Value of n	Value of temp	Returns
p2(4)	4	Not created yet	?

What is the final value returned from the call of p2(4)? What simple mathematical function does this method compute?

2. What will happen if sumOfFirst is called with argument value 0?

Programming Exercises

1. Write a simple application program that calls the sumOfFirst method with some arbitrary argument value. Then modify the sumOfFirst method by removing the test for the base case so that infinite recursion will result. Then run your program. What message do you eventually get that indicates you had infinite recursion? How long did it take to get it?

2. Write a recursive method that computes the nth value of the sequence defined by

$$F_n = 2F_{n-1} + n$$

What are the values for F_n for $n = 1, 2, 3,$ and 4? Write a simple applet with a text field for input and a label for output that you can use to test your method for different values of n.

17.4 MORE EXAMPLES

The best way to get proficient at writing recursive methods is to practice. To that end, here are a few examples that demonstrate how to design and implement recursive solutions to common programming tasks.

17.4.1 Search an Array for a Value

A common programming task is to search an array for a particular value. In general, the values in the array are not in any special order, and in fact depending on what kind of values are stored in the array, there may be no way to even define an order. Hence there is no other way to search for a particular value than to inspect each and every value in the array until you find it or have inspected every value and found that it isn't there. For simplicity let's assume that the value you are looking for is in the array and write a recursive method to find it.

First, let's describe in words how the recursion works. It is rather simple. The basic idea is to look at the first element of part of the array. If it has the value you are looking for, then you are done. If it doesn't, then search the rest of the array, that is, the elements of the same array except for the one you just checked. Since we are assuming that the value we are looking for is in the array somewhere, eventually the base case (a match) will occur. In addition, we are always searching a smaller array each time, so we will be getting closer to the base case all the time.

The Java method that does the search will have two obvious parameters, the array and the value to be searched for. To make it general, let's assume that the array is an array of `Object` that has the `equals` method defined. Via polymorphism this method will search for any kind of object since all objects are defined by classes that are a subclasses of `Object`. To make this method general, let's assume that the search can be limited to a specific range of elements (i.e., not necessarily the whole array), and give the method two more parameters—the index of the first element to be checked and the index of the last element to be checked.

Finally the method will return an index to the matching element. We could instead have had the method return a reference to the matching object, but whoever is using this method may want to make a change to the array (e.g., to delete the value), so returning the index is more general. The user of the method can always get the reference to the object itself from the array, so in defining the return value this way we don't lose any functionality (Code 17.6).

CODE 17.6

```
public int find(Object [] array, Object target,
                int first, int last) {
    if (target.equals(array[first])) {
        return first;
    }
    else {
        return find(array,target,first+1,last);
    }
} // end of find method
```

The base case. This will be true eventually, because a match is assumed.

Return whatever the search of the one smaller array finds.

Assume that find is called the first time with first = 0 and last = 10. Then it will check element 0 to be equal to target, and if it is, return 0 as the result of the search. If not, it will call find again, passing the array and the target again, but this time passing 1 and 10 as the limits of the array to search. The first comparison, having failed to match, has eliminated element 0 from consideration, so the rest of the array, from 1 to 10, will be searched recursively.

The key to recursive methods such as this that work with arrays and whose recursion involves using smaller and smaller parts of the array is to have parameters, like first and last above, that define the part of the array that is still under consideration. We will see this pattern over and over.

It is often desirable to have a simple form of the find method that does not need first and last. The assumption is that every element will be searched, so why bother to specify them. If so, then an additional find method can be defined that simply calls the recursive one above and supplies 0 and array.length as limits (Code 17.7). Notice that the method name find is overloaded, but easily distinguished by the number and types of the parameters.

CODE 17.7

```
public int find(Object [] array, Object target) {
    find(array,target,0,array.length);
} // end of find method
```

17.4.2 Binary Search of an Array

When the values in an array have an ordering relationship between them (i.e., the array is in "ascending" or "descending" order), then there is a much faster way to search for a particular value. The idea is to pick a middle element of the array and see if that is the desired value. If not, then because the array is in order, you will know which half of the array the element must be in.

Recursively, the procedure is to first check the middle element of the part of the array being searched. If it is the desired element, you are done. If not, then determine which remaining half of the array the desired value must be in, and search it. Clearly the part of the array being searched each time gets smaller, and, assuming the value is in the array somewhere, eventually the remaining array will be just one element, which will have to match.

If the objects referred to by array elements are ordered, then there must be a method that will let us compare them to see whether they are equal, and if not, which is smaller or larger. Let's call this method compareTo, and assume it returns an integer that is less than 0 if the first object is less than the second, 0 if they are equal, and greater than 0 otherwise (Code 17.8).

The diagram in Figure 17.1 shows the array and the values of first, middle, and last in each of the four recursive calls to binarySearch. For simplicity I assumed each element contained a reference to an Integer object, and simply showed the value in the object in the array.

CODE 17.8

Find the index of the element closest to the middle.

```
public int binarySearch(Object [] array, Object target,
                        int first, int last) {
    int middle = (first + last) / 2;
    int compareResult = target.compareTo(array[middle]);
    if (compareResult == 0) {
        return middle;
    }
    else if (compareResult < 0) {
        return binarySearch(array,target,first,last-1);
    }
    else {
        return binarySearch(array,target,first+1,last);
    }
} // end of binarySearch method
```

Compare it with the target object.

If target before middle, search lower half.

Otherwise search upper half.

FIGURE 17.1

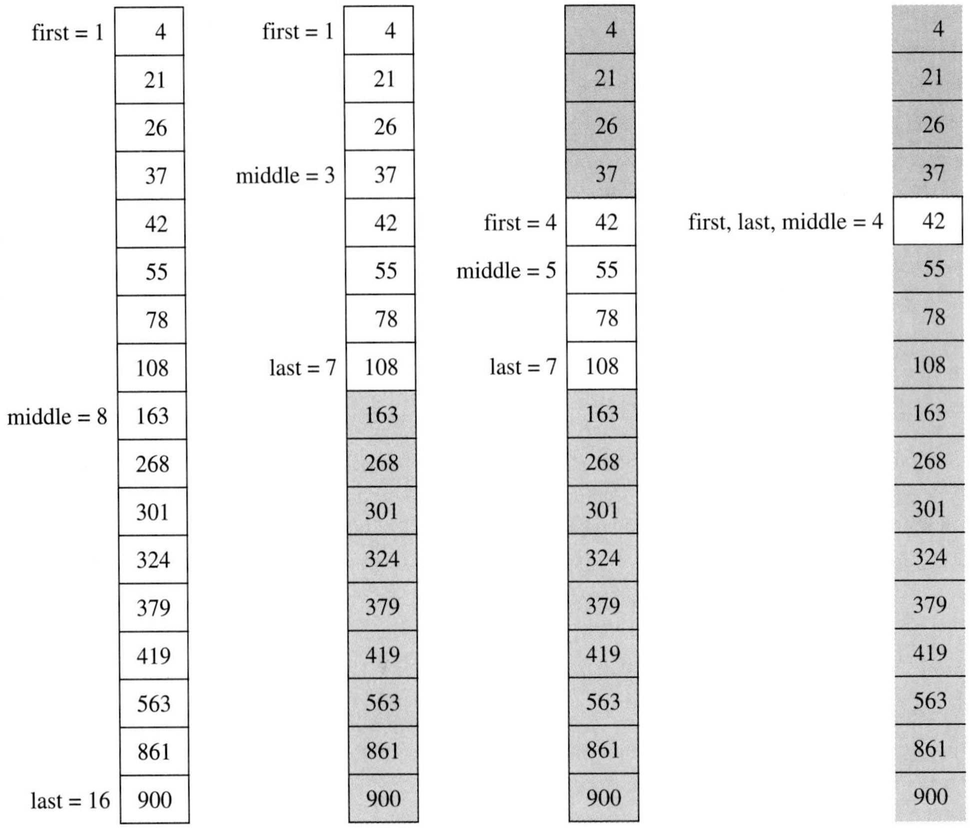

	first = 1	first = 1					
first = 1	4	4		4		4
	21	21		21		21
	26	26		26		26
	37	middle = 3 37		37		37
	42	42	first = 4 42	first, last, middle = 4 42
	55	55	middle = 5 55		55
	78	78	78		78
	108	last = 7 108	last = 7 108		108
middle = 8	163	163	163		163
	268	268	268		268
	301	301	301		301
	324	324	324		324
	379	379	379		379
	419	419	419		419
	563	563	563		563
	861	861	861		861
last = 16	900	900	900		900

At each step the part of the array that no longer needs to be searched is shown with a shaded background. Note that `middle` is simply the average of `first` and `last`, and because of integer division, it is always an integer. When the last call in the example finds the target, it returns its index to the previous call, which returns it to the previous, etc. all the way back to the first call, and the recursion is done.

This technique called **Binary search,** is a very efficient way of finding something in an array that is ordered. As you can see, each time approximately one-half of the remaining elements to be searched are eliminated. For example, suppose the array contains approximately 1 million elements. Then after one call, approximately one-half a million elements no longer need to be searched. After two calls, approximately three-quarters of a million elements have been ruled out. If you continue this, you will discover that it will take no more than 20 recursive calls to `binarySearch` to find the element you are looking for. This is enormously better than searching one element at a time from the beginning to the end of the array, called **linear search,** which could take as many as a million recursive calls. Of course, the objects in the array must be able to be ordered, and they must be in order in the array for it to work. If the objects are not ordered, then the very slow linear search method must be used.

17.4.3 Sorting an Array

A very simple technique for taking an unordered array of objects and putting them in increasing order goes as follows: Find the smallest value in the part of the array under consideration, exchange it with the value in the first element of the array, then sort the rest of the array (not including the first element). The first call will put the smallest value in the first element of the array, the second call will put the second smallest value in the second element, the third call will put the third smallest value in the third element, etc. The recursion stops when the part of the array still under consideration consists of just one element (which by that time will contain the largest value).

The code for this is pretty simple. I'll assume that we already have a method (called `findSmallest`) that is given an array and limits to work with and returns the index of the element containing the smallest value (Code 17.9).

The base case occurs when there is only one element left in the part of the array under consideration, and that is easily detected when the index of the first element of the rest of the array is equal to the index of the last element of the rest of the array.

17.4.4 Towers of Hanoi

The towers of Hanoi is a classical recursion problem based on a simple game. The game has three posts with a stack of different-diameter disks on one of them, as shown in Figure 17.2.

CODE 17.9

```
public void sort(Object [] array, int first, int last) {
    if (first == last) {
        return;
    }
    else {
        int smallIndex = findSmallest(array,first,last);
        Object temp = array[first];
        array[first] = array[smallIndex];
        array[smallIndex] = temp;
        sort(array,first+1,last);
    }
} // end of sort method
```

If `first` is equal to `last`, there is only one element left, so this "small" array is already sorted.

Find the index of the smallest value.

Swap the first value with the smallest.

Sort the rest of the array.

FIGURE 17.2

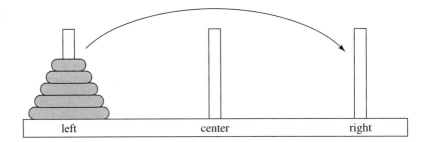

left   center   right

The object of the game is to move all the disks to the rightmost post according to the following two rules: Only one disk may be moved from one post to another at a time, and at no time can a large disk be put on top of a smaller one. The legend says that if you start with 64 disks on one post, then, when you are done, the world will end!

There is an extremely simple recursive solution to this problem. It goes as follows. To move n disks from the "source" post to the "destination" post, first move $n - 1$ disks from the source post to the "other" post, then move the last disk from the source post to the destination post, and finally move the $n - 1$ disks from the other post to the destination post. Hence if you can move $n - 1$ disks, then by the above three steps you can move n disks. This is the general case. The base case is when there are no disks to move ($n = 0$), in which case you do nothing. Figure 17.3 shows how this works.

Code 17.10 is a recursive method that prints out the sequence of steps used to move n disks from one post to the other. It assumes that the posts are strings labeled "left," "center," and "right." The three parameters are, first, the name of the post to move from; second, the name of the post to move to; and third, the name of the post to use as a temporary holding place.

Step 1:

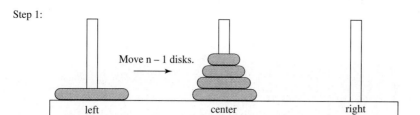

Move n – 1 disks.

left   center   right

Step 2:

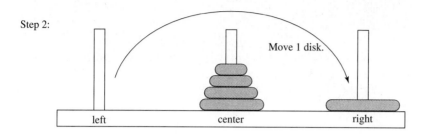

Move 1 disk.

left   center   right

Step 3:

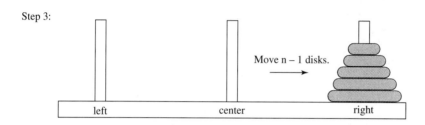

Move n – 1 disks.

left   center   right

FIGURE 17.3

CODE 17.10

```
public class HanoiDemo {

    public static void main(String [] args) {
        HanoiDemo hd = new HanoiDemo();
        hd.hanoi(3,"left","right","center");
    } // end of main method

    public void hanoi(int n, String from, String to,
                      String temp) {
        if(n>0) {
            hanoi(n-1, from, temp, to);
            System.out.println(
                "move disk from " + from + " to " + to);
            hanoi(n-1, temp, to, from);
        }
    } // end of hanoi method

} // end of HanoiDemo class
```

Move $n - 1$ disks from from to temp, using to as a temporary.

Move one disk from from to to.

Move $n - 1$ disks from temp to to, using from as a temporary.

HanoiDemo
Prints directions of how to move three disks from the left post to the right post.

When the program is executed, the output will be

```
move disk from left to right
move disk from left to center
move disk from right to center
move disk from left to right
move disk from center to left
move disk from center to right
move disk from left to right
```

You might want to follow these steps through by hand to convince yourself that it works.

Although I won't prove it, the number of single disk moves performed by this method to move n disks is $2^n - 1$. When n is 64, $2^n - 1$ is 18,446,744,073, 709,551,615. If you could make one move a second, this amounts to almost 600 billion years. There is a good chance that the world would end by then since the sun is supposed to burn out long before that!

As promised earlier in this chapter, this is a problem that has an almost trivial recursive solution. A nonrecursive solution is quite a bit harder, and I'll leave it as an exercise to write one. Once you do, decide for yourself whether using recursion is best for some problems.

Programming Exercises

Each of the following problems requires you to write a recursive method that performs some operation on an array. To test your methods, first write an application program that reads from a file some number of strings, one per line, into an array of strings, then via a GUI inputs whatever arguments are needed for a call of the corresponding method. Also either provide a display of the return value of the method, or write the modified array to another file so you can see if it did the right thing.

1. Modify the recursive method find to return -1 if the target value is not found in the array. *Hint:* There are now two base cases, one when the target value is found, the other when there is no remaining array to look in.

2. Modify the recursive binarySearch method to return -1 if the target value is not found in the array.

3. Write a recursive method to find the smallest value in an array.

4. Write a recursive method to reverse the values in an array.

5. Write a recursive method to find the largest value in an array using the following approach: Find the largest value in the array consisting of everything except the first element, then return the larger of that value and the value in the first element.

6. Write a recursive method to find the largest value in an array, using the following approach: Find the largest value in the lower half of the array, then

find the largest value in the upper half of the array; then return the larger of those two values. Is this any better than the approach in the previous problem? If so, why?

Summary

- Recursive methods call themselves on smaller and smaller problems until a simple solution on a very small problem is arrived at.
- Recursion is a powerful programming technique.
- Recursion is not necessary, but can make for a very simple, elegant solution where a nonrecursive solution would be very difficult to write.
- Every recursion has a general case and a base case.
- The general case usually does something simple and uses itself on a smaller problem to complete the task.
- The base case stops the recursion, usually when the task becomes so small that there is a trivial, nonrecursive action or result.
- Infinite recursion results when either the recursive call does not work on a smaller problem or the base case is never achieved.
- Binary search is a very efficient searching technique when the array being searched is in order.

Glossary

Base Case A situation that causes a recursion to terminate.

Binary Search A search technique that keeps eliminating half of the remaining values on each step. It requires that the array being searched be in order.

General Case A solution that does something simple, but also uses itself on a smaller problem.

Linear Search A search technique where each value in an array, from the first toward the last, is checked. It is not very efficient, but is necessary for unsorted (or unsortable) arrays.

Recursion Definition of something in terms of itself.

Recursive Method A method that calls itself, either directly or indirectly.

Java Reserved Words

abstract	continue	float	long	short	**true**
boolean	default	**for**	native	**static**	**try**
break	**do**	goto	**new**	**super**	**void**
byte	**double**	**if**	**null**	switch	volatile
case	**else**	**implements**	package	synchronized	**while**
catch	**extends**	**import**	**private**	**this**	
char	**false**	instanceof	**protected**	throw	
class	**final**	**int**	**public**	throws	
const	finally	**interface**	**return**	transient	

The reserved words in bold are explained and used in the text.

Java Primitive Types

B.1 INTRODUCTION

Java defines many primitive types. These differ from classes, and are not part of the class hierarchy headed by `Object`. This text uses several, but not all, of Java's primitive types. This appendix summarizes all Java's primitive types, explains their underlying representation using binary values, and shows how to define literals of each type.

B.2 BINARY NUMBERS

All computers represent primitive data types using the binary, or base-2, number system. Binary numbers use only the digits (bits) 0 and 1. Whereas in the decimal, or base-10, number system each digit in a number represents a power of 10, each bit in a binary number represents a power of 2. So, for example, the decimal number 1982 is

$$1 \times 10^3 + 9 \times 10^2 + 8 \times 10^1 + 2 \times 10^0 = 1000 + 900 + 80 + 2$$

and the binary number 1101 is

$$1 \times 2^3 + 1 \times 2^2 + 0 \times 2^1 + 1 \times 2^0 = 8 + 4 + 0 + 1 = 13$$

Suppose you have a decimal number and want to find its binary equivalent. Here's a simple method. Divide the number by 2 and write down the remainder (0 or 1). The remainder is the rightmost bit of the binary number. Then take the quotient of that division, divide it by 2, and write down the remainder to the left of the previous remainder. This second remainder is the next-higher bit of the binary number. Keep repeating this process of dividing the quotient by 2 and writing the remainder to the left of the previous one until the final quotient is 0. The sequence of remainders is the binary equivalent. For example, find the binary equivalent of decimal 23:

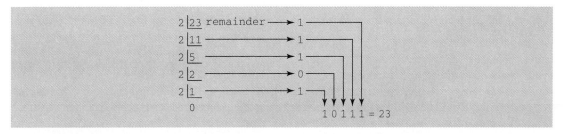

A computer allocates a fixed number of bits to store a binary number (different types use a different number of bits). The leftmost bit is reserved to represent the sign of the number, with 0 meaning positive and 1 meaning negative. Hence if there are *N* bits available to store a binary number, then one of them is the sign and $N - 1$ are used for the magnitude. A number that will not fit in N bits (including the sign) cannot be stored in a variable of a type that only allocates N bits.

Just as adding leading zeros to a decimal number does not change its value (that is, 17 and 00017 are the same value), adding leading zeros to a binary number does not change its value (that is, 10111 = 00010111). When a binary value like 10111 (+23) is stored in a variable that allocates 32 bits, the binary value will start with 27 zeros (the first of which is the sign). Note that the binary equivalent of 23 (10111) cannot be stored in 5 bits because the upper bit would be interpreted as the sign, which unfortunately would be 1, meaning negative. The largest positive binary value that can be stored in 5 bits is 01111, which is 15 in decimal.

Negative numbers are represented in the following way. The leftmost bit is still the sign bit, with 1 representing negative, but the remaining bits cannot simply be treated as the binary equivalent of the rest of the number. Instead, the binary equivalent of a negative number is found by adding 1 to the number, taking its absolute value, converting its absolute value (which is now a positive number) to its binary equivalent, and finally changing each 0 to a 1 and each 1 to a 0. For example, to find the binary equivalent of -24, first add 1 to get -23, then take the absolute value of -23 to get 23, now convert 23 to binary (say, 8 bits) to get 0010111, and finally change all 0s to 1s and 1s to 0s to get 11101000. Notice that the leftmost bit, which still represents the sign, is a 1, meaning negative.

To find the decimal equivalent of a negative binary number, you simply do the steps above in reverse. First change all the 0s to 1s and the 1s to 0s, convert the number to decimal, make it negative, then subtract 1. For example, the binary number 11111011 becomes 00000100, then 4, then -4, then -5, which is its decimal equivalent.

Using this notation for representing negative number results has the rather unexpected property that the smallest negative number is not the negative of the largest positive number. Instead it is 1 smaller than the negative of the largest positive number. For example, in 8 bits the largest positive number is 63, but the smallest negative is -64. You can figure this out yourself by first noticing that the smallest negative 8-bit number, in binary, is 10000000, and then converting it to decimal to get -64 (not -63).

This seemingly unusual way of representing negative numbers is called *twos-complement* notation. It is used because it makes building electric circuits that do binary arithmetic quite simple.

B.3 THE `int` TYPE

An `int` variable is represented by a 32-bit binary number. The largest positive value is 2,147,483,647, and the smallest negative value is $-2,147,483,648$. This range of values is sufficient for most applications. If it isn't, for example, if you are keeping track of the U.S. national debt, or the total capacity of a modern hard drive (well over 20 billion bytes), Java has another primitive type called `long`, which is described in the next section.

Literals consisting of a sequence of digits are of type `int`. However, starting a nonzero literal with the digit 0 alters the meaning, so don't do it unless you understand what is going on (for example, 037 and 37 do *not* represent the same value in Java).

B.4 THE `byte`, `short`, AND `long` TYPES

Java provides the `byte` and `short` primitive types for situations in which memory space is limited and the range of values that must be stored in a variable is small. A `byte` variable uses 8 bits to store a signed integer, with values ranging from -128 to 127. A `short` variable uses 16 bits, with values ranging from $-32,768$ to 32,767.

There is no way to write a `byte` or `short` literal. All sequence-of-digit literals are assumed to be of the `int` type. However, if you create a `byte` or `short` variable and immediately assign it an integer value, and if that value fits in the space allocated, then the Java compiler will not complain. For example, the following are legal:

```
byte tiny = 49;
short notSoTiny = -30000;
```

In all other situations you must use a cast to convert an `int` value to a `byte` or `short`.

Java also has a `long` type that stores an integer in 64 bits. This largest positive value is 918,734,323,983,581,183, and the smallest negative is −918,734,323,983,581,184. Java also allows `long` literals to be written in programs by immediately following the sequence of digits with an L or l (no space between the last digit and the L or l). For example, 387652396406537L and −2983777238471 are both `long` literals.

B.5 THE `double` AND `float` TYPES

A number expressed in scientific notation as $a \times 10^b$ is actually stored as though it were expressed as a number in the form $1.m \times 2^e$, where the conversion of a and b to m and e is beyond the scope of this text. A `double` value stores m and e in 64 bits, using 53 bits for m (one being the sign bit) and 11 bits for e (again using up 1 bit to handle positive and negative values of e). The largest positive double value is approximately 10^{308}, the least negative double value is approximately $-(10^{308})$.

This range of values more than suffices for most situations. However, of greater importance is the accuracy with which a double value is expressed. A double value has approximately 15 decimal digits of accuracy.

If memory space is tight but accuracy is not critical, the `float` type can be used instead of double. A `float` value stores m and e in 32 bits, using 24 bits for m and 8 bits for e (i.e., one-half as much space as a double). The largest positive float value is approximately 10^{38}, the least negative float value is approximately $-(10^{38})$. A float value has approximately 7 decimal digits of accuracy.

A double literal is written in one of three ways. The first is simply a sequence of digits with a decimal point. The decimal point may preceed the digits (for example, `.483`), may be between digits (for example, `3.14`), or may be at the end of the digits (for example, `1492.`).

The second is a form of scientific notation, consisting of a sequence of digits with an optional decimal point, followed by the letter e or E, optionally followed by a plus or minus sign, followed by a sequence of digits (for example, `4.8e-12`, which represents 4.8×10^{-12}). Other examples are `1E5` (10^5), `.76e-1` (0.76×10^{-1}), and `42.e+5` (42.0×10^5).

The third is to immediately follow any integer, or double literal formed in one of the above two ways, with the letter d or D (for example, `3D`, which represents 3.0).

A float literal is written almost exactly the same as a double literal. The only difference is that a float literal has an f or F at the end instead of a d or D (for example, `4.3f`, `2e-6f`, `3f`).

B.6 THE `char` TYPE

Every character is represented in the computer by a numeric code and is allocated 16 bits. For example, the code for the letter A is 65 (or 0000000001000001 in binary). The actual code value is usually of no consequence to programmers, and a complete list of codes is not shown here (there are 65,536 possible codes).

Table B.1

Sequence	Meaning
\n	New line
\t	Tab
\b	Backspace
\r	Return
\f	Form feed
\\	One backslash
\'	Single quote
\"	Double quote

A `char` literal consists of a single quote character, followed immediately by an arbitrary single character (or one of the special two-character sequences shown in Table B.1), followed immediately by another single-quote character. For example, 'A' is the `char` literal for the letter A, '\t' is the `char` literal for a backspace, and '\'' is the `char` literal for a single quote.

B.7 THE boolean TYPE

Java does not specify how a value of the `boolean` type is represented. It only specifies that a boolean value is either true or false, represented by the literals (and reserved words) `true` and `false`, respectively.

B.8 String LITERALS

A `string` is an object, not a primitive type. However, Java does allow `String` literals to be expressed. A `String` literal represents a `String` object and must be used where an object reference is expected.

A `String` literal is a sequence of characters enclosed between double-quote characters ("). Any character may appear between the double quotes, except a double quote. A `String` literal can also use any of the special two-character symbols shown in Table B.1.

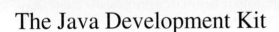

The Java Development Kit

C.1 INTRODUCTION

The Java Development Kit (JDK) from Sun Microsystems is the original collection of tools used to compile and execute Java programs. There have been many improvements and additions to Java and the tools over the years, and new releases of the tools have appeared regularly. This process continues. The basic use of the tools, however, has not changed much in this time. Hence the description of the use of the tools below will likely be accurate for the foreseeable future.

The JDK is available for free download from Sun Microsystems' website (www.java.sun.com). It also goes under the name SDK, so be aware when you are looking for the correct link to follow to the download Web page. Sun distributes and supports versions of the JDK that run on the following platforms (architecture/operation system):

- Sparc/Solaris
- x86[1]/Solaris
- x86/Linux
- x86/Windows (95/98/2000/NT 4.0)

Sun's website also has links to versions of the JDK that run on many other platforms. As of early 2001 the list consisted of the following:

- AIX (IBM)
- DG/UX4-2 (Data General)
- DYNIX/ptx 4.4.2 forward (Sequent)
- HP-UX (Hewlett-Packard)
- IRIX (Silicon Graphics)
- Linux (Blackdown.org)
- MaxOS (Apple)
- OpenVMS (Compaq)
- OS/2 (IBM)
- OS/390, OS/400 (IBM)
- SCO (SCO)
- Tru64 Unix (Compaq)
- UnixWare (SCO)

---

1. The x86 architecture is used in what are commonly called PCs and PC-compatibles.

The use of an integrated development environment (IDE) is neither recommended nor discouraged. The JDK tools certainly suffice, but are command-line-based and do not offer a GUI that can streamline the editing/compiling/executing/debugging process. However, most IDEs require considerable setup, both when first installed and every time a new program is begun, and the somewhat steep learning curve may frustrate the beginning student.

In the remainder of this appendix I'll assume you are not using an IDE.

C.2 EDITING JAVA PROGRAMS

The JDK does not provide tools for typing in and editing Java programs. You'll have to find out what is available on the computer you are using.

Be aware that most word processors (e.g., Microsoft Word) expect that you are entering English, not Java, and hence may try to format your code in strange ways. They also do not automatically save a Java program in a form that can be understood by the Java compiler. It may be possible to change various settings to turn off the automatic formatting and to get your file in the proper form, but you are probably better off using the simplest text input program you can find (e.g., Microsoft Notepad).

Most UNIX-based systems (e.g., Linux, Solaris) have text-oriented editors that are much better suited to entering and editing Java programs. Most systems have an editor called vi, many have Emacs. Free GUI-based versions of them (vim and xemacs) also exist but may have to be downloaded from various distribution sites. These versions also have options to automatically indent your programs, to use different colors for various things in your program (e.g., reserved words, identifiers, literals, comments), and to notify you when you have unmatched parentheses, quotes, etc. Some of these editors are also available on other platforms (e.g., Windows).

C.3 COMPILING JAVA PROGRAMS

When using the JDK, you must put your Java program in a file whose name begins with the same name as the public class defined in the file, then has a dot (period), followed by `java`. For example, if your file has the public class name `JavaDemo`, then the file it is in *must* be called `JavaDemo.java`.

Once you have entered your code and saved this file, you can compile it by entering the following command at a prompt:

```
javac JavaDemo.java
```

If the compiler finds any errors, it will list them after this line. If not, the compiler will create a file for every class defined in the file. Each file's name will be the class name followed by a dot followed by `.class`. To continue the example above, if the file `JavaDemo.java` also has a class name `Listener` in it, then the files `JavaDemo.class` and `Listener.class` will be created by the compiler. If an old version of a `.class` file exists, the compiler will replace it.

C.4 EXECUTING JAVA PROGRAMS

C.4.1 Application Programs

An application program is executed by typing the `java` command and following it with the name of the class (not the `.class` file) that contains the `main` method. To continue our example, if the `JavaDemo` class in the `JavaDemo.java` file has the `main` method in it, and the file has been compiled without error, then type

```
java JavaDemo
```

Be *especially* careful *not* to put `.class` after the class name. The `java` command essentially adds it for you when looking for the proper file. If you do put `.class` after the class name, you will get an error message saying something to the effect that a class is not found.

C.4.2 Applets

An applet is executed by typing the `appletviewer` command and following it with the name of a file that contains information about the `.class` file that contains the class that `extends JApplet`. This file can have any name you like except that it must end with `.html`. It is common to give the `.html` file the same name as the class that `extends JApplet`. Hence by our example, and assuming that `JavaDemo` class `extends JApplet`, this file would be called `JavaDemo.html`; but names such as `test.html` or `MyExample.html` will work just as well.

The `.html` file must contain what is called an *applet tag*. Here is an example:

```
<applet code=JavaDemo.class width=500 height=600> anything </applet>
```

The size of the applet window is specified after `width` and `height`, and the name of the file containing the compiled class that `extends JApplet` must appear after `code` (this time with `.class` left on). The word `anything` can be replaced with whatever you like, including nothing. It is ignored by the `appletviewer` command. A short comment indicating what the applet does is a nice touch.

Note that the applet tag need not all be on one line. For example, you could also write

```
<applet
        code=JavaDemo.class
        width=500
        height=600
        >
this is my best applet
</applet>
```

C.5 JAVADOC

The `javadoc` command takes a Java source file with doc comments and produces a `.html` file that can be displayed with a Web browser. For example, if you have a file `Abstraction.java`, then typing

```
javadoc Abstraction.java
```

will produce the file `Abstraction.html` for the Web browser.

The Animator

D.1 INTRODUCTION

The Animator is a collection of classes that provides an environment in which simple to complex animations can be constructed. It has two threads of execution: one repeatedly redraws the animation background (sky, grass, and surface) and calls the draw method; and another initializes the animation, calls the setup method (if there is one), and has methods that the user can call to get information about the animation scene (sizes, positions), display debugging or other textual information, and get input from the user.

The buttons appearing below the animation scene control the speed of the animation, that is, how often the draw method is called. To get the animation to start, click on the button labeled "go." To stop it, click on "pause." To cause it to call the draw method once, click on "stop." To make it run faster, click on "faster"; to make it run slower, click on "slower."

Below the buttons is the region in which the animation program can display textual information. It displays the last several lines written (in black) and echoes whatever was input (in dark green).

Below the text output region is the input region. It is normally gray but turns yellow when the program is expecting input. The region will not accept input until it is yellow. The mouse must be clicked in this region after it turns yellow before anything can be entered.

D.2 EXTENDING THE ANIMATOR CLASS

An animation program is created by defining a class that extends Animator. The Animator class is abstract and hence must be extended. It has default, empty method definitions for setup and different variations of an overloaded draw method that can be overridden by the extending class. At least one of the draw method variations should be overridden, or nothing will be animated.

The startup method is called once before the animation begins. It has no parameters and returns void. It is usually used to get information from the user that the program needs to vary the appearance or operation of the animation.

The variations of the overloaded draw method are as follows:

```
public void draw(Graphics g)
public void draw(int clock, Graphics g)
public void draw(int x, int y, Graphics g)
public void draw(int clock, int x, int y, Graphics g)
```

The first variation simply provides a reference to a Graphics object that is used to draw simple shapes (lines, ovals, rectangles, etc.) in the scene, and is generally used to draw things that remain the same throughout the animation.

The second variation also supplies an integer that is increased every time the draw method is called, simulating a ticking clock. This variation is used for things whose position and/or appearance may change over time.

The third variation has no "clock," but does provide the x and y coordinates of where things should be drawn. The y coordinate will always be the distance of the surface from the top of the scene (even if the animation window is resized), and the x coordinate is controlled by the left and right buttons below the scene, which the user clicks on to make the things defined by this `draw` method move left or right.

The fourth variation supplies the clock value and the x and y coordinate values. It is used in situations where all are needed.

The animation program usually overrides just one of these methods, even if it has things that are static, time-varying, and position-varying. The clock and coordinate values are simply ignored when drawing static things, the coordinate values are ignored when drawing time-varying things, and the clock value is ignored when drawing position-varying things. Of course, things can be drawn that are both time-varying and position-varying, in which case all values will be used.

If an animation program chooses to override two or more of the `draw` methods, then the methods are called by the Animator in the order shown above. Extending more than one draw method is not recommended as it gives less control over the order in which things are drawn. For example, if the first variation is used to draw a static thing and the second variation is used to draw a time-varying thing, the static thing will always be drawn first and hence will always appear behind the time-varying thing, should they overlap.

D.3 ANIMATOR METHODS

The Animator has several methods that can be called to get information about the scene, display debugging or other textual information, and get input from the user. Table D.1 lists these methods.

Table D.1

Method	Argument Type(s)	Return Type	Description
`Animator.getSceneHeight`	None	int	Returns the height of the scene, in pixels
`Animator.getSceneWidth`	None	int	Returns the width of the scene, in pixels
`Animator.getSurface`	None	int	Returns the y coordinate of the surface of the scene
`Animator.readDouble`	None	double	Returns a double entered by the user
`Animator.readInt`	None	int	Returns an int entered by the user
`Animator.readString`	None	String	Returns a String entered by the user
`Animator.write`	int, double, or String	Void	Writes the argument
`Animator.addClickListener`	A reference to a `ClickListener` object	Void	Tells Animator which object has a `click` method (see D.4)

The three `get` methods return values for the current size of the animation window. If the window is subsequently resized, then those values will no longer be correct. Hence it is best if the animation window be given the desired size before these methods are called. The `write` method is overloaded so that int, double, or String values can be displayed.

D.4 ANIMATION EVENTS

The Animator will react to the mouse being clicked in the animation scene by calling a method called `click` that appears in some object's class definition. Before this will work, the program must inform the Animator which object (a listener object) has the `click` method by calling

```
Animator.addClickListener(reference)
```

where `reference` is a reference to the object whose class definition includes a `click` method.

The `click` method has two integer parameters, the x and y coordinates of where in the scene the mouse was when it was clicked. This method must be defined in a class that `implements ClickListener`.

D.5 RUNNING THE ANIMATOR

The Animator is an applet, so you'll need an `.html` file to specify the class file and window size (see Appendix C.4.2). Once execution is begun, the `startup` method is called first, then the `draw` method(s), under control of the speed buttons. An animation is terminated by quitting the Applet Viewer.

INDEX